Property Problems
From Genes to Pension Funds

W.G. Hart Legal Workshop Series

Property Problems
From Genes to Pension Funds

Editor

J.W. Harris

LONDON–THE HAGUE–BOSTON

Published by
Kluwer Law International Ltd
Sterling House
66 Wilton Road
London SW1V 1DE
United Kingdom

Kluwer Law International Ltd incorporates
the publishing programmes of
Graham & Trotman Ltd
Kluwer Law & Taxation Publishers
and Martinus Nijhoff Publishers

Sold and distributed in the USA
and Canada by
Kluwer Law International
675 Massachusetts Avenue
Cambridge MA 02139
USA

In all other countries, sold and distributed
by Kluwer Law International Ltd
P.O. Box 322
3300 AH Dordrecht
The Netherlands

ISBN 90-411-9643-9
Series ISBN 90-411-9642-0

©Kluwer Law International Ltd
First published in 1997

British Library Cataloguing Publication Data
A catalogue record for this book is available from the British Library

Library of Congress Cataloguing-in-Publication Data is available

This publication is protected by international copyright law. All rights reserved. No part of this publication may be reproduced, stored in a retrieval system or transmitted in any form or by any means, electronic, mechanical, photocopying, recording or otherwise, without the prior permission of the publishers.

Typeset in Times 10.5pt by Carrigboy Typesetting, Bantry, County Cork, Republic of Ireland.
Printed and bound in Great Britain by Arrowhead Books Ltd, Reading, Berkshire.

Preface

The essays in this collection are based on papers first delivered at the W. G. Hart Legal Workshop which was held at the Institute of Advanced Legal Studies in London in July 1993. On behalf of all the contributors, I should like to thank the Institute's former director, Professor Terry Daintish, and its current director, Professor Barry Rider, for their encouragement and assistance in arranging for the publication of this volume.

A glance at the contents list, or at the summary of the contributions which I have attempted in the introduction, will show the range of intriguing property problems covered. We were fortunate in receiving papers from varying perspectives and from different parts of the world. The annual W. G. Hart Legal Workshops provide occasions for scholars to foregather and exchange views about some topic of interest to lawyers, philosophers and social scientists. I hope that this collection on property demonstrates the productive possibilities of such encounters.

J.W. Harris
Keble College Oxford

Contents

Preface .... *v*
Contributors .... *ix*

1 Introduction: Property Problems *by J.W. Harris* 1

PART I: THE FRONTIERS OF PROPERTY

2 Patenting Human Genes: Legality, Morality, and Human
   Rights *by Deryck Beyleveld and Roger Brownsword* 9
3 Human Dignity and Property Rights in Human Body Parts
   by Stephen R. Munzer 25
4 The Legal Status of the Pre-Embryo: Some Comparative
   Considerations Prompted by Davis v. Davis
   by Antonello Miranda 39
5 Theft of Information and the Concept of Property in the
   Information Age *by Deborah Fisch Nigri* 48
6 Compulsory Expropriation and Company Law
   by Gerard McCormack 61
7 Property: Assets or Power? Objects or Relations as Substrata
   of Property Rights *by Wolfgang Mincke* 78
8 Pensions as Property and Pensions as Contract
   by Richard Nobles 89

PART II: CHALLENGES TO ORTHODOXIES

9 Long-Term Leases as an Alternative to Ownership
   by Joshua Weisman 105
10 Security Interests as Property: Relocating Security Interests
   within the Property Framework *by Alison Clarke* 118
11 Property and Unjust Enrichment *by W. J. Swadling* 130
12 Things as Thing and Things as Wealth *by Bernard Rudden* .. 146
13 Hohfeldian Use-rights in Property *by J.E. Penner* 164
14 What is Non-Private Property? *by J.W. Harris* 175

PART III: RELOCATING PROPERTY'S ROLE

15 Theories of Property and Economic Development
  by Joshua Getzler 193
16 Telling Stories: Rights and Wrongs of the Equity of Redemption
  by David Sugarman and Ronnie Warrington 207
17 Pragmatism and Property by Alan Ryan 225
**18 Socio-Legal Concept of Property Rights in Town Development:
   a Critical Approach to Comparative Studies on Urban
   Planning Laws in Eastern and Western Countries**
  by Michiatsu Kaino 242
19 Hegel and the Social Dynamics of Property Law
  by M.G. Salter 257
20 Hegel on Private Property and Public Access
  by William N.R. Lucy 274

Important published works of contributors 291
Index 297

Contributors

J.W. Harris

J.W. Harris is Professor of Law at the University of Oxford. He studied law at Oxford and qualified as a solicitor. He was a lecturer at the London School of Economics and has been a tutorial fellow at Keble College, Oxford since 1973. He has been a Mellon Research Fellow at Princeton, Allen Allen and Hemsley visiting professor at Sydney, and visiting professor at the Universities of Hong Kong, Singapore and Palermo. His publications cover property law, property theory and legal philosophy.

Deryck Beyleveld

Deryck Beyleveld is Professor of Jurisprudence at the University of Sheffield and Director of the Sheffield Institute of Biotechnological Law and Ethics (SIBLE). He studied biochemistry at the University of the Witwatersrand and philosophy and social and political sciences at the University of Cambridge before taking his doctorate in philosophy and social theory at the University of East Anglia. His publications span criminology, legal and moral philosophy, contract law, product liability law, international human rights law, and law and ethics of biotechnology.

Roger Brownsword

Roger Brownsword is Professor of Law at the University of Sheffield where he has worked since he graduated from the London School of Economics in 1968. His best-known papers are in the fields of common law and legal theory, focusing most recently on the relationship between law, morality and rationality. For the past six years, Professor Brownsword has edited the case-note section of the *Modern Law Review*.

Stephen Munzer

Stephen Munzer is Professor of Law at the University of California at Los Angeles. He has postgraduate degrees in both philosophy and law. His main work has centred on moral, political, and legal philosophy, and has appeared in philosophical journals, law reviews, and collections of essays. His interests include the philosophy of biology and Christian theology.

Antonello Miranda

Antonello Miranda is currently Acting Professor of Private Comparative Law at the Faculty of Law, Palermo University. He has been researcher of civil and private comparative law at the Department of Private Law, Palermo University. Professor Miranda holds a degree in law from Palermo University and studied modern English law at the London School of Economics. He is an Associate of the Institute of Advanced Legal Studies as well as being a member of both the Italian Association of Comparative Law and the Associazione Siciliana per la Comparazione Giuridica "E Amari".

Deborah Fisch Nigri

Dr Deborah Fisch Nigri graduated from the Federal University of Rio de Janeiro in 1986 obtaining a degree in Juridical and Social Sciences. In March 1990 she participated in a research programme in the Information Technology Law Unit at Queen Mary and Westfield College, obtaining a PhD in 1993. She has worked and researched extensively in the area of data protection and is currently a consultant in Sao Paulo in the area of intellectual property law.

Gerard McCormack

Gerard McCormack is a Reader in Law at the University of Essex. A graduate of University College Dublin, he has held posts as Lecturer in Law at Queens' University Belfast and at the University of Southampton. He has published extensively, particularly in the areas of company law and commercial law.

Wolfgang Mincke

Wolfgang Mincke studied law in Munster and Tubingen from 1963–1968 and then in Helsinki from 1969–1970. He was assistant professor in Munster from 1974–1985 and from 1985–1991 was Professor for Private Law in Gottingen. He has been visiting professor in Georgetown, Washington D.C. and has practiced law in Germany. He is sometime Professor for Legal Informatics in Rovaniemi, Lapland and is currently professor of Dutch private law in Maastricht.

Richard Nobles

Richard Nobles is a Senior Lecturer in the Law Department of the London School of Economics. He teaches jurisprudence and property and has written extensively on pension law.

Joshua Weisman

Joshua Weisman is currently a Professor in the Faculty of Law at the Hebrew University of Jerusalem. He has been a British Council Scholar, a Fulbright Scholar, and a Visiting Scholar at Harvard University. He has also been a Fellow of the Inns of Court and of the Institute of Advanced Legal Studies. He has held the position of Dean of the Faculty of Law, Hebrew University of Jerusalem, as well as being visiting professor at the New York University School of Law, the University of Southern California, Los Angeles, Tulane University and London University.

Alison Clarke

Alison Clarke is currently Senior Lecturer in Law at University College London. She has been a solicitor in private practice, a Lecturer in Law at King's College London, University of Southampton and a member of the Southampton Institute of Maritime Law. Alison Clarke was seconded to the Law Commission in 1985–1987 to work on the reform of land mortgages project.

William Swadling

William Swadling is a Fellow and Tutor in Law at Brasenose College and a Lecturer in Law at the University of Oxford. He previously held posts at the University of Southampton, Queen Mary and Westfield College, London and University College London. He has published a number of articles and chapters on tort, contract, public law, property and restitution and is a contributor to *Halsbury's Laws of England*. For a number of years he was a member of the Standing Conference on Legal Education (a sub-committee of the Lord Chancellor's Advisory Committee on Legal Education and Conduct).

Bernard Rudden

Bernard Rudden, has since 1979, been Professor of Comparative Law in the University of Oxford and Fellow of Brasenose College. Previously, he was Fellow and Tutor at Oriel College, Oxford. An English solicitor, he has been Visiting Professor at several universities in Asia, Europe and the United States.

J.E. Penner

J.E. Penner, is currently Lecturer in Law at Brunel University. He has degrees in science (honours genetics) and law and is a Doctor of Philosophy.

Joshua Getzler

Joshua Getzler is a Fellow and Tutor in Law at St Hugh's College, Oxford. He completed history and law degrees at the Australian National University in 1989 and a Doctor of Philosophy in law at Oxford in 1993. His researches embrace legal history from Roman to modern times, equity and commercial law and economics law. He has published articles on recent and ancient equity, on the history of hunting and enclosure law, and on the economics of the common law. His latest work investigates the transformation of trust and fiduciary law by the new global capital markets, and the impact of these changes on the regulation of the welfare state.

David Sugarman

David Sugarman is currently Professor of Law, Department of Law, at Lancaster University. He was formerly Senior Lecturer in the Department of Law at Lancaster University.

Ronnie Warrington

Prior to his death in 1994, Dr Ronnie Warrington was Senior Lecturer in Law at Lancaster University.

Alan Ryan

Alan Ryan has been Warden of New College, Oxford since 1996. He was Professor of Politics at Princeton University from 1988–1996 and before that Reader in Politics at Oxford and a Fellow of New College. He was elected a Fellow of the British Academy in 1986. He writes on a broad range of subjects including contemporary American politics, children's books and the novels of Patrick O'Brien. He reviews widely, for the *New York Review of Books*, *Dissent*, *The New York Times*, *The Times Literary Supplement* and *The Times Higher Education Supplement* among others. When allowed to do so, he sails small boats very badly.

Michiatsu Kaino

Michiatsu Kaino, is a graduate of the Law School, University of Tokyo. He was Associate Researcher and then Associate Professor of the Institute of Social Science at the University of Tokyo from 1966 until 1975. In 1975–1976 he was a Visiting Scholar at the Institute of Advanced Legal Studies, University of London. Professor Kaino was Associate Professor, Professor and then Dean of the School of Law at Nagoya University until 1995, and was Visiting Professor of Japanese Law at the School of Law, University of Warwick in 1990–1991.

Michael Salter

Michael Salter teaches jurisprudence, property law and human rights law at the University of Lancaster. He graduated from the University of Southampton with a Bachelor of Law degree in 1978 and with a Doctorate of Philosophy from the University of Sheffield in 1988.

William Lucy

William Lucy teaches jurisprudence and contract at the Law School, University of Hull. He has written a number of essays about theories of adjudication, the philosophy of the common law and the political philosophy of property.

1

Introduction: Property Problems

J.W. HARRIS*

For all its familiarity in day-to-day and commercial life, "property" is an elusive idea. Its analysis raises many problems – conceptual, ideological and justificatory.[1] The essays published in this volume contribute fresh insights to some of these problems.

Part I deals with the frontiers of property. Are there resources which could be (but should not be), or which should be (but as yet are not), brought within the scope of property institutions? Technological progress and other developments in modern life force such questions on legislators and judges.

Consider derivatives and parts of the human body. Throughout most of human history, the right thing to do with a corpse or any part of it has been to dispose of it, one way or another, reverently and hygienically. That required the imposition of duties upon kin, priests and other public functionaries; but not the conferring of property rights. The common law accordingly recognises property in a corpse only in very rare instances.[2] Nowadays, however, human bits and pieces may be put to many "valuable" uses: in transplant operations; in fertility treatment; or as the material base for academic and commercial research in the burgeoning field of biotechnology. Could there be a satisfactory regime of "property" suitable to all these ends?[3]

In their essay Deryck Beyleveld and Roger Brownsword question the readiness of the European Patent Office to grant patents in respect of human gene sequences. The European Patent Convention denies patentability when the exploitation of an invention would be "contrary to morality". Beyleveld and Brownsword contend that the examiners should be guided by a critical cultural European morality, centred on human rights; and that they have not as yet taken seriously the charge that such patents infringe the human right to dignity.

Stephen Munzer makes a qualified Kantian case against the commercial sale of human body parts. The case is qualified since, as he recognises, it depends crucially on the following assumption: market language would, in such a context, inevitably offend a defensible (Kantian) conception of human dignity.

---

* Professor of Law at the University of Oxford and Fellow of Keble College.
[1] See J.W. Harris, *Property and Justice* (1996).
[2] *Dobson v. North Tyneside Health Authority* [1996] 4 All E.R. 474, C.A.
[3] See Harris, *op. cit.* above, n.1, pp. 351–361.

Antonello Miranda focuses on the pre-embryo, fertilised human ova stored by an agency pending use. Does the woman from whom they came have the sole prerogative to decide whether they should be implanted in her womb, in defiance of the wishes of the "father"? A Tennessee court has ruled "no". Miranda submits that the same answer should be reached in Italian law, by a proper reading of those provisions of the Italian Civil Code which deal with natural modes of acquiring ownership of property.

What part should property play in the age of the expanding information industry? For over a century common law courts have grappled, indecisively, with the question whether information is, in some sense and for some purposes, a species of "property".[4] Deborah Nigri argues that, at least in the commercial context, piecemeal protection of information is not enough. In disagreement with recent English and Canadian case law, she suggests that traditional criminal law rules prohibiting theft should be adapted so as to bring commercially valuable information within the scope of this crime.

As to intangible property more generally, common lawyers have no doubt that there is such a thing as "intellectual property"[5] and that contractual rights of some kinds ("choses in action") are also property.[6] Does that mean that those rules of a property institution which deploy "ownership" and other proprietary concepts in relation to tangible items apply also, in some closely analogous way, to intangible rights?

Take shares in companies. We trade in them and inherit them in much the same way as with other forms of property. Gerrard McCormack, in his essay, raises the question whether that rule which prohibits expropriation without fair compensation has any significant role to play in the context of company law provisions which allow majority shareholders to force minorities to sell their shares. He concludes that the attitude of the European Human Rights Commission and the case law of English courts suggests that it does not.

It should not be supposed that the boundaries of intangible property are problems only for common lawyers. In his essay Wolfgang Mincke notes that for some systems – such as the English and the French – a single concept serves for both objects (land and goods) and for certain relations (debt, patent, copyright etc.); whilst in others – such as the German or the Dutch – different concepts are employed, depending on whether the substrate is an object or a relation. The problem is that, while bank balances and other contractual claims are (of economic necessity) treated as part of a person's assignable assets, German law cannot apply the term "property" ("eigentum") to these things because German legal science finds in them only power-relations, not "objects". Mincke proposes that "naked value" might itself be treated as a transferable object; but he recognises that this would raise new problems (similar to those encountered by common lawyers when they chew over the limits of the term "chose in

---

[4] *ibid.* pp. 341–350.
[5] *ibid.* pp. 42–47, 296–299.
[6] *ibid.* pp. 50–52, 58–62.

action"). When do contracts create this transferable "naked value", and when do they not?

If all the pensions we were ever to receive were fixed by public law, or by contracts with the state, and if the rights they conferred could never be anticipated or encashed or pass into the hands of others, the familiar rules of property institutions would not apply to them. But what of claims to pension funds set up by privately owned enterprises? English law has recently had to respond to situations in which something goes wrong, for example, the fund is criminally dissipated.[7] Equally perplexing problems may arise when things go well. Suppose the fund is advantageously invested so that, after each contributor's contractual rights have been fully met, there is a surplus. Do the members of the scheme own it, so that they can dictate what is to be done with it? Does the enterprise own it, so that it can use it for its general business or distribute it to its shareholders? Or does no-one at all stand to it in that special relationship we call "ownership"?

Richard Nobles explores such questions in his essay. He examines the perspectives which underlie judicial interpretations of the minutiae of fund-constituting instruments. He concludes that, on the whole, neither employees nor employers have succeeded in convincing English courts that "ownership" should represent the dominating ideological perspective. That role should be filled, he suggests, not by a proprietary, but by a role, conception – that of good employer/employee relationships.

The essays in the second part of this collection challenge certain orthodox assumptions about property – political, doctrinal, or philosophical.

Twenty years ago a section of the British Labour Party published a pamphlet advocating the "nationalisation" of land, not by State take-over, but by substituting long leases for freeholds.[8] "New Labour" is unlikely to support such an idea; but it has been a recurrent theme of radical politics. The proponents and the vociferous opponents of this proposal were at one in supposing that its consequences would be of two kinds: ideological change, since people would no longer regard their dwellings as "owned" by them; and innovatory controls, as the State would be able to negotiate covenants restricting land-use instead of relying on the present battery of public law restrictions.

Joshua Weisman's essay provides fascinating comparative material for this debate. He examines the situation in Israel and other jurisdictions where long leases are the normal form of landholding. He discusses the "ideological" arguments – which, in Israel, take a religious form – and the "utilitarian" arguments favouring long leases over "ownership". He concludes that it is by no means obvious that it makes all that much difference which system is adopted.

Security interests (mortgages, charges, pledges, liens) are granted as much protection by our law as are ownership interests. They are enforced, not merely

---

[7] *Bishopsgate Investment Management Ltd (in Liquidation) v. Homan* [1995] 1 All E.R. 347, C.A. Chancery 211.
[8] Brocklebank *et al.*, *The Case for Nationalising Land* (Campaign for Nationalising Land, 1973).

against successors to the burdened property, but against the mortgagor's trustee in bankruptcy in preference to all unsecured creditors. Alison Clarke argues that they are thereby mislocated within the overall property framework. Holders of such interests would still have the advantage of being able to enforce loans against specific assets of solvent debtors, even were they denied their present priority in bankruptcy proceedings. She contends that economic considerations commonly advanced to support the existing rules are in fact skewed by the doctrinal presupposition that a security interest must constitute a share of the ownership of the asset in question.

William Swadling pitches into another doctrinal orthodoxy. Suppose someone is vested with property which, for one reason or another, he ought not to keep. It is, in his hands, an "unjust enrichment". The law's response, in many situations, has been to grant a proprietary remedy to the person "at whose expense" the enrichment has come about; and some commentators advocate a wider application of this approach.[9] Swadling submits that neither principle nor policy justify awarding the fruits of wrongdoing to such a claimant in priority to all other creditors of the wrongdoer. *In personam* restitutionary relief should suffice.

Bernard Rudden in his essay attacks doctrinal assumptions on a wider front. Lawyers distinguish between real and personal (immovable and movable) property; but they overlook a more fundamental distinction. Some facets of a property institution – concepts like ownership, possession, publicity and servitudes – are concerned (he argues) with "things as things". More complex conceptions – such as estates, interests under trusts, and most of the law of intellectual and intangible property – deal with "things as wealth". Those who transact in terms of these latter conceptions are concerned with funds, not with allocating competing uses over tangible resources.

Since the early years of this century, property law theorists in the English-speaking world have generally accepted a "bundle of rights" analysis of the concept of ownership, following the lead of W. N. Hohfeld.[10] Some judges have done the same.[11] James Penner challenges this approach. He contends that our institutional practices deploy a claim to the "exclusive use" of a thing, which is a single right, not a bundle of rights. Viewing ownership as a single right (he maintains) enables us to focus on the specific interest which property law seeks to protect. There is a single duty not to interfere with other people's property, not a myriad of duties relating to each and every item owned by each and every other member of the community.

My own essay contests the assumption commonly made by philosophers who investigate the subject, that there are three parallel ideal types of property institution: private property; common property; and state (or collective) property.

---

[9] Harris, *op. cit.* above, n.1, pp. 336–341.
[10] *ibid.* pp. 120–125.
[11] See *R v. Morris* [1984] A.C. 320 at 331, *per* Lord Roskill.

Introduction: Property Problems

I contend that "private property" is the logically prior concept. It is presupposed by all varieties of non-private property.

Part III of the book contains essays which seek to relocate the role of property within wider fields of historical, comparative and philosophical research.

Classical economics takes it to be axiomatic that clear definitions of property rights are essential for well-functioning markets. Joshua Getzler condemns as ahistorical the hidden assumption that markets themselves call property rights into existence. He reminds us that Max Weber had noted the English counter-example to any straightforward correlation between market needs and the evolution of property-holdings: England achieved capitalist supremacy without a formally rational catalogue of proprietary conceptions. Weber explained the aberration by reference to the different castes of functionaries who controlled legal development. Getzler suggests that, instead, we should focus on the adaptability of old institutions to meet new economic demands; the internal capacity of the common law to eliminate arcane forms; legislative initiatives; and the stability of expectations resulting from a constitution which circumscribed centralised authority.

In their essay David Sugarman and Ronnie Warrington concentrate on that very strange common law beast, the equity of redemption. Equity set aside contractual terms whereby property was forfeit if a mortgage was not repaid, and any provisions which might inhibit redemption; and, pending redemption, it treated the mortgagor as vested with a fully-fledged proprietary subject-matter. The familiar story locates this development within the sphere of personal morality – equity springing to the aid of a luckless borrower in the toils of a ruthless moneylender. Sugarman and Warrington tell a different story. The equity of redemption was both a practical device for securing the hegemony of the landed aristocracy, and also a potent symbol. It resonated with images, religious, cultural and constitutional. It was part of the narrative of a specifically English identity wherein the honour of a worthy elite was safeguarded.

The recent revival of interest in the pragmatic philosophy of John Dewey prompts Alan Ryan to locate property rights within the wider implications of the Deweyan perspective. Following this approach, property rights can only be understood and evaluated in the light of the social functions we expect property to serve. If, for example, they present an obstacle to co-operation between management and labour, then they are not really "rights". Ryan regards this functionalist analysis as appropriate for most kinds of property rights although not, as Dewey's own writings suggest, for other more important kinds of rights.

Urban planning law in Western countries takes place against a background of individual or group privately owned and marketable land-holdings. Michiatsu Kaino juxtaposes to this feature of property institutions in the West a distinctive Asian perspective. He recognises that Western conceptions have been introduced into Asian jurisdictions, either by imitation or through colonisation. He argues, however, that indigenous communal property notions have not disappeared; and that the future welfare of urban populations requires property conceptions which, unlike Lockean individualism, incorporate responsibility for non-owners' interests.

One of the alleged merits of a property institution is freedom: proprietors can exercise autonomy in ways which nothing but resource-ownership could facilitate. The philosopher most often invoked in this connection is Hegel. Indeed, Hegel seems to have knocked Locke off the perch as primary apologist for private property. However, Hegel upholds a picture in which, although ownership freedoms may be seen as absolute at the "moment" of abstract right, they are by no means so when this moment is taken up within those of morality and ethical life.[12] The last two essays in this volume cut through Hegel's metaphysics to show how his insights may be applied.

Michael Salter claims that "ethical life", as depicted by Hegel, remedies the abstract quality of the prior moments. It does this by focusing upon the historically specific and contextual features which shape both subjective and objective aspects of property relations. It follows (he argues) that, from a Hegelian analysis, legal recognition of private property rights is valid only in so far as it makes a positive contribution to the wider project of cultural self-determination – a project which must overcome unjust features of social life, such as homelessness, systematic poverty and pervasive social alienation.

William Lucy applies Hegel's analysis to the potential conflict between claims to private property in land and assertions of public access rights. He interprets Hegel's justification of private property in terms of the individual's need to acquire an autonomous and disciplined will. He suggests that the same considerations may underlie demands for public access. He notes that Hegel himself had allowed for the sphere of free contract, established within the moment of abstract right, to be circumscribed within "ethical life"; and argues that, by parity of reasoning, society may derogate from absolute ownership in favour of access rights.

---

[12] Harris, *op. cit.* above, n.1, pp. 232–238.

Part I
THE FRONTIERS OF PROPERTY

2

Patenting Human Genes: Legality, Morality, and Human Rights

DERYCK BEYLEVELD* and ROGER BROWNSWORD**

Introduction

According to a recent survey, over 1,000 patents (worldwide) have been granted for human gene sequences, of which about half have been granted by the European Patent Office (EPO).[1] It is surprising, perhaps, that the EPO should have taken a leading role in granting patents of this kind. For, unlike some patent systems, the European Patent Convention (EPC) expressly excludes granting patents where it would be contrary to morality; and, above all, it has been moral concerns about patents on life that have bedevilled attempts to harmonise patent law within the European Union.[2] Yet, when the morality of granting patents on human gene sequences was put to the test in the *Relaxin* case,[3] the EPO gave short shrift to the opponents' arguments. In a robust judgment, the Opposition Division declared that it was absurd to liken patents on human genes to slavery; and it emphatically rejected the opponents' contention that patents on life were being granted – DNA, as the Opposition Division put it, is merely "a chemical substance which carries genetic information and can be used as an intermediate in the production of proteins which may be medically useful."[4]

In this paper, we consider whether the EPO is right to take such a "liberal" view of the patenting of human gene sequences. In the first part of the paper, we discuss the moral responsibilities of the EPO, restating and refining the thesis

---

* Professor of Jurisprudence, Faculty of Law, University of Sheffield, and Director of the Sheffield Institute of Biotechnological Law and Ethics.
** Professor of Law, Faculty of Law, University of Sheffield, and member of the Sheffield Institute of Biotechnological Law and Ethics.
[1] See Thomas, Davies, Birtwistle, Crowther, and Burke, "Ownership of the Human Genome" (1996) 380 *Nature* 387.
[2] Culminating, in 1995, in the European Parliament's rejection of the draft EU Directive on the Legal Protection of Biotechnology. For the earlier history of the Directive, see Beyleveld and Brownsword, "Patentability of Genetically Engineered Animals: The Emerging European View" (1995) 8 *Asia Business Law Review* 19; and, for brief comment on the resuscitated version of the Directive, see our concluding remarks below.
[3] [1995] O.J. 388.
[4] *ibid*. para. 6.3.4.

that we advanced in *Mice, Morality and Patents*[5] – namely, that the examiners should be guided by a critical cultural European morality of human rights before defending our position against Edward Armitage and Ivor Davis's[6] objection that the drafters of the EPC intended to exclude a patent as immoral only exceptionally (essentially, where Europeans would think it inconceivable that a patent should be granted). Having clarified the moral jurisdiction of the examiners, we deal in the second part of our paper with the specific question of the morality of patenting human gene sequences, focusing in particular on the *Relaxin* case.

1. Morality and Article 53(a) of the European Patent Convention

Patentability, for the purposes of the EPC, is determined initially by Article 52(1), which provides:

> "European patents shall be granted for any inventions which are susceptible of industrial application, which are new and which involve an inventive step."

However, the technical criteria in Article 52(1) must be read in conjunction with the exclusionary provisions of Article 53. First, Article 53(a) provides that patents shall not be granted for:

> "inventions the publication or exploitation of which would be contrary to 'ordre public' or morality, provided that the exploitation shall not be deemed to be so contrary merely because it is prohibited by law or regulation in some or all of the Contracting States."

Secondly, Article 53(b) provides that patents shall not be granted for:

> "plant or animal varieties or essentially biological processes for the production of plants and animals; this provision does not apply to micro-biological processes or the products thereof."

Both limbs of Article 53 have given rise to interpretive difficulties in the face of patent applications involving genetic engineering – notably, in the *Oncomouse*[7] application (which concerned a transgenic test animal for cancer research), and subsequently in the *Plant Genetic Systems* case[8] (which concerned a genetically modified herbicide-resistant plant). However, with regard to patents on human gene sequences, Article 53(a) is the key exclusionary provision and, for present purposes, the crucial question is how we are to interpret "morality".

We can deal with this question in three steps: first, we will outline the interpretation that we gave in *Mice, Morality and Patents*; next, we will draw

---

[5] Beyleveld and Brownsword, *Mice, Morality and Patents* (1993).
[6] Armitage and Davis, *Patents and Morality in Perspective* (1994).
[7] [1989] O.J. 451, first decision by examiners; [1990] O.J. 476, Board of Appeal; [1992] O.J. 590, reconsidered decision by examiners.
[8] Opposition Proceedings EPO 242 236 B, Opposition Division; T 0356/93, [1995] E.P.O.R. 357, Board of Appeal.

out the implications of the Contracting States' recognition of human rights (to expose the depth of the moral commitment represented by Article 53(a)); and then we can respond to Armitage and Davis's criticism of our interpretation.

(a) The interpretation of Article 53(a) given in Mice, Morality and Patents

Elsewhere,[9] we have relied on Alan Gewirth's argument that any agent or prospective purposive agent (PPA) must accept the Principle of Generic Consistency (PGC) (requiring PPAs to respect the generic features of agency) on pain of contradicting that he/she/it is a PPA[10] from which it follows that all principles that PPAs may rationally take as guides for their conduct must be consistent with the PGC (which, thus, functions as the supreme principle of both morality and legality). Had we adopted this argument in *Mice, Morality and Patents*, we would simply have said that "morality" in Article 53(a) of the EPC must incorporate the PGC. However, we did not argue in this way. Instead, we suggested that we could arrive at substantially the same conclusion by a less controversial strategy. Effectively, this strategy involved two complementary approaches – one approach scrutinising the text of Article 53(a), the other focusing on the intentions of the Contracting States.

With regard to the first of these approaches, we were faced with virtually a *tabula rasa* at the time of writing *Mice, Morality and Patents*. The text of the EPC offers little help, giving no definition of either "ordre public" or "morality". The EPO Guidelines, by contrast, suggest that examiners should "consider whether it is probable that the public in general would regard the invention as so abhorrent that the grant of patent rights would be inconceivable"[11] and a letter bomb is given as an example of an invention that could not be patented without being universally condemned as outrageous. However, the Guidelines are not binding; patents on letter bombs are some distance removed from patents on the products and processes associated with modern biotechnology; and, in the *Oncomouse* examination (the first test case on Article 53(a)), the examiners balanced the moral costs and benefits of granting the patent rather than asking whether granting the patent would be inconceivable.

With the jurisprudence of Article 53(a) in its infancy, our first approach was to draw up a short-list of four candidate "moralities". This short-list comprised: (i) a specific established moral theory (utilitarianism, Kantianism, or the like); (ii) the personal morality of the examiners; (iii) the cultural morality of the Contracting States; and (iv) the critical cultural morality of the Contracting States (or, the morality of right-thinking persons in the Contracting States). We eliminated the first two possibilities summarily – the first on the ground that such

---

[9] See, *e.g. Law as a Moral Judgment* (1994) (for the concept of law); "Privity, Transitivity, and Rationality" (1991) 51 M.L.R. 48; and "Impossibility, Irrationality, and Strict Product Liability" in Howells and Phillips (eds.), *Product Liability* (1991) p. 75 (for examples of application to doctrinal questions).
[10] Gewirth, *Reason and Morality* (1978).
[11] EPO Guidelines (C–IV, 3.1).

a specific theory would have been explicitly identified had it been intended to serve as the governing morality, and the second on the ground that such a delegation of moral authority was simply implausible. We also rejected the third possibility – partly on the ground that this would entail cumbersome and possibly unreliable procedures (as the examiners sought to take stock of prevailing views, whether by employing questionnaires or by inspecting legislation or whatever) and partly because the proviso in Article 53(a) suggests that the examiners are not tied to local cultural standards, at least to the extent that such standards find expression in prohibition "by law or regulation in some or all of the Contracting States." This left the critical cultural morality of the Contracting States. On this reading of Article 53(a), it would not be sufficient that certain positive or negative attitudes prevailed in the Contracting States; such attitudes would have to be checked for their sincerity, coherence, consistency, stability and the like. As Ronald Dworkin has put it, so-called "morality" should count in legal argumentation only where it is free from "prejudices, rationalisations, matters of personal aversion or taste, arbitrary stands, and the like".[12] In *Mice, Morality and Patents* we suggested that such a reading best captures the sense of Article 53(a), by making the morality of the Contracting States the general frame of reference and yet giving the examiners a distinctive role in assessing what that morality might rationally amount to in any particular case.

Contrary to our view, many patent practitioners favour the "inconceivability" test,[13] sometimes arguing that the text of Article 53(a) supports such an interpretation. One such claim is that the use of the word "contrary" is suggestive of the requirement that there should be an overwhelming consensus against granting a patent.[14] However, this is unconvincing. More promisingly, there is an argument that the proviso in Article 53(a) signals that the EPO should exclude a patent on moral grounds only exceptionally. According to this argument, Article 53(a) contemplates two moral jurisdictions, one at the EPO (excluding patents that would be unhesitatingly condemned as immoral in the Contracting States) and the other in the Contracting States (each Contracting State being free to impose more stringent moral regulation if it so wishes). We suggest, however, that the proviso only supports this view if it is read selectively. Insofar as the proviso states that regulation in *some* of the Contracting States does not determine whether an invention is immoral under Article 53(a), this might be thought to signal that the EPO's moral jurisdiction is minimal, operating only on the lowest common denominators of agreement amongst the

---

[12] Dworkin, *Taking Rights Seriously* (rev. ed., 1978) p. 248. It is also Dworkin's view that those who hold opposed moral positions should at least respect the fact that the other side holds a moral position. Such mutual respect might then serve to defuse otherwise aggressive oppositions such as those concerning the morality of abortion and euthanasia: see Dworkin, *Life's Dominion* (1993).

[13] As per the EPO Guidelines and as adopted by the Opposition Division in both *Plant Genetic Systems* (Opposition Proceedings EPO 242 236 B1) and *Relaxin* [1995] O.J. 388.

[14] See Armitage and Davis, *op. cit.* above, n.6, at p. 81.

Contracting States. However, the proviso also states that the morality question in Article 53(a) is not determined even where *all* the Contracting States regulate against the invention. Yet, if regulatory prohibition in all the Contracting States is not sufficient to exclude the patent as immoral, we might wonder what better evidence there could be of "inconceivability".

If the text of Article 53(a) incorporates the critical cultural morality of the Contracting States, we need to identify the cornerstone moral commitments of the Contractors. In *Mice, Morality and Patents*, we suggested that the commitments of the Contracting States to human rights (as evidenced by their agreement to the European Convention on Human Rights (ECHR) and other international human rights instruments) would be one of the principal features of such morality and that, if that morality is to be read critically, we must give full weight to its recognition of human rights. In short, Article 53(a) must be read as a charter for human rights in the specific field of patent law.

So much for textual considerations; but, what of our second approach towards the interpretation of Article 53(a)? Briefly, our suggestion was that there was a line of argument that ran from the Contracting States' acceptance of human rights (most proximately evidenced by their acceptance of the ECHR) through to Article 53(a) of the EPC such that the spirit and purpose of the EPC must be taken to be consistent with the Contracting States' prior commitments to human rights. Accordingly, whatever else Article 53(a) might mean, it must be read in a way that respects human rights. Our next step is to spell out more fully what this line of argument involves and how treating Article 53(a) as a charter for human rights brings the PGC into play.

(b) The significance of recognising human rights

Our second approach in *Mice, Morality and Patents* is underwritten by a "dialectically contingent"[15] argument that can be employed where human rights are accepted. Here, we contend that anyone who claims that anyone has any human rights must, on pain of contradicting this claim, accept that conformity with the PGC is necessary for permissible action. This contention involves two distinguishable components. First, it involves the claim that if any human rights

---

[15] Gewirth's argument to the PGC is "dialectically necessary" – *dialectical* because its premise is a claim made by an interlocutor (namely, the claim of a PPA to be a PPA); and *necessary* (for any PPA) because (a) the PPA cannot coherently deny that it is a PPA, and (b) all steps in the argument are strictly necessary (employing only purely logical principles and/or considerations adduced solely by analysis of the concept of being a PPA). This is to be contrasted with a "dialectically contingent" procedure (such as that in the text). The latter form of argument is propounded relative to some claim made by an interlocutor (and is, thus, dialectical) but (a) the claim is one that the interlocutor can coherently reject, *or* (b) the connection between the premise (claim) and the conclusion is contingent. Both dialectically necessary and dialectically contingent arguments are to be contrasted with assertoric procedures, in which considerations with free-standing validity (*i.e.*, independent of claims made by interlocutors) are adduced for the acceptance of conclusions.

are attributed to some being X, then the rights granted by the PGC must be granted to X. Secondly, it involves the assertion that if these rights are granted to any being X, they must be granted equally to all human beings (and, indeed, to all PPAs).

The argument[16] may, therefore, be presented on the basis of a human being claiming that he or she has human rights (the content of which may be anything at all), and the demonstration will be that this person must, on pain of contradicting this claim, accept that all human beings (and, indeed, all PPAs) have a right to the generic features of agency (GF).[17]

A human right is a claim-right[18] possessed by a human being simply by virtue of being human. That is to say, where it is the case that X is human is sufficient to justify that X has claim-right R, then claim-right R is a human right.

Suppose then that X claims:

(1) I (*i.e.* X) have human rights R.

It follows from the definition of a human right that X is asserting

(1a) X is human → X has R-rights (*i.e.*, X being human is a sufficient reason why X has R-rights).

The logical principle of universalisability now requires X to assent to

(2) Y is human → Y has R-rights, which entails

(2a) All human beings have R-rights.

Now

(3) Any human being has a right to r → that human being has a right to the necessary means to exercise r.

From

(4) There are GF (which are necessary means to the exercise of r, whatever r might be), it follows that X must assent to

---

[16] The presentation of this argument draws on Beyleveld, "Legal Theory and Dialectically Contingent Justifications for the Principle of Generic Consistency" (1996) 9 *Ratio Juris* 15.

[17] Gewirth (*op. cit.* above, n.10, at pp. 52–63) divides the generic features often referred to as "freedom" and "well-being" into two categories: (a) conditions that are necessary in order to be able even to attempt to act (these include the capacities of free choice as it is involved in action, life itself, and sufficient mental equilibrium to translate desires into action), and requirements, interference with which threatens these conditions (in humans, these are things like food, clothing, and shelter); and (b) things that are conditions required for successful action regardless of the purposes involved which (in humans) include various kinds of information, not being lied to, and various freedoms such as freedom of movement, and other civil liberties. See, further, Beyleveld, *The Dialectical Necessity of Morality: An Analysis and Defense of Alan Gewirth's Argument to the PGC* (1991) pp. 18–21.

[18] Claim-rights or "strong" rights are correlative to duties on the part of others not to interfere with the possession or doing of that to which the rights-holder has the right.

(5) Whatever any human being has a right to, that human being has a right to have the GF.

Thus, it follows from (2a) that X must assent to

(6) All human beings have a right to have the GF, whatever R-rights are,

and to

(7) All humans have a human right to have the GF.

However,

(8) Any being granted a claim-right must be capable of exercising it,[19] and in order to be able to exercise a right a being must be a PPA.

It follows that X must assent to

(9) All PPAs have a (claim-)right to have the GF, (which is the PGC).[20]

What bearing does this dialectically contingent argument have on the interpretation of the EPC? The answer is remarkably simple. Once human rights are recognised *within a particular legal system*, it is an entirely straightforward logical implication of the dialectically contingent argument that, *within that legal system*, the PGC must be treated as the criterion of legal validity. By the same token, where human rights are recognised by the signatories to an international treaty or convention, those signatories must treat the PGC as the criterion of legal validity. Of course, the implications of accepting human rights might not have been so appreciated by the signatories. Nevertheless, given that the EPC Contracting States had already accepted human rights (*e.g.*, by signing the ECHR), the logic of such acceptance is clear: the Contracting States (and those who interpret their actions) are constrained by the PGC.

To the extent, however, that our second approach is rooted in the Contracting States' acceptance of the ECHR, it might be doubted whether the ECHR is to be correctly characterised as a "human rights" instrument in the sense required by the dialectically contingent argument. One source of doubt can be removed immediately: for, the ECHR clearly respects the essential idea that being human is the sufficient property for possession of human rights. Thus, according to Article 14:

> "The enjoyment of the rights and freedoms set forth in this Convention shall be secured without discrimination on any ground such as sex, race, colour, language, religion, political or other opinion, national or social origin, association with a national minority, property, birth or other status."

---

[19] "May" implies "can" just as much as "ought" does.
[20] Importantly, it also follows that the essential or relevant property of humans with respect to their having rights must be that they are PPAs, which means (at least, in the first instance) that "human" must be interpreted as "having the capacities of agency".

It is also the case, however, that the argument requires such "human rights" instruments to be consistent with the PGC; and, given that the ECHR is not a carbon copy of the PGC, we might anticipate some difficulties concerning, for example, the priorities between competing rights, the adequacy of the reasons for restricting rights, and the absoluteness of particular rights.

There is no real problem here, however. First, the absence (from the ECHR) of a specific criterion for dealing with conflicts between rights *at least* does not contradict the construction required by the PGC that the more important rights are those that are more necessary for action *per se* and for successful action in general (with the rights that are necessary for the former being more important than those that are merely necessary for the latter). Secondly, although the ECHR cites, *inter alia*, the needs of public order, crime prevention, and the like, as conditions justifying the restriction of human rights, it is far from implausible (as, indeed, it is necessary) to see the justification of such restrictions as lying in the protection of the rights of others afforded by the satisfaction of such needs. Thirdly, even though non-derogable rights (such as those provided by Articles 3, 4, and 7 of the ECHR[21]) are not absolute under the PGC,[22] they are extremely fundamental within its structure. It is not unreasonable, and almost certainly wise, where the PGC is being operationalised as a political legal instrument, to present the most important of the PGC's protections as absolute in order to protect against member states being tempted to abuse the right to derogate.

Of course, if interpretation in line with the PGC becomes very strained, it might be preferable to reject specific provisions as mistakes. However, it is suggested that the ECHR may be viewed as a rough guide to the rights required by the recognition of human rights (*viz.*, the rights required by the PGC); and there is no reason, therefore, to think that the dialectically contingent argument cannot be earthed in landmark human rights instruments of this kind.[23]

Assuming that the dialectically contingent argument is valid, it has an important sting in the tail. This is that, if the EPC must be read as subject to recognised human rights (and the PGC), such qualifications are to be read in automatically. Accordingly, even if Article 53(a) did not appear in the EPC, a morality exclusion (centred on human rights and the PGC) would nevertheless have to be implied. It follows that those patent practitioners who would like to see the

---

[21] Art. 3 grants the right not to be subjected to torture or inhuman and degrading treatment or punishment. Art. 4 grants the right not to be held in slavery or servitude. Art. 7 grants the right not to be subject to retroactive punishment.

[22] Under the PGC, there is at most one absolute right (*viz.*, the right not to be killed against one's will).

[23] Similarly, the UN Universal Declaration of Human Rights can be regarded as broadly compatible with the PGC. Indeed, in his most recent book, Gewirth suggests that "the generic rights ... can be construed as a rational reconstruction of the UN's list of rights", with "the generic rights based on the PGC [coinciding] extensionally with the UN Declaration of Human Rights": see Gewirth, *The Community of Rights* (1996) p. 29.

deletion of Article 53(a) from the text of the EPC would not thereby alter one jot the meaning of the Convention – if not explicit, the morality exclusion would be implicit.[24]

(c) Armitage and Davis's criticism

In *Patents and Morality in Perspective*, Edward Armitage and Ivor Davis argue that the patent system is centred on inventiveness not morality; that patent examiners are not qualified to solve moral conundrums; and that Article 53(a) should be invoked only in the most exceptional of cases where it would be inconceivable that a patent should be granted. As for the much-debated *Oncomouse* balancing approach, Armitage and Davis concede that it is "useful" but with the reservation that:

> "... it should be applied to determine not whether the invention falls to one side or the other of a moral mid-point but whether it is so far to one end of the spectrum as to make the grant of a patent the likely receptacle of public outrage."[25]

Moreover, this reservation is underlined in the authors' concluding remark that:

> "What Article 53(a) is dealing with is not inventions which are slightly on the wrong side of a moral mid-point, but those which are clearly contrary to morality – i.e. right at one end of the scale."[26]

Although support for this position can be found in both the EPO Guidelines and in some of the EPO's decisions, most tellingly, Armitage and Davis pray in aid of their position their first-hand knowledge of the intentions of the drafters of Article 53(a). Briefly, according to Armitage and Davis, the original intent of the drafters was to put in place a light regulatory regime; and, although the morality of granting patents on genetically engineered products had not been considered by the drafters of the EPC, Armitage and Davis suggest that they would have seen no reason to draft a more stringent regulatory regime for such applications.

If we have no reason to doubt the accuracy of Armitage and Davis's account of the intentions of the drafters (which we do not), then surely our thesis in *Mice, Morality and Patents* must be mistaken. We think not.

First, Armitage and Davis presuppose a legal positivist framework for their "original intent" thesis, thus disallowing any "external" moral constraints on

---

[24] In its report, *Human Tissue: Ethical and Legal Issues* (1995), the Nuffield Council on Bioethics recommends the adoption of a Protocol to the EPC, setting out in detail the criteria to be used when applying Art. 53(a) to patents in the area of human and animal tissue (see paras. 11.43 and 11.47). Pending adoption of such a Protocol, the Council prefers the maintenance of a "light approach" by the EPO (para. 11.43). Far from having, as the Council puts it, "the advantage of not requiring a change in the law" (para. 11.41), however, the light approach would (on our analysis) maintain a state of affairs that is not supported by law.

[25] *op. cit.* above, at pp. 47–48.

[26] *ibid.* at p. 81.

their understanding of the (subjective) intentions of the drafters of (legal) instruments. As legal idealists, we should not allow such a thesis to pass. However, on this occasion, we will respond to Armitage and Davis on their own terms.

Secondly, if original intent rules, whether applied to the language or the purpose of the instrument, it can only rule insofar as intent is clearly established. On Armitage and Davis's own admission, however, patent applications involving modern biotechnology simply were not anticipated by the drafters of the EPC – their horizons were limited to plant varieties and cross-bred animals; genetic engineering, gene therapy, and the like was still the stuff of science fiction. Nevertheless, Armitage and Davis argue that we should accept the interpretation of Article 53(a) that the drafters would have intended had they foreseen applications such as that in the *Onco-mouse* case. Even for supporters of the original intent theory, this counter-factual qualification must weaken the force of the argument.[27] After all, would Armitage and Davis want to say that in 50 or a 100 years' time the hypothetical intentions of the original drafters should still govern the interpretation of Article 53(a)? For the sake of argument, however, let us concede that Armitage and Davis's view is still defensible.

Thirdly, we come to the fundamental problem with Armitage and Davis's interpretation. Even if original intent (or hypothetical intent) governs, it can only govern in so far as the authors of the instrument in question have lawful authority. What Armitage and Davis assume is that the Contracting States to the EPC had a free hand in agreeing to the terms of the Convention. It follows, on this assumption, that the interpretation of Article 53(a) rests entirely on the intentions of the Contracting States. In the light of our discussion, however, it will be appreciated that this is where we must take issue with Armitage and Davis. Our view is that the drafters of the EPC did not have a free hand; for, to the extent that the drafters were already bound by their own (positive) commitments to human rights, they could not lawfully put in place a patent regime that ignored those commitments. The fact that the drafters neither adverted to their prior moral obligations nor intended Article 53(a) to be read as a token of their commitment to human rights is immaterial. If the drafters tried to legislate against their prior human rights commitments, they acted *ultra vires*; whereas, if they simply did not advert to their prior moral commitments, then such inadvertence must be remedied by construing Article 53(a) consistently with those commitments.

(d) Summary

The moral reference point for Article 53(a) is the critical cultural morality of the Contracting States. Such a reading is in line with the text of Article 53(a). More importantly, however, such a reading allows the EPC to be read in a way that is consistent with the Contracting States' prior commitment to human

---

[27] *cf.* Ronald Dworkin, *A Matter of Principle* (1986) Chap. 1, especially at pp. 13–16.

Patenting Human Genes: Legality, Morality, and Human Rights 19

rights. Having recognised human rights, the Contracting States must also accept the PGC, which now becomes the governing principle of the EPC. On such an analysis, the actual intentions of those who drafted the EPC are relevant (and lawful) only insofar as they are consistent with the background moral commitments of the Contracting States.

2. The morality of patenting human genes

Many of the standard arguments for and against patenting genetic material apply to the patentability of all forms of genetic material;[28] however, it is arguable that procedures involving the human genome give rise to special concerns. So, for example, Article 6 of the latest draft of UNESCO's Universal Declaration on the Human Genome and Human Rights provides: "No scientific advances in the fields of biology and genetics should ever prevail over the respect for human dignity and human rights".[29] Moreover, such concerns are clearly in evidence in the *Relaxin* opposition,[30] the leading case at the EPO on the specific issue of the patentability of human genetic material.

In the *Relaxin* opposition, the patent in question covered claims, *inter alia*, to "a DNA fragment encoding a polypeptide having human H2-relaxin activity".[31] The opponents argued for revocation of the patent in its entirety, largely on the ground that it offended against Article 53(a).

Three arguments were put by the opponents[32]: first, that the "isolation of the DNA relaxin gene from tissue taken from a preganant woman is immoral, in that it constitutes an offence against human dignity to make use of a particular female condition (pregnancy) for a technical process oriented towards profit"; secondly, that patenting genes of this kind "amounts to a form of modern slavery since it involves the dismemberment of women and their piecemeal sale to commercial enterprises throughout the world" thereby infringing "the human right to self-determination"; and, thirdly, that the "patenting of human genes means that human life is being patented", which is "intrinsically immoral". The Opposition Division rejected all three arguments.

Generally, the position of the Opposition Division seems to have been that the opponents' arguments were good in principle but bad on the facts, for it conceded that the patenting of human DNA would be immoral "if it were true that the invention involved the patenting of human life, an abuse of pregnant women, a return to slavery and the piecemeal sale of women to industry."[33] Having so conceded, however, the Opposition Division rejected the specific allegations.

---

[28] See, *e.g.* Macer, "Whose Genome Project?" (1991) 5 *Bioethics* 183, especially at pp. 194–201.
[29] CIP/BIO/96/COMJUR.6/2 (Prov. 5) (1996). Similarly, see the Preamble to, and Art. 1 of, the Council of Europe's Convention on Human Rights and Biomedicine (November, 1996).
[30] [1995] O.J. 388.
[31] Claim 3 of 21.
[32] See para. 6.1 of the decision.
[33] See para 6.3 of the decision.

In relation to the first argument, the Opposition Division pointed out that those who had donated the tissue (that made it possible to isolate the gene) had done so consensually; and, moreover, there was no reason to doubt the morality of procedures of this kind (for many life-saving substances, such as blood-clotting factors, had been developed in this way). The second argument, it was said, betrayed a fundamental misunderstanding. A patent covering DNA encoding human H2-relaxin did not confer on the proprietor a right to any part of any particular human being. No woman was enslaved by the patent; the right to self-determination simply was not affected. As for the idea that the patent entailed the dismemberment and piecemeal sale of women, quite the contrary was the case – the whole point of the invention was to enable human H2-relaxin to be produced in a technical manner outside the human body. Finally, the Opposition Division dismissed the argument that patents on genes (even on the whole human genome) amounted to the patenting of human life. There is, the Opposition Division said, more to a human being than the sum of its genes. Furthermore, if the opponents had no objection to the patenting of human proteins, they could not consistently object to the patenting of human genes encoding such proteins.

Although the points taken by the Opposition Division are convincing enough on their own terms, full engagement with the opponents' arguments was avoided. What precisely the opponents wanted to say is, of course, a matter of interpretation. However, if we treat European critical cultural morality as the reference point for debate under Article 53(a), the thrust of the opponents' objection is clear enough. It is that the patenting of human genes violates human rights (notably the right to human dignity and the right to self-determination) and is, thus, intrinsically immoral in the sense that it would be wrong to resort to goal-based (*e.g.* utilitarian) consequentialist arguments to justify the grant of the patent.

Now, instead of asking whether the patenting of human genes would violate European critical cultural morality (in particular, human rights), the Opposition Division applied the EPO Guidelines ("inconceivability") test. Thus, "the opponents' general assertions concerning the alleged intrinsic immorality of patenting human genes" was said to be "founded on the premise that there is an overwhelming consensus amongst the contracting states that the patenting of human genes is abhorrent and hence prohibited under Article 53(a)."[34] Without too much difficulty, the Opposition Division was able to point to a complex ongoing public debate which, given the inconceivability test, undermined the opponents' general position.

To understand how the Opposition Division and the opponents talked past one another in the *Relaxin* case, consider three rival frameworks for argumentation under Article 53(a), namely: the cultural morality of the Contracting States, the inconceivability test, and the *critical* cultural morality of the Contracting States. Formally, these frameworks differ from one another in two respects: first, in the

---

[34] See para. 6.4.3 of the decision.

extent to which positive and negative evaluations are subjected to critical processing before they are treated as "moral" judgments; and, secondly, as to whether (and how) the level of popular support for a view counts. In a sense, each of these features represents a threshold requirement, one concerning quality, the other quantity. We can deal briefly with each of these matters.

Simple cultural morality imposes no quality threshold – it is enough that some act or other is considered to be "moral" ("right") or "immoral" ("wrong"). If only 51 per cent of New Zealanders "agree with" the patenting of genetic material extracted from plants and animals,[35] and if 69 per cent of respondents in Switzerland oppose such patents,[36] then we can read the cultural morality of New Zealand and Switzerland off these attitudinal survey results. Similarly, to take a famous example in the United Kingdom, if the general public declares an instinctive repugnance to the idea that foetal eggs should be used for infertility treatment, then this so-called "yuk" factor can be equated with simple cultural morality on this particular issue.[37] *Critical* cultural morality, by contrast, refuses to treat such evaluations as "moral" judgments unless various tests of sincerity and rationality are satisfied. However, this does not necessarily channel all moral judgments to a shared view – in principle, *critical* cultural morality allows for protagonists reasonably to disagree with one another.[38]

The inconceivability test apparently speaks to consensus more than to the quality of the consensual view although, to be sure, a test based on "abhorrence" evokes a fairly strident chorus of disapproval and, thus, it seems to be a version of cultural morality. In practice, however, the EPO has applied the inconceivability test with some quality control. As we have seen in the *Relaxin* case, for example, the Opposition Division said that negative evaluations must be based on a correct appreciation of the science, must be consistent with other (positive) evaluations, and must be reasonably stable.[39]

Turning to the quantity threshold, whereas the inconceivability test makes the level of negative evaluation decisive, cultural morality needs a quantity threshold to be specified before it can be put into operation. In principle, cultural morality might be coupled with one of a variety of quantity thresholds, ranging from a low-threshold precautionary approach (in which case, patents would be excluded under Article 53(a) if cultural morality displayed some doubt about the matter at issue) to a high-threshold permissive approach (of the kind

---

[35] See Macer, "Whose Genome Project?" 5 *Bioethics* (1991) 183 at p. 194–195.
[36] See T 0356/93, [1995] E.P.O.R. 357 (Board of Appeal in *Plant Genetic Systems*), para. 15.
[37] See, generally, Human Fertilisation and Embryology Authority, *Donated Ovarian Tissue in Embryo Research and Assisted Conception* (Public Consultation Document, January 1994). For reaction in the USA, see Kolta, "Reproductive Revolution is Jolting Old Views", *New York Times*, A1 (January 11, 1994).
[38] *cf.* n.12 above.
[39] *cf.* above T 0356/93, [1995] E.P.O.R. 357 (Board of Appeal in *Plant Genetic Systems*), where the Board gets quite close to adopting a test of European critical cultural morality, talking about norms that are deeply rooted in European culture, and controlling for bias, stability, and consistency (see especially paras. 6, 14, 15, and 17).

associated with the inconceivability test). With regard to critical cultural morality, however, it hardly makes sense to talk about a quantity threshold. Of course, *critical* cultural morality is founded in the settled convictions of the community (which presupposes some level of acceptance) but, beyond this, interpretation takes over and numbers no longer matter unless the content of the particular critical cultural morality makes numbers count.

In the light of these distinctions, we can detect problems in the *Relaxin* case in relation to both the quality and the quantity thresholds. Most obviously, the Opposition Division imposes a quantity threshold on the opponents' arguments when this is wholly inappropriate. The point is that, if it is judged that patents on human gene sequences violate human rights, then such patents are intrinsically immoral and the presence or absence of an overwhelming consensus condemning such patents is irrelevant. Less obviously, the Opposition Division employs a quality threshold in a one-sided manner. As we have said, the Opposition Division exposes inconsistencies and factual errors in the opponents' position, all the time weakening the (reconstructed) objection that the grant of a patent would be inconceivable. However, an examination of critical cultural morality demands that all arguments are subjected to the same quality scrutiny.

The one-sidedness of the Opposition Division's quality scrutiny is symptomatic, perhaps, of a reluctance to get drawn into a moral balancing approach of the kind associated with the *Onco-mouse* case. However, if the critical cultural morality of the Contracting States is the standard, the EPO is legally required to weigh the moral arguments on both sides; at any rate, it is required to do so if the patent involves violating a prima facie human right, for the patent could only be justified then by reference to more compelling human rights served by the grant. Again, UNESCO's draft Universal Declaration on the Human Genome and Human Rights shows the way, pointing out that whilst human rights to health and well-being can be served by research on the human genome, such research must proceed in a way that respects human dignity and with due regard to human rights.[40]

Had the Opposition Division in the *Relaxin* case dealt with the opponents' objections in this way, the result might well have been no different: it might have been ruled that the patent did not violate any human rights, or that any prima facie violations were overridden by more compelling rights (as determined by the hierarchical ordering of rights within the PGC). However, without such an examination of the issues, the Opposition Division failed fully to engage with the questions raised by the case.

Conclusion

The patenting of human genes looks set to remain problematic. Because of the complex technical checking requirements, patent offices may be unable to

---

[40] See the Recitals and Arts. 4–6.

process applications as quickly as applicants would wish; doubts about whether the technical criteria are satisfied may increase; and, above all, moral opposition to such patents is unlikely to diminish. Recently, for example, in the United States, a coalition of over 250 women's and public health groups has been formed to lobby against the patenting of human genes.

In Europe, the cutting edge of the debate lies with the latest attempt to formulate a revised Directive on the Legal Protection of Biotechnology. Here, the patentability of human genes is tackled from two sides. First, Article 3(1) of the revised draft relies on the standard distinction between "invention" (which is patentable) and mere "discovery" (which is not patentable) to provide: "The human body and its elements in their natural state shall not be considered patentable inventions."[41] Secondly, if human genes are implicated in an invention rather than a mere discovery, then Article 9(2) – drawing on a morality test (Article 9(1)) that runs in terms that are virtually identical to those in Article 53(a) of the EPC – specifically declares that "methods of human treatment involving germ line gene therapy" are to be treated as unpatentable. Thus, the strategy of the draft Directive with regard to applications to patent human genes is to exclude (a) mere discoveries and (b) inventions associated with germ line gene therapy, but otherwise to remit ethical objections (such as those raised in the *Relaxin* case) to the general morality test in Article 9(1). Whether this draft Directive will succeed where its predecessor failed remains to be seen.[42]

For reasons both practical and legal, it is imperative that the terms of the Directive harmonise with those of the EPC. Moreover, given that the members of the European Union share the EPC Contracting States' commitment to human rights, the logic of the argument in this paper is that the Directive must incorporate the same morality as the Convention. That morality, we have argued, is European critical cultural morality, centred on respect for human rights, and (on the basis of the dialectically contingent argument) entailing the PGC. On this analysis, the inconceivability test is, at worst, illegal (notwithstanding Armitage and Davis's appeal to the intentions of the drafters of the EPC) and, at best, a desperately poor way of formulating the correct questions. It follows that European patents should not be granted where they are contrary to PGC-compatible human rights, including the right to dignity. No doubt, the concept of human dignity is open to interpretation and the fact that the revived Directive, unlike its failed predecessor, dispenses with any reference to human dignity, perhaps testifies to its complexity. Nevertheless, if we want to place a moral

---

[41] See, further, para. 53 of the background notes:
"[P]atent law may not, in itself, affect the fundamental principle excluding all rights of ownership in respect of the human being. A gene or a cell, in their natural state, must be excluded from patentability because they cannot be regarded as patentable inventions. In this respect, patent law does not have to adopt an ethical stance for reasons of public policy or morality. It has only to observe its own principles."

[42] Even at the time of publication, significant changes to the draft Directive are being mooted. In particular, there is a school of thought that favours deleting the morality test altogether before the draft is presented to the European Parliament.

question mark against the patenting of human genes, then the concept of human dignity is as good a way as any of highlighting and focusing our reservations.[43] It is a cause for concern, therefore, that the right to human dignity is not more securely established in the jurisprudence of the EPO as well as in the European Union.

---

[43] In fact, this might be too weak a way of expressing the matter, for the concept of human dignity lies right at the root of Gewirthian thinking about agency and human rights: see, *e.g.* Alan Gewirth, *The Community of Rights* (Chicago, University of Chicago Press, 1996) passim but especially at p. 66. For further analysis of the relationship between dignity and human rights, see Deryck Beyleveld and Roger Brownsword, "Human Dignity, Human Rights, and the Human Genome", paper given at Second Meeting of EU Project PL 950207, Sheffield, April 1997.

3

Human Dignity and Property Rights in Human Body Parts

STEPHEN R. MUNZER*

1. Introduction

This essay deals with property rights in human body parts that can be exchanged in a market. The inquiry arises in the following context. With some exceptions, the laws of many countries permit only the donation, not the sale, of body parts. Yet for some years there has existed a shortage of body parts for transplantation and other medical uses. It might then appear that if more sales were legally permitted, the supply of body parts would increase, because people would have more incentive to sell than they currently have to donate. To allow sales is to recognise property rights in body parts. To allow sales, however, makes body parts into "commodities" – that is, things that can be bought and sold in a market. And some view it as morally objectionable to treat body parts as commodities.

I present a qualified case against property rights in body parts that are transferable in a market. As used here, the term "body parts" includes any organs, tissues, fluids, cells, or genetic material on the contours of or within the human body, or removed from it, except for waste products such as urine and faeces. The qualified case rests on a Kantian argument concerning human dignity. But the case is uneasy. There is no swift transition from the mere existence of a market in body parts to a sound objection in terms of commodities and Kantian dignity.

Instead, there is a complicated route strewn with difficulties. Here is a map. Section 2 clarifies why, from a Kantian point of view, sales of body parts are sometimes inappropriate. Section 3 describes three different ways of offending Kantian dignity. Section 4 then shows how to avoid the fallacy of division – a logical error that a Kantian perspective may seem prone to commit. Section 5 comments on two recent contributions to the literature. Finally, Section 6 concludes my uneasy case. Since I cannot exclude the possibility of other or less difficult arguments, this article offers only *an uneasy* case against property rights in body parts.

---

* Professor of Law, University of California at Los Angeles.

I do not offer knockdown arguments for bold conclusions. I do contend that it is morally objectionable for persons to sell their body parts if they offend dignity by transferring them for a reason that is not strong enough in light of the nature of the parts sold. Furthermore, it is morally objectionable to participate in a market for body parts, as (say) a buyer or broker, if by doing so one offends the dignity of oneself or others. Lastly, it is morally objectionable for a market in body parts to exist if its workings offend the dignity of enough participants in the market. These contentions raise a moral objection based on dignity rather than the existence of a moral objection all things considered. That an action or institution is morally objectionable does not entail that one lacks a moral right to do it or participate in it, or that the State or others have a moral right to interfere with the action or institution. I state these qualified results here so that readers who cannot abide any but the most dramatic conclusions will see what is coming and lay this essay aside with the least expenditure of time.

In a previous, inadequate approach to property and persons in *A Theory of Property*,[1] I touched on this topic only sufficiently to question the view that to speak of property rights in the body is to treat persons as "things" or "commodities." I also argued that it is unconvincing to hold that property-talk somehow demeans people by undercutting their autonomy.

This approach is inadequate because, *inter alia*, I did not consider whether people might have property rights in various *parts* of their bodies, and, if they do, which parts and which rights those might be. In a recent essay I identified three different Kantian arguments against property rights in body parts,[2] but I did not develop a promising reconstructed version of one of these arguments. Hence, there is much unfinished business so far as I am concerned. This essay is an effort to remedy some of the shortcomings of my previous discussions. Since whole bodies and their uses raise somewhat different (though related) issues, I do not take up such matters as slavery, indentured servitude, baby-selling, prostitution, surrogate motherhood, or the market for labour.

2. A Kantian starting point

The works of Kant suggest several arguments against property rights in human body parts. One of them – the argument from human dignity – runs as follows. Human beings have dignity (*Würde*). Dignity is an unconditioned and incomparable worth. Entities with dignity differ sharply from entities that have a price on a market.[3] If human beings had property rights in body parts and exercised those rights, they would treat parts of their bodies in ways that conflict with

---

[1] Munzer, *A Theory of Property* (1990) pp. 55–56.
[2] Munzer, "Kant and Property Rights in Body Parts" (1993) 6 *Canadian Journal of Law and Jurisprudence* 319.
[3] Kant, *The Groundwork of the Metaphysic of Morals* (1785) (trans. by Paton as *The Moral Law*, 1948) pp. 96–97.

their dignity. They would move from the level of entities with dignity to the level of things with a price.

This argument, as just presented, is entirely too sketchy to be convincing. To fill it in, one must at least (1) unpack Kant's understanding of dignity, (2) explain his account of persons and their bodies, (3) clarify so far as possible the difference between sales and donations, and (4) articulate preliminarily the connection between selling a body part and being vulnerable to moral objection. I intend the resulting argument to be broadly Kantian in spirit. I do not claim that Kant scholars will find it faultless, or that it is consistent with everything that Kant says.

1. Persons have dignity just by virtue of being human.[4] This dignity is not lost even if a person acts immorally.[5] Moreover, dignity is "unconditioned"[6] – that is, it does not depend on needs, consequences, or other contingent facts. Dignity is also an "incomparable worth," for it is "exalted above all price" and "admits of no equivalent".[7] Thus, one cannot counterbalance an offence against dignity by any increase in price. Dignity is therefore priceless.[8]

Dignity is an attribute not mainly of isolated individuals but of persons as "ends in themselves"[9] who are members of a "kingdom of ends".[10] Persons so understood belong to a moral community in which dignity and autonomy must be ascribed to every rational person with a will. Accordingly, the construction of a legal system for these persons must observe the dignity of each individual.[11]

Let us now join these reflections on dignity with the idea of moral and legal rights. I suggest that Kant's understanding of dignity proceeds from an effort to wrestle with the question of how we must reciprocally recognise individuals in a moral and legal order that affords them equal rights. His answer is that we must ascribe to them the attribute of dignity if a practice of universal equal rights is to make sense. This attribute is transcendentally necessary. That is, ascribing dignity to oneself and others is a necessary condition of the possibility of universal equal rights.

---

[4] See, *e.g. ibid.* pp. 96–97; Kant, *The Metaphysics of Morals* (1797) (trans. Mary Gregor, 1991) pp. 216–217, 230–231, 254–255.

[5] See, *e.g.* Kant, *Lectures on Ethics* (1775–80) (trans. Louis Infield and foreword by Lewis White Beck, 1963) pp. 196–197.

[6] Kant, *Groundwork of the Metaphysic of Morals*, above, n.3, at p. 97.

[7] *ibid.* at pp. 96, 97.

[8] For a sensitive exposition and use of Kant's views on dignity, see Thomas E. Hill, Jr., *Dignity and Practical Reason in Kant's Ethical Theory* (1992) pp. 10, 47–50, 56, 166–167, 178, 202–217, 246–247.

[9] Kant, *Groundwork of the Metaphysic of Morals*, above, n.3, pp. 97–98.

[10] *ibid.* at pp. 98–100.

[11] See Hill, *op. cit.* above, n.8, at pp. 178, 208–209, 246–247, as well as Hill's the general treatment of the "kingdom of ends" at pp. 58–66.

Kant's use of the notion of dignity rests on an innovative reaction to predecessors in the history of political theory.[12] One tradition identifies dignity with honour. Under an ethic of honour, only some persons have dignity. Other persons, who belong to lower orders of moral attainment or of society, lack dignity in the sense of honour, and do not have moral rights equal to those who possess honour. Kant redefines "dignity" in such a way that all persons have it just by virtue of being human. Accordingly, they are all bearers of equal moral and legal rights.

Kant is also reacting to a different tradition, represented by Hobbes, that identifies dignity with price. More precisely, Hobbes separates both "worth" and "dignity" from "honour". Honour he associates with power. Worth is the value of a person as set by his or her price, and dignity is that person's value as set by the commonwealth. In terms of the contrast with Kant, it is what Hobbes technically calls "worth" that is more relevant, and Hobbes insists that "as in other things, so in men, not the seller, but the buyer determines the Price".[13] Kant responds in effect that Hobbes, while he eschews the older honour-ethic, cuts off the branch on which he is sitting. One cannot achieve universal equal moral rights if one appeals only to worth in Hobbes's sense and if persons can have different values or "prices" on the market. Hence, Kant redefines dignity so that, as against Hobbes, it differs from price, and so that, as against the aristocratic ethic of honour, it undergirds universal equal moral and legal rights.

2. If these remarks help to explain Kant's understanding of dignity, they do little to elucidate the complicated, and not terribly clear, account of body parts, whole bodies, selves, and persons on which the argument seems to rest. Although Kant often makes stronger statements,[14] his deepest objection, I think, is only to property rights in some body parts as defined in my introduction. He comments that the "body is part of the self; in its *togetherness* with the self it constitutes the person".[15] He also appears to distinguish between body parts that are organs, such as kidneys or testicles, and body parts that are not organs or otherwise integral to the functioning of the body, such as hair.[16] His emphasis, then, is on the integration or "togetherness" of the various parts that make up a human person. And the core of his protest is against the sale of any part that is integral to the normal biological functioning of that person.[17]

---

[12] James Tully suggested to me this way of looking at Kant's position.
[13] Hobbes, *Leviathan* (1651) (ed. Pogson Smith 1909) Pt. I, Chap. 10, p. 67. Actually, a willing buyer and a willing seller would jointly determine the price.
[14] Munzer, *op. cit.* above, n.2, surveys the stronger pronouncements and suggests ways of using Kant's general moral theory to soften them.
[15] Kant, *Lectures on Ethics*, above, n.5, at p. 166 (emphasis added); *cf. ibid.* at pp. 147–148.
[16] Kant, *The Metaphysics of Morals*, above, n.4, at p. 219.
[17] For a more careful textual reconstruction of this and other Kantian arguments, see Munzer, *op. cit.* above, n.2.

One way to develop this Kantian argument is to distinguish between isolated sales and frequent exchanges in a market. Kant would have concern about both. Even isolated transactions could offend the dignity of the few individuals involved. Yet frequent exchanges pose a graver risk to the dignity of many individuals. If a market is an arrangement in which sellers and buyers make exchanges, and if commodities are items that can be bought and sold in a market, then a market for those body parts integral to normal biological functioning, such as kidneys, would be quite worrisome for Kant. Specifically, the existence of such a market could transform attitudes that human beings have toward themselves and others. They might come to think of one another not so much as moral agents with inherent dignity, but more as repositories of organs, tissues, and other bodily substances. They might dwell heavily on the price that healthy organs would fetch on the market. In sum, a Kantian argument from dignity raises, at least prima facie, a concern about body parts as "commodities" that are exchangeable in a market.

3. But now it is necessary to clarify the difference between sales and donations. Ordinarily, it is easy to distinguish between them. Sales are transfers for value received in return. Donations are gratuitous transfers. An arrangement for donating body parts is not a market, and does not make body parts into commodities.

Yet sometimes the line between sales and donations can be fuzzy. Suppose that A needs bone marrow and B needs a kidney. Their tissues are compatible. A agrees to transfer one of her kidneys to B. B agrees to transfer some of his bone marrow to A. Does it make a difference whether these transfers are characterised as "mutual donations" or "mutual sales"?

It does, but the line can be hard to draw. Sometimes one can draw it. If each says that he or she will transfer even if the other does not, and if one has good grounds for believing both, then the transfers are mutual donations. No commodities are in play and no moral objections arise. But suppose that B realises that it is harder to find histocompatible bone marrow than kidneys and surmises that he may be able to obtain a kidney elsewhere. B then agrees to the mutual transfer with A only if A pays B $20,000. Here the transfers are mutual sales – or at least the transfer from B to A is a sale. Here at least the bone marrow is a commodity, and one can debate whether B's action is morally objectionable. Differently, suppose that neither A nor B requests any cash, but each says that he or she will transfer only if the other does. Here it is hard to make a uniquely convincing case for either the label "mutual donations" or the label "mutual sales." Perhaps "barter" is apt. It is also harder to assess the morality of the motives and actions of A and B.

4. Yet even if the line between sales and donations is clear enough, it is necessary to articulate the connection between selling a body part and being vulnerable to moral objection. Recall that the core Kantian protest involves, in

effect, two strands: selling body parts and losing body parts needed for normal biological functioning. A thought experiment can separate these strands and force consideration of what it is about selling that might be objectionable. Imagine that in the distant future artificial organs and other body parts are plentiful. Only a small subgroup of humans needs natural organs as replacements for organs that have become diseased or injured. A member of the larger group sells various natural organs to members of the subgroup, and immediately receives artificial organs in risk-free surgical procedures. He makes money in these transactions because the price for his natural organs far exceeds the cost of the artificial replacements and the surgeries. Hence, in this hypothetical example, the strand of losing a body part necessary to healthy functioning drops out as a pertinent consideration.

What, then, might be objectionable about selling as such? It will not do to say that the hypothetical seller should get a job rather than sell natural organs for a living. The seller may well be leading a shallow life and not fulfilling the possibilities of a genuinely human existence. Even if that is so, the objection appears to be, not to selling as such, but rather to leading a shallow and unfulfilling life. Nor will it do to say, in the case of some organs or body parts, that they are so bound up with the seller's personal identity that they should not be sold. Examples of such organs or parts might include the brain, face, genitals, hands, tongue, and larynx. Once again, if there is a sound objection, it relates, not to selling as such, but to the transfer of intensely personal parts of the body.

A better answer invokes the *strength of the reason* for selling the organ or body part. Getting money is a superficial reason for transferring a body part, at least when the seller has morally unproblematic ways of earning a decent living. Compare Kant's remark that it is objectionable "to have oneself castrated in order to get an easier livelihood as a singer".[18] Kant's thought here may be that if a somewhat less easy livelihood is still possible, one does violence to the humanity in one's person by becoming a castrato. The hypothetical seller's reason differs from deeper or nobler reasons, such as donating an organ to save the life of a member of the subgroup. Furthermore, receiving money would be an especially superficial reason for transferring an intensely personal part of the seller's body. For such parts, the reason could be deeper if the recipient were the seller's identical twin, though here donating betokens a nobler class of reasons and associated motives than selling.[19] It is, of course, possible for a reason for donating a body part also to be insufficiently strong.

---

[18] Kant, *The Metaphysics of Morals* at p. 219.
[19] Scott, *The Body as Property* (New York, Viking Press, 1981) pp. 222–223, mentions a testicle transplant between identical twins.

As a first approximation, then, selling a body part might be morally objectionable if the strength of the reason for selling is insufficient in relation to the nature of the part sold. This preliminary result should be understood against the background of the following points. First, money is just a medium of exchange. Thus, receiving money in return for a body part is not inherently or always morally objectionable. One has to look at the reason for which the seller wants the money. Secondly, even if selling is morally objectionable, it does not follow that the seller lacks a moral right to sell. Here as in other situations, persons sometimes have a moral right to do what is morally wrong, objectionable, base, ignoble, or degrading.[20] Thirdly, it is logically possible for an entity to have both a dignity-value and a market-value.[21] Nevertheless, it may not be psychologically possible for someone to think of an entity as simultaneously having both and still retain the attitudes typically exhibited toward entities regarded as possessing dignity. And there can be a kind of social split-mindedness if many regard some persons – *e.g.* women or children – as simultaneously having both kinds of value.[22] Fourthly, even if a body part is salable and hence is a commodity, it does not follow that the body part is *only* a commodity. Fifthly, this preliminary result has nothing to do with some familiar Marxian themes. The result does not suppose that anyone is exploiting the seller. Neither does it rest on the idea that exchange-value swamps or undercuts use-value. For instance, if kidneys can be bought and sold, then they have an exchange-value. But this fact does not interfere with their use-value, for sold kidneys, if successfully transplanted, will perform the same functions in the recipients that they did in the sellers. Sixthly, so far only a possible objection to selling body parts has emerged. Lacking at the moment is any account of how buying body parts or the existence of a market for body parts could offend dignity.

3. Three ways of offending dignity

The Kantian starting point has not got us far. It proposes a definitional connection between a market for body parts and a view of body parts as commodities. It suggests that the lack of a sufficiently strong reason is what can make selling body parts morally objectionable. And it introduces some speculative worries about the impact of a market for body parts on dignity. Yet the previous section does not explain how this market, or participating in it, can offend dignity. Providing such an explanation is the next order of business.

---

[20] See Waldron, "A Right to Do Wrong" (1981) 92 *Ethics* 21.
[21] Kant seems to oscillate on this point. In one passage he says that "everything has either a price or a dignity". Kant, *Groundwork of the Metaphysic of Morals*, at p. 96 (emphasis omitted). In another work he writes that man regarded as a natural being can have a "price" even while, regarded as a "person", he has a "dignity". Kant, *The Metaphysics of Morals*, at p. 230 (emphasis omitted).
[22] *cf.* Walzer, *Spheres of Justice: A Defense of Pluralism and Equality* (New York, Basic Books, 1983), Chap. 4.

I shall describe three ways of offending dignity by buying or selling body parts. The classification is consistent with but does not stem from Kant's writings. The first way affronts, insults, or demeans dignity. The offence is direct. The second and third ways degrade the sense of dignity. Here the offences are indirect. They relate proximally to the sense of dignity and only distantly to dignity itself. I shall elaborate.

The first way of offending dignity occurs if and only if an action affronts, insults, or demeans dignity, but does not reduce it. Kantian dignity, it will be recalled, is an unconditioned and incomparable moral worth that all persons have just by virtue of being human. It relates to a transcendentally necessary attribute of human beings. Consequently, this first offence against dignity does not reduce the worth of a person. It cannot do so. Unless the action kills the victim, or produces a mental disintegration that destroys the victim's capacity to act as a rational moral agent, the victim will survive as a person. And were the victim destroyed as a person, the dignity would be destroyed rather than merely reduced.

This first offence against dignity is significant because it is a specially disrespectful form of treatment. If one commits the offence against oneself, one exhibits a disregard for one's own inherent worth. However, I do not agree with those passages in Kant that suggest, for example, that by engaging in prostitution or selling oneself, one "jettison[s] [one's] person" and becomes a "thing" or a worm.[23] These actions, even if they are morally wrong, do not have a once-and-for-all effect. If others commit this offence against a person, indignation and resentment are appropriate. Suppose that a shop foreman upbraids a female employee, calls her a "typical stupid woman", and screams that her job "should be done by a man". She is entitled to protest and rebuke the wrongdoer and defiantly to reaffirm her worth in the face of such treatment.[24] It is a tricky matter to say what sort of intention is necessary to offend dignity in this first way. The verb "affront" suggests that the intention selects dignity as its target. The verbs "insult" and "demean" probably require some less selective or precise intention to offend dignity.

Explaining the second and third offences against dignity requires a pair of additional concepts. One is the *sense of dignity*: an awareness of unconditioned and incomparable worth. This awareness is connected to Kant's understanding of self-respect, which I take to be a sense of inner moral worth that comes from acting on principles rationally derived from the moral law.[25] Unlike dignity, the sense of dignity is partly subjective, since it rests on a person's awareness of his or her moral worth. Furthermore, unlike dignity, the sense of dignity is susceptible of being reduced.

---

[23] Kant, *Lectures on Ethics*, p. 124. But see *ibid.* at pp. 196–197.
[24] See Hampton, "Forgiveness, Resentment and Hatred" in Murphy and Hampton, *Forgiveness and Mercy* (1988) pp. 35–87. Her chapter offers a fuller discussion of the varieties of human worth than can be attempted here.
[25] See Munzer, *op. cit.* above, n.2, at pp. 329.

The possibility of a reduced sense of dignity brings into play the other concept: *degradation*. Elsewhere I have suggested that degradation is treating someone or something in such a way as to reduce, or to attempt to reduce, him, her, or it to a lower level or degree.[26] There are many sorts of degradation. In the present context, a lower level or degree of sense of dignity is meant. So the thought is that to recognise and exercise property rights in body parts might sometimes be to lower a person's sense of dignity.

With these two concepts in hand, I return to the remaining offences against dignity. The second way of offending dignity occurs if and only if an action has, and is intended to have, the outcome of degrading someone's sense of dignity. For instance, if an organ broker in a Third World country intended to make a prospective seller of a kidney feel of lesser moral worth, and if the broker succeeded, the broker would have degraded the prospective seller's sense of dignity. Of course, those who deal in body parts may not have such refined intentions as to undermine a person's sense of moral worth. They are more likely to intend to make money by dealing in organs. But whenever the appropriate intention is present, and the intended outcome is achieved, the second offence against dignity arises.

The third way of offending dignity occurs if and only if an action has, but is not intended to have, the outcome of degrading someone's sense of dignity. Here the person who degrades does not intend to lower a person's awareness of moral worth, but lowers it through some lapse, fault, mistake, misjudgment, or the like. Suppose that you are a medical worker. Through insensitivity, you treat me as a repository of organs and tissues to be sold on the market. I am fragile and my sense of dignity declines. You have offended dignity in this last way.

The relevance to morality of this threefold classification of offences against dignity is as follows. From the standpoint of consequences, the last two offences are more serious than the first. From the perspective of the appraisal of intentions, the first two offences are more serious than the third. Of course, the third offence may still exhibit a kind of moral fault that is distinct from consequences. It can be blameworthy to have allowed oneself to develop, say, the insensitivity to treat others badly without intending to lower their sense of dignity.

Some might argue that the first offence does not amount to much. This "no harm, no foul" approach might work for basketball, but it is not in order here. If I have an unconditioned and incomparable worth, and if you insult that worth by treating me as a repository of body parts, you have offended my dignity even if I have the strength to resist your impositions. I suspect that the root appeal of arguments couched in terms of dignity and the sense of dignity is not to consequences. Rather, it is to the moral inappropriateness of treating human beings in a way that does not comport with their equal moral worth in a community of moral agents.

---

[26] *ibid.* at p. 322.

The general payoff of this section is that participating in a market for body parts can sometimes undercut the distinction between dignity and price, and thus sometimes undermine the practice of mutual recognition as equal rights-bearing citizens. To appreciate this general point, one should, however, attend to the three different ways in which buying and selling body parts can offend dignity. Otherwise, one can fall into using such words as "demeaning" or "degrading" without noticing that they can apply to different situations requiring careful discrimination. In contrast to the previous section, we now have a tentative explanation of how market activities in addition to selling might sometimes offend dignity.

To prevent misunderstanding I should offer these points about the argument thus far. First, offences against dignity, as understood here, are offences against the dignity of particular persons – whether sellers, buyers, brokers, or other participants in a market for body parts. They are not offences against an abstract or general dignity that floats as a brooding omnipresence in a Kantian sky. Second, that the sense of dignity is in some measure subjective requires no apology. Evidently, it can be tricky to discover the extent to which the second and third offences reduce a person's sense of dignity. Still, an inquiry of this sort is no more troubling than that into any moral position that recommends beneficence or contains a principle against harm. In all such cases one has to discern the existence and extent of an impact on one person of the actions of others. I am not claiming that all persons who buy or sell body parts have negative subjective reactions that one can call reductions in their sense of dignity.

4. The fallacy of division

Any sound argument against property rights in body parts that uses a concept of dignity must avoid the fallacy of division. Those who commit this fallacy make the mistake of arguing that what is true of a whole must also be true of its parts. In the present context, the fallacy comes up in this way. Human beings have dignity. Human beings can also suffer offences against dignity in three different ways. But it is fallacious to argue that, in consequence, human body parts have dignity or can suffer offences against dignity. Similarly, even if a living human being has an unconditioned and incomparable worth, it does not follow that parts of that human being's body do. And even if persons lack property rights in themselves or their whole bodies, it does not follow that they lack property rights in their body parts or that those parts are not commodities.

Now some may respond that no serious thinker could be tempted by such obviously faulty reasoning. But Kant is a serious thinker, and some passages suggest that he succumbed to this temptation. For example, he writes that a man "is not entitled to sell a limb, not even one of his teeth." Part of his argument for this position is that "a person cannot be a property and so cannot be a thing which can be owned, for it is impossible to be a person and a thing, the proprietor and the property".[27] But even if persons cannot have property rights in the whole of their persons or their whole bodies, it hardly follows that they lack property rights in parts of their bodies. The quoted passages do not reflect Kant's best or considered thinking on this topic. Still, they indicate that this sort of logical blunder can attract a sober and intelligent, if momentarily unwary, philosopher.

To avoid the fallacy of division, one or both of two related strategies might be pursued. The *integration strategy* insists on the unified organisation of the various body parts, of widely different kinds, that make up a living human being. The broadly Kantian view sketched in Section 2 exemplifies this strategy. Pursuing the matter in this way suggests a gradient of concerns about body parts as commodities. The concern is less serious for hair and for replenishable fluids such as blood and semen. It is more serious for a single paired but non-renewable organ such as a kidney. And it is more serious still for single nonrenewable organs such as the heart, liver, or pancreas. This gradient of seriousness is an attractive consequence of the integration strategy.

The *derived-status strategy* invokes the fact that the various body parts are, or were, parts of a living human being and can have more or less personal connections with that human being. The status of the part has something to do with the status of the whole and its role in the whole. A gradient of appropriateness of treatment as a commodity suggests itself, and concern about the ultimate use of the part is relevant. Here are some examples. If sold blood is used for transfusion, the concern is minimal. But if sold blood is used as a movie prop in place of so-called Technicolor blood, the concern rises. If sold skin becomes a graft for a burn victim, the concern is minimal for cadaveric flesh but rises for skin supplied by a living person. And if sold skin is used for upholstery, the concern is great indeed. Differently, a sold kidney raises fewer concerns about appropriateness, because the function of a kidney is not especially personal. Concerns rise in the case of a sold testicle because (*inter alia*) any child conceived through it will have the genetic makeup of the seller rather than the recipient. If, fancifully, one could, while alive, sell one's face with the transfer to take effect at death, concern would be great, because one's face is intensely personal. This gradient of appropriateness of treatment is an appealing consequence of the derived-status strategy.

The latter strategy may seem problematic for two reasons. First, degrading uses are not confined to human beings or human body parts. For instance, one could degrade an original painting by Rembrandt by urinating on it or using it as a dart board. One is then no longer treating it in a way appropriate to a work of art. Now I agree that various objects can suffer degradation. And Section 3 observes that there are many sorts of degradation. Still, my argument in no way requires that *only* body parts or persons be vulnerable to degradation. But persons alone are susceptible to the sort of degradation that involves a reduction in the sense of dignity.

---

[27] Kant, *Lectures on Ethics*, p. 165. See also Munzer, *op. cit.* above, n.2, at pp. 7, 8–10.

Secondly, the derived-status strategy reflects concern about specific uses rather than treating body parts as commodities. Thus, it would also be objectionable to use *donated* blood as a movie prop or *donated* skin as upholstery. Now I agree that such uses of donated body parts are objectionable. All the same, I wish to argue that there is something particularly objectionable about *selling* body parts for uses of these sorts. The argument rests on a point made in Section 2 – namely, that sometimes receiving money in return for a body part is an insufficiently strong reason for selling, especially when the part sold is to be used in an inappropriate way. Hence, a special concern arises when body parts both suffer degrading uses and are commodities. It is, though, in no wise a feature of my argument that only sold body parts can be put to degrading uses.

I do not claim that obtaining money is always a frivolous, trivial, superficial, or shallow reason for transferring a body part. Modest need can be reason enough for selling blood or semen. And dire need can justify the sale of other body parts. There are reports of a vast market in kidneys and maybe even eyes and skin from the Persian Gulf to China.[28] The sellers are the desperately poor. The ultimate recipients are affluent patients with renal or corneal disease or severe burns. These transactions can involve an offence against dignity. Yet it does not follow that, all things considered, the desperately poor lack ample justification for the sales. Writ large, a market in body parts may be prima facie objectionable, but on balance barring such a market may not be justified. Doubtless some redistribution of income and wealth is the most effective way to restore hope. Yet, short of that, sellers should recognise that they are worth *incommensurably more* than the amount their body parts would bring on the market. They are human beings with an unconditioned and incomparable worth. This self-recognition is a reason for holding on to a sense of dignity in the face of assaults on their struggle to live.

5. Property, politics, and language

In a discussion elsewhere, I tried to identify the different participants in a market for body parts and to investigate the impact on dignity of using the language of the market.[29] I stand by that discussion.

Just enough space is available here to comment on a pair of new contributions to the literature.[30] In a thoughtful and elegant article, Mark F. Grady stresses the dangers of *politicising* body parts.[31] He does not address market transactions

---

[28] See, *e.g.* Wallace, "For Sale: The Poor's Body Parts" *Los Angeles Times*, August 27, 1992, p. A1.

[29] Munzer, "An Uneasy Case against Property Rights in Body Parts" (1994) 11 *Social Philosophy & Policy*, pp. 259–286, at pp. 277–284, 285, 286.

[30] I do not take up Radin, *Contested Commodities* (1996), because most of her book weaves together previously published articles. Munzer, "Uneasy Case," pp. 263–266, *op. cit.* above, n.29, at 270–271, addresses some of her views.

[31] Grady, "Politicization of Commodities: The Case of Cadaveric Organs" (1994) 20 *The Journal of Corporation Law* 1, pp. 51–68.

for present delivery of body parts from living human sellers ("spot sales"). Rather, for purposes of contrast he targets "forward sales" of cadaveric organs. Grady is as aware as most that dangers may lurk in the "commodification" of cadaveric organs as a result of forward sales. But his central point is that the administrative allocation of cadaveric organs could damage our discourse more than a market could.

Grady provides some analogies. One is gasoline in the 1970s. In response to the oil crisis, the federal government made administrative allocations and imposed price controls. As a result, "gasoline stopped being a commodity and was invested with many of the attributes that society normally reserves for merit goods".[32] Another analogy is rent-controlled apartments in Santa Monica, California, in the 1970s and 1980s. Such apartments tended "to fall into shortage at the regulated price".[33] In both cases the consequences, according to Grady, were regrettable. Grady worries that government regulation of cadaveric organs, in the form of disallowing forward sales, harms public discourse more than would the language of the market.

With some reservations, I accept Grady's point. The analogies of gasoline and apartments to cadaveric organs are only partial. Until there exists a market in forward sales of cadaveric organs, it is difficult to know whether the language of the market would be more, or less, regrettable than the language of politics and administrative bureaucracy. Yet surely Grady is right to say that some forms of "politicising" body parts might be quite unfortunate.

In a lucid and concise volume, E. Richard Gold devotes systematic attention to the implications of what he calls "property discourse".[34] He contends that property discourse, in its application to body parts, is likely to drive out other forms of discourse.

To my knowledge, Gold's work is the first book-length treatment of body parts that pays special attention to property and the language of the market. For that reason alone it is a welcome contribution. Readers will find much of interest in his discussions of such famous cases as *Moore v. Regents of the University of California*[35] and *Diamond v. Chakrabarty*.[36] In addition, his chapter on "Translating Value" brings some philosophical sophistication to the analysis of different scales of value and to the distinction between commensurability and comparability.[37]

I express three reservations. First, Gold defines "property discourse" too narrowly as "the sum of the assumptions, conceptions, and language used by

---

[32] Grady, *op. cit.* above n.31, at p. 62.
[33] *ibid.* p. 65 (footnote omitted).
[34] Gold, *Body Parts: Property Rights and the Ownership of Human Biological Materials* (1996).
[35] 51 Cal.3d 120, 793 P.2d 479 (1990), *cert. denied*, 499 U.S. 936 (1991). See Gold, *op. cit.* above, n.34, at pp. 23–39, 44, 46, 48, 138–140, 156–157, 161, 177, 181–185.
[36] 447 U.S. 303 (1980). See Gold, *op. cit.* above, n.34, at pp. 78, 80–85, 108, 115, 145, 165, 198–199.
[37] Gold, *op. cit.* above, n.34, at pp. 144–163.

judges, lawyers, and legislators in allocating rights of control over goods".[38] Legal officials play by far the most important role in setting up and modifying discourse relating to property. But the use of this discourse by everyone determines whether it adversely affects the dignity of individuals. Secondly, Gold presents inadequate arguments for the proposition that "any supplementary discourse would likely be drowned out by property discourse".[39] His main arguments appear in the final chapter and are largely conceptual in character.[40] What one also needs, and Gold does not provide, is empirical evidence regarding the use of market and non-market language. Thirdly, Gold offers no deep account of the nature of an alternative to property discourse concerning body parts. He tends to work from the non-market elements – *e.g.* of a shared life or a socially sanctioned relationship – in several perspectives on property.[41] Lacking is a well-articulated alternative that is anchored in philosophical bedrock. The Kantian view pursued in this essay may have appeal precisely because it rests on a subtle and probing view of human dignity.

6. The uneasy case concluded

This case against property rights in body parts is uneasy. One reason is the difficulty in clarifying what is objectionable about selling as such. A second reason is that a market in body parts has varied participants as well as many who do not participate at all. Hence, the extra-linguistic effects on them will vary significantly. Yet another reason is that our understanding of the effects of the language of the market, *for this sort of market*, is sketchy. There is, then, no rapid and cogent move from the mere existence of a market in body parts to a sound objection, in terms of commodities and Kantian dignity, to that market.[42]

---

[38] Gold, *op. cit.* above, n.34 at p. 7.
[39] *ibid.* at p. 17.
[40] *ibid.* pp. 164–177
[41] See Gold, *op. cit.* above, n.34, at pp. 166–168.
[42] This essay reproduces about half of Munzer, *op. cit.* above, n.29, which is reprinted in full in *Property Rights* (Ellen Frankel Paul, Fred D. Miller, Jr., and Jeffrey Paul, eds.,1994). My views on this topic have not changed in the meantime. Section 5 of the present version is new.

For help with this essay I am indebted to Richard L. Abel, Ellen Brostrom, Evan Caminker, David Copp, Ralph A. DeSena, David Dolinko, John Martin Fischer, Gary Gleb, Mark F. Grady, Rebecca Gudeman, Kenneth L. Karst, M. B. E. Smith, and James Tully. I also owe debts to my colleagues and seminar students, to members of the Law and Philosophy Discussion Group, and to the participants in the W. G. Hart Legal Workshop in London (July 1993) and in the Social Philosophy and Policy conference on property rights in Palo Alto, California (April 1993). I am thankful for a fellowship from the National Endowment for the Humanities and financial support from the Academic Senate and the Dean's Fund at the University of California, Los Angeles. (Copyright 1994 Social Philosophy and Policy Foundation. Reprinted with the permission of Cambridge University Press.)

4

The Legal Status of the Pre-Embryo: Some Comparative Considerations Prompted by *Davis v. Davis*

ANTONELLO MIRANDA*

1. *Davis v Davis*[1]: Facts and questions concerning a new artificial insemination case

The development of artificial insemination techniques has given rise to various issues complicating, from a legal point of view, the subject of affiliation which is in itself problematic.

As is well-known,[2] the most important question to have arisen concerns the topic of "surrogate" affiliation and motherhood or "womb-leasing" – of which

---

* Acting Professor of Comparative Law, Department of Private Law, Palermo University, Italy.
[1] *Davis v. Davis*, Tennessee Ct of Appeals, September 13, 1990, Lexis, p. 642.
[2] There is a great deal of writing about artificial insemination and its related problems. We can point out: Lojacono, "voice Inseminazione artificiale", in *Enc. dir.*, XXI, Milano, 1971, p. 751; Trabucchi, "La procreazione ed il concetto giuridico di paternità e maternità", in *Riv. dir.civ.*, 1983, II, p. 780; Palazzo, "Esperienze straniere, raccomandazioni del Consiglio d'Europa e prospettive per la regolamentazione in Italia della fecondazione in vitro", in *Quadrimestre*, 1984, p. 653; Pellegrino, "L'inseminazione artificiale – un dato che il diritto continua ad ignorare", in *Stato civ.*, 1984, p. 702; Santosuosso, "Riproduzione umana artificiale e diritto", in *Iustitia*, 1985, p. 345; Tortorici, "Spunti per una regolamentazione dell'inseminazione artificiale", in *Riv. dir. fam.*, 1984, p. 1058; Alpa, "Appunti sull'inseminazione artificiale", in *Riv. crit. dir. priv.*,1985, p. 333; "Comporti, Ingegneria genetica", in *Iustitia*,1985, p. 312; Del re, "Inseminazione artificiale, fecondazione in vitro e trapianto di embrione: alla ricerca dei genitori perduti", in *Temi rom.*, 1985, p. 352; Dogliotti, "Inseminazione artificiale – Problemi e prospettive", in *Giur.it.*, 1985, IV, p. 417; Lombardi Vallauri, "Manipolazioni genetiche e diritto", in *Iustitia*, 1985, p. 1; Piccoli, "Tecniche di fecondazione artificiale e 'nascituri' – Necessità di una normativa sulla bioingegneria", in *Riv. notar.*, 1985, p. 687; Semizzi, "Rilievi giuridici sulla fecondazione artificiale", in *Riv. dir. fam.*, 1984, p. 360; Auletta, "Fecondazione artificiale: problemi e prospettive", in *Quadrimestre*, 1986, p. 1; Gandolfi, "Profili civilistici della fecondazione artificiale", in *Giur. it.*, 1986, IV, p. 84; Milan, "La madre su commissione. Problemi giuridici, in Manipolazioni genetiche e diritto", in *Quaderni Iustitia*, Milano, 1986, p. 314; Scannicchio, "One way return. Da Roe aWebster, Libertà di scelta e controllo statale nella giurisprudenza costituzionale americana sull'interruzione della gravidanza", in *Riv. crit. dir. priv.*, 1990, p. 506; Busnelli, "Il diritto e le nuove frontiere della vita umana", in *Jus*, 1988, 1, pp. 27–53; Zatti, "Quale statuto per l'embrione?", in *Riv. crit. dir. priv.*, 1990, p. 437.

the case *Re Baby M.*[3] is emblematic – and the matter of "heterologic" insemination.

Despite all the efforts made and the legislative projects which were proposed[4] and even implemented,[5] the problems which had to be confronted were rarely solved in a satisfactory way, while new questions were posed. This shows that when such complex elements are involved, the statute law, especially if it is prohibitive, can really do little.[6]

Conversely, so-called "homologous insemination", that is the treatment which uses a wife's ovules and her husband's sperm, seemed to avoid causing particular problems (in instances where the wife subsequently wishes to terminate the pregnancy); and it seemed to have dispelled and solved all the doubts and questions about the certainty of paternity which, obviously, by this supposition was put beyond doubt. But, even in this quiet little room far from the violent polemics of artificial insemination, a "small" and absolutely unexpected development produced new doubts and problems.

This development was considered in the well-known judgment delivered by the Court of Appeals of Tennessee in *Davis v. Davis*. The court had to determine to whom, as between a husband and wife, then divorced, belonged the "custody" of, and the right to take care of and make decisions about, seven ovules fertilised by a homologous process and cryo-preserved pending a possible implantation in the uterus.

The question has aroused considerable interest because it has ethical, moral and biological aspects. As far as legal analysis is concerned, against the background of the lack of full recognition of the legal status of the "pre-embryo", there are explosive implications for the various practical and theoretical considerations.

The Court of Appeals of Tennessee, amending the judgment delivered at first instance[7] in favour of the woman, (a judgment which had, in a certain sense,

---

[3] The American judgment relative to the *Baby M.* case may be read in *Riv. dir. fam.*, 1987, p. 1515, with comment by Miranda, which is recommended for further bibliographical references.

[4] The reference is clearly relative to the project Santosuosso, *i.e.* an Italian Reform Commission asked to realise a legislative project on artificial insemination (Italy has not yet a statute or any other rule in this field).

[5] On the English law about artificial insemination see Criscuoli, "La legge Inglese sulla 'surrogazione materna tra' riserve e proposte", in *Riv. dir. fam.*, 1987, p. 1029.

[6] Here it is not possible to deal in depth with the problem. However, I believe that a law that is prohibitive of any kind of artificial insemination, cannot be an obstacle for new questions and cannot solve those which have already arisen. It is enough to think that the Italian prohibition of heterologous insemination, would draw people towards those countries where it is allowed, as has happened (and happens) in the case of abortion. Also, admitting the possibility of a prohibition and the punishment of those involved (the doctor?, the"surrogate parents"?, the biological ones?), there would remain the problem of guaranteeing protection to the most innocent party: the child.

[7] The text of the judgment is published in *Riv. dir. fam.*, 1990, p. 829, with notes by Di Pietro and L. Eusebi. See *Davis v. Davis* 15 Family Law Reporter 9092.

The Legal Status of the Pre-Embryo

recognised the human subjectivity of the embryo from the moment of fertilisation), held that both the custody and the right to choose the destiny of ovules fertilised by the homologous process belonged to both persons who contributed to the fertilisation.

The decision is articulated in four fundamental propositions:

1. A fecundated and cryo-preserved ovule, composed of a number of identical cells, variable from a minimum of four to a maximum of eight, even though it can contain all the genetic patrimony of the future human being, is not yet "differentiated", but remains in a "cellular" condition. Consequently this ovule cannot be considered in the same way as a foetus or as an embryo already implanted in the uterus (which itself is less protected than a born child).
2. The fertilised and cryo-preserved ovule, however potentially vital, is not "living" and cannot be considered from a narrow legal point of view in the same way as a "person".
3. If it is true that there is a constitutionally protected right to procreate, there is also a constitutionally protected right not to procreate; it is therefore necessary to balance these two rights according to circumstances and observing the terms of the law.
4. Both parties, the woman and the man, have equal interest in fertilised ovules and consequently both the custody and the right of control and disposition must be exercised jointly by both of the persons who contributed to the fertilisation.

The judgment further cites laws and precedents about the right to procreate and about the custody of the embryo in order to emphasise the peculiarity of the point at issue before the court, in comparison with the precedents.

The court justifies its own decision "distinguishing" the facts from the previously expressed hypotheses.

2. The logical-deductive pattern of the judgment: The choice of the concrete solution most coherent with the system

The problem in itself may be considered and perhaps also solved in each of the various aspects which it involves. I shall not attempt here to deal with the biological, ethical and moral aspects of the question. This will avoid confusing different analysis criteria and distorting the reading and comprehension of data caused by mixing more or less consciously moral, ethical or religious opinions with the technical-legal ones.

The decision of the American court can be fully accepted, if considered from a strictly legal point of view and if put within the frame of a pre-existing set of rules. Besides, we can observe how those judges were able to deal with such an insidious case whilst trying to come to a solution which is harmonious with the system.

Before coming to a more specific examination of the decision it is necessary to emphasise that the judges of the Court of Appeals of Tennessee wanted, first of all, to solve the controversy of establishing who should decide the fate of those seven fertilised ovules. In doing this they did not carry their analysis of the facts beyond the logical-systematic continuity of the system; in other words the court, in order to solve the question, decided to apply only legal parameters and to disregard moral, ethical and political impediments.

The mistake made by the court of first instance (if it is possible to speak about a mistake) would be that of giving rise to a remarkable example of judge-made law, by dictating new rules for the future rather than deciding the specific question – "usurping" the legislator's prerogatives. Even in common law systems, this law-making power of judges does not go so far as to allow delivering judgments which are not integrable with the system.

On the contrary, on account of the characteristics of those systems,[8] the work of the law aims at a careful reconstruction of the system which takes place through the interpretation of needs and expectations of a developing society but not with the aim of effecting this development[9] which is a political task.

Just this anxiety is expressed in the words of the Court of Appeals: "We are asked to solve the problem which was submitted to us in conformity with the Tennessee legal system and with the constitutional rights granted to the parties". For the court the solution of the case cannot be but the solution most in conformity with the existent set of rules, that is, the solution most likely to avoid trauma and the raising of other problems and complications.

3. Gradation and balance of different rights

However, one of the most controversial aspects of the decision may be the one in which the fundamental scientific and legal difference between fertilised ovules and the already implanted embryo is ascertained (we mean the pre-embryo that is something hardly more developed than a simple cell).

It is important to notice how this distinction made by the court is less important in view of the equally serious consideration that the embryo is not protected by the law in the same way as a "person". Quite apart from the demonstration of the scientific and legal difference between the pre-embryo and the embryo, it could be argued that in any case we would not be confronted with a subject who is fully entitled to his rights.

---

[8] On the English system, the paradigm of common law systems, see an Italian work, Criscuoli, *Introduzione allo studio deldiritto inglese, Le fonti*, Milano, 1980.

[9] For reflections on the theme and for bibliographical information see: Miranda, "Codificazione e common law", in Atti Accademia Lett. *Scienze ed Arti di Palermo*, 1987, II, p. 135 (8 *bis*). See below, n.12.

One of the most important points is the observation that both the law and the cited precedents assert that the protection of the foetus is always a partial protection, less than that which is granted to a "person" born alive. For example, among the authorities cited by the court such as the federal and Tennessee laws, as well as the cases *Roe*[9a] and *Webster*[9b] some recognise a certain protection for a foetus implanted in the uterus for at least three months. This protection is, however, less than the consideration given to the well-being of the mother. Furthermore, other laws do not consider the foetus or the embryo to have the same rights as a "person"; this is, for instance, the case with the Tennessee Wrongful Death Statute which, in order to give compensation for damages, makes a clear distinction between the protection granted to a person born alive and the lesser protection afforded to the foetus.

Apart from the question of whether the fertilised ovule must be considered an embryo or not, the court observes that the system provides a gradation of protections and acknowledgements which may be shared or not but which, in any case, exist and must be observed; the mother's right to health takes precedence over the right of the foetus to be born; the right of the mother to terminate her pregnancy prevails over the right to life of the (less than three-months-old) foetus; the right not to procreate of each parent prevails over the right of the unborn child.

The American constitutional idea itself leaves out "a legitimate correlation between the existence of the 'subject' and the purely factual moment of conceiving (*i.e.* the legal relevance and importance of the interests of the conceived)".[10]

As the judgment states: "this legislative pattern shows that developed embryos are granted some protection and greater respect than simple human cells ... but they are not granted a status equivalent to that of an already born child".

We must notice that this statement is not the same as saying that "the life of the embryo begins when the child is born", nor that the life of the embryo is postponed "until the moment in which the foetus is able to be independent outside the mother's uterus".[11]

The court, indeed, did not want to deal with the question of vitality or not of the embryo at all, nor with the question of "personal existence" or the beginning of human life after conception. The court limited itself to notice that the laws and precedents clearly distinguish between the embryo and the born child, according two different kinds of protection to them. The court fully recognises the legal protection of the human embryo. Nevertheless, this protection is, with-

---

[9a] *Roe v. Wade* 410 U.S. 113 (1973); 35 L. Ed 2d 147.
[9b] *Webster v. Reproductive Health Services* 400 U.S. 173 (1991); 114 L. Ed 2d 233.
[10] This is Scannicchio's statement. See "One way return. Da Roe a Webster. Libertà di scelta e controllo statale nella giurisprudenza costituzionale americana sull'interruzione della gravidanza", *op. cit.*, above n.2, at p. 506.
[11] Di Pietro, "Sette embrioni in cerca di una madre: nuova sentenza dello Stato del Tennessee", in *Riv. dir. fam.*, 1991, p. 102.

out doubt less clearly defined than that granted to a born child and, furthermore, it does not prevail over other constitutionally granted rights such as the mother's right to health.

Even if the fertilised ovules may be considered in the same way as an already implanted embryo, their protection should always be compared not only with the constitutional rights granted to the mother but also to the father's constitutional rights. In fact, it is possible that, in the Tennessee legal system, the law fixes different parameters of protection, granting freedom and rights to some persons rather than to others. So the system is free to consider when, how and in what measure the embryo's right to life (or that of the foetus, or of the fertilised and implanted ovule) does not prevail in comparison with man's freedom to procreate, without denying in any case a protection or a specific advantage.

4. The "property" in the pre-embryo and the scheme of fructification: A new perspective for Articles 820 and 821 of the Italian Civil Code

If it is the law-making context which justifies the behaviour of the Court of Appeals, we have to ask why the American court confirmed the fundamental difference between the fertilised and cryo-preserved ovule and the already implanted ovule. This distinction is based on the fact that the latter may be considered as a human being while the former might be considered as biological material. In my opinion the court held this opinion for two reasons. The first is that by this maintained difference it is possible to distinguish whether pregnancy has started or not. The court wants to emphasise that "no pregnancy is being carried out"; this is an important point because the mother's right to choose depends on it. The court supports this position by affirming that fertilised but not implanted ovules are juridically different from an embryo. The court does not consider that pregnancy has started at the moment of fertilisation but more exactly, until implantation (something which may be postponed for a long period). Until that moment, both a man's and a woman's right *not* to procreate exists.

After implantation, the right of a woman to choose should prevail, at least, according to the precedents set down in *Roe v. Wade* and *Webster v. Reproductive Health Service*,[12] until it would be possible to interfere with this freedom to choose. Such interferences should aim at defending the potential human life.

The precedent in *Roe v. Wade* (and those derived from it) in fact, apply only in cases in which the ovule is already implanted in the uterus with the consequent prevalence of the mother's right of choice. The "biological father" could

---

[12] For a deeper examination of the two decisions see: Scannicchio, *op. cit.* above, n.10, See also Criscuoli, "L'opposizione del marito all'aborto voluto dalla moglie: dai casi 'Paton' e "Danforth' all'art. 5 della legge n. 194 del 1978", in *Riv. dir. fam.*, 1979, p. 222.

The Legal Status of the Pre-Embryo

not intervene at all except before the beginning of the pregnancy and after a certain period from the beginning of the pregnancy. Since the fertilised and cryo-preserved ovule was not yet implanted in the uterus, it would still be at both of the subjects' disposal. This means that the right to procreate or not, of both a man and a woman, would be equal and so neither of them would have a greater protection or a greater acknowledgement under the law.

The second reason is directly linked to the first one. In fact, it is necessary to establish to whom belongs the right of care and disposition, and for what reason. The position the court prefers, the one which considers the fertilised ovules as "biological material", is the only one which justifies technically the attribution of the power of disposition to both the interested parties.

In my opinion, this case would be analogous to what the Italian legal system asserts for separated parts of the body. Hence, we must consider the application of the natural modes of acquiring ownership to these separated parts:

1. It is not by the old conception of *ius in se ipsum*[13] – which would be inapplicable because it would not be possible to bring within the sphere of self-ownership those parts which, once separated, have been joined to others of different origin, creating in this way something new and different[14];

2. It is not by the conception which considers these parts *res nullius* as a consequence of *derelictio*, and consequently, subject to acquisition by occupation[15] – also this mode of acquisition would be inapplicable, either because, as has been pointed out,[16] it would first be necessary to show "through the verification of the *modus acquirendi*" that the subject is vested with a right, or because in the case under consideration it would be difficult to demonstrate the hypotheses of *derelictio*, or because we would face a more complex problem; in fact, we should suggest the acquisition by those who are interested in using them, that is the doctor or health service involved;

3. It is not by the thesis of *derelictio*[17] – inapplicable in this case, either because *derelictio* would not be one of the typical cases provided for acquisition[18] or because, in the case under consideration, it would be necessary to reckon with two *derelictio* which give rise to something new and different in comparison with the single separated part; but

---

[13] On the theme see: Bianca, *Diritto civile*, 1, Milano, 1978, p. 163; De cupis, *I diritti della personalità*, II ed., Milano, 1982, p. 168; D'addino Serravalle, *Atti di disposizione del corpo e tutela della persona umana*, Camerino, 1983, 129; Criscuoli, *L'acquisto delle parti staccate del proprio corpo e gli artt. 820 e 821 c. c.*, in *Riv. dir. fam.*, 1985, p. 266.

[14] See Criscuoli, L'acquisto . . . , *op. cit.* above, n.13, at p. 268.

[15] *cf.* Bianca, *op. cit.* above, n.13, at p. 163 s.; Dogliotti, *Le persone fisiche*, in *Trattato di dir. priv.*, 2, Torino, 1982, 81.

[16] Criscuoli, *op. cit.* above, n.13.

[17] De Cupis, *op. cit.* above, n.13, at p. 178.

[18] Criscuoli, *op. cit.* above, n.13, at p. 270.

4. It *is* by the scheme of "fructification"[19] as provided in Articles 820 and 821 of the Italian Civil Code. Consistently with this scheme we should consider "fruits" all those goods whose existence "derives from mother-thing and that, correlatively to this origin, have the stigma of new-good that is an independent good, as a structural entity and as a source of exploitation".[20]

In the case under consideration both these characteristics are present. There is no obstacle in "the consideration of body as "thing" or "mother-thing" because this term, as used in the rule, has a clearly metaphorical meaning referring to every entity, living or not, capable of productivity".[21]

As far as concerns entitlement to the property we may refer to Article 821 of the Italian Civil Code which allows that the "fruit" is originally acquired by separation from the subject owner of the mother-thing and consequently admits, in abstract, the possibility of a "co-ownership" for an hypothesis like the one under examination, supposing that it would be possible to give a symbolic and not exclusive or selective meaning to the literal reference to the right of property.[22] The fertilised ovules would be as available as the single ovule, the single seed, the blood or an organ (parts considered "viable" but not living and composed of cells containing the genetic patrimony of human beings); but their availability would be subject to the co-ownership of the parties that contributed to fertilisation.

The unilateral decision to postpone the joint determination of the parties obviates certain complications; we should think of the problem of trying to avoid at least the legal consequences deriving from this "paternity" when it is ordered in favour of the implantation of ovules against the "father's will"; or the problem of justifying technically the "gift" of these ovules (which, if considered "persons", they could not be given, sold or even surrendered); or the problem of establishing if all seven ovules or only some of them will be implanted.

Secondly, the unilateral choice is not exclusive in itself; it does not exclude that the ovules in question might be given, one day, to other sterile couples so that they could be led to achievement. In this way, the objection of those who maintain that the bilateral control of the ovules could be justified only if it is supported by the intention of both the parties to do everything to secure their survival, would fail. In my opinion this would be considered a laudable intention from an ethical or religious point of view, but completely irrelevant from a legal perspective. Perhaps my attitude, and that of the court, could seem reductive and cynical because it aims at dealing with this delicate subject only from a strictly legal point of view. It tries to find a solution which (in the "tragic

---

[19] Criscuoli, *op. cit.* above, n.13, at p. 272.
[20] *cf.* Barcellona, voice Frutti (dir. civ.), in *Enc.dir.*, XVIII, Milano, 1969, p. 215.
[21] Criscuoli, *op. cit.* above, n.13, at p. 272.
[22] Criscuoli, *op. cit.* above, n.13, at p. 274.

choice" which one must make) can cause the least trauma possible, even at the cost of sacrificing deserving positions of tutelage. But I believe this is the only way to give concrete, functional and sure answers, in line with current developments, to the requests of a scientifically and technically evolving society.

5

Theft of Information and the Concept of Property in the Information Age

DEBORAH FISCH NIGRI*

This paper demonstrates why it is necessary to attribute proprietary rights to information for criminal purposes, and considers the consequences of such an attribution. Special attention is devoted to the importance of information in our computerised world, and the need for effective protection from possible misuses. The paper also discusses why it is difficult to apply traditional concepts of criminal law to information.

1. Introduction: Computers in the information age

Computers are a valuable asset because of the information they can store and retrieve in a fraction of a second. As computers have become faster and easier to operate, society has gained from their use. Information travels across nations and business transactions have become dependent on these machines.

The alliance of computers and telecommunications produced further developments such as the use of telex, facsimile services, teletext, and vast networks such as the Joint Academic Network (JANET) which links universities for exchange of information and realisation of advanced research. Along with all the facilities at scientific levels, technological advances led to the computerisation of offices and business increasing their potential with the aid of such machines. Now the Internet has firmly taken its place in the computer world.

The rapid growth of the computer industry raised fundamental questions regarding storage of confidential information, privacy, data protection and crime. Traditional criminal law is not well-adapted to meet these problems.

In this paper I shall consider the intrinsic characteristics of information and the need to grant proprietary rights to information, at least for the purposes of the criminal law.

Information is a special kind of asset capable of being exploited by criminals. Because information comprises an *intangible* asset it does not attract proprietary rights, therefore the level of protection given to it is extremely thin,

---

* Solicitor and independent consultant, Rio de Janeiro, Brazil. This paper was written in 1993 for presentation at the W.G. Hart Workshop.

especially in English law. To address this problem we need a new theory of "criminal information law" as developed by several renowned researchers.[1]

The theory of criminal information law recognises information as a new economic, cultural and political asset, and as having a "specific danger potential". In adopting and recognising such a theory, information will be considered as an asset in its own right, disassociated from the rules governing tangible and corporeal objects. The holder of the information will be protected by the law guaranteeing the integrity, accessibility and availability of such information.

In a federal provincial study in Canada, the notion that protection of information should be based on proprietary rights was rejected. The practice adopted was based on an *entitlement* approach where an analysis of why a particular type of information should be protected, why persons should or should not have access to certain types of information, and what limitations should be imposed in such circumstances.[2] In Canada this viewpoint is well-illustrated by the decision of *R v. Stewart*.[3] A decision was reached in this case by the Ontario Court of Appeal stating that information could be stolen, but it was later overturned by the Supreme Court generating passionate debates.[4]

The law of theft in England does not cover theft of information as decided in *Oxford v. Moss*.[5] The decision in *Oxford v. Moss* makes it clear that removing an important paper in itself can be theft, provided the necessary *mens rea* is proved, but removing a paper with intent to return it after copying or memorising the information contained on it does not constitute criminal conduct. The inadequacy of such a decision becomes obvious when we consider that the paper itself is worthless, but the information it contains is invaluable and such information *becomes* worthless once the element of confidentiality is lost by the appropriation of the paper.[6] The reluctance of English courts to consider information as property was reiterated in *R v. Absolom*,[7] where it was decided that trade secrets could not be stolen.

---

[1] Sieber, Bing, Vivant and Vandenberghe.
[2] See Piragoff, *National Report for Canada*, in the proceedings of the AIDP Colloquium on Computer Crime and Other Crimes Against Information Technology, (1992) at p. 29.
[3] (1983) 5 C.C.C. (3d) 481, C.A. reversed by (1988) 1 S.C.R. 963, S.C.
[4] There has been a lot of criticism regarding both decisions. For criticism regarding the Court of Appeal decision see Brown, "Computer-Related Crime Under Commonwealth Law and the Draft Federal Criminal Code" (1986) 10 C.L.J. 376; Hammond, "Theft of Information" (1984) 100 L.Q.R. 252, and "Electronic Crime in Canadian Courts" (1986) 6 O.J.L.S. 145. For criticism of the Supreme Court decision see Doherty, "Stewart: When is a thief not a thief? When he steals the 'Candy' but not the 'Wrapper'" (1988) 63 *Criminal Reports* (3d) 322. For further discussion see Hughes, "Computers, Crime and the Concept of 'Property'" (1990) 1 (3) *Intellectual Property Journal* 154; and Magnusson, "Kirkwood and Stewart: Using the Criminal Law Against Infringement of Copyright and the Taking of Confidential Information" (1983) 35 *Criminal Reports* (3d) 129.
[5] *Oxford v. Moss* (1978) 68 Cr. App. R. 183.
[6] See Weinrib, "Information and Property" (1988) 23 (2) *University of Toronto Law Journal* 140.
[7] *The Times*, 14 September 1983. See Coleman, *The Legal Protection of Trade Secrets*, (1992) p. 96.

In the United States, Public Law 102–561 amended the Federal Criminal Code to impose felony sanctions for the infringement of *any copyrighted work*. It seems that the original amendment was specifically directed to computer programs but the scope has now been extended to deter piracy of "motion picture, sound recordings, computer programs and other original works of authorship".[8]

I shall argue that effective criminal remedies should be provided in relation to any *kind of information*, especially information held in digital form, and not only copyrighted work.

2. Information and changing the concepts of legal property

In adopting a traditional definition, *property* is "anything that can be owned". The *Oxford Concise Dictionary of Law* makes a "distinction between *real property* (land and incorporeal hereditaments) and *personal property* (all other kinds of property), and between *tangible property* (that which has a physical existence, *e.g.* chattels and land) and *intangible property* (*choses* in action and incorporeal hereditaments)". The definition goes on to say that "For the purpose of the law of theft, property includes all real, personal and intangible property. For the purposes of the law of criminal damage, property does not include intangible property".[9]

The desirability of applying the concepts of property and ownership to information is becoming more evident. However, the concept of property is itself a difficult legal concept. Nevertheless, there is an imminent need to recognise that the modern conception of property must be fully "de-physicalised."[10]

The common law conception of property at the end of the eighteenth century[11] saw property as an absolute dominion over things. Property was "that sole and despotic dominion which one man claims and exercises over the external things of the world, in total exclusion of the right of any other individual in the universe".[12] This was a "physicalist" concept of property that required some external thing to serve as the object of property rights and such absolutist concept gave the owner the sole and despotic dominion over the thing. A basic distinction was made between real property, which was fixed and immovable, such as land, and personal property, which was movable, such as goods and money.

The creation of a new concept of property started with the necessity to create non-physical forms of property and the definition started to shift to embody

---

[8] See (1993) 9 *Computer Law and Security Report* at 94. Penalties comprise imprisonment for five years if at least 10 infringing copies have been made during a 180 day period where the copies have a retail value in excess of $2,500. The infringing act must be done for a commercial advantage or private financial gain.
[9] *Oxford Concise Dictionary of Law* (2nd) at p. 322.
[10] See Weinrib, *op. cit.* above, n.6, at p. 118. See also Vandevelde, "The New Property Approach of the Nineteenth Century: The Development of the Modern Concept of Property" (1980) 29 *Buffalo Law Review* 325.
[11] William Blackstone *Commentaries on the Laws of England* (1765).
[12] *ibid.*

rights over values rather than over a thing. By the end of the nineteenth century legal property rights were given to business goodwill, and lately in trademarks and trade secrets, courts created property rights where nothing tangible existed leading to the *dephysicalisation* of property.[13] Today the path is leading in the same direction regarding proprietary rights over information.

Although the main issue in this paper is to discuss information as property under the concepts of traditional criminal law the problems of ownership of information are equally present in the civil law sphere. However, civil law has a primary goal to provide protection to the owner of the property by means of financial recompense. Such loss might be recovered from the person who caused it. Civil law is designed to cover the relationship between individuals. The role of criminal law is quite different. Criminal law exists to protect both individuals and society as a whole, and such protection highlights its public nature. It is in the public interest that the State exercises its powers to deter the law breaker and society expects a prompt response against any abuse. In that sense criminal law is more ample and its deterrent powers are stronger than civil law.

Property consists of rights, privileges, and powers that the law recognises over a particular subject-matter. For the purpose of this paper, property rights are taken to include rights over access and use of information stored in computers. Practically, this means that the concept of property should not involve only the so-called *enjoyment of access*, but should also involve the *control over access*.

The importance of protecting the computer environment and the system's integrity is highlighted as being of paramount importance. According to one author

> "[O]ur social institutions exist to further certain ends: if property rights are assigned, the expectation must be that such an assignment will achieve a more desirable result than would otherwise be the case. The law of property is thus purposive. In economic terms, the protection of property rights serves as an incentive to encourage conduct we consider desirable by regulating the actions of others in relation to that protected interest".[14]

Following this assertion, it can be said that it is in the interest of society at large, which is dependent on computers and which is essentially made up of computer users, that appropriate and strong protection should be given to the assets computers hold.

(a) The developing nature of property concepts

Property rights to tangibles are well established. However, the concept of property should not be static. The law does not exist in a vacuum and therefore cannot remain unaffected by the large changes in the communication of

---

[13] See Vandevelde, *op. cit.* above, n.10, at p. 335.
[14] See Weinrib, *op. cit.* above, n.6, at p. 121.

information. Some may argue[15] that the notion of property is relative and that the relativity of property is not simply a matter of time and place. The extent of resources in relation to which proprietary rights may be affirmed varies according to the advance of modern technology.

The moves in English law to recognise property rights in information have been very slow. The attribution of proprietary status to information both for criminal and civil purposes allows judge and jury to construct exclusive rights in a manner that such information will be effectively protected against any appropriation by improper means.

(i) *Civil Law*   In 1769 Yates J. wrote: "Nothing can be the object of property which has not a corporeal substance".[16] Such an assertion might have been the correct one to make then, but today it is quite difficult to accept. Equally, from the commercial reality, it is difficult to accept that "*in general, information is not property at all. It is normally open to all who have eyes to read and ears to hear*".[17] A more hopeful approach was expressed by Lord Hodson:

> "I dissent from the view that information is of its nature something which is not properly to be described as property. We are aware that what is called 'know how' in the commercial sense is property which may be very valuable as an asset. I agree with the learned judge and with the Court of Appeal that the confidential information acquired in this case can be properly regarded as the property of the trust".[18]

Although civil law as it developed was able to extend the concept of property to intangibles such as business goodwill and trademarks, courts often have to supplement legislation to unprotected intangibles. This was the case with the famous US Supreme Court decision in *International News Service v. The Associated Press*.[19] In this case the protection granted by the court was related to the plaintiff's rights to property.

It is argued, in the context of this paper, that *information* includes information at private level, and confidential information at business level, such as trade secrets. If a trade secret, which gives a certain company supremacy over its competitors is misappropriated, disclosed or unlawfully used, it is imperative that in addition to the protection already provided by civil law, criminal provisions should apply. Confidential information should also gain proprietary rights as confidential information of commercial value is a form of intangible property. Indeed, one area of law which establishes a premium on the assertion of control over the access of strangers to the benefits of a distinct resource is the legal protection of confidential information.[20]

---

[15] Kevin Gray, "Property in Thin Air" (1991) 50 (2) *Cambridge Law Journal* 252 at p. 296.
[16] Cited by Weinrib, *op. cit.* above, n.6, at p. 122.
[17] Lord Upjohn, in *Boardman v. Phipps* [1967] 2 A.C. 46 at p. 127.
[18] *ibid.* at p. 107.
[19] 248 U.S. 215 (1918). In this case "news items" was considered by the court as *quasi* property.
[20] See Gray, *op. cit.* above, n.15, at p. 300.

In considering the importance of confidential information in cases of industrial and commercial espionage, where computers play an important role, it is believed that penal trade secret protection supported by adequate civil provisions concerning unfair competition should be established. It seems that a conceptual objection to the categorisation of confidential information as property lies in the fact that information disappears or "evaporates", as one author writes, "when it reaches the public domain, or when third parties, whether independently or by reverse engineering, make the same discovery"[21]. Nevertheless, there are a few examples of property rights that can disappear if certain events occur: property rights in a trademark disappear when it becomes widely used generically; copyright and patent protection are lost after a specified time.[22]

In the United States, the US Supreme Court ruled that the taking of confidential information such as a trade secret constituted the taking of property. In *Ruckelshaus v. Monsanto*[23] and in *Carpenter v. United States*[24] the right of exclusive use of confidential information as a property right was recognised. The court, however, made clear that such property right is extinguished if such information is public knowledge or generally known in an industry, at which stage it ceases to be a trade secret.

In England the issue of attributing proprietary rights to information is controversial, both in civil and criminal law. Nevertheless, in the civil law sphere, early English authorities spoke about property in confidential information.[25] The most distinguished case was *Prince Albert v. Strange*[26] where a set of drawings made by Queen Victoria and her husband were sent to a printer to be engraved. Copies of the engravings came into the hands of the defendant who prepared a catalogue describing the works that were being prepared for a public exhibition. The court said that the plaintiff had a common law right of property in the drawings. Such protection extended to the information describing the work, which he was "entitled to keep wholly for his private use and pleasure, and to withhold altogether, or so far as he may please, from the knowledge of others".

Other early authorities are *Exchange Telegraph Co. Ltd v. Gregory and Co.*,[27] *Exchange Telegraph Co. Ltd v. Central News Ltd*,[28] and *Exchange Telegraph Co. Ltd v. Howard and Manchester Press Agency Ltd*.[29] The three cases concerned a plaintiff who was involved in the business of collecting information such as stock prices, horse races and sporting news respectively, who took

---

[21] R. G. Hammond, "Quantum Physics, Econometric Models and Property Rights to Information" (1982) 27 *McGill Law Journal* 47.
[22] See Weinrib, *op. cit.* above, n.6, at p. 128, n.43.
[23] 467 U.S. 986 (1984).
[24] 484 U.S. 19 (1987).
[25] See Weinrib, *op. cit.* above, n.6, at pp. 130–131.
[26] (1849) 2 *De Gex and Smale* 683 at 697.
[27] [1896] 1 Q.B. 147.
[28] [1897] 2 Ch. 48.
[29] (1906) 22 T.L.R. 375.

action against a defendant who secretly obtained information from one of the plaintiff's subscribers and used it in his own business. The plaintiff obtained an injunction restraining the defendants from copying the information on the basis that he had property rights in the information.

In *Exchange Telegraph Co. Ltd v. Howard and Manchester Press Agency Ltd*, Buckley J. made a statement that illustrates how important any kind of information can be for its *owner*. He said:

> "The plaintiffs carry on the business of collection and distributing information. The knowledge of a fact which is unknown to many people may be the property of a person in that others will pay the person who knows it for the information as to the fact. In unpublished information there is a right of property, or there may be in the circumstances of the case. The plaintiffs here sue, *not in copyright at all, but in respect of that common law right of property in information which they had collected and were in a position to sell*. Their case is that the defendant stole their property, that he has surreptitiously obtained that which belonged to them and used it in rivalry with them" (emphasis added).[30]

(ii) *Criminal law* The definition of crime embraces two basic elements to characterise the wrong and establish a cause of action: the *mens rea* that is the required intention, and the existence of the *res*. The concept of *res* is related to the concept of *property*. The traditional concept of *property* can cause confusion in the courts as it embraces the specific differences between tangible and intangible property, as seen above.

Traditionally property theory divided property into real or personal property. The area of personal property embraces rights and privileges, which comprise an abstract *dominium* protected in Roman law. Roman law developed the absolute right of supremacy over *res*, which could be corporeal or incorporeal. The intangible *res* is the right itself.[31] Therefore, property in Roman law included not only the property itself but all rights involved in that property. It seems that such concept was not integrated in the modern concept of property for criminal purposes.

Tangibility is usually integral to the notion of property. However, certain intangible property can be the object of illegal appropriation. Intangible property includes patents, trademarks, trade secrets and copyright. Nevertheless, the fact that intangible property can be stolen does not mean that anything that is intangible can be stolen. In relation to computerised information the problems start here. *Information* is not qualified as property as it cannot be owned. Hence, information held in a digital form imposes certain restrictions to the application of traditional criminal law.

---

[30] For further details see Libling, "The Concept of Property: Property in Intangibles" (1978) 94 L.Q.R. 103.
[31] See Dunning, "Some Aspects of Theft of Computer Software" (1980) 4 *Auckland University Law Review* 292.

The unauthorised removal of information from a computer system is usually regarded as theft. There are some jurisdictions that consider such an act as a related offence, such as larceny or stealing.[32] Traditionally, theft is the dispossession of a tangible item belonging to another with the intention of retaining it. In relation to theft of information, it seems that the whole problem centres on the word *dispossession*.

In a *traditional* theft a person steals property belonging to another and retains this property. The victim does not hold the property any longer. In the computerised world, the tangible property, *i.e.* the medium containing the information, if stolen, would comprise the traditional offence of theft. However, in cases of software theft or pure theft of information, dispossession does not occur. The perpetrator usually copies the information contained in the disk. The "owner" of the information, technically speaking, does not lose anything. Another problem faced by *dispossession* is that if information is not regarded as property in the first instance as it cannot be owned, how can the holder of the information be dispossessed? If information is removed and the system itself is not damaged by any physical interference, difficulties are expected for the prosecution.

A useful comment by J. C. Smith[33] might elucidate the question of ownership in relation to appropriation of information. On referring to the law of theft the author mentions that *"stealing has never impaired the ownership of the victim of the offence. The owner in nearly all cases remained owner of the stolen property. So it is a perfectly logical conclusion that there might be a theft though the owner in fact loses neither ownership nor possession of the property"*. Clearly, those assertions could prove correct if information *per se* be considered as a special kind of intangible property.

In several European countries the requirement is that the offender takes an *item of another person's property*.[34] In the United States, in some jurisdictions, property is interpreted in conjunction with the notion of *thing of value* that includes intangibles such as computer programs.[35] In *Hancock v. State*,[36] considered the first major case to deal with computer abuse, an employee of Texas Instruments Automatic Computer Corporation was convicted of theft of 59 computer programs and of trying to sell them to one of the company's clients. The defendant argued that the programs did not constitute corporeal

---

[32] In Australia, the New South Wales and South Australian legislation retains the common law offence of larceny meaning that the defendant takes and carries away personal goods of another with the intention of depriving the owner of the property without the owner's consent. In the Crimes Act 1958 (Victoria), s.72, the concept of stealing is preserved. See Hughes, "Computers, Crime and the Concept of 'Property'" (1990) 1 (3) *Intellectual Property Journal* 154.
[33] [1988] Crim.L.R. 611 at 614.
[34] Belgian Penal Code, ss.461, 463; French Penal Code, art.379; German Penal Code, ss.242, 246; Greek Penal Code, ss.372, 375; Italian Penal Code, s.624; Penal Code of Luxembourg, s.461.
[35] Such as in *U.S. v. Girard* 601 F.2d 69 (2nd Cir., 1978).
[36] *Hancock v. State*, 402 S.W. 2d, 906; 379 F.2d, 552 (1967).

personal property because no original documents were removed from his employer's premises and therefore could not be the subject of theft. His arguments were dismissed as the court found that the Texas Penal Code, Article 1418, which defined property subject to theft, included "all writings of every description, provided such property possesses any ascertainable value", therefore software came within the definition of the statute.

On appeal the defendant argued that computer software could not be construed as a corporeal personal property and that the real value was the trade secret contained within the documents, but trade secrets were non-corporeal property. However, the court accepted the judicial construction of the State law and concluded that in "light of the Texas court there was ample evidence that Hancock committed the offense for which he was indicted."[36a]

The English Theft Acts of 1968 and 1978 also provide the above requirement. In England, the Theft Act 1968 replaced the old law of larceny (Larceny Act 1916) that required the occurrence of the physical movement of a thing. The Theft Act 1968 depends mainly upon the appropriation of *property*. Section 1(1) of the Act provides that "A person is guilty of theft if he dishonestly appropriates property belonging to another with the intention of permanently depriving the other of it, and thief and steal shall be construed accordingly."

Under section 1 of the Theft Act 1968, the offence of theft will depend on the appropriation of property rather than the removal of a thing. Section 3 defines appropriation as "any assumption by a person of the rights of an owner" and property is partially defined in section 4(1) as to include "money and all other property, real or personal, including things in action and other intangible property".[37]

Prior to the Theft Act 1968, the old law of larceny required the physical movement of a thing, thereby intangibles could not be stolen. Today, the expression "things in action" covers personal rights of property such as company shares, trademarks, bank balances or copyright. Patents are considered as being other intangible property according to section 30(1) of the Patents Act 1977 and not things in action. The concept of theft of intangible property is confusing as it does not include the theft of anything that is intangible. The intangible item must fall within the definition of property and qualify as such.

Apart from the problems that the expression things in action may bring, some serious problems arise in relation to information held by computers. Information held in digital form suffers an enormous limitation regarding the applicability of the law of theft to cases of computer-related fraud, for instance. The information stored by computers nowadays is of important and sensitive value, commercially and personally. As seen above, it seems that information cannot be

---

[36a] *ibid.* at p. 553.
[37] Other provisions of s.4 embrace questions of theft of land, or things forming part of land, theft of certain plants and theft of wild animals.

owned, therefore it does not fall within the definition of property protected by the law of theft. The most famous case that confirmed the fears that section 1 of the Theft Act 1968 could not provide protection for copying of intangibles in the computer context was, indeed, not a computer-related case as mentioned above.[38]

Although there are strong arguments stating that *information* is a different kind of intangible property not capable of being stolen like bank balances, it must be appreciated that to a greater extent, *information* has become an object in its own right. The necessity to associate information with a medium, a physical object in a book, or a disk is becoming difficult to assimilate. It is true that to provide information with the status of property is a quite courageous approach and may cause confusion.

However, whenever a company invests in the development of a software product, for instance, thousands of pounds are spent in research, time, and engineering skills. When the product is ready to reach the market it is often sold at very high prices. If the high quality software is *stolen* and consequently sold for an inferior price, the manufacturer and the retailer are losing a substantial amount of money. Computer software contains useful information and it is bought and sold as any other product. The intangible information contained in a computer program has thereby an immense commercial value. In fact the product is bought because of the relevant information it contains. Therefore why not consider it as property if there is a considerable amount of profit to be obtained from such intangible assets? It seems that in considering computerised information as a corporeal object a lot more could be achieved in the legal sphere. Although copyright laws were adopted to offer legal protection against unauthorised reproduction and use of software products, little has been achieved on the criminal front.

If certain information is commercially valuable, such as industrial information, a product of research and intellectual efforts by one company, and that information is acquired by a competitor, but he simply copies the information from a disk and returns the disk, does this mean that nothing has been stolen? It seems that under current law the answer is yes, nothing was stolen. If the competitor profits from this unlawful taking wouldn't he be guilty of an offence? Clearly, he is depriving the original owner of the information of his profit. In the English Criminal Law, the Law Commission proposals on computer misuse have not recommended changes in the interpretation of the Theft Act in order to give to some kinds of information the condition of property. Some may argue that to do so in English law "would involve reading the Theft Act in a very robust way for the purposes of producing a dramatic new offence".[39] Maybe by deciding to do so, many successful prosecutions could be achieved.

---

[38] *Oxford v. Moss* above *op. cit.*, n.5.
[39] Griew, *The Theft Acts 1968 and 1978* (5th ed., 1986).

(b) Balancing interests in the property approach

The employment of proprietary rights to information may have the disadvantage of creating a monopoly over information for private benefit. However, from a legal perspective, the main challenge is to balance private and public interests in providing protection to information.

Defining information as property demands drawing this balance between private interests, third party's interests, and social interests in the free flow of information. Nowadays there is an eager demand to promote better and faster expansion of information in the interests of science and to build an open society. Free flow of information plays an important part in that demand being recognised as a vital element for the democratic society. In contrast to these strong claims, there is an urgent need to grant proprietary rights to information. Such a move will provide exclusive rights to those associated with property rights in tangible and corporeal objects. The approach developed in this paper advocates the necessity to provide strong and effective protection to information in the computerised environment without preventing access to information to lawful beneficiaries.

In the United States it seems that two different approaches have been advocated and can be used to equalise the above interests.[40] One approach is concerned with defining rights in case-specific analysis and uses a so-called "transactional balancing". This approach of decision-making assumes that competing interests need to be viewed in each particular context or in a particular transaction. For example, in copyright issues the balancing is most explicit in the context of "fair use" situations. Nevertheless, in the copyright context, one may say that some balance needs to be found between the interests of copyright owners in controlling modifications to their works and the interests of the consumers who are able nowadays to take enormous advantage of the flexibility or "plasticity" of works represented in digital form.[41] Works stored in computerised form can be easily corrected, changed, altered, and more usefully, updated. In the digital world one typical example is the relatively easy way that computer programs can be reversed, engineered or decompiled in the process of being transformed into unrecognisable forms.

The second approach uses a "categorical balancing". In this case property conceptions are evaluated and defined on a balance of interests. If it is decided that there is a property right, such right can easily be enforced without any further inquiry whether the right *should* exist. One can still ask if in a particular case the preconditions for creating such right actually exist, but the property right exists independently. In the categorical approach there is a clear rule stating that the

---

[40] See Nimmer and Krauthaus, "Information as Property – Databases and Commercial Property" *International Journal of Law and Information Technology*, Vol. 1, No. 1, at p. 10.
[41] See Samuelson, "Digital Media and the Law" (1991) 34 (10) *Communications of the ACM*, at p. 25.

right exists. It seems that when a commercial interest is at risk the latter approach is preferable.

Because information can be considered, in principle, as a *public good*, there are some doubts whether property rights should be extended to it in full scale. In the criminal law context all interests described above that need to be balanced and equally protected by the law, may suffer some kind of misuse. Private interests of the creator, assembler, or holder of information might be violated through unauthorised access and copying of an entire database or computer file. In the electronic database domain, piracy is greatly facilitated by the use of modern communication networks. Society's interests as a whole might be at risk if a database containing information about AIDS or HIV is accessed and misused placing human lives at risk. In that situation it is in the public interest that such misuse does not occur. Therefore it can be seen that the balance of interests, which is often divided between public and private interests, in reality are blended into one common interest, which is to protect information itself from any kind of abuse.

The law will have the responsibility to regulate and to avoid the unfair impacts of technology. Sometimes the law will act protectively, such as in the case of copyright protection of software, and sometimes the law will serve to punish, such as in cases of theft or fraud. Theft of information is a complex area that needs both preventative and punitive measures to provide deterrence which existing legislation does not provide.

3. Final remarks

The misuse and abuse of information, especially of information held in digitalised form, has extended beyond civil law into areas of criminal law. More important than extending old criminal law concepts to fit theft of information is the consideration of extending proprietary rights to information, and to consider information as an asset in its own right. Reliance on traditional criminal statutes covering property offences, even though somewhat adapted through judicial interpretation, will not suffice as far as theft of information is concerned, nor will a simple expansion of the definitions of property in established theft provisions. Instead, a comprehensive legislative program is necessary. The argument that special recognition is not needed for such an asset overlooks basic needs which enable laws to be passed to remedy improper conduct.

In this paper, it is submitted that the traditional concepts of tangibility and property ought to change to provide an adjustment of the law to the information technology era. A complete reconstruction of old ideas is needed in view of the new information technology law age. The concept of dispossession in cases of software theft or theft of information must also change. It is suggested that dispossession occurs when software or information is duplicated and such duplication is unlawful. Therefore, if information is obtained in an unfair way for the victim, this information must be regarded as property for the purposes of a successful prosecution. It is further suggested that reliance on copyright laws to tackle such questions is insufficient because traditional copyright law does not cover unauthorised access, use or damage to information.

For criminal law itself, the early thesis that property is necessarily associated with "things" has been weakened. The argument that information deserves proprietary protection has been reinforced over the years. In the United States, the view that trade secrets can entail property rights has become more widely held. Criminal law began to address more directly the concept of information as property for that body of law. Furthermore, for criminal law, there is an emergent need to re-define the concept of theft taking into account the problems of information stored in digital form. In the United Kingdom, as has been seen, regarding theft of intangibles such as digital information, it is contended that the law must change significantly. For instance, the concept of "permanently depriving", stated in the Theft Acts of 1968 and 1978 would have to be revised. Although the provision of the Theft Act 1968 defines property to "include money and all other property real or personal, including things in action and other intangible property", the offence still seems to be addressed to tangible objects.

Apart from restricting unauthorised access to information, which in the United Kingdom is covered by the Computer Misuse Act 1990, there is a need to provide effective protection for assets held in computers. The intention is mainly to achieve protection above and beyond existing and old fashioned concepts of criminal law. The gist of the law should be to acknowledge that it is better to provide protection to *information* in the first instance than not to have it at all. Granting proprietary rights to information beyond existing concepts of the criminal law sphere fulfils this aim.

6

Compulsory Expropriation and Company Law

GERARD McCORMACK*

This paper looks at the power of compulsory expropriation in the company law context. The focus is on the position of a shareholder within a company and the limits of property ownership.

A shareholder may be bought out against her wishes in a couple of situations. First, there is statute-backed expropriation. A takeover bidder who acquires 90 per cent of the shares in a company is permitted by statute to acquire the remainder compulsorily, at a fair price. This may be regarded as equivalent to the power of eminent domain where land is acquired for public purposes. The analogy soon falls down, however. In the eminent domain context public interests are at stake, whereas, in this context, the interests of one private party are given precedence over those of another. Such ordering may seem questionable and the compatibility of the relevant statutory provisions with the European Convention will be addressed.

The second situation of compulsory expropriation arises by private contractual arrangement. The constitution of a company, a contractually-constituted document, may permit one shareholder to be bought out against her wishes in certain circumstances. The proper limits on contractual stipulations of this nature will be considered.

Compulsory expropriation by statute

As noted at the outset of this paper, statute provides a mechanism whereby a takeover bidder whose bid has met with almost complete success may acquire the remaining shares compulsorily. The relevant provisions are now contained in sections 428–430F of the Companies Act 1985 (Part XIIIA). Part XIIIA was inserted into the Companies Act 1985 by section 172 and Schedule 12 of the Financial Services Act 1986 to supersede a less detailed and sophisticated set of procedures already in place. The legislative provenance of the compulsory acquisition regime may be traced back to the Companies Act 1928 where the

---

* Reader in Law, University of Essex.

provisions were introduced as a result of the recommendations of the Greene Committee.[1] The committee said:

> "It has been represented to us that holders of a small number of shares of the company which is being taken over . . . frequently fail to come into an arrangement which commends itself to the vast majority of their fellow shareholders with the result that the transaction fails to materialise. In our opinion this position – which is in effect an oppression of the majority by a minority – should be met".[2]

The provisions have been somewhat amended over the years. Nevertheless, the basic principle remains the same – a dissentient minority may be bought out compulsorily where a takeover bid has achieved at least a 90 per cent acceptance level. One of the main changes brought about in this area by the Financial Services Act 1986 was to allow a minority to serve a "reverse acquisition notice". In effect the minority may change their minds once they realise the extent to which a takeover bid has been successful and the takeover bidder may be compelled to buy them out.[3]

Compulsory expropriation and the European Convention

Although Britain has not incorporated the provisions of the European Convention on Human Rights into its domestic law it is bound by the terms of the Convention on the international plane.[4] The Convention along with many written constitutions explicitly protects private property rights. Part XIIIA divests a shareholder of what might loosely be described as property rights against her wishes. The question therefore arises as to the compatibility of the provisions of Part XIIIA with the Convention. Article 1 of Protocol 1 to the Convention is in the following terms:

> "Every natural or legal person is entitled to the peaceful enjoyment of his possessions. No one shall be deprived of his possessions except in the public interest and subject to the conditions provided for by law and by the general principles of international law.
>
> The preceding provisions shall not, however, in any way impair the right of a State to enforce such laws as it deems necessary to control the use of property in accordance with the general interest or to secure the payment of taxes or other contributions or penalties."

---

[1] Cmnd. 2657 (1926).
[2] *ibid.* at para. 84.
[3] Such a change was suggested as long ago as 1945 by the Cohen Committee who pointed out that the position of a small minority in a subsidiary company may be anything but satisfactory – Cmnd. 6659, para. 141.
[4] As Lord Ackner explained in *Brind v Home Secretary* [1991] 2 W.L.R. 588 at 603–604 the Convention may be deployed for the purpose of resolving an ambiguity in English primary or subordinate legislation. Moreover, it may be regarded as an articulation of some of the principles underlying English common law.

How does Part XIIIA fit into all this? We have a taking of property against the wishes of the property owner but no apparent public purposes. In fact, somewhat similar provisions came before the European Commission in *Bramelid and Malmstrom v. Sweden*[5] and the Commission ruled that the compulsory acquisition regime passed muster. According to the terms of Swedish law when a company itself or through a subsidiary owned more than 90 per cent of the shares and more than 90 per cent of the votes in another company, it had the right to purchase the remainder of the shares in that other company. Where the purchasing company had acquired the majority of the shares by virtue of a takeover bid, the Companies Act 1985 laid down that the purchase price should be fixed as the offer price, unless there were special reasons for deciding otherwise. The applicants complained about having to sell their shares at the offer price, because they claimed, and the arbitrator appeared to accept, that this price was considerably less than the "true" value of the shares.

The complaints were found to lack substance. In the first place the compulsory transfer of property between individuals was a feature of many laws. Examples were cited, *inter alia*, of the seizure and sale of goods in the course of execution proceedings. Stress was laid on a notion of balance. According to the Commission a State must not create an imbalance between persons which would result in one person arbitrarily and unjustly being deprived of his goods for the benefit of another. The Swedish legislation did not fall down on this score. The Commission emphasised that that the price of the applicant's shares was fixed by qualified arbitrators in a carefully reasoned decision and following criteria which did not appear either arbitrary or unreasonable.[6]

In the light of this decision of the European Commission it is difficult to conceive how Part XIIIA of the 1985 Act might be successfully challenged. To justify this statement fully it is appropriate to look in more detail at the relevant provisions of English law.

More detailed examination of the English position

On being served with a compulsory acquisition notice by a successful takeover bidder, section 430C of the Companies Act 1985 gives a minority shareholder the option of applying to the court. The court may, of course, reject the application or else it may make one of two orders in favour of the applicant, *e.g.* (a) that the offer or shall not be entitled and bound to acquire the shares, or (b) specifying terms of acquisition different from those of the offer. There is a relative wealth of authority on the circumstances that might prompt the court to intervene. Generally speaking, the onus is clearly on the applicant to suggest grounds for court intervention. The *locus classicus* is *Re Hoare and Co. Ltd*[7] where

---

[5] (1982) 5 E.H.R.R. 249. For an analysis of the case see Forde (1984) XIX *Irish Jurist* (N.S.) 277 at 278–280. See also McCormack [1994] *Anglo-American Law Review* 161 at pp. 163–169. This chapter is a shortened version of that article.
[6] *Malstrom v. Sweden* (1982) 5 E.H.R.R. 249 at 257.
[7] (1933) 150 L.T. 374.

Maugham J. stated that the reasons for inducing the court "to order otherwise" are reasons which must be supplied by the dissentients who take the step of making an application to the court. The onus was on them to give a reason why their shares should not be acquired by the transferee company.[8]

The observations of Maugham J. have been sanctified by acceptance in subsequent case law. *Re Press Caps Ltd*[9] may be cited in this connection. Here the shares in question were quoted on the stock exchange and the offer price was pitched slightly in excess of the stock exchange price. Wynn-Parry J. said that prima facie the stock exchange markings could be taken as a satisfactory indication of the value of the shares in question. It followed that to succeed the applicant had to go behind the stock exchange prices and that was a heavy task which he had not managed to discharge.[10]

Stress is laid on fairness and the meaning of this term has been elaborated upon in a number of cases. In *Re Grierson, Oldham & Adams Ltd.*[11] it was held that the test of fairness is whether the offer is fair to the offerees as a body and not whether it is fair to a particular shareholder in the peculiar circumstances of his own case. The rationale of this rule was explained by Plowman J.:

> "It would quite obviously be impossible, at any rate in most cases, for the offeror to know the circumstances of every individual shareholder and, therefore, to frame an offer which would necessarily be fair to every individual shareholder in the peculiar circumstances of his case."[12]

Moreover, the courts appear to have accorded the takeover bidder a considerable margin of appreciation in applying the test of fairness. In *Re Sussex Brick Co. Ltd*[13] Vaisey J. said:

> "I think that the scheme must be obviously unfair, patently unfair, unfair to the meanest intelligence . . . A scheme can be effective to bind a dissenting shareholder without complying to the extent of one hundred per cent with the highest possible standards of fairness, equity and reason."

It should be noted, however that this dictum was described by Hardie Boys J. in the New Zealand case of *Re Deans*[14] as a rather enthusiastic overstatement of what is required. He added that the applicant does not need to show that the majority were "morons".[15]

A fertile field for a minority shareholder is to allege lack of disclosure of information by the offeror. This was the case in *Re Evertite Locknuts (1938) Ltd*[16] though the judge treated the minority shareholder somewhat harshly.

---

[8] *ibid.* at 375.
[9] [1949] Ch. 434.
[10] *ibid.* at 447.
[11] [1968] Ch. 17.
[12] *ibid.* at 33.
[13] [1961] Ch. 289 at 292.
[14] [1986] 2 N.Z.L.R. 271.
[15] *ibid.* at 274.
[16] [1945] Ch. 220.

Vaisey J. said that in the absence of proof that the proposed scheme was unfair, the mere fact that a shareholder was not provided with all the materials upon which he could come to a just conclusion in regard to the proposal was not a sufficient ground for the court to interfere.[17]

An approach more favourable to a minority shareholder was adopted by Hoffmann J. in *Re Lifecare International plc*.[18] He suggested that if a shareholder can show that the board recommendation to accept a takeover offer was based on erroneous advice, this goes some way towards discharging the onus of proof upon the shareholder. Moreover, some doubt was cast on the correctness of the decision in *Re Evertite Locknuts (1938) Ltd* by Browne-Wilkinson V-.C. in *Re Chez Nico (Restaurants) Ltd*.[19] He said that the fact that 90 per cent of the shareholders have accepted the bid cannot carry decisive weight if it is shown that their acceptance was obtained in ignorance of facts of which they should have been informed. Furthermore, the takeover bidders in this case were corporate insiders in possession of information that was denied to the ordinary shareholders. General Principle 4 of the City Takeover Code provided:

> "Shareholders must be given sufficient information and advice to enable them to reach a properly informed decision and must have sufficient time to do so. No relevant information should be withheld from them."

Browne-Wilkinson V.-C. noted that the code does not have the force of law. Nevertheless, he said that for the purposes of section 430C the code was a factor of great importance. Substantial infringements of the provisions of the code as to disclosure negatived any presumption that the offer was fair because 90 per cent of the shareholders had accepted it.

It may be that there is a substantial identity of interest between the offeror and the shareholders who have accepted the offer, in which case the burden of proof lies on the offeror to show that the minority should be bought out compulsorily. In point is *Re Bugle Press Ltd*.[20] Here there were three shareholders in the company with two holding 90 per cent of the shares between them. The duo offered to buy out the third shareholder, one Treby, but the latter refused to sell. The majority shareholders then incorporated a company which proceeded to launch a takeover bid for the shares in Bugle Press. The duo accepted the offer in respect of their shareholdings in Bugle Press so that the 90 per cent acceptance level was achieved but Treby again refused to sell. The question arose whether the compulsory acquisition power could properly be exercised. The Court of Appeal refused to sanction compulsory acquisition.[21]

---

[17] *ibid*. at 224.
[18] [1990] B.C.L.C. 222.
[19] [1992] B.C.L.C. 192.
[20] [1961] Ch. 270. See also *Esso Standard (Inter-America) Inc. v. J.W. Enterprises Inc.* (1963) 37 D.L.R. (2d) 598.
[21] [1961] Ch. 27 D at 286–287. There are indications from the Privy Council that the statutory acquisition procedure is one that is to be narrowly construed. In *Blue Metal Industries v. RW Dilley* [1970] A.C. 827, Lord Morris said the procedure entailed the involuntary acquisiton by

To conclude, Part XIIIA provides for compulsory acquisition at the original offer price but the court has a discretionary power to refuse to sanction expropriation on the application of a minority shareholder and this power has been exercised on a number of occasions. The provisions represent a regulation of the relationship of shareholders *inter se*, but the majority are not left with unfettered power. A balance is sought to be struck. In these circumstances it is suggested that no infringement of Article 1, Protocol 1 of the European Convention arises.

Compulsory expropriation in other statutory situations

There are other means whereby a compulsory buy out of dissentient shareholders may be achieved and these are potentially less protective of the minority than Part XIIIA. First, one might mention schemes of arrangement under section 425 of the Companies Act 1985. The basic design of this section is to facilitate corporate reorganisations but on occasion the section has been used to buy out minority shareholders compulsorily. A scheme of arangement under the section requires court sanction and a majority in number representing 75 per cent in value of the shares in question must accept the scheme. Provided, however, that these conditions are met the arrangement becomes binding on abstainers or dissenters. In *Re National Bank Ltd*[22] the facility was used to accomplish the compulsory elimination of minority shareholders. Moreover, the court rejected the proposition that a 90 per cent acceptance criterion should be imposed as a condition of approving the scheme. According to Plowman J. a contrary view would involve imposing a limitation or qualification either on the generality of the word "arrangement" or else on the discretion of the court under the section. The legislature had not expressly laid down any such limitation.[23]

In *Re Hellenic and General Trust Ltd*,[24] on the other hand, the court refused approval for a scheme of arrangement that envisaged expelling a minority of shareholders precisely because to do so would undermine the requirements of Part XIIIA. Templeman J. said that where one had in effect a Part XIIIA scheme, then putting it at its lowest, there must be a very high standard of proof on the part of the applicant to justify obtaining by section 425 what could not be obtained by Part XIIIA.[25]

It is submitted that the approach adopted by Templeman J. in *Re Hellenic & General Trust Ltd* derives implicit support from the opinion of the Privy Council

---

a private interest of the property of another. This was an exceptional interference with rights of individual ownership and the procedure was not one designed to achieve the concentration of property interests generally.

[22] [1966] 1 W.L.R. 819.
[23] *ibid.* at 829–830.
[24] [1976] 1 W.L.R. 123.
[25] *ibid.* at 129. For contrasting analyses of these two cases see Prentice (1976) 92 L.Q.R. 13 and Hornby (1976) 39 L.Q.R. 207.

in *Blue Metal Industries Ltd v. RW Dilley*.[26] He laid emphasis on the fact that Part XIIIA had to be strictly adhered to. He added that there was nothing in the scheme of philosophy of the companies legislation to suggest that the legislature intended to permit this power of compulsory expropriation to be exercised merely because a majority, even an overwhelming majority, thought fit to agree to it.

"Squeeze-outs" in the course of a reduction of capital

A possible means whereby a company may continue in effective existence yet still squeeze out a dissentient minority is provided by section 135 of the Companies Act 1985.

This section stipulates that subject to confirmation by the court a company may, so long as it is authorised by its articles, reduce its share capital in any way. The section can be used to secure the elimination of whole classes of shares on the same terms as was done in *House of Fraser plc v. ACGE Investments Ltd*.[27] It might conceivably be used to accomplish the elimination of a particular individual shareholder, so to speak. A case in point is *Re Robert Stephen Holdings Ltd*[28] where the facts are somewhat exceptional. The case involved a public company that had failed to achieve the objectives that lay behind it going public and there was a general feeling that the company should revert to its original status as a family company. The company passed a special resolution that reduced its share capital by cancelling shares held by persons outside the family. The resolution was only opposed by one small shareholder and even he failed to turn up at the court hearing that considered the reduction. The court approved the reduction in the unusual circumstances but a caveat was issued that what was done in this case should not be followed as a general practice. Plowman J. opined that it was desirable in cases like the present to proceed by way of a scheme of arrangement. While it was true that a dissentient minority shareholder could come to the court and object to confirmation of a reduction, nevertheless the interests of the minority shareholder were better protected under what was now sections 425–427. The weakening of that protection, he said, was not something that the court ought to encourage.

Compulsory expropriation and the articles of association

The statutory protection against squeeze-outs of minority shareholders in takeover situations seem like an extraordinary work of supererogation if the articles of association of a company provide for compulsory expropriation. A successful takeover bidder could use such a clause to get rid of a dissident

---

[26] [1970] A.C. 827.
[27] [1987] A.C. 387. See also *Re Saltdean Estate Co. Ltd* [1968] 1 W.L.R. 1844.
[28] [1968] 1 W.L.R. 522. See also *Re Rank Radio and Television Ltd, The Times*, November 19, 1963.

minority so why all the fuss about Part XIIIA? Compulsory expropriation provisions might be in the corporate constitution on initial incorporation or incorporated therein by subsequent alteration. The question arises as to the permissibility of such provisions. A freedom of contract theorist may say to the minority shareholder that the expropriation clause is there as a result of a freely-expressed bargain between the parties.[29] The rules of the game were set when the shareholder joined and the shareholder cannot now cry foul when it is sought to activate the clause. After all, the shareholder agreed to the clause. In the same way, the rules of the club are alterable by a more than 75 per cent majority vote. The shareholder should have known of this facility for alteration when she joined. She cannot now complain about an alteration that is to her detriment. To address this issue further it is necessary to do a little theorising.

First, it is true to say as one commentator does[30]: "Companies are voluntary associations, in the sense that nobody can make you join one, and the hallmark of such associations, where a legal relationship exists between their members, is contract." Moreover, section 14 of the Companies Act 1985 specifically invests the memorandum and articles of association of a company with contractual status.[31] The section embodies a contract between members *inter se* and also between members and the company that is enforceable both by members against the company and by the company against members.[32]

But company law is not completely contractarian in nature. Shareholders do not have a completely free hand in laying down the memorandum or articles of association. Their freedom is constrained in that company law contains a substantial mandatory element. The law imposes fiduciary duties on directors and senior officers of a company. The Companies Act 1985 in section 310 limits attempts to contract out of such fiduciary duties in the articles of association of companies. A director is obliged by statute, irrespective of what the articles may say, to disclose her interest in contracts with the company on pain of committing a criminal offence. So there is a non-excludable core of company law. The big question is how far that core extends and whether it serves to invalidate compulsory expropriation clauses in the memorandum or articles.

---

[29] The contractual approach to companies dates back to Coase, "The Nature of the Firm" (1937) 4 *Economica* (N.S.) 386. For more modern contractual perspectives see Alchian and Demsetz, "Production, Information Costs, and Economic Organisation" (1972) 62 Am.Econ.Rev. 777; Fama and Jensen, "Separation of Ownership and Control (1983) 26 J.L. & Econ. 301; Jensen and Meckling, "Theory of the Firm: Managerial Behaviour, Agency Costs and Ownership Structure" (1976) 3 J.Fin.Econ. 305; Klein, "The Modern Business Organisation: Bargaining Under Constraints" (1982) 91 Yale L.J. 1521 and Williamson, "Corporate Governance" (1984) 93 Yale L.J. 1197. There is a symposium on the issue in (1989) 89 *Columbia Law Review*. See also Prentice, (1988) 8 O.J.L.S. 55 and Riley, (1992) 55 M.L.R. 782.

[30] See Drury, [1986] C.L.J. 219.

[31] For a sample of some of the literature see Wedderburn, [1957] C.L.J. 194; Goldberg, (1972) 35 M.L.R. 362 and (1985) 48 M.L.R. 158; Prentice, (1980) 1 Co. Law 179; Gregory, (1981) 44 M.L.R. 526 and Drury, [1986] C.L.J. 219.

[32] The *locus classicus* is *Hickman v. Kent or Romney Marsh Sheep-Breeders Association* [1915] 1 Ch. 881. See in particular the statement of Astbury J. at 897.

Hitherto we have been talking about mandatory rules contained in statutes. One of these impinges directly on the area that we are considering. Section 9 of the Companies Act 1985 allows a company freely to alter its articles by special resolution. Section 16 however provides that a member is not bound by an alteration in the articles made after the date on which she became a member if and so far as the alteration:

(a) requires her to take or subscribe for more shares than the number held by her at the date on which the alteration is made; or

(b) in any way increases her liability as at that date to contribute to the company's share capital or otherwise to pay money to the company.

What about judicial intervention to constrain contractual freedom in the context of articles of association of companies? Reasons for non-intervention spring readily to mind. There is an immediate antipathy against allowing judges the latitude to rewrite freely agreed-upon contractual terms but the matter may not be as simple as all that. An inter-shareholder agreement represents a long-term contractual enterprise. As one commentator puts it[33]: "The parties are bound up in the same enterprise, and thus have to do business with each other over a long period of time." The provisions may not have been drafted with each and every contingency in mind for it is quite impossible to foresee future events with precision. One is concerned with a fluid long-term relationship and the parties' conception of future events at the time of contractual formation may not encompass what actually transpired. Furthermore, articles of association of companies tend not to be consistent for either clarity or consistency.[34] Often they consist of a complicated mishmash of provisions and sometimes they are supplemented by shareholder agreements that exist outside the articles and even by informal understandings.[35]

Contractarians might counter this line of reasoning by suggesting that the terms of the corporate constitution will be reflected in the price paid for shares in the company.[36] If certain provisions of the articles of association are particularly disadvantageous to a shareholder this will be reflected in the price paid for shares.

Others talk about informational imperfections.[37] It may be unduly simplistic to suggest that all members share informational equality when it comes to assessing the likely future impact of clauses in the articles of association or that such clauses are necessarily reflected accurately in the share price.

---

[33] See Drury, [1986] C.L.J. 219 at 222. For a general analysis of relational contracting see Macneil, *The New Social Contract: An Inquiry into Modern Contractual Relations* (New Haven, 1980).

[34] See, for example, the comments of Lord Goff in *Guinness plc v. Saunders* [1990] 2 A.C. 663 at 698.

[35] See, generally, Riley, (1992) 55 M.L.R. 782 at 785–786.

[36] See, generally, Easterbrook and Fischel, "The Corporate Contract" (1989) 98 *Columbia Law Review* 1416.

[37] See, for example, Bebchuk, (1989) 98 *Columbia Law Review* 1395 at pp. 1406–1408.

Be that as it may, there seems little justification for an automatic and inflexible rule invalidating compulsory expropriation clauses in the articles of association. If the clause is operated oppressively or capriciously or in a manner that was unforeseen at the time of incorporation, then there is a case for a long-stop remedy. This comes in the shape of section 459 of the Companies Act 1985 which allows members to seek redress in situations of unfairly prejudicial conduct.[38] The precise relief granted may be tailored to the requirements of a particular individual case. Given the flexibility that section 459 affords, the case for an outright ban on compulsory expropriation clauses at the time of incorporation is distinctly uncompelling. In fact, the courts have shirked imposing such a ban. A leading case in point is *Phillips v. Manufacturers Securities Ltd.*[39]

The case concerned a company that had been formed with the express object of furthering the interests of a certain trade federation, namely the association of bedstead manufacturers. The plaintiff, who was a member of the federation, became a shareholder in the company. The plaintiff resigned from the trade federation and was then expelled from the company pursuant to a clause in the articles of association. His shares in the company were compulsorily sold at the price of one shilling per share whereas they were worth considerably more. The Court of Appeal refused to set aside the expropriation resolution on the ground that it was actuated by a malicious motive. Lord Cozens-Hardy M.R. was unperturbed by the fact that the resolution may have been passed to punish the plaintiff.[40]

It is quite common for non-profit associations and family firms to have expulsion clauses in their articles. *Gaiman v. National Association for Mental Health*[41] serves as an example. In this case, Megarry J., in rejecting a challenge to an expulsion resolution, propounded the well-accepted notion that directors are subject to a duty to exercise their powers in what they bona fide believe to be the interests of the company. He went on to say, however, that there was no superadded obligation to observe the requirements of natural justice in considering the expulsion resolution. The judge said:

> "[P]rovisions in the articles of a company for expropriation or expulsion are valid, even though they deprive the member of valuable property rights."[42]

What about the position when compulsory expropriation clauses are introduced by amendment of the articles?

---

[38] For general analyses of s.459 see Prentice, (1988) 8 O.J.L.S. 55; Hannigan, [1988] L.M.C.L.Q. 60 and Riley, (1992) 55 M.L.R. 782.
[39] (1917) 116 L.T. 290.
[40] *ibid.* at pp. 296–297.
[41] [1971] 1 Ch. 317. See also *Walsh v Cassidy* [1951] Ir. Jur. Rep. 47.
[42] [1971] 1 Ch. 317 at 336.

Compulsory expropriation and alteration of the articles

The articles of association of a company are declared freely alterable by statute.[43] Some theorists would argue that there are good reasons for so doing.[44] In one sense there is a case for laisser-faire and freedom of contract.[45] A member has joined an association the rules of which she knows may be changed at some future stage against her wishes. She has subjected herself to the will of the majority and the will of the majority may branch out to encompass amendments to the basis of association. On the other hand, if the power of the majority was completely unfettered that might appear to be a recipe for dictatorship. The problem of informational imperfections is particularly acute in this sphere. A would-be member of a company may have grave difficulty in foreseeing the likely scope of future amendments to the corporate constitution. Of course, it is theoretically possible for an individual member to protect herself against future constitutional alterations by making a contract outside the articles as to how each would vote on a resolution to alter the articles. There is nothing objectionable in such a provision. The recent decision of the House of Lords in *Russell v. Northern Bank Development Corp Ltd*[46] is to this effect. The House of Lords held that although a provision in a company's articles of association which restricted its statutory power to alter those articles was invalid, an agreement outside the articles between shareholders as to how they would exercise their voting rights on a resolution to alter the articles was not necessarily invalid.

Another way in which an individual shareholder might protect herself against prejudicial alterations of the articles would be to press for the inclusion in the articles of a clause investing her shares with enhanced voting power on any resolution to alter the articles. Section 303 of the Companies Act 1985 allows a company to dismiss a director by ordinary resolution. In *Bushell v. Faith*[47] however, a provision in the company's constitution was upheld which gave the shares of a director greater voting power on any resolution to remove him. The effect of the provision was to circumvent the operation of section 303, yet this was held to be insufficient ground for striking it down. Similarly, the shares of a particular individual shareholder might have added weight on any resolution to change the articles.

Be that as it may not all shareholders possess sufficient foresight or clout to safeguard themselves in these ways from adverse alterations of the articles. Are there alternative means of protection available through the courts? In resolving this issue it is necessary to highlight a tension between two long-established

---

[43] Companies Act 1985, ss.9 and 16.
[44] See Bebchuk, "Limiting Contractual Freedom in Corporate Law: The Desirable Constraints on Charter Amendments" (1989) 102 Harv. L.R. 1820.
[45] See Easterbrook and Fischel, "The Corporate Contract" (1989) 98 *Columbia Law Review* 1416 at pp. 1442–1444.
[46] [1992] 3 All E.R. 161.
[47] [1970] A.C. 1099.

authorities namely *Pender v. Lushington*[48] on the one hand and *Allen v. Gold Reefs of West Africa*[49] on the other. First, *Pender v. Lushington*. This case concerned a company whose articles limited the number of votes to which any one shareholder was entitled. To maximise his voting power Mr Pender split his shareholding among nominees. At a general meeting the chairman nevertheless refused to accept the votes of nominees. It was held that the chairman's conduct was an actionable wrong. Jessel M.R. pointed out that the right to vote was a property right which a shareholder might exercise for whatever reason he thought fit.

So Victorian values of self-interest prevail. We may pass to another Victorian case, *Allen v. Gold Reefs of West Africa*, where a greater degree of disinterestedness was required of a shareholder in voting for a resolution to alter the articles.

Lindley M.R. said:

> "[T]he power ... must like all other powers, be exercised subject to those general principles of law and equity which are applicable to all powers conferred on majorities and enabling them to bind minorities. It must be exercised, not only in the manner required by law, but also bona fide for the benefit of the company as a whole ..."[50]

The words "bona fide for the benefit of the company as a whole" have generated considerable controversy. In a couple of first instance decisions the expression has been relied on to strike down constitutional alterations that encompassed compulsory expropriation clauses. The first case is *Brown v. British Abrasive Wheel Co.*[51] Here a company was in great need of further capital. The majority who represented 98 per cent of the shares were willing to provide this capital if they could acquire the shares of the 2 per cent minority. They failed to achieve this objective by agreement and then proposed to alter the articles so as to enable them to purchase the minority shares compulsorily. The terms of the acquisition were fair but nevertheless Astbury J. looked askance at the proposed alteration. He said:

> "I find it very difficult to follow how it can be just and equitable that a majority, on failing to purchase the shares of a minority by agreement can take power to do so compulsorily."[52]

To the same effect is *Dafen Tinplate Co Ltd v. Llanelly Steel (1907) Ltd.*[53] In this case the shareholders in the defendant company were principally companies and persons manufacturing tinplates who were originally invited to become shareholders on the understanding that, although under no legal obligation to do so, they were to take the steel bars required for their tinplates from the defendant

---

[48] (1877) 6 Ch. D. 70.
[49] [1900] 1 Ch. 656.
[50] [1900] 1 Ch. 656 at 671.
[51] [1919] 1 Ch. 290.
[52] *ibid.* at 295–296.
[53] [1920] 2 Ch. 124.

company. The plaintiff company was a founder shareholder of the defendant company but subsequently withdrew its custom and transferred it to a new rival steel company. An unsuccessful effort was made to acquire the plaintiff company's shares. Thereupon the defendant company passed special resolutions altering its articles and introducing a power enabling the majority of the shareholders to determine that the shares of any member (other than a certain named company) should be offered for sale by the directors to such persons as they should think fit, at a fair value.

According to Peterson J. the question of fact he had to consider was whether the alteration was for the benefit of the company. He said:

> "To say that such an unrestricted and unlimited power of expropriation is for the benefit of the company appears to me to be confusing the interests of the majority with the benefit of the company as a whole."[54]

In his opinion the altered article was too widely drawn.

These first-instance decisions have suffered somewhat at the hands of the Court of Appeal and it is by no means certain that they are good law. *Sidebottom v. Kershaw Leese and Co. Ltd*[55] is a case in point. The case involved a private trading company in which the majority of the shares were held by the directors. The company altered its articles by enabling the directors to require any shareholder who competed with the company's business to transfer his shares, at their full value, to nominees of the directors. The validity of the resolution was upheld. Some doubt was cast on the judgment of Astbury J. in *Brown v. British Abrasive Wheel Co.*[56] According to the Court of Appeal "bona fide" and "for the benefit of the company as a whole" meant two things and not one. Lindley M.R. in the *Allen* case[57] was laying down a single composite expression. The conclusions of fact arrived at by Astbury J. in Brown were dubious. Lord Sterndale displayed some partiality to the following formulation for assessing alterations:

> "[T]he alteration must not be such as to sacrifice the interests of the minority to those of a majority without any reasonable prospect of advantage to the company as a whole."[58]

In *Shuttleworth v. Cox Brothers & Co. (Maidenhead) Ltd*[59] the Court of Appeal categorically rejected the proposition based upon the judgment of Peterson J. in *Dafen Tinplate Co. v. Llanelly Steel Co.*,[60] that the question is not what the shareholders think, but what the court thinks is for the benefit of the

---

[54] *ibid.* at 141.
[55] [1920] 1 Ch. 154.
[56] [1919] 1 Ch. 290.
[57] [1900] 1 Ch. 656 at 671.
[58] Above, n.55, at 162. The reference comes from *Buckley on the Companies Act* (9th ed.) p. 25.
[59] [1927] 2 K.B. 9.
[60] [1920] 2 Ch. 124.

company. Scrutton L.J. observed that to adopt that view would be to make the court the manager of the affairs of unnumberable companies instead of the shareholders themselves. The judge also stated:

> "The absence of any reasonable ground for deciding that a certain course of action is conducive to the benefit of the company may be a ground for finding lack of good faith or for finding that the shareholders, with the best motives, have not considered the matters that they ought to have considered. On either of these findings their decision might be set aside."[61]

So the first instance decisions have come in for some hierarchical criticism.[62] On the other hand they derive some implicit support from the decision of the Court of Appeal in *Re Bugle Press Ltd.*[63] In that case the court refused to allow the majority to use what is now sections 428–430 of the Companies Act 1985 so as to bring about the compulsory acquisition of a minority member's shares. The court seemed to think that making use of the statutory procedure in this manner would be to contravene fundamental principles of company law. If the same result could have been achieved by alteration of the articles then why all the fuss?[64]

It should be noted that *Re Bugle Press* derives some support from the decision of the High Court of Australia in *Gambotto v. W.C.P. Ltd.*[64a] In this case it was held that an alteration of articles so as to confer upon the majority power to expropriate the shares of a minority must be made for a proper purpose and also is required to be fair in the circumstances. Fairness in this context had both a procedural and substantive dimension. Substantive fairness was concerned largely with the price offered for the shares whereas procedural fairness required the disclosure of all relevant information. The proper purpose principle meant that an expropriation was only justified where it was reasonably apprehended that the continued shareholding of the minority was detrimental to the company, its undertaking or the conduct of its affairs, and expropriation was a reasonable means of eliminating or mitigating that detriment. The majority of the court also took the view that the conferring of taxation and administrative benefits could not by themselves constitute a proper purpose for a resolution altering the articles to allow for expropriation of a minority shareholder's shares.

The English Court of Appeal has not been terribly successful in propounding a principle for judging amendments to the articles. The most valiant effort was made in *Greenhalgh v. Arderne Cinemas Ltd*[65] where Evershed M.R.

---

[61] [1927] 2 K.B. 9 at 23.
[62] See, generally, F.G. Rixon (1986) 49 M.L.R. 446 at 460–461. This article contains an excellent analysis of the conflicting case law on the power of companies to alter their articles.
[63] [1961] 1 Ch. 270.
[64] See *Gower's Principles of Modern Company Law* (5th ed., 1992) at p. 598. It may be however, as Gower points out, that the beliefs or assumptions of those who frame Acts of Parliament are an unsure guide as to what the law actually is.
[64a] (1995) 182 C.L.R. 432; on which see Prentice, (1996) 112 L.Q.R. 194.
[65] [1951] Ch. 286.

struggled with alternative formulations. On the one hand he laid down an "individual hypothetical member" test. It is asked whether, in the honest opinion of those who voted in its favour, a particular resolution is for the benefit of an individual hypothetical member.[66] Some people would say that this test is unworkable because the individual hypothetical member is a character deprived of substance. In a company divided into rival camps the effect of a resolution will depend upon whether the particular individual member is in the majority or minority camp.[67]

The alternative test suggested was that of discrimination. It was said that a special resolution altering the articles might be impeached if its effect were to discriminate between majority and minority shareholders, so as to give the former an advantage denied to the latter. Critics say that while the court barked it did not bite. It is argued that the effect of the resolutions under challenge in the particular case was to discriminate between majority and minority shareholders.

A discrimination test seems uncommonly like an unfair prejudice test.[68] If something is discriminatory as between minority and majority shareholders and there are no objective grounds for the discrimination then surely it is unfairly prejudicial with respect to the minority shareholders. Unfair prejudice on the other hand does not necessarily involve discrimination. If a shareholder is complaining about actual or proposed alterations to the articles then the most procedurally convenient course would seem to be to bring an unfair prejudice petition pursuant to section 459 of the Companies Act 1985. In this way other matters of complaint can be adjudicated upon at the same time and there are no difficulties about *locus standi* and framing an appropriate action. On the other hand, the invariable remedy granted to a successful petitioner under section 459 is for her connection with the company to be severed on payment of a fair price for her shares.[69] If the gravamen of the complaint is the introduction of a compulsory expropriation clause into the articles then the petitioner may go away empty handed from the court unless the terms of the expropriation are unfair.

There have in fact been a number of unfair prejudice petitions that have centred around the issue of valuation clauses in the articles.[70] Objections have been raised by respondents to many unfair prejudice petitions on the basis that the

---

[66] *ibid.* at 291.
[67] See, *e.g.* Gower, *op. cit.* above, n.64, at pp. 600–601.
[68] See Rixon, (1986) 49 M.L.R. 446 at 472–475.
[69] This approach has been criticised by some commentators, *e.g.* Ruth Redmond-Cooper, (1988) 9 Co. Law 169 at 171. It has been argued that the approach fails to take account of the interests of the company as distinct from those of the members, with the result that the "trouble" complained of by the minority shareholders will be allowed to continue unchallenged and the company may ultimately find itself in insolvent liquidation, causing loss to both creditors and employees. Lord Simonds in *Scottish Co-operative Wholesale Society v. Meyer* [1959] A.C. 324 at 349 stated that the aim of granting relief is not the bringing to an end of matters complained of, but, by ordering the purchase of the petitioners shares to put them in a position where they are no longer able to complain.
[70] See, generally, Riley, (1992) 55 M.L.R. 782 at 798–802. See also, Prentice, (1986) 102 L.Q.R. 179 and Hannigan, [1987] *Business Law Review* 21.

articles contain share valuation machinery and the petititioner should go down this route rather than seeking to invoke the court's jurisdiction under section 459. Although intially sympathetic to these arguments[71] the courts have become increasingly wary of the dangers of out of court valuations. The dangers are particulary acute if the out of court valuation is to be carried out by auditors who may be close to the company management. Moreover, the valuer will in the generality of cases act as an expert rather than as an arbitrator. In consequence, reasons adduced for the particular valuation will be thin on the ground and so render the decision virtually impregnable. The change in judicial attitude was manifested in *Virdi v. Abbey Leisure Ltd*[72] Here the petitioner's primary claim was for winding up on the grounds of justice and equity rather than for relief on the basis of unfair prejudice. Nevertheless, the basic principle holds good. The Court of Appeal said that there was a risk that an accountant in conducting a valuation under the terms of the company's articles might value the petitioner's shares at a discount because he was a minority shareholder. There was nothing unreasonable in the petitioner refusing to accept this risk. Consequently, an application to strike out the petitioner's claims for relief as being manifestly ill-founded was dismissed.

The same judicial approach was adopted by Harman J. in *Re a Company (No. 00330 of 1991), ex parte Holden.*[73] The judge pointed out that a valuation of the company's shares under the articles was to be carried out by an expert who would not be obliged to give reasons for his decision. Moreover, there was no provision for any representations to be put before the expert and there was no way in which the shareholder whose shares were being valued could know what matters had been taken into account. In these circumstances an aggrieved shareholder was not acting unreasonably in presenting an unfair prejudice petition rather than relying on the share valuation machinery contained in the articles.

Conclusion

A successful takeover bidder faced with an intractable minority in the company being taken over has a couple of options for eliminating the dissidents. One is to use the statutory procedure provided for in Part XIIIA of the Companies Act 1985. The mechanism has been kept within narrow bounds by the courts. The other option is to make use of compulsory expropriation clauses in the articles of association of the company. It is submitted that there are no independent self-standing principles that automatically invalidate compulsory expropriation clauses. There are no grounds for objection if the compulsory expropriation

---

[71] See, for instance, *Re a Company (No 007623 of 1984)* [1986] B.C.L.C. 362, *Re a Company (No 004377 of 1986)* [1987] B.C.L.C. 94, *Re a Company (No 003843 of 1986)* [1987] B.C.L.C. 562, *Re a Company (No 003096 of 1987)* (1988) 4 B.C.L.C. 80, and *Re a Company (No 006834 of 1988), ex parte Kremer* [1989] B.C.L.C. 365.
[72] [1990] B.C.L.C. 342.
[73] [1991] B.C.L.C. 597.

clause was in the articles when the company was first incorporated. If the clause has been introduced by alteration of the articles then it is unobjectionable if framed so as to protect a company from conduct by a shareholder that is detrimental to the interests of the company. An unfettered power of expropriation appears equally unexceptionable if the price payable for the shares is a fair one though a different view was taken by the High Court of Australia in *Gambotto v. W.C.P. Ltd*.[73a] who require that an expropriation must be made for a proper purpose. In England the test for judging alterations of the articles has collapsed into a discrimination test which is quite akin to an unfair prejudice test. A shareholder aggrieved because of alterations to the article may bring an unfair prejudice petition under section 459 of the Companies Act 1985. There is little prospect of success however with such an action if the articles provide for severance of a shareholder's connection with the company at a fair price; such price to be arrived at after an independent, impartial and fully-reasoned valuation process. Common law, equity and statute are at one in this sphere.[74]

[73a] (1995) 182 C.L.R. 432.
[74] A different version of this paper has appeared in [1994] *Anglo-American Law Review* 161–194.

7

Property: Assets or Power? Objects or Relations as Substrata of Property Rights

WOLFGANG MINCKE*

Concepts of property

Property does not seem to enjoy popularity as a topic in comparative law. A lot of literature exists on the law of obligations and its more specialised branches; but when it comes to property law, we do not find much.[1] One might conclude that property as a concept is not very interesting for comparative purposes.

Yet, at first glance, property may seem to be so basic a concept in private law that it should be universally accepted. The French name it *propriété*, the Germans *Eigentum*, the Netherlanders *eigendom*, the Swedish *egendom*, and the Finnish *omaisuus*; translators would not hesitate to use these words as equivalents. But when a lawyer approaches the concept and looks at it through the magnifying glass of his science the opposite impression might arise: the concept varies widely. Perhaps it is more appropriate to speak about concepts in the plural, not about one single concept. This complexity of the matter might explain the reluctance of comparative legal writers to deal with property.

As a first superficial distinction, the different concepts of property can be placed into two groups. In one group are very comprehensive concepts of property such as the English and French ones. The English 'property' and French *propriété* comprise a variety of things that are objects of a right: land, tangible and non-tangible movable things such as chattels and debts; and patents and copyrights. In the other group we would have the German *Eigentum* and the Dutch *eigendom*. Both are limited to indicating the most extensive rights a person may have in land or other tangible (corporeal) things.

If in German or Dutch law one looks for a comprehensive concept for the remaining group of rights (obligations, intellectual property) there is a word indicating the subject that has such a right. Such a subject is called an *Inhaber*

---

* Professor of Private Law, University of Maastricht, Netherlands and the University of Rovaniemi, Finland.
[1] Recently in the Netherlands there appeared a comprehensive comparative study of French, English and German property law by Zwalve, I *Hoofdstukken uit de Geschiedenis van het Europese Privaatrecht – Inleiding en Zakenrecht* (1993).

in German or a *rechthebbende* in Dutch. But both legal terminologies lack a word for the right such a subject has, at least it is not *Eigentum* or *eigendom*.

Dutch law is of special interest. It had a comprehensive term until 1992, when a new patrimonial law came into force. Under their old law the Dutch used the word *eigendom* in much the same way as the French use the word *propriété*. The new law follows the German terminology limiting *eigendom* to the right in land or corporeal movables.

On the other hand Dutch law has not committed itself totally to the German concept. Germany has special statutory rules for the transfer of different rights in different parts of the *Bürgerliche Gesetzbuch*. The transfer of debts is regulated separately from the transfer of movables, etc.[2] The Dutch go their own way when it comes to the transfer of rights. Dutch law has the same basic rule for the transfer of all kinds of rights in Article 84 of Book 3 *Burgerlijk Wetboek*. In the articles which follow, this rule is modified for different objects.

Another oddity concerning German law has to be added. When the German constitution protects *Eigentum* (Art. 14 *Grundgesetz*), this protection is not limited to property in the restricted sense of the *Bürgerliche Gesetzbuch*. It is very clear that this protection covers the wide field of rights that is comparable to the English property or French *propriété*.

Swedish and Finnish law have a special characteristic concerning property. In both their legal terminologies two words exist for what elsewhere is simply named "property", *propriété* or *Eigentum*. The two distinct words indicate whether the substratum of the right is indicated, or the right itself. When they speak about the substratum of the right they use the word *omaisuus* (Finnish) or *egendom* (Swedish); but when the right itself is indicated, the word is *omistus* (Finnish) or *äganderätt* (Swedish). This distinction is usually not expressed in other languages, though the distinction certainly exists. (English terminology has a compound concept expressing the same distinction, "property ownership". This term sounds somewhat pleonastic to the ears of a Dutch or German lawyer.)

There is something remarkable regarding the range of these words in Swedish and Finnish terminology. When the word for the right is used (*omistus* or *äganderätt*), it is restricted to the right in corporeal things, movable or not.[3] The words *omaisuus* and *egendom*, on the other hand, are used in the broader sense, similar to "property" or *propriété*.[4]

One could go on and look for further consequences of such differences in the concept of property in more detail, but that is not the goal of this article. Instead, I shall try to show some differences in underlying ideas that can be seen as reasons for these different conceptions.

---

[2] § 398 of the *Bürgerliche Gesetzbuch (BGB)* provides for assignment of debts, § 873 for the transfer of rights in land, § 929 ss. for the transfer of corporeal movables; a general rule is found – somewhat hidden – in § 413 for the transfer of rights for which there is no special provision.

[3] Kivimäki-Ylöstalo, *Suomen siviilioikeuden oppikirja, yleinen osa* (1981) 34 *ff*. Malmström-Agell, *Civilrätt* (1990) 47 *ff*.

[4] Kivimäki-Ylöstalo, op. cit. above, n.3, p. 30, 211; Malmström/Agell, *op. cit.* above, n.3, p. 50.

Different categorisations of rights

In the beginning of the last century a discussion started in German legal science that lasted for the rest of the century.[5] This discussion concerned the concept of "subjective" rights (*subjektive Rechte*). The topic is closely related to the law of property since property rights can be seen as a sub-category of subjective rights. This discussion never had a clear conclusion: the *Bürgerliche Gesetzbuch* – in force since January 1, 1900 – did not decide the unanswered questions. It apparently avoided the problems. And this century has not seen much progress in the resolution of the open questions.[6]

Any concept of subjective rights has a major problem: it has to provide the framework for two different types of right. On the one hand we find the rights that clearly have an object, such as property rights in respect of a corporeal thing, and on the other hand we find rights where an object is not so apparent, such as rights arising from obligations. The whole problem of the concept of subjective rights can be seen to reside in the question whether these two groups are sufficiently similar to justify a common notion of "subjective rights" and what the criterion would be for deciding into which group a specific right falls.

Traditionally there are two approaches to the classification of rights. According to one approach they are classified as *iura in re* and *iura in personam*.[7] According to the other approach the rights are classified as "*absolute*" or "*relative*".[8] When the classification into *iura in re/iura in personam* is used, an object to which a person is entitled seems to be emphasised. This is clear with *iura in re*, where the Latin preposition "in" is used with the ablative, indicating that it is the *res* to which one is entitled.[9] This is not so clear with *iura in personam*, where the use of the preposition "in" with the accusative indicates a direction. Indeed the question: "to what is one entitled by a *ius in personam*, what kind of asset has the creditor?" has been most puzzling and has to this day no clear answer.

The classification into absolute or relative rights seems to encounter fewer difficulties. When a right is characterised as absolute or relative, there is no immediate need to determine an object of that right. It is said that an absolute right is potentially directed against everybody; a relative right, on the other hand, is directed against a certain debtor only. This classification views rights in terms of relationships created between persons. The question to what one is

---

[5] It should be noted that the discussion flourished only after the French Civil Code had come into force.

[6] For an account of the state of play concerning the question see Larenz, "Zur Struktur 'subjektiver Rechte'" in *Beiträge zur Europäischen Rechtsgeschichte und zum Geltenden Zivilrecht, Festgabe für Johannes Sontis* (1977) 129 *ff*.

[7] In German terminology one refers to *dingliche Rechte* as opposed to *persönliche Rechte*.

[8] A warning to take note of is that "absolute" in this sense is not used in the same way as the English "absolute title". Absolute in this sense does not indicate that the right is not limited by rights of others. "Absolute" is contrary rather to "relative" or "privity of contract" (when taken into account that "relativity" refers to a right, whereas "privity" refers to the contract as a juridic act).

[9] In English this is obscured by the use of the term *iura in rem*, as "in" with the accusative indicates a direction and thus a mere relationship.

entitled by the right falls outside the scope of this classification. It focuses on the power which exists when a right vests in somebody. This approach appears simpler, and furthermore, it continues a tradition of Roman law, where the central concept in legal thinking was the *actio*. It can also be connected with the system of writs in early English law.

The classification of rights in terms of relationships created between persons, seems to have been the most popular so far. Thibaut, one of the first who wrote about the conflict between these two approaches in Germany, defended the classification into absolute and relative rights as the primary one.[10] The "pandectists", at least implicitly, had to take a position in this conflict. Most of them adhered to the basic characterisation of rights as relative and absolute. Most influential for further development in Germany has been Windscheid. He formulated a subjective right as a discretionary power given by the legal order, by which the command of the legal order is converted into commands of private legal subjects.[11] This interpretation of subjective rights as commands clearly reveals the relational character of rights.

The German Civil Code seems to follow the doctrine of Windscheid. This explains why *Eigentum* in this code is a narrower concept than "property": relationships can be shown in all instances of subjective rights. But if the underlying substratum of all subjective rights is a relationship, this relationship is insufficient to explain *Eigentum*. The relationship as such, absolute or relative, does not assist in explaining an increase in the patrimony of the right holder. In addition to the relationship, regard must be had to the valuable object, in the case of a *ius in re* it would consist of a piece of the material world, such as a piece of land or a corporeal movable thing. But no such object can be shown to accompany the relationship underlying a *ius in personam*.

Indeed, it seems to be this reasoning that leads to the narrower concept of property in Germany or the Netherlands. And this theoretical background is not limited to these countries. In most discussions of the structure underlying subjective rights the idea seems to prevail that such rights consist of relationships. This also applies to French and English legal science. It seems that German and Dutch law are only more consistent in avoiding a concept of property in which no clear object is indicated.

The most consistent solution found so far has gained ground in Scandinavia during recent decades. There the starting point of discussion has been different. Legal realism in Scandinavia had disputed the concept of subjective rights in general. To them the concept of subjective rights was a misled, idealistic, metaphysical notion. The Danish legal philosopher Ross offered a way out:[12] in place

---

[10] Thibaut, "Über Dingliches und Persönliches Recht" in II *Versuche über Einzelne Theile der Theorie des Rechts* (1801) 25 and 36.
[11] "Eine von der Rechtsordnung Verliehene Willensmacht, durch die sich der Befehl der Rechtsordnung in Befehle der Einzelnen Rechtssubjekte Verwandelt." *Cf.* Windscheid, I *Pandektenrecht* (1891) § 37 n 3.
[12] Ross, *Ejendomsret og Ejendomsovergang med særligt Henblik paa dansk Retspraksis* (1935). The idea is not at all new in common law countries.

of subjective rights he saw bundles of claims. The right is nothing but a loose abstraction of such a bundle of claims. The right is defined by the claims of which it consists.

The most spectacular consequence of this view becomes visible in the transfer of a right. There is no longer the need to transfer the right in its entirety. The right can pass gradually, claim by claim. A further consequence of this view seems to be that the distinction between rights *in re* and rights *in personam* must disappear. And indeed there is a tendency in Scandinavia to blur the difference between the rights *in re* and rights *in personam*.[13] The outcome of this is to the detriment of the rights *in re*, which are in danger of disappearing as a special category.

The need of an object for obligations

Even though there might be a wide consensus in seeing rights in terms of relationships, this situation is not satisfactory at all. The argument has already been used that this view can explain the power of an owner or a creditor, but has difficulty in explaining how a right can confer property. In the case of rights *in re* this difficulty could perhaps be overcome by some further relationship existing between the parties and the piece of land or the movable thing concerned. But how can this view explain that a creditor is enriched by others' indebtedness to him? That an obligation is enough to enrich the creditor is admitted everywhere: one of the first things we imagine, when we hear that somebody is rich, is a high bank balance. But against the bank we have no right *in re*, the legal relationship with the bank is personal. Even economists allow us to write the claims we have arising out of contracts on the credit side of the balance sheet. There must be something more than a relationship. Power is not enough either. There must be an asset that is worth money.

Another argument carries perhaps even more weight, at least for those who care about scientific standards: relationships cannot be transferred. What may happen is that one person succeeds another in a relationship, but this would not constitute a transfer. Only objects can be transferred and in a sense a relationship is just the opposite of an object.[14] Debts are nevertheless transferred all the time.

It seems that Roman lawyers had a very subtle feeling for the problem. They saw obligations as relationships (*in personam*), consequently they denied the possibility of transferring obligations. Instead they used the procedure of *novatio* whereby the parties were exchanged. This seems to be an appropriate solution, perhaps the only one in the case of relationships. The relational character

---

[13] In Denmark and Norway traditionally the difference is not emphasised – see Kruse, I *Ejendomsretten* (1951) 192 *ff*. In this sense Ross has given a theoretical explanation for his national law.

[14] Rudden has apparently seen this point (*cf*. Lawson and Rudden, *The Law of Property* (2nd ed.) p. 16). The predicament is stated by Werner in *J. Staudingers Kommentar zum Bürgerlichen Gesetzbuch und dem Einführungsgesetze* vol. 2 *Recht der Schuldverhältnisse* (1930) Einl (I 1) before § 398.

of obligations might also be the reason why Roman lawyers did not develop a general concept of *"ius subjectivum"*. Perhaps for them *iura in re* and *iura in personam* were too different in character to be put together in a common class.

Surely we cannot return to the standpoint of Roman law. We need to be able to transfer obligations. Our economy would come to a halt without that possibility. So we have to model our legal tools according to this need. The outcome seems clear. It must be something like the general concept of property or *propriété* as it is found in English or French law. The problem is how this can be construed. The simplest solution would be to find an object for obligations. This object must have a value that enriches the creditor. It could serve as the object for transfer. It should allow a uniform approach for *iura in re* and *iura in personam*.

Indeed, since the discussion started at the beginning of last century, there have been endeavours to find an object for obligations. There were some legal writers who used the division into *ius in re* and *ius in personam* as the starting point, and they felt the need to construe an object for obligations. Savigny defined the object as the performance of the debtor.[15] This view was also accepted by his disciple Puchta.[16] This proposal has not been accepted by legal science, and it has been rejected with good reason. An object thus construed may satisfy formal requirements. But a right to determine the behaviour of another person would again only be a power, it could not explain the obligation as a property right, and surely in the transfer of the right it is not the action of the debtor that passes from the assignor to the assignee.

Jhering, too, saw the need for an object for obligations. He criticised Windscheid, because he found no "concrete substratum" (*gegenständliches Substrat*) in Windscheid's "discretionary power". Only such a substratum would give the commanding will a content. This "concrete substratum" demanded by Jhering can be understood as the object of the obligation. Jhering himself proposed as object of obligations the interest that is legally protected.[17]

One could argue that Jhering's interest is not very concrete either. One could object that this definition is somewhat circular. Since the legal protection is the result of the right it should not be an attribute of its object. Furthermore, this interest seems to be a rather general concept. It may just be, however, that this generality might show the way for a solution in the search for an object for obligations. Indeed, an interest that is specific enough could have value for purposes of enrichment. It could be an object which could be transferred and it could satisfy structural needs too.

Jhering's proposal has not been taken further.[18] Nevertheless, the quest for an object of obligations has continued. Though this is not one of the great

---

[15] Von Savigny, I *System des Heutigen Römischen Rechts* (1840) §§ 53, 58.
[16] The sixth chapter (about obligations) of Puchta's *Pandekten* had the title "Die Rechte an Handlungen" (rights to actions).
[17] Von Jhering, III *Geist des Römischen Rechts* (1888) §§ 60 *ff.*
[18] If we do not take the so called "Interessenjurisprudenz" (legal doctrine of interests) as initiated by this conception. But this doctrine does not consider the problem that is discussed here.

topics of discussion of today's legal science, important writers have reminded us that subjective rights generally can and must be seen in the light that they add to property (*Vermögenszuordnung*).[19]

After so much energy has been spent on the problem of a general structure for subjective rights that would comprise rights *in re* as well as obligations, it may seem that all possible solutions have been explored – none to our satisfaction. Lawyers could be doomed to live with this predicament. But even though lawyers might be accustomed to predicaments this is no reason to avoid the challenge. Indeed, it has been demonstrated that obstinate problems have only existed as a result of a reluctance to abandon supposed preconditions that were actually unnecessary. This might be the case with our problem too.

The categories rearranged

In an article published in 1961 Raiser[20] proposed a new arrangement of the criteria to systematise subjective rights. He did not develop a whole system of subjective rights in that article. He concentrates on rights *in re*, but he expressly does not exclude obligations. He does not say much about systematisation, but the hints that can be found in his article seem worth fathoming.

Raiser introduces a new dichotomy, "primary rights" and "secondary rights". This distinction does not separate different subjective rights from each other, it refers to a structure *within* the rights. This structure is most visible in rights *in re*. One can see on the one hand the independent legal position of the owner, his legally protected competence to determine on his own the fate of the object. This is his primary right. On the other hand the owner has power to realise that position. There are actions with which he can defend his position against interference from others. These are the secondary rights. In this explanation one can see the primary right representing the concept of property and the secondary right representing the aspect of power. It is a short step to saying that the primary right is absolute because the owner has it in regard to everybody. The secondary rights can only be exercised against intruders and therefore are always relative to them.

One thing becomes clear in this explanation. The distinction between absolute and relative does not classify rights at all, it shows certain aspects of every right. Rights *in re* contain apparently both aspects. When one looks now at rights *in personam*, one of the aspects, the relative side or – to use the terminology of Raiser – the secondary rights, are clearly visible. These are the claims of the creditor against the debtor, whereby he gives effect to his right. The question is what the absolute side of obligations consists of.

So far this construction has not provided us with an answer to the question of what the object of an obligation is. What it does, however, is to refute the

---

[19] See Wieacker, "*Die Forderung als Mittel und Gegenstand der Vermögenszuordnung*" [1941] D.R.W. 49 ff.; Westermann, *Sachenrecht* (1966) § 2 II; Larenz I *Lehrbuch des Schuldrechts – Allgemeiner Teil* (1982) § 33.
[20] Raiser, "Der Stand der Lehre vom Subjektiven Recht" [1961] *Juristenzeitung (J.Z.)* 465 *ff*.

argument that an answer is impossible since obligations are relative in contrast to absolute rights *in re*. To illustrate this a scheme may help:

	iura in re	*iura in personam*
primary rights (absolute, object)	*uti, frui, abuti*	?
secondary rights (claims, relative, power)	*reivindicatio actio negatoria*	claims for payment and delivery

The upper right quadrant is still empty.[21]

The object of obligations

It does not seem very promising to go on searching for an object of obligations in the outside world. Various candidates have been examined without a satisfactory result. Other writers have tried to find something absolute for obligations inside law. They proposed the "reification of obligation", an "obligatory competence" or a "right in the obligation".[22] All these proposals have one major flaw: they do not propose an object *of* obligations but try to see the obligation itself as an object. This is not the solution we are looking for. It is useless to put relationships into a hat and then pull out an object.

I prefer a different approach. Since it is not possible to find a real object for obligations in the outside world and since the object will have an institutional reality only, the question arises whether one should not simply determine the object according to our needs and then verify whether this object has enough institutional support.

One thing we can say without a great deal of consideration is that the object must have some value. It is the obligation's value that causes it to be considered as property. The problem is that there is no real object to bear that value. But this is not as strange as it might seem. We are well used to values that are independent of the real objects which bear that value. An example of this is money, in which case the value of the money is independent of the paper and the colour used. The same holds true for cheques and bills of exchange. It is possible that in the case of a normal obligation even this little bit of

---

[21] The scheme given here might remind one of the famous "scheme of opposites and correlatives" of Hohfeld, "Fundamental Legal Conceptions as Applied in Judicial Reasoning" [1913] *Yale Law Journal* 16; Reprint *Westport* [1978] 36. The scheme used here differs from the aforesaid scheme by introducing the concept of an object of rights; Hohfeld expressly looks at rights as relationships only.

[22] *cf.* Dulckeit, *Die Verdinglichung obligatorischer Rechte* (1951). Karl Larenz, I *Lehrbuch des Schuldrechts – Allgemeiner Teil* (1982) § 33 III; II *Besonderer Teil* (1981) § 72 I a. Oertmann, "Zur Struktur der Subjektiven Privatrechte" [1925] *Archiv für die civilistische Praxis* (AcP) 129 *ff*, 145 *ff*.

materiality is abandoned. The institutional support for the execution of the obligation would be sufficient to convey that value. In the case of an obligation we would be dealing with a "naked" value that is not materialised at all.

The value of the obligation is created when the parties enter into the contract; it disappears with performance. This is the reason why the free creation of values by obligations is economically acceptable. The value has only provisional and temporary existence. This is different if an obligation is created with the intention of letting it circulate. In such cases the obligation may have the same effect as injecting currency into the economy that may lead to inflation. (Economists are the experts regarding the difficulties which are experienced when calculating the national income, where normal obligations are not taken into account but obligations of longer duration may well be.)

English lawyers should be able to intuitively accept the notion that a naked value can form the object of an obligation. The only thing that a promisee in English law can count on is that he can receive institutional support for a claim for money. Thus what they have as promisees is only the claim for the value of the expected performance. More conditions have to be fulfilled before specific performance can be demanded. If specific performance can be demanded, a promisee no longer requires a claim for the value since he is deemed in equity to have a right in the thing itself, a right *in re*.

Even in civil law countries where specific performance is the point of departure, it is generally accepted that the buyer of, for example, a piano, has no piano at all before performance is rendered. In these countries, too, until performance is rendered, what a creditor has is the value of the piano, only. This can be seen in cases of misrepresentation. If the debtor is liable for damages, those damages are calculated with reference to the value of the object as misrepresented. (Perhaps the debtor is also liable for further damage or loss caused by his misrepresentation; but these damages would be calculated differently. These damages will have to be measured in accordance with the normal principles of the law, and not with reference to the value created by the contract.)

A value as object of an obligation has specific characteristics. The creditor's property is more secure than any corporeal object. The value cannot be damaged or stolen. What can happen is that the debtor may have agreed to render performance of more value than he is able to meet. (This situation resembles inflation on a national level where the amount of money surpasses national performance.) Nominally the debtor will be obliged to perform as agreed; economically his obligations have to be re-evaluated. This happens in bankruptcy, where the bankruptcy leaves the nominal value of the obligation untouched, yet economically it might be desirable to free the debtor from his obligations.

The proposal to see a "naked" value as the object of obligations may lead to speculation. Before the idea of such an object can be mooted, it must be possible to attribute value independent of an object bearing such value. This presupposes some measure of value. Such a measure is money. Consequently, obligations themselves would presuppose a culture where money is known and used. It should be possible to test this assumption in history. The result would give a strong argument for or against the proposal presented here.

The argumentation used here has not been very systematic, as the intention was to present the idea that value is an object of obligations. The property element in obligations is found in their value. In the scheme given above this value would take the place of the object of the primary right of obligations and thus complete it. This means that a general structure for subjective rights can be shown. The English and French comprehensive conception of property appears to be well founded. The theoretical doubts that have led to the restricted concepts of *Eigentum* and *eigendom* in German and Dutch law respectively would seem surmountable. Obligations do not represent only relationships between creditor and debtor, and they do not only give a power to the creditor. They have an object and this makes them transferable like other assets.

Further consequences

Explanations in law are often like a blanket that is too short. One has the choice as to whether the shoulders or the feet are cold. The explanation that has been given above has this same characteristic.

Having given a general structure for subjective rights, there is a danger that the general structure of contracts has been lost. The value, as the creditor's property, is the object of an obligation. The obligation is the product of a contract. Is it necessary in all cases that a contract produces a value in the hands of the creditor? Or do we now have to distinguish between contracts which create such a value and those that do not?

This question is not new. Windscheid has already discussed it[23]: Two neighbours agree that one will not play the trumpet after 6 p.m. and the other will pay 20 DM per month in exchange. Does the neighbour who expects to enjoy quiet evenings derive any property out of this contract? Perhaps he has the power to suppress any trumpet sounds, but does this constitute value in his hands? Is there anything that he can transfer by assignment to somebody else?

Not even such far-fetched examples have to be used. If I hire a room for a month, do I have any property after conclusion of the contract? Does it constitute value in my hands? Has value been created or transferred by the contract? One could doubt it and say that I acquire value only through my own actions, if and when I use the room. Again the question would arise, whether I have any object to transfer.

Other examples could be mentioned. One such example is a contract where services are promised. Do we have to concede that some contracts do not result in perfect obligations creating value and power, but that some create only power?[24] (In all these cases the explanation that such contracts have a strong

---

[23] Windscheid, II *Lehrbuch des Pandektenrechts* (1891) § 250, n.3.
[24] This way we would have two classes of "imperfect obligations", one where the creditor has value but no power, as in the case of a prescribed claim, the other where the creditor has power but no value.

personal element, is not very convincing.) The gap we have closed in the doctrine of rights would reappear in the doctrine of contracts or the doctrine of obligations. Would we have to revive the kind of distinctions that Roman lawyers made between *contractus* and *pactum* or between consensual and real contracts?

A further difficulty in another field appears. The identification of value as the object of obligations suggests that the distinction between rights *in re* and rights in *personam* relates to rights in substance and rights in value respectively.[25] The question is whether these two categories are mutually exclusive. Indeed, rights *in re* can be seen as rights where the value is of no importance. The right of ownership is not affected at all, if the value of a car or a house declines. My ownership of a "Blue Mauritius" will not change at all if tomorrow thousands of specimens of this stamp are found. Whenever the value of something in law plays a role, it is on the basis of an obligation. That is why all claims for compensation are *in personam*.

The strict separation of substance and value rights can indeed be found in most civil law countries. It is one of the functions of accessory rights (as "hypothec" and pledge) to overcome this separation.[26] Nevertheless, some rights are found that violate this principle. In Germany it is the *Grundschuld*, a right similar to the hypothec which, though a right *in re*, has itself a certain value. In the Netherlands the new civil code has a so called *kwalitatieve verbintenis* (qualitative obligation) that has the characteristics of a right in land. Both rights are not traditional but have been created by lawyers who were not conscious of any violation of a legal principle. In both cases it has to be asked whether the creation has been an achievement. I would doubt it in both cases.

The multitude of rights in land in England could be interpreted as a trend to create separate value rights in land and to convey each as an independent object.[27] Again this would violate the principle of strict separation of substance rights and value rights. Though English law perhaps would not accept such a principle, some of the dissatisfaction with this situation in land law might stem from the fact that such rights merge elements of both categories.

Certainly there are more fields where the view of obligations as rights in a value together with a strict separation between value rights and substance rights will cause difficulty. Only further discussion can reveal whether this view will result in confusion or in a better understanding of property law.[28]

---

[25] A distinction between rights in substance and rights in value has been made by Kohler in "Substanzrecht und Wertrecht" [1901] *AcP* 155 *ff.*, though in a different way.

[26] See Mincke, *Die Akzessorietät des Pfandrechts* (1987) pp. 103 *et seq.*

[27] Lawson and Rudden *op. cit.* above, n.14, at p. 226 *ff.* discuss physical objects as things and investments. They maintain that when things are seen as investments their money value alone is relevant. In the context of the distinction between substance and value rights, the value of a thing would be relevant in obligatory relationships only.

[28] This article has been published before in [1996] *Journal of South African Law (Tydskrif vir die Suid-Afrikaanse Reg)* s.255 *ff.*

8

Pensions as Property and Pensions as Contract

RICHARD NOBLES*

Introduction

The overwhelming majority of members of occupational pension schemes belong to what are called "defined benefit" schemes.[1] These schemes provide benefits defined by reference to a member's salary at the date of their retirement or, if they change jobs, the salary paid just prior to their leaving.[2] This paper examines claims by scheme members that the funds which secure these pensions represent their deferred pay, and that these funds are, in some meaningful sense, their property. The first part of the paper considers what it means for employees to claim ownership of pension funds or pension scheme benefits. In particular, it examines the scope for such claims to influence court decisions on the extent and manner in which employers should be allowed to benefit from pension funds. The second part of the paper examines the courts' increasing use of contractual analysis to resolve disputes over the respective entitlements of employers and employees.

I. PENSIONS AS PROPERTY

1. Lay perceptions of pensions as property

A pension fund, from the perspective of the Confederation of British Industry,[3] is like a mortgage. The assets which exceed the amount necessary to secure the benefits promised to the members are the equivalent of the mortgagor's equity, with the employer as mortgagor. In the light of this, the Confederation of British Industry would like to see the following statutory statement:

---

* Senior Lecturer, Department of Law, London School of Economics.
[1] By contrast with money purchase schemes, in which the size of the trust fund, or at least a member's individual share of that fund, defines the size of the pension received.
[2] 93 per cent of pension scheme members belong to final salary schemes. See National Association of Pension Funds Annual Survey of Pension Schemes (1994) p. 5.
[3] See Confederation of British Industry, Evidence to the Goode Committee, "Occupational Pension Schemes: Securing the Future".

> "a pension fund is not to be regarded as a conventional trust with the beneficiaries having an interest in the assets of the fund, but as a guarantee fund supporting the employer's promise."[4]

By contrast, the Charter For Pension Fund Democracy (an organisation which represents 3.5 million employees) views pension funds as the employees' property. It has stated that:

> "This reform [majority member-appointed trustees] is essential to ensure that pension fund assets are entirely separate from employer assets and that trustees act in the best interests of members. The best judges of members' interests are the members themselves. Increasingly, scheme members do not perceive employers as suitable guardians of *their trust funds*."[5]

How do these perspectives and their non-specialist conceptions of property impact upon the current law of pensions, or the manner in which that law might be reformed?

2. The lawyers' view of pensions as property

To practising pension lawyers, looking for an "owner" of the pension fund, is likely to be viewed as political rhetoric – relevant to the process of reform – but irrelevant to the establishment of existing legal rights.[6] Looking at the pension scheme as a whole, one cannot find employees or employers enjoying the ownership of pension funds in the sense in which ownership might be generally understood by lay persons: that is the right to alienate, manage and enjoy property.[7] Instead of anything as simple as laymens' views of ownership, we find assets held under the terms of the pension scheme, which amounts to a type of private constitution. The trustees hold the legal title to assets, under a duty to manage them in the best interests of the beneficiaries,[8] and in accordance with the scheme's rules. The trustees exercise the scheme's investment powers. The scheme actuary advises on the contribution rate necessary to meet the cost of benefits. The employer will typically covenant to pay such contributions as the actuary decides,[9] but reserves the right to discontinue the scheme and thus make no further contributions. The employer may also reserve the right to veto any increase in the pension benefits. With such powers, the employer can not only

---

[4] Above, n.3, at p. 14.
[5] The Charter for Pension Fund Democracy's Submission to the Goode Committee, at p. 31, para. 5.2 (emphasis added).
[6] Knott J. in *LRT Pension Fund Trustee Company Ltd v. Hatt* [1993] Pension Law Reports 227 at 267, stated that it was "quite impossible, as well as simplistic, to try to identify the owner or owners of a [pension fund] surplus".
[7] The sort of understanding which would be contained within a statement like "He owns that umbrella". See Honoré "Ownership", in Guest (ed.), *Oxford Essays in Jurisprudence: A Collaborative Work* (1961) Chap. 5.
[8] *Cowan v. Scargill* [1985] Ch. 270.
[9] Escolme, Hudson, and Greenwood, *Hoskings Pension Schemes and Retirement Benefits* (6th ed., 1991) para. 3–07.

Pensions as Property and Pensions as Contract

prevent its liabilities under the scheme from being unilaterally increased by the trustees, but can ensure that it benefits from investment returns. If investments do better than expected, and benefits are not increased, the employer will be able to pay less contributions in the future. If the scheme is wound up with more assets than are needed to fund the accrued benefits, and the employer can veto benefit increases, then the "surplus" which then arises will be available to be returned to the employer. The power of amendment is often shared between the employer and the trustees, with the employer having power to suggest amendments, and the trustees to veto them, or vice versa.

In various disputes scheme members have sought to establish that the parties whose actions may directly affect the security and amount of their benefits (trustees, actuaries, financial advisers and employers) have duties towards them. These disputes have mostly concerned the use of assets which are not considered necessary to secure the members' fixed benefits: "surpluses". Two kinds of surpluses have been involved: surpluses arising on final winding up, and surpluses arising within ongoing schemes when the actuary's periodic valuation indicates that the current level of funding exceeds the current value of the schemes' benefits (the latter kind of surplus has been termed an "actuarial surplus"). Establishing the existence of both kinds of surplus, and deciding which parties are to benefit from them, involve the exercise of discretionary powers. These powers may be given to trustees, or to the employer, or the actuary, or shared between these parties. In those cases which have come to court, the court has had not only to establish how a particular power has been allocated,[10] but also what duties affect the manner in which that power may be exercised.[11] Identifying how a power has been allocated, and the duties attached to it, requires the court to look outside the law itself, to different perspectives. One of these perspectives is an ideology, which approximates to lay understanding of ownership set out above.

3. The need for perspectives

An example will serve to demonstrate the need for perspectives when deciding pension disputes.

---

[10] In *Re Courage Group's Pension Schemes; Ryan et al. v. Imperial Brewing and Leisure Ltd et al.* [1987] 1 All E.R. 528, the court had to decide whether the power to amend had been given solely to the employer, or shared between the trustees and the employer. In *Stannard v. Fisons* [1992] I.R.L.R. 27, C.A., the court had to consider whether the calculation of a bulk transfer payment was a matter solely for the scheme actuary, or also required the trustees to satisfy themselves that the amount transferred was "fair".

[11] In *Cowan* above, n.8, the court had to decide whether the trustees' duty to act in the members' best interests allowed them to take into account the members' interest in continued employment in the coal industry. In *Stannard v. Fisons*, above, n.10, the Court of Appeal gave directions on what needed to be considered by trustees when deciding how "fairly" to divide a pension fund on the sale of subsidiary companies. In *Imperial Tobacco Group Pension Trust Ltd v. Imperial Tobacco Ltd* [1991] 2 All E.R. 597 the Court examined how an employer might exercise its veto over benefit increases. For a discussion of the way in which duties of care relate to the exercise of powers see Cullity, "Judicial Control of Trustees' Discretions" (1975) 25 U. of Toronto L.J. 99.

Re Courage Group's Pension Schemes[12]

In this case, Hanson plc. had sold the Courage group of companies to Elders plc. The Courage pension schemes had a surplus of £80 million. The sale agreement provided that unless Elders were able to transfer the surplus back to Hanson, the purchase price would increase by £50 million. To get the surplus to Hanson, Elders asked the trustees of the pension scheme to execute an amendment substituting Hanson as "employer" under the scheme rules, in place of the Courage parent company. As the named employer, only Hanson's employees could then be scheme members. Thus the pension scheme, and its surplus, would be separated from the Courage employees, who would no longer qualify as scheme members. The court had to decide whether the scheme's rules gave the power of amendment to the employer, with the trustees being required to concur, or whether the power was joint, with the trustees having the right to withhold consent. The relevant clause stated that:

> "The company may at any time . . . add to, delete or vary all or any of the provisions of this Deed or the rules and the [trustees] shall concur in executing any such deed".[13]

Elders argued that the word "shall" in this clause was a mandatory provision, meaning "must." The provision anticipates that the trustees might take a different view from the company, but provides that their opposition will be overridden. Yet Millett J. held that the trustees not only had a right to refuse to execute a deed of amendment, but in the particular circumstances of the case, he felt that they were under a duty to refuse. He interpreted the word "shall" to mean that amendments would not be valid unless the trustees complied:

> "to exclude any discretion in the [trustees] would not only deny any effective protection to the members, but would make nonsense of the careful allocation found elsewhere in the trust deed and rules. What is the point of conferring a power on the [trustees] or requiring the [trustees] consent to be obtained, if the power can be assumed by the company, or the [trustees'] consent can be dispensed with by an amendment made by the company alone in which the [trustees are] bound to concur".[14]

The "point" from the employer's perspective is that ultimate control rests with the company. Millett J. was not denying that this could be desired by an employer. He was simply unwilling to grant the employer such overriding control.

This example not only demonstrates that ambiguity in the division of power is possible, it also illustrates the way in which ambiguities are resolved, and the importance within that resolution of judicial perspectives on what the entitlements of the various parties ought to be. The judge looks to the words to find the intention of the drafting parties, and looks for an intention which is judged to be probable. In forming a view as to what is probable the judge looks at the

---

[12] [1987] 1 All E.R. 528.
[13] [1987] 1 All E.R. 528 at 535.
[14] *ibid.*

implications of different interpretations. Ideally, the interpretation given to a form of words will be an acceptable interpretation in terms of syntax, a reasonable provision to find alongside the other rules of the scheme, and represent a reasonable interpretation of the intention of the parties, which produces just results. Within this process, the judge's perspective on what the entitlements of the parties ought to be forms a crucial background matrix to the interpretation of the words in dispute. Such perspectives do not determine the outcome, in the sense that they overwhelm all forms of words and all arrangements of rules. But they do influence the outcome, in the sense that the duties and powers found within pension schemes will be affected by the judicial view of what entitlements the parties can reasonably expect to enjoy. One of these perspectives is the ideology of property.

4. The ideology of property

Cotterrell has written about the ideological significance of claiming to be the owner of something held in trust.[15] This claim operates as a claim to exercise power, without having to justify that power, simply by being identified as the owner of a thing. The owner of a thing may exercise power represented by that thing without further justification in terms of needs, deserts, etc. Thus, in the context of pension schemes, to the extent that members can establish themselves as the owners of the pension fund, they should expect to exercise the power represented by that fund, without the need for further justifications. As the beneficiaries of a trust the members should not ordinarily expect to exercise that power directly. But they may expect the power to be exercised on their behalf, again, not because they are in need, or deserve such protection, but simply because it is their property.

> "... what appears as a highly technical and esoteric part of property law doctrine is actually a concept of wide influence in popular consciousness. The idea of a fiduciary obligation of the trustee harnesses to the legal doctrine a moral conception of great social significance and induces us to see the trust beneficiary not as the possessor of property-power but as a person meriting protection; a person to whom moral as well as legal obligations are owed. The trust-form, concentrating and guaranteeing property-power, not only fails to impose moral obligations on the powerful [the beneficiaries], but actually encourages us to think of *moral obligations owed to them* because of their beneficial entitlements."[16]

The ideological conception of property identified by Cotterrell presents itself as a form of moral argument which can be used to justify legal decisions.[17] If

---

[15] Cotterrell "Power, Property and the Law of Trusts: A Partial Agenda for Critical Legal Scholarship" in Fitzpatrick and Hunt *Critical Legal Studies* (1987). K235 C93
[16] *ibid.* at p. 88.
[17] Other concepts of property lack this persuasive force. Analysis such as that by Calebresi and Melamed, "Property Rules, Liability Rules, and Inalienability: One View of the Cathedral" (1972) 85 *Harvard Law Review*, 1089, which identify property by the remedies granted in

"I" am the owner of an identifiable thing, then I deserve the protection of the law for my enjoyment of that thing. The law can only protect me by recognising that I have rights against other parties. Thus, to the extent that I can present myself as being the owner of a thing, I can legitimately claim rights that protect my enjoyment of that thing. This process contributes towards the tendency for rights to agglomerate in whichever party can present themselves as the owner of the thing in question.[18]

By claiming the ownership of their pension fund, members are making the same form of "moral" argument. Pension scheme members cannot ask for a sympathetic interpretation of the rights granted to them by their pension scheme on the basis that they are an exploited section of the workforce, or at least not by comparison with those workers (part-time, temporary or full-time employees working in small firms)[19] who do not have access to occupational pension schemes. But if they can identify rights which are recognisable as property rights, they can expect their enjoyment of those rights to be protected. To be recognised as property rights, a bundle of rights needs to be presented in a form which approximates to the lay understanding of ownership: as a definite thing which a given person or persons can claim to own. In the family trust, the beneficiaries are able to present the assets in the control of the trustees as "their" property, and this operates as a powerful claim for protection in many contexts.[20]

5. The role of property ideology in developing pension trust doctrine

(a) Ownership of the fund

The ideology of property ("thing-ownership") has played an important part in the courts' assimilation of the pension fund into legal doctrine. First, employees have been impeded from claiming that their labour has given them property rights in the pension fund, by their inability to point to the fund as a "thing" which they can be said, in any meaningful way, to "own".[21] Employees'

---

court, clarify what has been decided, and persuade, if at all, only by identifying the consequences of offering a remedy appropriate to property. Hoefeldian analysis, which treats property as relations between persons, with respect to things, has no persuasive force. It clarifies what is being claimed, and what claims have previously been accepted by the courts, but not whether any new claim should be granted.

[18] See Donahue "The Future of the Concept of Property Predicted from its Past" in Pennock and Chapman (eds.) *Property* (New York, 1980).

[19] *Occupational Pension Schemes 1987: 8th Survey by the Government Actuary* (HMSO 1991) para. 5.13.

[20] They can require the trustees to act in their best interests, and to avoid all conflicts of interest. They also enjoy considerable protection against loss through misappropriation by their right to trace trust assets.

[21] I do not mean to claim that employees must point to some material "thing" outside the law, to which they may lay claim through law. I accept that the "thing" which members are claiming is constructed through law (the assets of the pension fund are themselves legal constructs, and their grouping together in a single pension fund is also achieved through law). The use within

attempts to establish ownership of the pension fund have foundered on the fact that its value has to be shared with the employer. That part of the fund which the scheme actuary regards as more than sufficient to secure the scheme's existing liabilities (the surplus) will, in the ordinary course of events, lead to lower future employer contributions. There is no guarantee that any part of the surplus will lead to an increase in the current benefits of the existing members. In *Re Imperial Foods Pension Scheme*[22] the employer's right to benefit from this actuarial surplus was felt to be incompatible with the employees claim to own it. The case involved the division of a pension scheme following the sale of subsidiaries, and the transferring members' claim that their share of the fund should have included a share of the fund's surplus:

> "the fallacy . . . is . . . in assuming that the fund existing at the moment of separation belongs exclusively to the two classes of members, namely the transferring and the continuing members together, and to nobody else . . . the most cursory consideration will establish that this is not the case."[23]

The second way in which property ideology has operated has been through the court's inability to treat the members as the original owners of the employer's contributions to the scheme. Whilst these contributions may be earned by the members through their labour, and claimed by the members as their pay, the fact remains that immediately prior to being paid over by the employer they were the property of the employer. Unless the court accepts a momentary transfer of ownership to the members, in exchange for their labour, prior to the payment into the scheme, the members' claim to own these contributions must necessarily fail. In those schemes where employees make no contributions from their own wages, the members cannot enjoy property rights *except as beneficiaries*, under the rules of the scheme. Even where the members do pay contributions, their property claims are limited to those assets which represent their accumulated contributions, and would not include the assets generated through the employer's contributions, which are likely to be considerably larger.

The practical implications of the members' inability to show ownership of employers' contributions is illustrated by the development of doctrine in *Davis v. Richard & Wallington Industries*.[24] Scott J. was asked to decide who was entitled to a pension scheme's assets if its winding up rule failed to dispose of the same. (This was not relevant to the outcome of the case, as the winding up rule in the actual case, which he held to be validly introduced, was capable of disposing of all the assets.) Scott J. decided that any moneys not disposed of under the scheme rules should return to the employer under the doctrine of resulting

---

law of ideas which have parallel forms in other social spheres is not simple or straight forward, and may be best captured by systems' concepts such as "interference" and "coupling". See Teubner, *Law as an Autopoietic System* (1993) Chap. 5.
[22] [1986] 1 W.L.R. 717.
[23] *ibid.* at 728.
[24] [1991] 2 All E.R. 563.

trust. Whilst not relevant to the outcome of the case before him, it has implications in other cases where a scheme's winding up rule fails to dispose of the scheme's assets. In such cases, the employer will, if the reasoning in *Davis* is followed, claim all of the scheme's surplus assets for itself. Is this an example of anti-employee inclinations on the part of the judiciary, a refusal to give members the treatment which they deserve?[25] Or is it, as Cotterrell's analysis suggests, that the ideology of property short circuits the language of desert? If the money is paid in by the employer, and not disposed of by the trust, it can only be returned to a former owner. And if the employees did not enjoy anything barely recognisable as the thing-ownership relationship associated with property, they cannot claim to have been former owners of the employers' contributions. Thus, with regard to employers' contributions, they cannot, whatever the abstract justice of their claim, seek to benefit as *owners* from the employers' contributions if the pension trust fails to exhaust all of the trust funds.[26]

Whilst employees have not succeeded in convincing the courts that they should be treated as the owners of pension funds, they have managed to convince the courts that it is not entirely appropriate to treat the employer as owner either. Ownership claims by employers could arise in two ways. First, as the original owner of their contributions, and usually the party solely responsible for the drafting of the pension scheme, employers might wish to present themselves as "settlors". In family trusts, whilst the settlor plays no necessary role in the administration of the trust, the interpretation of the trust instrument, requires the courts to give effect to the intention of the settlor. Gardner attributes this to economic liberalism: a respect for the freedom of a property owner to do what it likes with its property.[27] A second way in which employers might raise ownership claims, is with respect to the surplus. If the employer has claims under a resulting trust for any undisposed surplus on winding up, and can expect to benefit from an actuarial surplus within an ongoing scheme through the reduction of its contributions, is there a sense in which the employer "owns" all surpluses?

Neither of these positions has been established. The employer is not the settlor. Indeed, in *Re Courage*, the concept of a single settlor was banished from pension trusts. There Millett J., whilst stating that there were no special rules of construction for pension trusts, proceeded to replace trust law's usual rule of construction (giving effect to the likely intention of the settlor) with one of "giving reasonable and practical effect to the scheme, bearing in mind that it has to be operated against a constantly changing commercial background".[28] Nor is

---

[25] See Nobles, *Davis v. Richard & Wallington Industries* (1990) 19 I.L.J. 24.
[26] But the judge's decision not to allow members of a contributory pension scheme to participate in the resulting trust on a pro-rata basis has been criticised as running contrary to property reasoning. See the report of the case in the [1990] Pension Law Reports 125.
[27] Gardner, *An Introduction to the Law of Trusts* (1990) p. 14.
[28] Above, n.10 at 537.

the employer sole beneficiary of the surplus. In *Mettoy Pension Trustees Limited v. Evans*[29] Warner J. interpreted a power to increase benefits which had been reserved to the employer (who was not a trustee) as a fiduciary power, and refused to allow it to be exercised by a receiver. As part of his justification for this decision he announced that: "One cannot in my opinion, in construing the rules of a "pension scheme", start from the assumption that any surplus belongs morally to the employer." In rejecting both these ownership claims, the courts have been influenced by the employees claim that pensions are their deferred pay. But this is not interpreted as a property claim. For the courts, the significance of deferred pay is simply that the employer's pension contributions, and the fund which they help to create, are both *earned* by the employees. They are part of their consideration. As such, whilst it may not be appropriate to treat the employees as owners of the pension fund, (due to the extensive rights over the fund enjoyed by the employer) it is also not appropriate to treat the employer as the owner of the fund, or even a part of it.

(b) Members' benefits as property

Whilst members' cannot show ownership of the whole fund, there is broad acceptance that the benefits promised under the scheme rules are a form of property – a thing which they own. And, in order to protect these property rights in the pension benefits, the courts have had to recognise members' rights over other aspects of the scheme. For example, in *LRT Pensions Fund Trustee Company Limited v. Hatt*,[30] the amalgamation of two pension schemes was achieved through the establishment of a new scheme using an interim deed. The interim deed empowered the employer to approve the new scheme's rules. This deed contained no express limitation on what might be approved. In Knox J.'s opinion restrictions had to be implied. The court:

> "should be vigilant to see that the [Employer's] duties, to have regard to the pre-existing rights of the members of the two funds which are being amalgamated, are properly observed and not to take away established property rights unless that is a proper incident in the process of amalgamation."[31]

In Knox J.'s view, the members' property rights included not only their accrued benefits, but some, though not all, of the provisions which increased the security of those benefits. On this basis he disallowed rule changes which removed the employer's covenant to make minimum contributions.[32]

---

[29] [1991] 2 All E.R. 513; [1990] 1 W.L.R. 1587 at 1619.
[30] Above, n.6.
[31] *ibid. The Report of the Pension Law Review Committee* (the "Goode Committee") CM 4243–I at para. 4.2.8 exhibits a similar concern with protecting the members' accrued rights.
[32] But allowed changes which gave the employer appointed chairman of the trustees a casting vote.

(c) The need for another approach

The decisions discussed above represent a stalemate in which the ideology of property cannot easily operate. Neither employer, nor employee have a right to have property power exercised in their favour simply because the pension fund is "theirs". And whilst employees may be considered to have property rights in their accrued pensions, the courts face considerable difficulty in identifying which additional rights should also count as property rights. If every rule which may affect the value or security of the accrued benefits is itself a members' property right, then no rule may be interpreted, and no power exercised, in a manner which allows the employer to benefit from the fund, or to increase its control over the fund. Affording such strong protection for the members' property rights in their accrued benefits would amount to accepting the members' claim to own the whole fund.

If the courts do not accept that the members own their fund, or that their property rights in accrued benefits must be protected from anything which affects their value, then the ideology of property will not indicate how disputes over the exercise of discretionary powers should be resolved. With the failure of this ideology to provide an adequate basis from which to identify the rights and duties appropriate to a pension scheme, the courts have turned to another legal perspective: the contract of employment.

II. PENSIONS AS CONTRACTUAL ENTITLEMENTS

Before exploring this perspective, one needs to make some preliminary remarks indicating what it is not. Contractual entitlements within pension schemes are not based upon a conscious agreement reached between the workforce, either individually or collectively through trade unions, and an employer. Negotiation of pension benefits is quite recent,[33] and such negotiations as do occur concentrate upon the benefits offered and pay little attention to the allocation and exercise of discretions.[34] Nor is the written contract of employment likely to introduce new obligations to those set out in the pension scheme itself, since the contract is likely to refer only to the employee's right to be a member of the scheme on its current terms. If one simply moved away from the ideology of property, in which members have reasonable expectations *because* they are beneficiaries, and tried to ground their expectations in some form of intentionality, one would not advance the members position.[35] Most members are singularly

---

[33] See Nobles, *Pensions Employment and the Law* (1993) p. 4.
[34] *ibid.* at p. 5.
[35] In *Armour v. Liverpool Corporation* [1939] Ch. 422, Simmonds J. was only prepared to recognise as common contractual terms those rules of the pension scheme of which *all* the workforce were aware.

Pensions as Property and Pensions as Contract

unaware of the benefits promised by their pension scheme, let alone the rules governing the exercise of discretions.[36]

What the contract of employment offers is both another method for protecting property rights and a new perspective from which to interpret the provisions of an occupational pension scheme. Contract offers a means of taking into account the employment relationship. This use of contractual analysis is not an alternative to treating pensions as property, but supplements it; both by providing an alternative remedy, and by offering a new perspective on what entitlements the employees should enjoy. In both cases property rights provide a starting point, or at least a point of reference, for the introduction of contractual restrictions on the manner in which discretions can be used.

1. Contract as a remedy: the use of contract to protect property rights

The use of contractual analysis to protect property rights is illustrated by the *Imperial Tobacco* case.[37] The Imperial Tobacco pension scheme ("the old scheme") had been closed to new members when the Imperial Group was taken over by Hanson. Imperial Tobacco was able to enjoy a contribution holiday with respect to this scheme as it had a surplus, at minimum, of £130 million. But new employees could not join the closed scheme. They had to have a new scheme set up to provide their pensions and, with respect to this scheme, Imperial Tobacco was having to make contributions. The new management of Imperial Tobacco tried to persuade the members of the old scheme to transfer their entitlements into the new scheme. If all the members transferred then all of the fund, including the surplus, would go with them. If they did so, then the surplus would then be in a scheme which was not closed to new members, and could therefore be used to fund the pensions of new employees. There was also an important difference in the two scheme's winding up clauses. The new scheme provided for any residual surplus on winding up to be returned to the employer. Thus, if the members transferred to the new scheme, not only would they reduce the likelihood that they would benefit from the surplus (since it would be used to fund the benefits of new members), but they would lose their right to receive benefit increases in the event of the old scheme being wound up. The members of the old scheme were led to believe that the only basis on which they could expect to enjoy benefit increases was if they transferred into the new scheme. But if the members had a right to benefit increases within the old scheme, then they had no need to transfer to the new scheme. The Vice Chancellor was therefore asked to decide on what basis, if any, the employer could refuse its consent to benefit increases within the old scheme.

---

[36] The Goode Committee found widespread ignorance amongst employees about pensions. See "Knowledge and Misconceptions about Occupational Pension Schemes", Chap. 6 of the *Report of the Pension Law Review Committee* (the "Goode Committee") CM 4243–II.

[37] Above. n.11.

The Vice Chancellor accepted that, were the requirement for consent given to an individual within a family settlement, it would ordinarily be expected to be exercisable as that individual saw fit. But pension trusts were different. *All* the powers of an employer under a pension scheme were subject to an implied duty of good faith not to undermine the relationship of trust and confidence which ought to exist between an employer and employees. This duty existed both in contract, and in trust, and was breached where "the sole purpose of refusing to consent to an amendment increasing benefits is the collateral purpose of putting pressure on members to abandon their existing rights".[38]

There was no need to use contractual analysis to achieve this result. The law of trusts restricts the use of powers other than for their intended purpose.[39] And the decision that a power should not be used to remove existing rights seems to owe as much to a property perspective as a contractual one: the members could point to the fund, in a winding up, as a thing which they owned, and which should not be taken away from them. As such, in this particular case, the use of contract was simply an alternative remedy to that already available in the law of property. However, by articulating the remedy in terms of an employer's general duty not to undermine their employees' trust and confidence, Brown-Wilkinson V.-C. also made it easier for future courts to have regard to the contract of employment as a perspective for deciding upon members' entitlements.

2. The perspective offered by the contract of employment

As stated before, the contractual perspective does not introduce a real agreement, or another oral or documentary source of rights separate from the pension scheme. It requires one to consider what is appropriate within an employment relationship. This might be expected to offer employees little by way of extra protection. If, for example, we accept Unger's view of the world of work as one structured through contractual and hierarchical relations,[40] then looking to the employment relationship might simply reinforce the expectation that the employer should exercise full control. However, as Moffat has pointed out,[41] the employment relationship is by no means as contractual as Unger's typology suggests. It has elements of trusting, and paternalism. As Fox has shown, the employment relationship contains an ideology based upon master-servant relationship, with the status of master carrying a responsibility for the general welfare of the servant.[42] The paradigm which underlies the master-servant relationship is not contract, but the idea of family, with the employer in the position

---

[38] [1991] 2 All E.R. 597 at 608.
[39] "It is trite law that a power can be exercised only for the purpose for which it is conferred, and not for any extraneous or ulterior purpose." *Re Courage* above, n.10, at 537.
[40] See Unger, "The Critical Legal Studies Movement" (1983) 96 *Harvard Law Review* 561 at 564–565.
[41] Moffat, "Pension Funds, a Fragmentation of Trust Law" (1992) 55 M.L.R. 123.
[42] Fox, *Beyond Contract: Work, Power and Trust Relations* (1974) pp. 185, 248–249.

of *paterfamilias*.[43] Pension provision can be seen as part of the employer's desire to create:

> "[a] style of personal relations cultivated by management, characterised by respect, consideration, and fair dealing, on the basis of which 'the good employer can establish a feeling of sympathy and cooperation between himself and his people akin to the old family feeling that existed between the master and his apprentices in the days before machinery and industrial centres'."[44]

There is some evidence that the courts have been influenced by this master-servant ideology, allowing discretions to be exercised by "good" employers who are concerned with the welfare of their workforce, but seeking to restrain "bad" employers who are concerned only with profit maximisation. The best example of this has been the court's antipathy to those employers who seek to exploit their power over the pension scheme of a company which they have recently acquired through a takeover. Millett J.'s judgment in *Re Courage*[45] captures this contrast between employers who can be trusted and those who cannot:

> "In the present case, the members of these schemes object to being compulsorily transferred to a new scheme of which they know nothing except that it has a relatively small surplus. While they have no legal right to participate in the surpluses in the existing schemes, they are entitled to have them dealt with by consultation and negotiation between their *employers with a continuing responsibility towards them* and the [trustees] with a discretion to exercise on their behalf, and not to be irrevocably parted from these surpluses by the unilateral decision of a *take-over raider with only a transitory interest in the share capital of the companies which employ them.*"[46]

However, if the court's willingness to restrain the employer's ability to control and exploit its workforce in the area of pension trusts is limited to that found in other areas of the employment relationship, it will not produce a high level of protection. Rather than hold all employers up to the standard expected of a model "good" employer, the courts have limited themselves to the restraint of actions regarded as wholly unreasonable.[47] Only where discretions are exercised in ways which are clearly seen as abuses are they going to be caught. Doubts have to be resolved in the employer's favour. As Collins has said of this approach in the context of unfair dismissal:

> " The [court] . . . simply endorses the practices of management in all but the most unreasonable and irrational abuse of managerial . . . power."[48]

---

[43] *ibid.* at p. 184.
[44] Fox, *op. cit.* above, n.42, at p. 196.
[45] [1987] 1 All E.R. 528.
[46] *ibid.* at 545 (emphasis added).
[47] In *Imperial Tobacco* above, n.11, Brown-Wilkinson V.-C. stressed that the duty of good faith did not require employers to act reasonably.
[48] Collins, *Justice in Dismissal* (1992) p. 39.

Conclusion

This paper has sought to identify the manner in which pension rights can be conceived of as property and the limitations of such conceptions, as part of the process of interpreting pension schemes. In the face of these limitations, neither employers, nor employees, are likely to be able to establish "ownership" of pension funds. The courts have similarly been unable to use property analysis, by itself, to solve the disputes which have arisen over pension trusts. They have been forced to look to the contract of employment, for standards which supplement trust doctrine, and restrain the employer's control of the pension scheme. These restraints will not serve to make employees into the owners of their funds, but will prevent employer practices which undermine the limited property rights which employees enjoy and/or are perceived as an abuse of the employer's power.[49]

---

[49] An earlier version of this paper was published as "Pensions as Property" in 14 *Legal Studies* (1994) at p. 345.

Part II
CHALLENGES TO ORTHODOXIES

9

Long-Term Leases as an Alternative to Ownership

JOSHUA WEISMAN*

Introduction

A land tenure system which is based on the principle that ownership of land is retained by the State while individual landholders are being granted, at most, long-term leases, is not very common among non-socialist countries. Yet, this kind of land tenure can be found in several places, *e.g.* in the Australian Capital Territory (Canberra), Singapore, Hong Kong[1] and Israel. Why in these countries were long-term leases preferred to the more accepted practice of conveying ownership (or freehold) to individual landholders? What are the advantages of a land tenure system based on leasing rather than conveying land? What has been the experience with long-term leases as substitutes for ownership of land? Were the goals set for long-term leases achieved? Did the implementation of this form of land tenure produce any unexpected side effects? These are some of the questions we propose to examine in this paper.[2]

I. Reasons for Adopting Long-Term Leases

Long-term leases were adopted by different countries in response to local socio-economic conditions. One would therefore tend to assume that the reasons for adopting this form of land tenure by different countries were as varied as were the conditions in those countries. Yet, this is not the case. Subject to some exceptions the reasons for adopting this form of land tenure were fairly similar in the different countries. Consequently, a review of these reasons in one country is,

---

* Professor of Law, The Hebrew University of Jerusalem, Israel.
[1] Neutze, "The Urban Leasehold System", (1988) 9 *Urban Law and Policy* 3; Cruden, *Land Compensation and Valuation Law in Hong Kong* (1986) p.3; Endocott, *A History of Hong Kong* (2nd ed.) pp. 28, 29, 44, 110, 111. The situation in Singapore was reported by Professor Tan Sook Yee, from the Faculty of Law, The National University of Singapore, in an interview held on January 16, 1992.
[2] We limit our study to cases in which the land tenure system does not permit private ownership of land. We do not intend to examine the question why in a legal system which permits private ownership of land, long-term leases are sometimes preferred.

practically, applicable also to the other countries where this form of land tenure was adopted.

We shall examine in some detail the Israeli case, although the situation under Israeli law differs from the situation in the other countries mentioned above in that in Israel the law does not, generally, prohibit private ownership of land. It is only with regard to one kind of land, named "Israel Lands",[3] that the law denies private ownership. However, in practical terms, in view of the fact that Israel Lands comprise about 92 per cent of the total area of the State,[4] it would seem appropriate to treat Israel as a country which, as a rule, and subject to some exceptions, denies private ownership of land.[5]

The grounds for support of long-term leases as a form of land tenure can be classified into ideological and utilitarian grounds. We shall briefly mention the ideological grounds and then dwell in greater detail on the utilitarian grounds.

1. Ideological grounds

(a) Religious motives

In 1960 Knesset (Israel's parliament) passed the Basic Law: Israel Lands, which prohibits transfer of ownership in Israel Lands.

When debating this law in Knesset several members of the house cited in support of the Basic Law the attitude of the Bible regarding private land ownership. According to the Bible a sale of rural land conveys only the right to use the land for the maximum period of 49 years (which is the term of the jubilee). At the expiration of this period all rural land reverts to its original owners. The underlying principle according to the Bible is that land cannot be privately owned: "The land shall not be sold for ever: for the land is mine; for you are strangers and sojourners with me".[6]

Does the fact that the biblical doctrine regarding private land ownership was referred to, during Knesset debate, indicate that, to quote Professor M. Elon's view, "the very essence of this law stems from Jewish religious law"?[7]

Admittedly, for some members of Knesset the biblical attitude towards land ownership was indeed the actual ground for their support of the Basic Law. However, it is submitted that for many others, citing the Bible in this context was merely to embellish their speeches rather than base their political stand in

---

[3] Defined as lands owned by the state, by the Developing Authority and by the Jewish National Fund. Basic Law: Israel Lands, s.1.
[4] Weisman, *Law of Property: General Part* (Jerusalem, 1993) p. 193 *et seq.* (in Hebrew). It is, perhaps, worthwhile mentioning that the ratio of State-owned land to privately owned land in Australia is quite similar. There, about 90 per cent of the land is State-owned. *Commission of Inquiry into Land Tenure, First Report, 1973* (Australian Government Publishing Service, Canberra, 1974) p. 39.
[5] On Israel Lands, and on exceptions to the rule denying private ownership in Israel Lands, see Weisman, *op. cit.* at p. 193 *et seq.*
[6] *Leviticus*, Ch. 25, v.23.
[7] Elon, *Religious Legislation* (Tel-Aviv, 1968, in Hebrew) p. 55.

this matter on religious grounds. For better or for worse, the great majority of Knesset members hardly consider themselves bound by the religious precepts of the Bible. There is therefore some exaggeration in the view (held, among others, by Professor M. Elon) that religious grounds are at the bottom of the Israeli land tenure system. While, admittedly, religious motives have played a part in this regard it would be wrong to assume that the Basic Law was adopted by the majority of Knesset members because of its conformity with the biblical attitude towards private land ownership.

(b) Socialist ideology

In the category of ideological grounds one finds also the socialist doctrine regarding land ownership. Supporters of the Basic Law which restricts private ownership of land have referred during Knesset debate on the Basic Law to the socialist doctrine of public ownership of means of production, and particularly of land.

Recent decline in adherence to either religious precepts, or socialist doctrine, has presumably eroded to some extent support for long-term leases as a substitute for private ownership of land, to the extent that such support was founded on either of these two ideological grounds.

2. Utilitarian grounds

(a) Public and private interests

The claim that long-term leases are superior to private ownership for utilitarian reasons was generally put forward from the public's point of view. There were hardly any supporters of long-term leases, on utilitarian grounds, whose main concern was the immediate interest of the individual land holder. Yet, the relatively small periodic payments of rent paid by tenants, as compared with the large amount a purchaser of land must pay, were sometimes pointed out as an advantage of long-term leases from the perspective of the individual landholder.

This advantage is doubtful. Even if we ignore pertinent economic considerations such as a comparison between the amount paid as purchase price, and the total amount of rent paid by a tenant over an extended period of time, or the distinction between payment towards acquisition of ownership and payment which does not accumulate an equity in an asset, and we confine our analysis to the sole aspect of periodic payments *vis-à-vis* payment of a one time amount, this is a questionable advantage. Often the acquisition of ownership is financed by a mortgage which is repaid by the purchaser by relatively small periodic instalments, while long-term leases often involve an initial payment of a substantial amount as capitalisation of future rent (a premium).[8]

---

[8] *Commission of Inquiry into Land Tenure, First Report*, 1973, above, n.4, at pp. 38–39.

Thus, the manner of payment of rent by a lessee is not necessarily an example, from the view point of lessees, of an advantage leases have over the acquisition of ownership.

The following are the more frequently cited grounds in support of long-term leases, from the perspective of the public's interest.

(b) Land use control

The most important claim in support of long-term leases is, probably, that they are a superior device for securing compliance with land planning requirements.[9] It is asserted that rather than rely on punitive sanctions provided by land planning statutes, it is preferable to apply contractual sanctions provided for by lease agreements (*e.g.* forfeiture of the lease), in case of violations of land control rules. Furthermore, leasing out land instead of sale has the advantage that it guarantees land reserves for the needs of future generations.[10]

Historical background   The use of lease agreements for the purpose of attaining planning objectives was common in Israel during the first half of the twentieth century, in its pre-Statehood period (*i.e.* prior to 1948). At that time the leadership of the Jewish community was devoid of governmental powers, and the only practical means for ensuring that land was used in accordance with the planning of the Jewish organisations which financed the purchase of land for use by settlers, was through lease agreements with the settlers. Consequently, lease agreements in those days incorporated provisions one normally finds in land planning statutes and regulations.

This practice was retained also after 1948, after the establishment of the State of Israel, although long-term leases were not required anymore for the purpose of enforcing planning objectives. The State now has elaborate planning legislation, and planning authorities, enjoying governmental powers. The continued practice of long-term leases which incorporate land planning elements is explained by the claim that in certain circumstances planning provisions by contract are preferable to statutory planning provisions.

The situation in Australia, Singapore and Hong Kong   The Israeli attitude regarding the role of long-term leases as a planning device was shared by some other countries as well. Also, in the Australian Capital Territory, Singapore and Hong Kong land is granted to individual holders within the framework of long-term leases, under the belief that a long-term lease is a better vehicle to achieve land use control.[11]

---

[9] Cruden, op. cit. above, n.1, at p. 16. Raison, "Land Tenure and Land Use Control in the Australian Capital Territory" (1978) 25 *Valuer* 290, 361; Raison, "The Perpetual Battle for Perpetual Leasehold in ACT" (1990) *Valuer* 105, 107.
[10] Raison, *op. cit.* above, (1978), n.9, at 290.
[11] Raison, above, n.9, at 105, 107; *Commission of Inquiry into Land Tenure, First Report,* 1973, above, n.4, at 69; Neutze, above, n.1, at 4, 6.

Experience with leases as a planning device The claim that long-term leases are a superior planning device cannot be easily verified.[12] It would seem that no study has hitherto compared the two methods, the statutory and the contractual, and come up with clear findings as to the advantages of either of them.[13] Factors which may render planning by legislation inefficient might also limit the efficiency of planning by contract. Thus, a politically weak local planning authority, which hesitates to cause discontent among its constituency, by enforcing restrictive statutory planning rules, would probably be also reluctant to apply contractual sanctions against infringers of similar planning rules, when incorporated in lease agreements.

The limited experience gained in Israel in this matter would seem to support the view that the efficiency of long-term leases as a planning device was, perhaps, overrated.

Thus, in Israel, lease agreements of State land provide that assignment of a lease is not permitted without the consent of the lessor and that rural State land must be cultivated by the lessee himself, to the exclusion of hired labourers. These provisions were frequently ignored by lessees. Attempts to enforce these undertakings by actions for breach of contract proved futile. Eventually, the solution resorted to was to convert these contractual restrictions into statutory provisions. During the debate in parliament it was admitted by the relevant administrative agencies that they encountered difficulties in enforcing lease agreements and that they were hopeful that with statutory provisions they would fare better and meet with greater compliance.[14]

It is interesting to note that an opposite development took place in Australia. The implementation of statutory land planning rules is, in Australia, the responsibility of local authorities. It was alleged that the manner in which these authorities exercised their discretion in planning matters left much to be desired. Consequently, it was suggested to resort to the enforcement of the lease agreements, on the assumption that this will prove more satisfactory. Of course, this suggestion could be made in view of the fact that the authorities in charge of implementing statutory planning provisions were not the same as those in charge of leasing State land.[15]

---

[12] See for the assertion that such a superiority is a myth, in: Raison, (1990), above, n.9, at 105, 107; *Commission of Enquiry into Land Tenure, First Report,* 1973, above, n.4, at 55.

[13] Compare: *Commission of Inquiry into Land Tenure, First Report,* 1973, above, n.4, at 55.

[14] *Divrey Haknesset* (Parliamentary Debates) vol. 47, p. 166 (in Hebrew).

[15] Neutze, above, n.1, at pp. 1, 6. The author indicates another advantage of long-term leases when compared with transfer of ownership. Upon transfer of ownership there is frequently pressure by the purchaser to amend the plan applicable to the land in order to enable a more extensive use of the land. This problem arises less frequently when leasing the land since an amendment of the plan which enables a more intensive use of the leased land would normally involve a raise of the rent (*ibid.* at p. 9). On the other hand, there is a certain advantage in statutory planning over contractual planning in that the interests of leasing authorities are different from those of planning authorities. A lessor is normally interested in the profit making of the property while the business of planning authorities is to promote public welfare (*ibid.* at pp. 20–21). The author also referred to the phenomenon of leasing authorities refraining from enforcing their rights under lease agreements (*ibid.* at p. 25).

A similar trend could be discerned also in Hong Kong where it was suggested that rather than rely on statutory provisions, when expropriating land for public purposes, it would be more efficient to have the land leased to individual landholders, subject to a condition that the lease would terminate should the land be required for public purposes. Interestingly, the experience with this technique was not encouraging and statutory expropriation was nevertheless preferred to "contractual expropriation".[16]

Positive planning In one respect planning by means of long-term leases seems to have a definite advantage over statutory planning. Normally, planning statutes operate in a passive manner. They do not instruct land owners what to do with their property. They are hypothetical in their approach. It is only *if* a land owner wishes to use his land that planning statutes come into play by telling the owner that certain rules must be observed. Planning statutes do not oblige an owner to develop his land if he prefers to let the land stay idle. It is in this respect that lease agreements can prove to be superior to statutory planning. Lease agreements can impose duties on the lessee to build, or otherwise develop the leased land in a prescribed manner.[17] Admittedly, in a land tenure system based on private ownership tax laws can be utilised to encourage an owner of land not to let his land remain undeveloped, but a tax provision will, normally, not be able to guarantee land development in a specific manner, according to a detailed plan. This can be achieved by a lease agreement.

Review of planning An additional aspect of leases as a vehicle for land use planning is the opportunity it offers, upon the expiration of a lease and before a new lease is granted, to review the planning of the site where the property is located. At this juncture there is an opportunity to introduce new planning ideas without the complexities which often arise when landholding is based on ownership, and when a duty could arise to compensate private owners for new constraints on their property.

However, to be of real value re-planning must extend to an entire neighbourhood. There is little advantage in the possibility of re-planning an isolated lot. To be able to achieve a meaningful re-planning, co-ordination is required of the terms of the leases in an entire neighbourhood, to ensure that they all expire at the same time.

(c) Source of revenue to the public

Leasing of land, as distinct from sale, enables the owner of the land to benefit from an increase in the value of the land, either during the term of the lease, or when renewing the lease after its expiration.

---

[16] Cruden, above, n.1, at pp. 9–10.
[17] Neutze, above, n.1, at p. 5.

An increase in the rent during the term of the lease is possible if the lease agreement provides for periodic review of the rent, or if it provides for an increase in the rent should a change in the use of the property take place (*e.g.* from residential to commercial use).[18]

Adjustment of the rent in case of an increase in the value of the property is, of course, possible at the expiration of the lease if the land is being leased again (subject to possible restrictions imposed by tenants protection statutes).

Thus, it is argued that the continued link between the lessor and the leased property enables the lessor to secure for himself certain advantages he would not be able to enjoy had he totally divested himself of the property by sale.

Criticism While there is some merit in the argument that certain advantages might accrue to a lessor as a result of his continued link to the leased property, this should not be overrated. Increase in value of land can benefit the public purse by means of property and betterment tax, even if land is absolutely transferred to private owners.[19]

Furthermore, it is not an easy matter for ministers in governments to raise rents paid by lessees of State-owned land. Such lessees are also the voters who elect the ministers into office. Also, raising rents can be of special difficulty for lessees whose incomes do not increase proportionately to changes in the land market. Such lessees, if organised, can form an effective pressure group against a rise in rent by government.[20]

The net result of all these factors is, in practice, that rent paid to State agencies is often considerably below market rates. This is supported by the experience both in Australia[21] and in Israel.

Premium Difficulties in collecting periodic rents have caused a move from periodic payments of rent to a payment of a lump sum (a premium), by lessees, upon the granting of the lease. This development took place in Australia as well as in Israel. In Israel the amount of the premium is 91 per cent of the value of the land. Under this system, which is designated "the capitalisation system", the lessee is not subject to a review of rent during the term of the lease. However, a certain payment is due if the lessee requests a change in the use made of the property during his term.

Naturally, this development, of periodic rents being replaced by a payment of a premium, narrows the gap between long-term leases and ownership.

---

[18] This is the case with lease agreements in use by the Israel Land Administration. Similar provisions in lease agreements can be found also in Hong Kong and in Australia. Cruden, above, n.1, at p. 3; Raison, (1990), above, n.9, at pp. 105, 106; *Commission of Enquiry into Land Tenure, First Report, 1973*, above, n.4, at p. 49.
[19] *Commission of Enquiry into Land Tenure, First Report*, 1973, above, n.4, at p. 52.
[20] Neutze, above, n.1.
[21] *Commission of Enquiry into Land Tenure, First Report*, 1973, above, n.4, at p. 53.

Furthermore, the assertion that when the term of a lease expires there is an opportunity for the lessor to adjust the rent of a new lease to changes in the value of the property, is based on the assumption that long-term lessees will indeed vacate the property leased to them upon the expiration of the lease. This is a questionable assumption. Experience in Israel indicates that long-term lessees tend to regard themselves as owners. Evicting them from "their" properties, at the expiration of the lease, could prove to be a difficult proposition.

The normal term of a lease of urban land, in Israel, is 49 years, with an option of a one time renewal for another term of 49 years. Since Israel is a relatively young country, it does not have, as yet, much experience with expirations of the second term of the lease (after 98 years). However, there is some experience with termination of the first term, of 49 years. Upon the termination of the first term the tendency has been to grant lessees the second term, conditioned on the payment of a yearly rent in the amount equal to only 1 per cent of the value of the land. The significance of this will be apparent when compared to the amount paid for the first 49 years – 91 per cent of the value of the land. In the opinion of the official land appraiser in Israel a payment of a similar premium, 91 per cent of the value of the land, is also justified when granting the second term.[22]

In view of the above, it seems that the claim that long-term leases have an advantage over transfer of ownership, in that they secure an income to the public in case of future increases in the value of the land, is exaggerated. This claim ignores the potential role of taxation in relation to privately owned land and it does not take full account of the difficulties which could be involved in collection and review of periodic rents.

(d) Prevention of speculation

It was hoped, in Israel as well as in the Australian Capital Territory, that if ownership of land was retained by the state, while individual landholders had only long-term leases, speculation in land prices would thereby be avoided.[23] However, experience has not confirmed this hope. The control lessors were able to exert over the land market was less effective than was assumed. In both countries prices of long-term leases of state-owned land were not substantially different from prices of long-term leases in privately owned land.[24] (A comparison of prices was possible in both countries since in Australia privately owned land is allowed outside the ACT, and in Israel about 8 per cent of the land is owned privately.) The State as lessor has the power to decide how much

---

[22] Cohen, *Institute of Land Use Research*, vol. 13 (5741), p. 15.
[23] Raison, (1978), above, n.9, at 289; Raison, (1990), above, n.9, at pp. 105, 106; Neutze, above, n.1, at p. 5.
[24] Raison, (1978), above, n.9, at p. 292; Neutze, "A Tale of Two Cities: Public Land Ownership in Canberra and Stockholm in the early 1980s", (1989) 6 *Scandinavian Housing and Planning Research* 189, at p. 194.

rent to charge when leasing its land but not, apparently, how much a lessee may charge when assigning his interest.

Admittedly, in a country like Israel, in which most of the land is owned by the State, prices of land can indeed be manipulated by the State. Yet, this influence has its limits and in practice it has not entirely eliminated speculation.

(e) Restricting acquisition of land by aliens

Is the system of long-term leases more efficient for the purpose of imposing restrictions on aliens in the acquisition of land, than is a system based on private ownership?

There is, perhaps, a feeling that legislating for such restrictions on aliens goes against liberal trends of our time, while as a provision in a contract such restrictions may seem to be less conspicuous, less disturbing, and therefore, perhaps, more acceptable.

Furthermore, if such restrictions are constitutionally challenged in court, would contractual restrictions not fare better than statutory restrictions?

Experience does not bear out such assumptions. A survey of countries in which aliens were restricted in the acquisition of land revealed that in many cases these restrictions were statutory rather than contractual and there were no indications that as statutory restrictions they were any less effective.[25]

The experience in Israel in this regard is of some interest. Several years ago (in 1980) a bill providing for restrictions on aliens in the acquisition of land was submitted to Knesset. It was met with vehement opposition by several members of the house, who argued that such restrictions are undemocratic and violate the principle of equality. In view of the opposition the bill was tabled and never became law. What happened instead was that restrictions were inserted in lease agreements of Israel Lands.

Perhaps one feels less comfortable when legislating for such restrictions than when having them as provisions in a contract. However, it is noteworthy that restrictions on aliens in the acquisition of land can be found in the statute books of many countries throughout the world.[26] It is therefore doubtful whether such restrictions are generally viewed unfavourably. Furthermore, if such restrictions are to be considered non-constitutional when in a statute book, it is doubtful that they would be approved by a court if included in a standard contract of a lease of State-owned land, which applies to more than 90 per cent of the total area of the State.

In view of the above, it is doubtful whether one can find support for long-term leases, because of the role they might play in restricting aliens in the acquisition of land.

---

[25] Weisman, "Restrictions on the Acquisition of Land by Aliens" (1980) 23 Am.J.Comp.L. 39.
[26] Weisman, *ibid.* at p. 40 n.9.

(f) Limiting the number of co-owners

A typical feature of land ownership is the possible increase in the number of its owners. If land is kept in the family for several generations the number of its co-owners could become substantial through successive devolutions. Such a development could give rise to difficulties when having to secure the consent of the co-owners for managing the land, or for making dispositions of the land.

English law, in its ingenuity, devised the "Trust for Sale", to cope with this problem. Under the trust for sale, which is imposed by law on every co-ownership of land, the maximum number of co-owners of the legal title is limited to four (the rest of the co-owners having only equitable interests). Other legal systems were less imaginative in dealing with this problem.[27]

Here again, a land tenure based on long-term leases may have a certain advantage over ownership. The very fact that a lease is limited in time reduces the potential number of successive transfers by succession and consequently the potential number of co-owners. Naturally, the shorter the term of the lease the more effective it is in limiting the number of co-tenants.

This leads us to the last topic of this paper, namely, the term of long-term leases.

II. THE TERM OF LONG-TERM LEASES

For a lease of land to serve as an alternative to ownership its term must be sufficiently long. The term must be for such a period that it would make sense for the lessee to develop the land having regard to the time limit the land would be at his disposal.

The life expectancy of ordinary buildings was sometimes a yardstick used when deciding the term of the lease.[28] It was estimated that 50 years was the life expectancy of an ordinary cement building.[29]

However, if a lease is for too long a period it undermines the reasons behind the policy of granting a lease rather than ownership. Also, a lease for a very long period could be perceived as fictitious, as ownership in disguise. Indeed, case law indicates that on many occasions courts have applied to long-term leases statutory provisions which were applicable to ownership of land.[30] In some other cases courts have adopted a more formal approach, and refrained from applying to long-term leases provisions in statutes referring to ownership.[31] The

---

[27] Lawson and Rudden, *The Law of Property* (2nd ed., 1982) p. 111.
[28] *Commission of Inquiry into Land Tenure, First Report,* 1973, above, n.4, at p. 60.
[29] Weisman, *Law of Property: General Part* (Jerusalem, 1993) pp. 256–257.
[30] *Electricity Company for Israel Ltd. v. Israeli Company for Refrigeration and Supply Ltd,* C.A.202/72 , P.D. 27(1) 661,667; *Basso v. Malach,* C.A.355/76, P.D.31(2) 359, at 363.
[31] *Aronov v. Eisen,* C.A.123/66, P.D.20(3) 440, at 444.

difference in approach can often be explained by the result sought by the court in each of these cases. Sometimes the different approach merely reflected the judicial temper of the judges who delivered the opinions, some of whom were less formal than others.

Be that as it may, the result is that very long leases tend to blur the distinction between ownership and leases and introduce uncertainty as to which rules courts will apply to them.

In some countries the duration of a lease of land is not limited by law. In other countries the law sets limits to the maximum term of a lease. Thus, in France the law limits leases of land to a maximum period of 70 years, and in some circumstances to 99 years. In Sweden, the law limits leases in urban areas to 60 years. In California, the term for urban land is 99 years, and that is the case also in several other states of the USA. In Canberra the term is 99 years and this is also the case in Hong Kong and in Singapore (but for commercial purposes the term in Canberra is 50 years, and in Singapore 30 years).[32]

Under Israeli law the only restriction with regard to the term of a lease is that it cannot be perpetual.[33] However, the practice of Israel Land Administration, which controls more than 90 per cent of the total area of the country, is to limit leases to 49 years. This term is based on the biblical jubilee: "A jubilee shall that fiftieth year be to you: ... In the year of this jubilee you shall return every man to his possession."[34] In addition, the lessee has an option to renew the term for one more period of 49 years. Accordingly, the maximum period of a lease in Israel Lands is 98 years, which is in line with the term in some of the other countries mentioned above.

The experience in Israel indicates that this period is too long. Lessees of Israel Lands tend to regard themselves as owners rather than as mere lessees.[35] The land market operates on the implied assumption that the lease is, for all practical purposes, unlimited in time. Thus, there is very little difference in price between ownership and long-term leases. Also, when selling a lease no reference is normally made to the period of the lease which had already elapsed, and the length of the remaining period of an assigned lease does not affect the price.

This disregard of the unexpired term of the lease results from a combination of factors. First, the excessive length of the term induces the feeling that the expiration of the lease is something remote and abstract. Secondly, the premium paid by lessees (80 per cent or 91 per cent of the value of the land), which is fairly close to the full price of the land, gives rise to the feeling that it would be unfair, and inconceivable, for the government to treat its lessees as mere tenants.

It is submitted that once large numbers of leases expire the reality will compel the State, as lessor, to deal with the situation as a socio-economic issue

---

[32] Weisman, "A Permanently Renewable Lease – a Panacea or a Delusion?", KARKA, (1987), 2 (in Hebrew); Cruden, above, n.1, at pp. 3, 7, 8; Raison, (1978), above, n.9, at pp. 289, 362.
[33] Section 3 of the Law of Property 1969.
[34] *Leviticus*, Ch. 25, v.10, 13.
[35] This has also been the experience in Canberra. Neutze, above, n.1 at p. 23.

rather than as a legal matter. The sooner officials of Israel Land Administration realise that, the better they may be prepared when this possibility becomes a reality.

Inherent difficulties of long-term leases

When regulating long-term leases one is confronted with an inherent difficulty. On the one hand, long-term leases, being limited in time, call for rules which are different from those applied to ownership. On the other hand, the extended duration of long-term leases requires the application of rules distinct from those which apply to short-term interests. The result is that neither the rules of ownership nor the regular rules of landlord and tenant are suited to long-term leases. Special rules, tailored to the distinctive features of long-term leases, are required. Existing law hardly responds to this need, although there are some attempts in this direction.

Another difficulty inherent in long-term leases is the constantly changing scope of the right. The initial term of a long-term lease diminishes daily. Legal rules which were justified on the grounds that they are to apply to a long-term interest will, at some stage of the lease, cease to be so justified. A long-term lease inevitably becomes a short-term lease. Should we change the legal regime applicable to long-term leases when the remaining period of the lease becomes sufficiently short, or should we continue to apply the same rules regardless of the actual length of the remaining period of the lease? Should, for example, an assignee of a remaining period of a lease, however short, be subject to the same rules which applied to the lease in its inception, when it was a long-term lease, although from the point of view of the assignee his lease might never have been for a long-term?

Conclusion

The case for long-term leases as a substitute for ownership is debatable. Utilitarian arguments in support of it are often inconclusive. Its merits as a land planning device are overrated, although it does have certain advantages, particularly in that it can impose positive acts (land development) rather than mere observance of planning constraints when there is a wish to develop the land.

Ideological grounds in support of long-term leases, such as religious or socialist grounds, are in their nature less refutable than utilitarian grounds. However, so also is the ground for support of ownership of land which is based on the urge of human beings to own their place of residence. The immense popularity in our generation of condominium as a legal framework for housing attests to this strong desire to own one's home rather than have any of the substitutes, such as long-term leases.

In countries where long-term leases are the rule one should attempt to avoid fixing too long a term for the lease and payment of too high a premium by the lessee. In Israel, where the normal term of the lease is 98 years, and where the premium paid by the lessees is up to 91 per cent of the value of the property, lessees tend to regard themselves as owners of the property, which must create serious difficulties at the expiration of the lease.

A shorter term of the lease, and the payment of a premium which is considerably lower than the full price of the land, might help in maintaining a clear distinction between ownership and long-term leases, a distinction which is the *raison d'être* for those who are in favour of long-term leases as a land tenure system.

10

Security Interests as Property: Relocating Security Interests within the Property Framework

ALISON CLARKE*

1. Property categorisation problems

Most property categorisation problems are problems at the margin. Property lawyers are interested in drawing lines between property and non-property and, understandably, the arguments tend to centre on "new" property in some form or another. The typical question is whether a new candidate for inclusion into the species is to be categorised as property or not, or perhaps whether a new doctrinal development is or is not really just property after all.

There is a property categorisation problem about security interests, but it is of a different nature. We are accustomed to thinking of security interests – mortgages, charges, pledges, liens – as coming high on the scale of established property interests, and indeed many would argue that that is the whole point of them. I am certainly not suggesting that they are *not* property interests, or that in some mysterious way we "wrongly" treat them as property when in fact they are no such thing (assuming such a logical possibility). What I do want to argue is that we in this jurisdiction have somehow come to mislocate them in the over-all framework of property interests. We over-value them, both in the sense that we talk of them as if they are worth more in financial terms than they are in fact worth (the "value aspect"), and also in the sense that we talk of them as if they comprised a bigger bundle of rights than they do in fact comprise (the "rights aspect").

2. Over-valuing security interests

(a) The value aspect

Within the property world no-one is seriously deceived. Even though mortgages are traded nationally and transnationally as if they were in themselves valuable commodities, presumably everyone involved appreciates that the value is in the underlying debt, not in the mortgage securing its repayment. Although a mortgage of a fee simple absolute in possession, or of a car, can be assigned, its value

---

* Senior Lecturer in Laws, University College London.

in the hands of the assignee is nil unless the underlying debt is also assigned.[1] And even in the simple case where the mortgage secures a debt owed to the mortgagee, the value to the mortgagee *of the mortgage* fluctuates depending on the likelihood of the mortgagor repaying the debt in full and on time, with – paradoxically – the value of the mortgage decreasing as the likelihood of default decreases.

By the same token, as Mr Justice Millett (as he then was) pointed out in *Re M. C. Bacon Ltd*,[2] a debtor does not deplete his assets or diminish their value by mortgaging all or any of them to a creditor. His equity of redemption in the mortgaged assets is worth precisely the same (to him) as his formerly unencumbered ownership. This is because, in our system at least, private property interests have what Honore has called the incident of liability to execution[3] – they are liable to be seized by creditors in satisfaction of a judgment debt. On this analysis, all that happens when a debtor mortgages an asset to one creditor is that that asset – formerly available via judicial process for the satisfaction of *any* debt – is now earmarked for the satisfaction of that creditor's debt in priority to all his other creditors. All that the debtor has lost is the freedom, if he chooses to sell the asset, to apply the proceeds of sale otherwise than in satisfaction of the secured debt. Consequently, it was held in *Re M. C. Bacon Ltd*[4] that a last-minute debenture granted to a bank creditor to secure continuation of a pre-existing overdraft facility was not challengeable by the debtor's liquidator as a transaction at an undervalue within section 238 of the Insolvency Act 1986. In section 238(4)(b) a transaction at an undervalue is defined as one where, *inter alia*, the value of the consideration provided to the debtor in money or money's worth is "significantly less than the value in money or money's worth of the consideration provided by the company". In the *M. C. Bacon* case, the consideration provided by the bank was the forbearance from calling in the overdraft and the agreement to continue the facility – *i.e.* a promise to honour cheques in the future up to the pre-existing overdraft limit. In these circumstances, said Mr Justice Millet, the attempt to characterise the granting of the debenture as a transaction at an undervalue was simply misconceived:

> "By granting the debenture the company parted with nothing of value, and the value of the consideration which it received in return was incapable of being measured in money or money's worth."[5]

---

[1] If O mortgages an asset to M1 to secure the payment of £X by O to M1, and M1 then assigns the mortgage to M2, M2 can enforce the mortgage but, either directly or indirectly, all proceeds of the enforcement will go to M1. There may, of course, be circumstances in which it is in M2's interests to ensure that M1 is repaid the amount owed by O, but in the absence of such circumstances the mortgage is valueless to M2.
[2] [1990] B.C.C. 78.
[3] Honore, "Ownership" from *Oxford Essays in Jurisprudence* (1961) (First Series, ed. A. G. Guest).
[4] [1990] B.C.C. 78.
[5] *ibid.* at 92. The decision on this point, and Mr Justice Millett's reasoning, was approved and applied by the Court of Appeal in *Menzies v National Bank of Kuwait SAK* [1994] B.C.C. 119.

This was undeniably hard on the debtor's other creditors. Before the granting of the debenture there was a substantial pool of assets owned by the debtor out of which their debts could have been satisfied. After the debenture was granted, and as a direct consequence of it, there was nothing left.[6] However, this was not because the pool of assets was worth any less to the debtor – simply that it was all diverted to meet the claims of a single creditor.[7] From the bank's point of view the debenture was certainly valuable, but this was not because it gave the bank an additional asset but because it gave them an additional and better device for collecting their pre-existing debt.

(b) The rights aspect

The same applies to the size or extent of the rights comprised in the interest. Property lawyers are not really deceived about the number of sticks in the security interest bundle. The common law mortgage – the most extensive of all security interests – may look like a major bundle of rights in that it involves the transfer of ownership or possession. But the subtraction from the bundle made by equity leaves a residue in the hands of the mortgagee which is barely distinguishable from a hypothecation. Whatever the position in theory, in reality security interest holders – even those holding property transfer mortgages – have very little more than contingent rights of management and alienation, exercisable on the happening of a future event which may never happen, and the happening of which is wholly outside their control and largely within the control of the grantor of the interest.[8] Put like this, security interests start to look distinctly marginal as property interests. The temptation to draw a comparison between them and rights of pre-emption is irresistible. The proprietary status of rights of pre-emption in land has long been controversial. Eventually in *Pritchard v. Briggs*[9] the Court of Appeal held that they are not property interests.[10] For

---

[6] This is not conjectural; according to the statement of facts given in the judgment, the debtor was a successful importer and wholesaler of traditional bacon, whose business swiftly collapsed when its principal customer first persuaded it to diversify into pre-packed manufactured bacon products and then abruptly withdrew its custom. Right up to the moment when the final collapse was imminent, the debtor had successfully resisted all attempts by the bank to obtain security for the overdraft: see *Re M. C. Bacon Ltd* [1990] B.C.C. 78 at 79.

[7] In other words, the real problem was that one creditor was being preferred to another, although there was held to be no voidable preference either, since in granting the debenture the company was not "influenced . . . by a *desire*" to prefer the bank, as required by s.239(5) of the Insolvency Act 1986; on the facts the directors concerned were simply giving in to commercial pressure – they knew that if the debenture was not granted the overdraft would have been called in – they manifestly had no desire whatsoever to improve the bank's position as a creditor in the event of the debtor's insolvency: *Re M. C. Bacon Ltd* above, n.4, at 89–91.

[8] This sweeping generalisation ignores foreclosure (on the basis of obsolescence) and possession (on the basis that the security interest holder must account for income and profits on taking possession under the wilful default rule).

[9] [1980] Ch. 338.

[10] The Court of Appeal explained away the fact that the 1925 property legislation frequently refers to rights of pre-emption as if they are property interests by saying that the legislators

Lord Justice Templeman, as he then was, the key element was control over the contingency on which the interest depended. He drew the distinction between options to purchase, which are undeniably property interests, and rights of pre-emption:

> "In the case of an option, the evolution of the relationship of vendor and purchaser may depend on the fulfilment of certain specified conditions and will depend on the volition of the option holder . . . In the case of a right of pre-emption, the evolution of the relationship of vendor and purchaser depends on the grantor, of his own volition, choosing to fulfil certain specified conditions and thus converting the pre-emption to an option. The grant of the right of pre-emption creates a mere spes which the grantor of the right may either frustrate by choosing not to fulfil the necessary conditions or may convert into an option and thus into equitable interest by fulfilling the conditions . . . The holder of a right of pre-emption is in much the same position as a beneficiary under a Will of a person who is still alive, save that the holder of the right of pre-emption must hope for some future positive action by the grantor which will elevate his hope into an interest."[11]

Thus, in the case of these particular contingent rights, the option to purchase and the right of pre-emption, the dividing line between property and non-property, depends on the ability of the interest holder to make the contingency happen. On this basis, if security interests do fall on the right side of the property line, it is not by very far. In principle, the mortgagee's right of recourse to the mortgaged asset is contingent on the mortgagor defaulting on the loan agreement. It would be unrealistic to suggest that the happening of this contingency is wholly within the mortgagor's volition, but it is certainly not within that of the mortgagee.

3. The property category misconception: the lay view and the bankruptcy view

It is outside the property law field that serious misconceptions about security interests begin to appear. This is strikingly common in non-lawyers; in lay terminology, aspiring property owners "get" a mortgage (a valuable commodity) from a bank or a building society, which may then allow the owners to "keep" the mortgage when they move house. And if there is a default in repayment, the bank or building society may then decide to "repossess" the property – as if taking back its own. These terminological oddities may or may not reflect a genuine misunderstanding of the rights of mortgagor and mortgagee in the mortgaged property, but it is difficult to believe that they do not at least colour borrowers' perceptions of their mortgagees' entitlements in relation to the mortgaged property.

---

got it wrong; it was held that none of the references in the 1925 legislation was apt to change the law – "they merely assume it to be what I would hold it was not", as Goff L.J. rather oddly remarked [1980] Ch. 338 at 398.

[11] *ibid.* at 418.

However, for present purposes the more significant misconception occurs in bankruptcy law.[12] In this jurisdiction bankruptcy law is quite extraordinarily respectful of property interests, and this respect is extended unquestioningly to security interests, to such an extent that secured creditors of a debtor are virtually unaffected by the bankruptcy of the debtor.

Bankruptcy classically prevents creditors from enforcing their individual rights to recover payment from their debtor. Instead, whether they want to or not, they must submit to a collective procedure for the collection and distribution of the bankrupt's assets. However, this applies only to unsecured creditors – or, rather, it applies to creditors only in so far as they have to rely on actions *in personam* to recover their debts. A creditor who has a right of recourse to the property of the bankrupt for the discharge of the debt is, in general, not a player in the bankruptcy game. Subject to some strictly limited restrictions, she simply goes ahead and realises her security as if the bankruptcy had never happened, taking out of the proceeds of sale whatever is owing to her, and acknowledging the bankruptcy only to the extent of paying over the balance to the bankruptcy official holding the bankrupt's estate, rather than paying it over to the bankrupt himself. If there is a subsequent security interest affecting the property, she does not even have to do that; she pays the balance to the next secured creditor in line.

This virtual isolation of the secured creditor from the bankruptcy process has had a profound effect on the development of bankruptcy law in this country in at least two respects. First, it has significantly hampered the development of a workable business rescue procedure. The insolvency regime introduced by the Insolvency Act 1986 provides four procedures which can be used as rescue vehicles (one for individuals and the other three for companies). None of these four restricts the right of secured creditors to be reimbursed in full up to the value of the security.[13] Administrative receivership, the one most commonly used, is really a debt collection procedure for a single secured creditor (the floating charge holder) rather than a collective bankruptcy procedure; the conduct of the procedure is put in the hands of the floating charge holder's nominee, whose prime function is to realise the assets for the benefit of his appointer. Of the remaining three rescue procedures – administration, individual voluntary arrangement and company voluntary arrangement – only the first two make any provision for an initial moratorium on enforcement of secured claims whilst rescue plans are being prepared and negotiated, and it is only in administration

---

[12] Using "bankruptcy" here in what I take to be the American sense, to cover any mandatory collective procedure imposed on (or invoked by) an insolvent legal person, whether human or corporate, as opposed to the English sense of a specific process usable only in relation to individuals.

[13] There is one relatively minor exception: an administrative receiver must pay the debtor company's preferential debts (set out in Sched. 3 of the 1986 Act) out of the proceeds of the floating charge in priority to the claims of the floating charge holder who appointed him: ss.40 and 59 of the 1986 Act.

(which anyway, can be vetoed by the holder of a floating charge[14]) that secured creditors' enforcement rights can be restricted throughout the rescue period. Even then, the restriction consists only of a provision requiring the creditor to obtain leave of the court or the administrator before enforcing the security,[15] and the courts have made it clear that in deciding whether to give leave, "great importance, or weight, is normally to be given to the proprietary interests" of the applicant:

> "The underlying principle here is that an administration for the benefit of the unsecured creditors should not be conducted at the expense of those who have proprietary rights which they are seeking to exercise, save to the extent that this may be unavoidable and even then this will usually be acceptable only to a strictly limited extent."[16]

In the interests of promoting business rescues, various attempts have been made to encroach on this insulation of the secured creditor from the bankruptcy process, but progress is painfully slow and strongly resisted.[17]

Even more significantly, but less often publicly acknowledged, the secured creditor's aloofness from the bankruptcy process has made bankruptcy virtually unusable for individuals whose only significant asset is a mortgaged house. In the vast majority of cases where an individual becomes insolvent, his financial affairs are settled by his bank or building society enforcing the mortgage over his house, leaving him with no assets to distribute to other creditors. There is simply no point in either he or his other creditors petitioning for his bankruptcy since everything will be taken by the house mortgagee. The bankruptcy legislation recognises the special significance of an individual bankrupt's home, and makes some – in fact rather ineffectual – attempt to preserve it from the bankrupt's unsecured creditors, at least for a limited period.[18] But these provisions can only apply if the property happens to be unencumbered by any mort-

---

[14] Insolvency Act 1986, s.9.
[15] s.11(3)(c) of the 1986 Act. In addition, both an administrative receiver and an administrator have power to dispose of charged property free from the charge – but the proceeds of sale *plus such amounts as may be necessary to bring them up to what the court determines to be the open market value of the asset* must be applied directly towards discharging the sums secured by the security: ss.15 and 43(3) of the 1986 Act.
[16] *Re Atlantic Computer Systems* [1992] 2 W.L.R. 367, C.A. at 395, *per* Nicholls L.J. (giving the judgment of the court) setting out guidelines as to when leave ought to be granted. He was here referring to the exercise of lessors' proprietary rights, but stated at 396 that "a broadly similar approach" would be applicable on an application to enforce security.
[17] See, for example, the Insolvency Service Consultation Documents *Company Voluntary Arrangements and Administration Orders* (1993); *Insolvency Law: An Agenda for Reform Justice* (1994); the Insolvency Service *Revised Proposals for a New Company Voluntary Arrangement Procedure* (1995). The government proposals would involve bolstering the company voluntary arrangement procedure by imposing greater restrictions on the rights of some secured creditors. To date, no draft legislation has yet been put forward by the government.
[18] See, in particular, ss.336–338 of the Insolvency Act 1986. The treatment of the family home in bankruptcy was discussed in an earlier W. G. Hart Workshop by Professor Stephen Cretney and by the writer, in papers now published in *Insolvency Law: Theory and Practice* (ed. Rajak) (1993) as Chapters 4 and 5 respectively.

gage or charge. In the (very likely) event that the bankrupt's family home is mortgaged these special provisions of the bankruptcy legislation are wholly irrelevant; the decision as to whether, when and how to sell the house and dispossess the bankrupt and his family lies solely with the mortgagee, and factors properly taken into account in making bankruptcy decisions, such as the needs of the bankrupt and his family, and the competing needs of other creditors, are ignored.[19]

4. Why can secured creditors opt out of bankruptcy?

There is considerable debate about precisely what it is that bankruptcy law is meant to achieve, but there is general agreement that at least one of its functions is to solve the common pool problem of a debtor's creditors. In other words, bankruptcy imposes on all creditors a collective collection and distribution procedure because this produces a better outcome for the creditors as a whole, than would be achieved if each pursued its claims individually.[20] But if this is the case, why then do we allow secured creditors to opt out of the procedure? There are at least three possible groups of argument for doing so, one based on what I argue is the property category misconception, one based on other aspects of bankruptcy theory not directly relevant here, and the third based on pragmatism. I am interested here primarily in the first, and will refer only briefly to the others.

5. The property argument

The conventional answer involves a two-step argument. The first step is incontrovertible. Bankruptcy entails a gross interference with private rights. In the bankruptcy process, regardless of the wishes of the bankrupt and his creditors, the bankrupt's property is confiscated and distributed rateably amongst his creditors in satisfaction of his debts to them. One of the first tasks of bankruptcy law must therefore be to distinguish what the bankrupt owns from what anyone else owns: only property of the bankrupt can justifiably be confiscated and given to his creditors, not property belonging to someone else.

It is in the second step of the conventional argument that the misconception becomes apparent. To interfere with the exercise of a secured creditor's rights to enforce her security over property of the bankrupt would (so the argument goes) be an infringement of the secured creditor's property rights, amounting to a confiscation of her property, which would then, quite wrongly, go to swell the pool of the bankrupt's property.[21]

---

[19] In the case of residential mortgages, the court's jurisdiction (under s.36 of the Administration of Justice Act 1970, as amended) to withhold or delay enforcement of the mortgage allows it to take into consideration only the likelihood of repayment.

[20] The classic exposition of this analysis is by Jackson in *The Logic and Limits of Bankruptcy Law* (1986).

[21] See Goode, *Principles of Corporate Insolvency Law* (1990) at p. 67 and also Jackson, *op. cit.* above, n.20, at pp. 91 *et seq.*

Security Interests as Property 125

This second step in the argument sounds entirely convincing for so long as one has in mind the basic model, grounded in common law, of security interests as major property interests transferring ownership or possession to the creditor. In such a model, the major property interest in the charged asset belongs to the secured creditor, leaving only vestigial property rights in the asset owned by the bankrupt. If, therefore, the secured creditor loses her security, the bankrupt's estate is wrongly augmented by adding to it the secured creditor's confiscated security interest. Whereas, before bankruptcy the bankrupt's estate included only an equity of redemption in the charged asset, now it includes the equity of redemption plus the mortgage, equalling 100 per cent of the bundle of ownership rights in the asset.

It becomes less convincing when one looks more closely at the real nature of the security interest. Taking first the value aspect, the valuable asset that the secured creditor holds is the debt, not the mortgage or charge securing repayment of it. It is the underlying debt that "belongs" to the secured creditor rather than to the bankrupt. To interfere with the secured creditor's right to enforce the security is indeed a confiscation of her property, but the important (valuable) property interest that is being confiscated is not the security interest but the debt (or, rather, the right to take action to recover the debt and the right to recover it in full up to the value of the asset). But this is exactly the same confiscation as that which is happening to all other creditors of the bankrupt: it is precisely this that bankruptcy does. To put it another way, if the secured creditor is prevented from enforcing her security, the bankrupt's estate is not globally increased in value to any significant extent. The only thing that is happening is that a smaller proportion of the estate will go to the secured creditor and a greater proportion of it will go to the other creditors.

The same thing happens if one looks at the rights aspect of the security interest. If a security interest is essentially a contingent right of recourse, exercisable on the happening of a future event, all that bankruptcy would be doing (assuming it was allowed to interfere with enforcement of the security) would be limiting the contingency. This certainly curtails the extent of the secured creditor's property interest, but it is difficult to see it as an augmentation of the bankrupt's estate by confiscation of the secured creditor's property. Indeed, it does not look different in kind from the curtailment of any other creditor's enforcement rights brought about by bankruptcy.

So, if there is a case to be made for allowing secured creditors to remain aloof from the bankruptcy process, it must depend on something other than the security interest's status as a property interest.

6. Other bankruptcy theory based arguments

There are other more sophisticated arguments, not directly relevant here, which are put forward by bankruptcy lawyers for respecting secured creditors' rights. None of these is wholly convincing. In particular, there is a contract argument to the effect that secured creditors having bargained (and paid) for a more favourable priority position on bankruptcy ought to be allowed to keep it.[22] This is part of a wider debate about the extent to which bankruptcy law ought to permit contracting out of the principle of *pari passu* distribution. Bankruptcy necessarily involves curtailment of contract rights; the debate is over how far this curtailment should go.[23]

In addition there is a linked argument that the fundamental purpose of bankruptcy law is subverted if pre-bankruptcy entitlements are not respected in bankruptcy. Whilst bankruptcy law may properly limit the *amount* that any creditor receives from the bankrupt estate, what it must not do is disturb that creditor's position relative to the other creditors, because any disturbance in relative positions provides an incentive for the advantaged creditor to maximise his own position by precipitating bankruptcy prematurely, thus leading to a worse deal for the creditors as a whole.[24] However, the basic premise of this argument is that the *only* proper function of bankruptcy law is to provide the most advantageous solution to the creditors' common pool problem as described above, a position doubted by those who put forward convincing arguments for a messier analysis.[25]

7. The pragmatic argument

The secured creditor's isolation from her debtor's bankruptcy may of course be justifiable pragmatically – it may be the case that if secured lenders' rights to enforce the security are abrogated or curtailed by the bankruptcy of the debtor, then secured lenders will no longer be willing to lend, or at least will lend less frequently, and/or will lend unsecured and hence more expensively. However, there are two things that can usefully be said about this. The first is that, even if it is a complete justification, it is almost certainly an *ex post facto* one. If, in this jurisdiction the central security interest had always been a *sui generis* right of recourse, transparently marginal and contingent, instead of the property transfer mortgage, it is questionable whether a desire to promote cheap lending would have been sufficient to persuade us to grant secured creditors immunity from bankruptcy.

---

[22] See, for example, Bridge, "The *Quistclose* Trust in a World of Secured Transactions" (1992) 12 O.J.L.S. 332 and Goode, "Is the Law Too Favourable to Secured Creditors?" [1983–1984] *Canadian Business Law Journal* 53 at p. 57.

[23] For the robust view of the Cork Committee (on whose recommendations the Insolvency Act 1986 was based) on this point, in so far as it affects secured creditors, see Report of the Insolvency Law Review Committee, *Insolvency Law and Practice*, Cmnd. 8558 (1982) paras. 1478–1483.

[24] See, in particular, Baird and Jackson, "Corporate Reorganisations and the Treatment of Diverse Ownership Interests: A Comment on Adequate Protection of Secured Creditors in Bankruptcy" (1984) 51 U.Chi.L.Rev. 97, developed more fully in Jackson, *The Logic and Limits of Bankruptcy Law* (1986).

[25] See, in particular, Warren, "Bankruptcy Policy" (1987) U.Chi.L.Rev. 775. She contrasts her "dirty, complex, elastic, interconnected" view of bankruptcy with the "rational, clean approach" of Baird and Jackson, characterising their view as "more chic" but hers as "more realistic and more likely to yield useful analysis" (at p. 811).

Secondly, it is based on an unspoken assumption that secured credit is a good thing. However, it is by no means clear that secured lending is efficient, or, if it is, that it is rendered inefficient or less efficient if rights to enforce the security are curtailed on bankruptcy. To take the first point first, intuitively it does seem likely that secured credit is efficient, if only because it has been so pervasive in free market economies for so long.[26] But efficient for whom? It seems fairly obvious that it is efficient for the secured creditor, in that the risk of not recovering the loan in full is decreased. This should result in lenders charging a lower rate of interest for secured loans, which suggests that secured credit is more advantageous for borrowers as well. However, whilst the risk of not being repaid in full is decreased for the secured creditor, it is correspondingly *increased* for all the unsecured creditors of the same debtor, because the secured assets are removed from the pool of assets out of which they can be repaid. So, at best, unsecured creditors will increase the rate of interest they charge the debtor by an amount corresponding to the discounted rate charged by the secured creditor and secured credit then becomes merely a "zero sum game". Even in such a case, the outcome is likely to be inefficient rather than neutral because setting up security arrangements is costly, so the debtor's total credit bill (*i.e.* adding together the costs of both the secured and the unsecured credit) will be greater in a world where secured credit is permitted than it would be in a world where it is prohibited. At worst – and this is rather more in line with what actually happens in the real world – some of the unsecured creditors will be unable to respond to the granting of secured credit by raising their interest rates (because they are involuntary creditors, or are not in a position to negotiate or re-negotiate the terms on which they extend credit). This benefits the debtor, but it does mean that the advantages to the debtor and the sophisticated and relatively affluent creditor are bought at the expense of the relatively poor and unsophisticated creditor.[27] In other words, it may be the case that secured credit is pervasive, not because it is efficient overall but because it permits "informed" creditors to capture wealth at the expense of "uninformed" ones.[28]

This, of course, is not the end of the matter. There are strong arguments that, notwithstanding the foregoing, secured credit produces other benefits for the enterprise (meaning here the debtor and all creditors collectively) and that these benefits outweigh any disadvantages – for example, that over-all costs of monitoring and/or regulating debtor behaviour are reduced,[29] and/or that valuable

---

[26] This argument is developed by White in "Efficiency Justifications for Personal Property Security" (1984) 37 *Vanderbilt Law Review* 473 at pp. 479–480.
[27] See Schwartz, "Security Interests and Bankruptcy Priorities: A Review of Current Theories" (1981) 10 J. Legal Stud. 1 and Scott, "A Relational Theory of Secured Financing" (1986) 86 *Columbia Law Review* 901 at pp. 904–912, both of which give excellent accounts of the arguments outlined in this and the following paragraphs.
[28] Scott, *op. cit.* above, n.27, at p. 908.
[29] See for example Jackson and Kronman, "Secured Financing and Priorities among Creditors" (1979) 88 Yale L.J. 1143.

financial management services are brought in by the secured creditor.[30] However, these explanations also are not wholly convincing.[31]

But even if secured credit is efficient, it does not necessarily follow that this desirable state of affairs is threatened by restricting the creditor's rights on bankruptcy. It seems likely that lenders take security for a variety of reasons, only some of which are connected with bankruptcy. Defaulting borrowers are not necessarily, or even usually, bankrupt. If security decreases the risk of default by non-bankrupts then it may still be worth taking even if it becomes ineffective on bankruptcy.

In fact, numerous arguments have been put forward in support of the proposition that security decreases the risk of default outside bankruptcy. It has been argued that security operates as a signalling device, enabling lenders to identify reliably and cheaply which potential borrowers are credit-worthy,[32] or alternatively, that it enables lenders to dispense with costly credit-checking at the outset and monitoring of behaviour during the security,[33] or conversely that (particularly in the case of those with floating charges or other blanket securities) it gives lenders access to information about the debtor's activities, so enabling them to take early action to safeguard their interests, and giving them control over decision-taking in the enterprise.[34] In addition, security undoubtedly has an important "hostage" function, and this applies *only* outside bankruptcy. Except where the debtor faces the loss of *all* assets in bankruptcy, fear of losing the secured asset provides an incentive for the debtor to behave in a way that most benefits the secured creditor – by, for example, conducting its business in a cautious manner, obeying instructions of the creditor, re-paying on time and in full, and paying the secured creditor ahead of other creditors when times are hard.

In addition to all of this, security also provides the creditor with an attractive alternative method of debt recovery – if the debtor defaults, it will still usually be cheaper, easier and more effective to obtain repayment by enforcing the security rather than by bringing an action on the debt, irrespective of the solvency of the debtor.

So, even if security became wholly ineffective on bankruptcy of the debtor, it would still have considerable attractions for lenders. Presumably, these would

---

[30] Scott, *op. cit.* above, n.27, and see also White *op. cit.*, above, n.26 for other reasons why security might nevertheless be efficient.
[31] See, for example, the criticisms made by Schwartz, *op. cit.* above, n.27.
[32] Contrary to what one might expect, the argument is that potential borrowers who offer security are signalling that they are *good* credit risks. For an explanation of this argument, which, at first sight, appears counterintuitive (the unsophisticated lender might be forgiven for thinking that the potential borrower who proffers security is signalling that he is unable to borrow unsecured) see Scott, *op. cit.* above, n.27, at p. 906 n.20.
[33] See, for example, Goode, *op. cit.* above, n.22, at p. 56 and Buckley, "The Bankruptcy Priority Puzzle" (1986) 72 *Virginia Law Review* 1393 at pp. 1395–1396.
[34] What Scott describes as "leverage": *op. cit.* above, n.27, at pp. 926–927.

not be sufficient in themselves to prevent a significant shift away from secured financing but this is not really the point. It would seem plausible that we could increase our present very minor bankruptcy restrictions on secured creditors' rights without this having a significant effect on the overall efficiency of secured credit outside bankruptcy, and equally plausible that more drastic restrictions would have significant effects but not necessarily to the overall detriment of the economy or society as a whole. The difficulty lies in deciding what the critical level of restriction is, and in predicting the outcome of going past that point.

8. Conclusion

For bankruptcy lawyers, the interesting question is how far secured creditors should be allowed to remain isolated from bankruptcy. It is property law, however, which has set the context for the debate. Because security interest holders have been treated as if they have major property interests, they have been given a prima facie total immunity from interference by bankruptcy law. As a result, the justification burden has rested on those arguing for a breach of that immunity. If our property law system was such that secured creditors had had to argue for special treatment on bankruptcy, one suspects that the end result would have been very different.

11

Property and Unjust Enrichment[1]

W.J. SWADLING*

1. Introduction

It is said that civilian systems maintain a complete opposition between property and unjust enrichment. For them, unjust enrichment forms a part of the law of obligations, with restitution always being effected through the grant of rights *in personam* and never by rights *in rem*. Taking the law of property as comprising the totality of rights *in rem*, unjust enrichment never appears within it. For such systems, therefore, it is quite natural to draw a line between property and unjust enrichment. But though there is meaning in such a distinction, the drawing of such an opposition is flawed, for unjust enrichment is an event and property the response to an event. It would be like trying to contrast tort and compensation. There is no logical reason why the event of unjust enrichment should not meet the response of rights *in rem*. It is simply a matter of observable fact that in civilian systems this never happens.

The thesis of this chapter is that it is highly desirable that, so far as possible, this should also be the position in English law. Restitution effected through the grant of proprietary rights should never, or almost never, happen. We should adopt the same position as civilian jurisdictions, not for the sake of harmonisation but because there is no compelling reason why proprietary rights should arise in response to unjust enrichment.

The award of a proprietary rather than a personal right has, for the restitutionary plaintiff, several favourable consequences. As the House of Lords has recently reminded us, only a proprietary right to restitution carries with it an award of compound rather than simple interest.[2] But more importantly, a proprietary right, provided the continued existence of the *res* in the debtor's hands, will take priority over the purely personal rights of third party creditors. The question which this chapter will address is whether a restitutionary plaintiff is ever deserving of the advantages of a proprietary right.

---

* Brasenose College, Oxford.
[1] Although the subject is also known as the Law of Restitution, it is unhelpful to describe it so, for restitution is simply a response to an event. And since the causative event of restitution is the unjust enrichment of the defendant, the subject is more properly known by that name.
[2] *Westdeutsche Landesbank Girozentrale v. Islington L.B.C.* [1996] A.C. 669.

2. What is proprietary restitution?

We must at the outset be clear as to what we mean by "proprietary restitution". Proprietary restitution occurs when rights *in rem* are generated in the plaintiff to reverse an unjust enrichment in the defendant. What is not included here is the situation in which there is a passive preservation of existing proprietary rights. In such cases, the plaintiff's proprietary rights will derive not from the defendant's unjust enrichment but from some other event. They will not be restitutionary, for survival of ownership is not restitution for unjust enrichment.[3] An example will illustrate the point.

In *Cundy v. Lindsay*[4] a rogue induced the plaintiff manufacturers to supply handkerchiefs to him on credit by pretending that he was a more reputable buyer already known to the plaintiff. The rogue then sold the handkerchiefs on to an innocent third party, the defendant. The plaintiff sued the defendant in conversion. The House of Lords held that the consequence of the mistake was that there was "no delivery of the goods with intent to pass the property".[5] Property in the handkerchiefs did not pass to the rogue and from him to the defendant who was therefore liable in conversion. But though the plaintiff had rights *in rem*, they were not rights *in rem* generated by the defendant's unjust enrichment. They were instead rights *in rem* which predated the receipt of the goods by the rogue and generated by some other event, in this case most probably a *specificatio*.[6]

A more controversial case arises where there is a substitution of one asset for another. Suppose that the rogue in *Cundy v. Lindsay* had first swapped the handkerchiefs for a horse and had sold the horse on to the defendant. Would a claim in conversion brought against the defendant in respect of the receipt of the horse be a claim in respect of a proprietary right generated by the unjust enrichment of the defendant? On one view, the answer is no, the reason being that the plaintiff's right in the substitute asset was not generated by the unjust enrichment of the defendant but merely reflected the persistence of property rights through substitutions. As Lord Ellenborough C.J. explained in *Taylor v. Plumer*, "the product of or substitute for the original thing still follows the nature of the thing itself, as long as it can be ascertained to be such, and the right only ceases when the means of ascertainment fail . . . ".[7] It is, however, probably more accurate to describe the plaintiff's right *in rem* to the horse as a

---

[3] For this reason, in *Macmillan Inc. v. Bishopsgate Investment Trust plc (No. 3)* [1996] W.L.R. 387 both Millett J. at first instance and the Court of Appeal were wrong to describe a claim by the beneficial owner of shares in respect of an interference with its equitable ownership as a claim "in restitution". In that case, the proprietary rights which the plaintiff sought to vindicate were generated by the intentional and prior act of the settlor in creating a trust in its favour and not by the defendant's unjust enrichment: see Swadling [1996] L.M.C.L.Q. 63.
[4] (1878) 3 A.C. 459.
[5] *ibid.* at 468, *per* Lord Hatherley.
[6] In many similarly structured situations the plaintiff will have acquired his proprietary rights by consent under a contract, but in this particular case the plaintiff had acquired raw materials and had manufactured the goods.
[7] (1815) 3 M. & S. 562 at 575.

new property right. But it does not necessarily follow that the new property right is one generated by the defendant's unjust enrichment. Novelty *per se* cannot be the criterion, for otherwise rights acquired by a person taking a mackerel from the sea would have to be described as restitutionary. But novelty in this particular context, does, according to one writer, mean we are within the domain of the law of restitution. Professor Peter Birks argues that:

> ".... if one person parts with an asset in circumstances in which the law gives him instead a right on certain conditions to revest it in himself, that power is something new. It is generated by the unjust enrichment of the alienee in order to effect restitution. Again, if one person is alleged to have used the value of another's property to acquire another asset, the question whether that is what he has in fact done being determined by the exercise of tracing, the right which the law raises in the new asset is restitutionary. It is raised to effect restitution of unjust enrichment. No amount of talk about tracing things, as though tracing were a hunt for the original asset, should be allowed to conceal the metaphor. Tracing is not a hunt for the original asset but an attempt to discover in which different asset the value of the original asset has been invested and is now located. The new asset implies a new right ... The new right has to be referred to a causative event. Generically, that causative event is unjust enrichment. The metaphor of hunting for things has concealed even the need for that explanation. So long as one seemed to be hunting for a thing, the same thing which one had at the beginning of the story, only the original right could be in question. There was nothing new to explain. Proprietary rights contingent on tracing are always restitutionary."[8]

Although the first part of this statement describes an instance which is incontestably an example of restitution being effected by the creation of rights *in rem*,[9] this is not so in the lines which immediately follow, in which Birks describes a situation which would include that of the plaintiff in our extended *Cundy v. Lindsay* scenario. In the case where the plaintiff's rights *in rem* in one asset are substituted for rights in another asset, it is doubtful whether the causative event of the substitution is the defendant's unjust enrichment.

One reason for doubt is that the defendant in such a case is never, at least as a matter of law, enriched at the plaintiff's expense.[10] At no stage does the horse become his, the plaintiff's title to the handkerchiefs being automatically transferred to the horse at the time when the exchange takes place. Thus, long before the horse came into the defendant's hands, the plaintiff had subsisting rights *in rem* in respect of it.[11] And if the defendant is never enriched, how can the cre-

---

[8] Birks (ed.), *Laundering and Tracing* (1995) pp. 318–319.
[9] It describes the right of a plaintiff in a case like *Car and Universal Finance Co. Ltd v. Caldwell* [1965] Q.B. 525, discussed below.
[10] See, further, Swadling [1996] L.M.C.L.Q. 63.
[11] It is not possible to do full justice to Professor Birks's thesis in this paper, but he would no doubt reply that my argument depends on a misconceived view of the nature of tracing. Tracing does not, he would argue, give a plaintiff a vested right in the substituted asset at the moment of substitution but instead a power to make the asset his own: see Birks, "Mixing and Tracing: Property and Restitution" 45(II) [1992] C.L.P. 69, especially pp. 89–95. Professor Birks does, however, admit that his view of tracing is novel and that the authorities where the question has

3. When will proprietary restitution be granted?

This is a difficult question to answer, made so because case-law in the area is minimal and the arguments for or against a proprietary award are only rarely addressed. Nor is there much academic writing on the subject.[12] This part of the chapter will attempt to give an overview of those situations in which a proprietary right has been granted. It is not, however, a comprehensive treatment,[13] for that would require at least a book, and not merely a chapter in a book.

For the purposes of exposition it will be convenient to distinguish between the five different reasons for restitution, *viz.* vitiated consent, qualified consent, free acceptance, policy-motivated factors and wrongdoing.[14]

(a) Vitiated consent

By vitiated consent we mean that the factor which calls for restitution, *e.g.* mistake, duress, undue influence, etc., impaired the plaintiff's intention to confer an enrichment on the defendant. Although proprietary restitution in this area is rare, it would seem that there are some cases, both at law and in equity, in which an impaired intention will generate a proprietary right to restitution. However, as the law presently stands, it is impossible to know precisely when this will occur. In the realm of mistaken transfers, one instance of proprietary restitution is provided by the case of a contract for the sale of goods vitiated by a non-fundamental[15] fraudulently induced mistake. An example is *Car and Universal Finance Co. Ltd. v. Caldwell*,[16] where the plaintiff was fraudulently induced to sell his car to a rogue in return for a worthless cheque. The Court of Appeal held that the plaintiff's later acts of informing the police and the Automobile Association of the fraud were enough to rescind the contract and thereby revest title to the car in him at common law to the prejudice of an innocent third party

---

been raised come down in favour of a vested interest theory. See also Matthews, "The Legal and Moral Limits of Common Law Tracing" in Birks (ed.), *op. cit.* above, n.8, 23 at pp. 57 *et seq.*

[12] One useful contribution is that of Fox, "The Transfer of Legal Title to Money" [1996] R.L.R. 60.

[13] No attempt is made, for example, to deal with the important topic of subrogation: see Mitchell, *The Law of Subrogation* (1994).

[14] The taxonomy adopted here is that of Birks, *Introduction to the Law of Restitution* (rev. ed., 1989).

[15] Where the mistake is fundamental, *i.e.*, as to the identity of the transferee or the subject-matter transferred, no property will pass to the recipient and any claim by the plaintiff will be to vindicate subsisting property rights and not property rights generated by unjust enrichment: text to n.4 above.

[16] [1965] 1 Q.B. 525.

purchaser who had in the meantime bought it from the rogue.[17] This ability to revest title being generated by the rogue's unjust enrichment, there can be no doubt that it is an example of proprietary restitution.[18]

The same process occurs in equity, though not only in the case of fraud.[19] In *Chase Manhattan Bank N.A. v. Israel-British Bank (London) Ltd*[20] the plaintiff, acting under a spontaneous mistake, paid US$2 million to the defendant, who, within a matter of days and after being alerted to the mistake, became insolvent. Goulding J. held that the plaintiff had a personal restitutionary claim for $2 million. But he also held that equitable title to the $2 million mistakenly paid remained in the plaintiff, who could therefore assert a proprietary right to this sum should it be shown, through the process of tracing, still to be present in the defendant's hands.[21] It should, however, be noted that the learned judge reasoned by analogy from the decision of the House of Lords in *Sinclair v. Brougham*,[22] a case which has since been overruled.[23]

When we move from mistake to duress, there seems to be no case, at least at common law, in which a grant of proprietary rights is made to reverse an unjust enrichment. Although there are cases in which the consequence that the transfer was made under duress has the effect of preserving the plaintiff's prior title,[24] these cases are, as we have seen, not examples of proprietary restitution. Nor does there seem to be any case of duress in which equity has taken a contrary view.[25] For both systems, property is either preserved in the transferor or passes to the transferee with no power of recall.

---

[17] This would also seem to be the position in Scottish law, where the rule is that "fraud passes against creditors": Bell, *Commentaries on the Law of Scotland and Mercantile Jurisprudence* (7th ed., 1870) Vol. 1, 299.

[18] Another is *Re Eastgate, ex parte Ward* [1905] 1 K.B. 465. Furniture was sold on credit to a purchaser who had no intention of paying for it. After delivery, the vendor discovered the deception and rescinded the contract of sale. He broke into the home of the purchaser and re-took possession of the goods. The purchaser had prior to this re-taking committed an act of bankruptcy. The action of the purchaser's trustee in bankruptcy in conversion against the vendor failed. Bigham J. held that though property in the furniture had initially passed to the purchaser, the vendor, because of the fraud, had a right as against the purchaser to revest it in him. The trustee in bankruptcy could, he held, be in no better position. The correctness of this decision was doubted by the Privy Council in *Re Goldcorp Exchange Ltd* [1995] 1 A.C. 74. It is, however, consistent with a long line of authorities in the area of rescission, none of which were cited to the court.

[19] For an example of rescission for fraud in equity, see *El Ajou v. Dollar Land Holdings plc* [1993] 3 All E.R. 717.

[20] [1981] Ch. 105.

[21] It could, of course, be argued that if equitable title never left the mistaken payer, this is an example of the enforcement of pre-existing proprietary rights and not one of proprietary rights raised to reverse an unjust enrichment. Against this is the argument that until the mistaken payment was received, the plaintiff had no equitable title at all: *cf. Westdeutsche Landesbank Girozentrale v. Islington L.B.C.* [1996] A.C. 669 at 706, *per* Lord Browne-Wilkinson.

[22] [1914] A.C. 398.

[23] In *Westdeutsche Landesbank Girozentrale v. Islington L.B.C.* [1996] A.C. 669.

[24] See, generally, in a criminal context, Hooper, "Larceny by Intimidation" [1965] Crim.L.R. 532 at 592.

[25] It is interesting to note that in one duress case in which an equitable proprietary claim was, albeit unsuccessfully, made, the claim was made in reliance on the rules relating to trusts for

But an area in which equity, though not the common law, does appear to give proprietary rights to reverse an unjust enrichment is that of undue influence. One example is the well-known case of *Allcard v. Skinner*.[26] A young woman transferred property to her spiritual adviser but later claimed that the transfer was made as a result of the transferee's undue influence. But for her delay, it seems that the remedy she sought, the re-transfer of the property concerned, would have been granted. But since no attack was made on the nature of relief, the case is no authority for the proposition that a proprietary remedy will issue in such cases.

(b) Qualified consent

When restitution lawyers talk of a qualified consent to transfer, they mean that the transfer, though consensual, was conditional upon the happening of some future event. Another name for this is "failure of consideration". An example would be advance payments made by a plaintiff under a contract which was subsequently frustrated. If the defendant has not performed his side of the bargain, the plaintiff can recover the pre-payment on the ground that the intent to transfer was not absolute but conditional on performance. The question here is whether the plaintiff has, in addition to his undoubted personal right to restitution, a proprietary claim. It might be thought that the answer would be no, the reason being that, realty apart, the law of property does not afford the facility of creating conditional estates in property. And in any case, if proprietary restitution is the exception in cases of vitiated intent, there would seem to be even less reason for giving the plaintiff a preferential status where there was a consensual decision to transfer. Despite this, there are a number of cases of qualified intent in which proprietary restitution has been awarded.[27]

One instance of proprietary restitution is said to be provided by *Re Abbott*.[28] A Cambridge don left a large sum of money on trust for his two deaf and dumb daughters. The money was stolen by the trustee and a family friend collected further moneys from well-wishers to provide for the children. A surplus remained after the children's death. A claim to it was made by their next-of-kin on the basis that the money belonged to the daughters absolutely. Stirling J. said that the money was intended to be applied for a particular purpose and was never intended to become the absolute property of the daughters. It was, therefore, held on resulting trust for the subscribers. Other cases in which similar

---

private (*i.e.*, non-charitable) purposes and not on the basis of the duress itself: *Universe Tankships Inc. of Monrovia v. International Transport Workers Federation* [1983] A.C. 366.

[26] (1887) 36 Ch.D. 145.

[27] One case concerned with the generation of proprietary rights following a failure of consideration is *Nesté Oy v. Lloyds Bank plc* [1983] 2 Lloyd's Rep. 659. However, the proprietary right there arose because of the defendant's knowledge of the reason for restitution and not simply because of the plaintiff's qualified intent to transfer.

[28] [1900] 2 Ch. 326.

reasoning was used include *Re Gillingham Bus Disaster Fund*[29] and *Re West Sussex Constabulary's Widows, Children and Benevolent Fund*.[30]

But are these cases of a resulting trust springing up after the failure of the purpose to give a restitutionary right *in rem*? One explanation might be that they are instead cases of trusts which fail *ab initio* and which give rise to automatic resulting trusts,[31] the equitable title to the fund never leaving the subscribers at all. If in *Re Abbott* the children were not intended to be absolutely entitled under the trust (as Stirling J. held), then the trust was either one for a private purpose (the maintenance of the daughters) and void from the start,[32] or involved the grant to them of a life interest with a resulting trust in respect of the remainder in favour of the donors. Either way, the money would be held on resulting trust for the contributors from the outset and not on the happening of the event which causes the consideration to fail.[33]

Yet another authority which seems at first sight to be awarding proprietary rights following a failure of consideration is provided by *Barclay's Bank Ltd v. Quistclose Investments Ltd*,[34] where a loan was made to enable the debtor to discharge a specific obligation, *viz*., the payment of a dividend to its shareholders. When it no longer became possible for that obligation to be discharged, the House of Lords held that the loan moneys were held by the debtor on trust for the creditor, who was thereby enabled to gain priority in the debtor's insolvency. But this was not a case of proprietary restitution; the rights created in favour of the creditor were not rights generated by unjust enrichment. Lord Wilberforce observed that "the intention to create a secondary trust for the benefit of the lender . . . is clear", a characterisation which Gummow J. in the Australian case of *Re Australian Elizabethan Theatre Trust* described as "indicative of an express trust with two limbs rather than an express trust in favour of the shareholders and a resulting trust in favour of [the creditor] . . . ".[35] And as Professor Birks has noted, "express trusts never create restitutionary beneficial interests".[36]

There are, however, two decisions in this field where a proprietary claim was sought but rejected. Neither is of much assistance. The first is *Guardian Ocean*

---

[29] [1958] Ch. 300.
[30] [1971] Ch. 1.
[31] In *Westdeutsche Landesbank Girozentrale v. Islington L.B.C.* [1996] A.C. 669 at 708 Lord Browne-Wilkinson cast doubt on Megarry V.-C.'s division in *Re Vandervell's Trusts (No. 2)* [1974] Ch. 269 of resulting trusts into the two categories of presumed and automatic resulting trusts. The point was, however, *obiter*, and the correctness of the division was not challenged by counsel.
[32] Accepting for the purposes of argument that *Re Denley* [1969] 1 Ch. 373 was wrongly decided. See Evans (1969) 32 M.L.R. 96.
[33] Although some of the money is usually spent, a defence of consent would have been available to both the trustees and recipients had the subscribers brought a *Re Diplock* [1948] Ch. 465 type claim.
[34] [1970] A.C. 567. See also *Rowan v. Dann* (1992) 64 P. & C.R. 202.
[35] (1991) 102 A.L.R. 681 at 691.
[36] Birks, *op. cit.* above, n.14, at p. 54.

Cargoes Ltd v. Banco da Brasil (No. 3),[37] where the Court of Appeal held that payments made in anticipation of a contract which never came into being, though generating a restitutionary right *in personam*, were not to be impressed with a trust. Although the case is of limited value, the authority for the plaintiff's claim, *Barclay's Bank Ltd v. Quistclose Investments Ltd*, being easily distinguished on the ground that there was no restriction on how the advance payments were to be applied, it does at least demonstrate that the court thought it necessary to find something beyond a mere failure of consideration to found a proprietary right. Likewise in *Re Goldcorp Exchange Ltd (in Receivership)*[38] the Privy Council held that moneys paid in advance for gold bullion were not impressed by a *Quistclose* trust because there was no condition attached to how the moneys were to be spent. And an argument based solely on failure of consideration also failed, but on the rather unsatisfactory ground that the transaction did not fail from the start. But as decisions like *Car and Universal Finance Co. Ltd v. Caldwell* show, it is no bar to subsequent revesting that the contract is terminated at a time after it comes into existence.

(c) Free acceptance

According to Birks, "a free acceptance occurs where a recipient knows that a benefit is being offered to him non-gratuitously and where he, having the opportunity to reject, elects to accept".[39] One of the on-going debates in the law of restitution is whether there is indeed such a ground of claim. It is not the business of this chapter to enter that controversy. All that can be said is that there is some doubt whether there is any personal right in such circumstances, and certainly no case in which a proprietary right has been awarded. But since this ground of claim depends on knowledge on the part of the recipient, it may well give rise to proprietary restitution should the argument concerned with knowledge-based trusts (discussed below) gain acceptance.

(d) Policy-motivated restitution

This is a miscellaneous category of cases in which the reason for restitution is not some defective or qualified intention on the part of the transferee, nor some unconscientiousness on the part of the recipient. Instead, what drives restitution in such cases is the furtherance of some other social interest.[40] An example is provided by *Woolwich Building Society v. Inland Revenue Commissioners*,[41] which concerned the recovery of taxes levied under an *ultra vires* statutory instrument. Although the payments were made under pressure, the type of pressure involved, the threat of legal proceedings for recovery, was not of a type

---

[37] [1992] 2 Lloyd's Rep. 193.
[38] [1995] 1 A.C. 74.
[39] Birks, *op. cit.*, above, n.14, at p. 265.
[40] Birks, *op. cit.*, above n.14, at p. 54 at 294–312.
[41] [1993] A.C. 70.

which would yield restitution. Nevertheless, restitution was allowed. Although the reason for restitution was nowhere made clear by the court,[42] one explanation is that it was to further a policy of adherence by the State to the rule of law.[43] Another example of restitutionary claims in this category are awards to salvors, the policy promoted being the preservation of property and human life. Although many salvors act through moral compulsion, many, particularly commercial salvors, do not.[44] They have, nevertheless, been allowed to recover.

In most cases under this head the award given is a personal right to restitution. The one exception is the award given to a maritime salvor, who is given the benefit of a lien on the salvaged property.[45] One possible explanation is that unless this were so, the policy that "seamen must be encouraged by awards of salvage to render assistance to property"[46] would be frustrated, for in such situations there will be neither time nor facility to enquire into the creditworthiness of the owner of the goods to be saved.

(e) Restitution for wrongs

All cases dealt with so far are examples of subtractive enrichments. In all of them the restitutionary plaintiff had, immediately prior to the defendant's enrichment, a proprietary right in the benefit transferred. That is not the case where the enrichment received is only "at the expense of" the plaintiff in the sense that it was obtained via the commission of a wrong against him,[47] as for instance where a fiduciary takes a bribe in breach of his duty of loyalty. There is no doubt that there are certain wrongs, breach of fiduciary duty among them, which generate restitutionary rights in their victims. But there is, as yet, no safe method of determining which wrongs give rise to restitutionary awards. The matter is complicated still further, however, for in those cases where restitutionary awards are made, there is no way of predicting in advance whether the award will be personal or proprietary. Sometimes it is both.

One case in which both personal and proprietary restitutionary rights were awarded to the victim of a wrong is *Att.-Gen. for Hong Kong v. Reid*.[48] The defendant, the Acting Director of Public Prosecutions in Hong Kong, had taken bribes to drop prosecutions. With the proceeds of those bribes he bought land in New Zealand. His employer argued that the bribes were held by the defendant on a constructive trust with the result that the land bought with the bribes

---

[42] See McKendrick, [1993] L.M.C.L.Q 88.
[43] Birks, "Restitution from the Executive: A Tercentenary Footnote to the Bill of Rights" in Finn (ed.), *Essays on Restitution* (1990).
[44] For an extreme example, see the facts of *The Medina* (1876) 1 P.D. 272.
[45] See, generally, Steel and Rose, *Kennedy's Law of Salvage* (5th ed., 1985) para. 1254.
[46] *The Telemachus* [1957] P. 47 at 49, *per* Wilmer J.
[47] For the two uses of the phrase "at the expense of" see Birks, *op. cit.* above, n.14, at pp. 23–24, 40–44; Birks, *Restitution – The Future* (1992), Chap. 1.
[48] [1994] 1 A.C. 324.

was likewise held for them on trust. The New Zealand Court of Appeal,[49] following the English case of *Lister v. Stubbs*,[50] held that though the defendant came under a restitutionary obligation to account for the proceeds of his breach of fiduciary duty, all that was generated between the parties was an equitable debt. The employer did not own the bribes themselves and so could not claim to own the things bought with them. The Privy Council disagreed. From the moment of receipt, the defendant, as well as owing the amount received to his employer, held the bribe on trust, a result reached through the application of the maxim that "equity looks upon that as done which ought to be done". Thus, so far as the law of New Zealand is concerned,[51] restitutionary plaintiffs claiming in respect of the wrong of breach of fiduciary duty have both personal and proprietary restitutionary rights to the enrichment.

4. Arguments in favour of proprietary restitution[52]

As noted above, in those cases in which restitutionary proprietary awards have been made, little or no attention has been paid to the justifications for such awards. There are, nevertheless, a number of arguments which have been advanced to support the grant of proprietary rights. There are four arguments from principle and two which, for want of a better word, we might describe as arguments from policy.

(a) Arguments from principle

(i) Underlying invalidity of the contract   In some of the cases discussed above, property has been transferred under a contract which is, for one reason or another, later rescinded. The effect of rescission will be to make the contract void *ab initio*. Does the fact that the contract is now void not also invalidate any transfer of property made pursuant to that contract? Although this view seems to have been accepted in a number of cases,[53] it is demonstrably wrong.

The mistake made by those who take the view that property cannot pass under a void contract is a failure to differentiate between the validity of the contract itself and the validity of the conveyance of property made pursuant to that

---

[49] [1992] 1 N.Z.L.R. 357.
[50] (1890) 45 Ch. D. 1.
[51] The decision has received a lukewarm reception in England and Wales: see the decision of the Court of Appeal in *Halifax Building Society v. Thomas* [1996] Ch. 217 and the cogent criticisms of Crilley [1994] R.L.R. 57.
[52] For a general discussion see Paciocco "The Remedial Constructive Trust: A Principled Basis of Priorities Over Creditors" (1989) 68 C.B.R. 315.
[53] The leading example is *Sinclair v. Brougham* [1914] A.C. 398, although it is often forgotten that the point was one which had been conceded by counsel in argument. But as we have seen, the case has since been overruled by the House of Lords in *Westdeutsche Landesbank Girozentrale v. Islington L.B.C.* [1996] A.C. 669 and was in any case decided *per incuriam* the decision of the Privy Council in *Ayers v. South Australian Banking Co.* (1878) L.R. 3 P.C. 548.

contract. In some cases, the thing which makes the contract invalid will also operate to nullify the conveyance. Such a case is *Cundy v. Lindsay*, where, as we have seen, the plaintiff's mistake of identity meant both that no contract was formed and that the subsequent act of delivery passed no property in the goods to the rogue. But in others, though the contract is void, property will pass. An example is *Singh v. Ali*,[54] where a lorry was delivered pursuant to a contract of sale void for illegality. The Privy Council held that property nevertheless passed to the purchaser, who could maintain conversion against the seller when the latter took it forcibly from the former. More recently, in *Westdeutsche Landesbank Girozentrale v. Islington L.B.C.*,[55] the House of Lords held that property passed in money payments made under a contract entered into between a bank and a local authority, despite the fact that the contract was *ultra vires* and void.[56] The invalidity of the contract can only affect the passing of property when it is the contract itself which operates as the conveyance of title. But contract is only one method of conveyance. Where title passes because of some other act, *e.g.* delivery, the invalidity of the contract pursuant to which it was transferred will not invalidate the transfer.[57]

(ii) Restitution and resulting trusts There is an argument which says, at least in the case of subtractive enrichments, that restitution can be effected through the device of resulting trust.[58] At the risk of over-simplification, the argument proceeds on the following basis. In the case of a gratuitous transfer of property from A to B, equity will raise a presumption of resulting trust in favour of A, which presumption can be rebutted by B proving that A intended to make a gift to him. Where A makes a mistaken payment to B, such a payment will *ex hypothesi* also be gratuitous, with the consequence that a presumption of a resulting trust will also arise in favour of B, which presumption will remain unrebutted because B will not be able to show an intention by A to make a gift.

I have argued elsewhere that this is wrong[59] and that view was endorsed by the House of Lords in *Westdeutsche Landesbank Girozentrale v. Islington L.B.C.*[60] It is wrong because it mistakes the nature of the trust which is raised upon a gratuitous conveyance. Such a trust is designed to reflect the actual intentions of the parties, there being a presumption that in such circumstances A intended B to be a trustee for him. But once evidence is given that the transfer was made by mistake, that in itself shows that no trust was intended and the presumption of resulting trust will thereby be rebutted. The argument in favour

---

[54] [1960] A.C. 167.
[55] [1996] A.C. 669.
[56] *ibid.* at 689–690 *per* Lord Goff of Chieveley.
[57] *Ayers v. South Australian Banking Co.* (1871) L.R. 3 P.C. 548 at 559, *per* Mellish L.J.
[58] The argument is that of Professor Birks. It is developed in full in Birks, "Restitution and Resulting Trusts" in Goldstein (ed.), *Equity and Contemporary Legal Developments* (1992).
[59] Swadling, "A New Role for Resulting Trusts?" (1996) 16 L.S. 110.
[60] [1996] A.C. 669.

of resulting trusts yielding restitutionary remedies only works if the sole evidence which can rebut the presumption of a resulting trust is evidence of a donative intent, but, as Lord Browne-Wilkinson has pointed out, "the presumption of resulting trust is rebutted by evidence of any intention inconsistent with such a trust, not only by evidence of an intention to make a gift".[61]

(iii) Trusts raised through knowledge   An explanation has recently been given which would explain the result, though not the reasoning, of a case like *Chase Manhattan v. Israel-British Bank*. It was said by Lord Browne-Wilkinson in *Westdeutsche Landesbank Girozentrale v. Islington L.B.C.*[62] that knowledge by the defendant bank of the mistake could make all the difference:

> "Although the mere receipt of the moneys, in ignorance of the mistake, gives rise to no trust, the retention of the moneys after the recipient bank learned of the mistake may well have given rise to a constructive trust."[63]

This view is difficult to justify. Not only is it unsupported by authority, it also fails to explain why the addition of knowledge on the part of the defendant of the unjust factor should elevate an otherwise personal right to restitution to a proprietary one to the detriment of the defendant's other creditors. Moreover, it both runs counter to *Re Goldcorp*,[64] where the fact that the defendants were acting in an unconscientious manner did not lead to the award of proprietary rights, and would support the actual result in *Sinclair v. Brougham*,[65] a case which Lord Browne-Wilkinson expressly overruled.[66] In the same case, Lord Goff, when talking about the award of proprietary rights, was careful to say that it was "particularly desirable that your Lordships should, so far as possible, restrict the inquiry to the actual questions at issue in this appeal, and not be tempted into formulating general principles of a broader nature".[67] Given that no argument was addressed by either side as to the correctness of *Chase Manhattan*, it is unfortunate that Lord Browne-Wilkinson did not heed this sensible injunction.

(iv) Equity considers as done that which ought to have been done   There is a further argument which would give proprietary relief in equity, though not in law. This is the one which we saw used to explain the proprietary award in *Att.-Gen. for Hong Kong v. Reid*.[68] Lord Templeman, delivering the opinion of the Judicial Committee of the Privy Council, said:

---

[61] *ibid.* at 708.
[62] [1996] A.C. 669. See, generally, Birks, "Trusts Raised to Reverse Unjust Enrichment" [1996] R.L.R. 3.
[63] [1996] A.C. 669 at 715.
[64] [1995] 1 A.C. 74.
[65] [1914] A.C. 398.
[66] [1996] A.C. 669 at 713.
[67] *ibid.* at 686.
[68] [1994] 1 A.C. 324.

"When a bribe is offered and accepted in money or in kind, the money or property constituting the bribe belongs in law to the recipient.... Equity however which acts *in personam* insists that it is unconscionable for a fiduciary to obtain and retain a benefit in breach of duty.... The false fiduciary who received the bribe in breach of duty must pay and account for the bribe to the person to whom that duty was owed.... But, if the bribe consists of property which increases in value or if a cash bribe is invested advantageously the false fiduciary will receive a benefit from his breach of duty unless he is made accountable not only for the original amount or value of the bribe but also for the increased value of the property representing the bribe. As soon as the bribe was received it should have been paid or transferred *instanter* to the person who suffered from the breach of duty. Equity considers as done that which ought to have been done. As soon as the bribe was received, whether in cash or in kind, the false fiduciary held the bribe on a constructive trust for the person injured."[69]

There are a number of problems with this reasoning, only two of which can be dealt with here.[70] The first is that it proceeds upon the mistaken assumption that the only way to strip a fiduciary of the profitable investment of a bribe is through a proprietary claim. In fact, there is no reason, either in logic or authority, to presume that claims in the second measure of restitution, *i.e.*, value remaining,[71] must be proprietary.[72] The second problem is that the argument mistakes the nature of the fiduciary's duty to account. As Lord Templeman acknowledges, the receipt by a fiduciary of a bribe generates an equitable debt between the fiduciary and his principal. This debt is a consequence of the fiduciary's duty to account. But that debt can be satisfied by the payment of money belonging to a fiduciary taken from any source. It is not only discharged by the handing over of the very money received. And since there is no duty to pay over the bribe *in specie*, the application of the maxim "equity considers as done that which ought to have been done" cannot give rise to any proprietary rights over those moneys, for payment over of the bribe itself is not that "which ought to have been done".

(b) Arguments from policy

(i) Plaintiff did not accept the risk of defendant's insolvency   There is a good argument for saying that those who trust in the solvency of their obligee should not be later awarded proprietary rights by the courts when it turns out that that trust was misplaced. The creditor had the opportunity to bargain for security but chose not to take it, this lack of security probably being reflected in the price.[73] For the court to now award proprietary rights would be to give him a benefit which was totally undeserved. Such an argument has sometimes been

---

[69] *ibid.* at 331.
[70] See, generally, Crilley [1994] R.L.R. 57.
[71] Birks, *op. cit.* above, n.14, at pp. 358–401.
[72] Examples of personal claims in the second measure include *Re Wrexham, Mold & Connah's Quay Railway Co.* [1899] 1 Ch. 440; *Boardman v. Phipps* [1967] 2 A.C. 46.
[73] As is well-known, the interest rate on an unsecured loan is far higher than on a secured one.

used to deny a restitutionary plaintiff proprietary rights where the ground of claim is failure of consideration, for there it might be foreseen that the condition of the payment would not be met. But the argument has also been turned on its head and used to justify the award of restitutionary proprietary rights. Thus, in a contemporary comment on *Chase Manhattan*, Professor Gareth Jones defended the grant of a proprietary remedy on the basis that "a person who pays money under mistake does not advance credit to another; he does not consciously take the risk that his recipient may become insolvent and that he may have to share the pickings of his estate with the general creditors".[74] However, this explanation fails to notice that there will be many other persons who will have only personal rights *vis-à-vis* the defendant but who also will not have taken the risk of his insolvency. The simplest example is that of the victim of the defendant's negligent driving. Although such a person will not have trusted in the tortfeasor's solvency, he will nevertheless be confined to a personal right in the event of the latter's insolvency. What this defence of *Chase Manhattan* fails to provide is any reason why the mistaken payer should be treated more favourably than the accident victim.

(ii) Enrichment a windfall What we might call the "windfall" argument is concerned to counter the argument that the restitutionary defendant's other creditors are prejudiced by the award of a proprietary right to the restitutionary plaintiff. The argument was also used by Professor Jones to defend *Chase Manhattan* and by Lord Templeman in *Att.-Gen. for Hong Kong v. Reid*. Professor Jones said that "The recipient's general creditors do not expect to be, and should not be, reimbursed from what is after all a windfall which should never have formed part of the recipient's trading assets. Only if a person has been induced to grant or extend credit because of the existence of assets materially swollen by the mistaken payment, is it arguable that his claim should rank *in pari passu* with that of the mistaken payer".[75] Lord Templeman put it more simply: "the unsecured creditors cannot be in a better position than their debtor".[76]

However, the argument that the general creditors should not have recourse to such a "windfall" (which, because it will also apply to payments made for a consideration which later fails, must be different from the argument that the restitutionary plaintiff did not trust in the solvency of the defendant) is also open to criticism. The defendant's creditors are not seeking to take a windfall: they are simply trying to have their losses made good.[77] And in any case, the argument ignores the fact that the defendant's assets will also be swollen by loans which he has failed to repay and by goods the price of which remains outstanding.[78] No-one has ever suggested that these creditors should also be given priority.

---

[74] [1980] C.L.J. 275 at 276.
[75] *ibid*.
[76] [1994] 1 A.C. 324 at 331.
[77] Crilley, [1994] R.L.R. 57 at pp. 67–69.
[78] Tettenborn, [1980] C.L.J. 272.

5. Arguments against proprietary restitution

What arguments of substance[79] are there in favour of confining restitutionary plaintiffs to personal rights? There are at least two, one from principle, another from policy.

(a) Argument from principle

In the majority of cases in which a restitutionary proprietary right is awarded, this will be in addition to a personal right to restitution. As we saw, the plaintiff in *Chase Manhattan* had both a personal right to repayment at law and a proprietary right in equity. But this is not simply a consequence of the law/equity divide, for in *Att.-Gen. for Hong Kong v. Reid* the plaintiff had both an equitable debt and an equitable proprietary right. This is logically inconsistent.[80]

The problem is that the plaintiff is in the same breath saying that the defendant both owes a certain sum to him and that the plaintiff owns that sum in the defendant's hands. The logical implication of such an assertion will be that satisfaction of one claim cannot affect the availability of the other, for if I both have a £10 note which belongs to you and in addition owe you £10, the repayment of the debt does not in any way mean that the specific £10 note no longer belongs to you. As Lindley L.J. pointed out in long ago *Lister v. Stubbs*, to say that one can have both types of right confounds "ownership with obligation".[81] The result is that the plaintiff gets the best of both worlds, for as Meagher and Gummow have pointed out, albeit in the context of *Quistclose*-type trusts:

> "As [owner] he could stand outside the liquidation and recover the property in full, yet if the [defendant] remained solvent but, without fault on its part, the fund had disappeared, the [plaintiff] could recover the money . . . as a debt."[82]

And the logic of this argument is not met by the pragmatic qualification that the court can always deny the plaintiff double-recovery.[83]

(b) Arguments from policy

The argument from policy is a simple one. It is one of equality of treatment in insolvency. As we have seen, the effect of the award of proprietary restitutionary

---

[79] One pragmatic argument which might be advanced is that proprietary awards should be restricted in the interests of certainty. But this is not an argument against proprietary restitution as such, for if certainty was our only goal, we might achieve it by holding that proprietary restitution should be available in all cases.

[80] *cf. Morley v. Morley* (1678) 2 Ch.Cas. 2, where it was held that a trustee was not a debtor to his beneficiary in respect of the trust property, so that when it was stolen from him without fault he was under no obligation to make good the loss. It is, of course, no defence to a claim in respect of a loan that the money was stolen after delivery.

[81] (1890) 45 Ch.D. 1 at 15.

[82] Meagher and Gummow, *Jacobs' Law of Trusts in Australia* (5th ed., 1986) para. 215.

[83] *Attorney General for Hong Kong v. Reid* [1994] A.C. 324 at 331 (Lord Templeman).

Property and Unjust Enrichment 145

rights is to give preference to one class of creditor at the expense of the others. No satisfactory reason has been advanced as to why this should be so. Indeed, as Professor Roy Goode has observed:

> "To accord the plaintiff a proprietary right to the benefit obtained by the defendant, and to any profits or gains resulting from it, at the expense of the defendant's unsecured bankruptcy creditors seems completely wrong, both in principle and in policy, because the wrong done to the plaintiff by the defendant's improper receipt is no different in kind from that done to creditors who have supplied goods and services without receiving the bargained-for payment . . . ".[84]

As we have seen, with the sole exception of maritime salvage, no good reason has yet been advanced for treating restitutionary plaintiffs any differently from the defendant's other unsecured creditors.

---

[84] Goode, "Ownership and Obligation in Commercial Transactions" (1987) 103 L.Q.R. 433 at p. 444.

12

Things as Thing and Things as Wealth

BERNARD RUDDEN*

1. Introduction

What the law does well is blind its servants. Judges, practitioners, and even jurists grow so accustomed to its rituals that they do not see how deeply weird they are. Take, for instance, the names of statutes. The English have a Supreme Court Act 1981, but they have no Supreme Court. They cannot learn the law of property from the Law of Property Act. The Animals (Boarding Establishments) Act 1963 defines animals to mean only dogs and cats. They have a lengthy Settled Land Act of 1925, although from 1882 to 1997 the one thing they could not settle was their land.[1]

Curiosities of this sort are not confined to the English. The May 1993 index to the 34 looseleaf volumes of the *Canadian Encyclopedic Digest* (Ontario) has, like its predecessors, no entry whatsoever for property. It contains nothing for "personal property", although the subset of "personal property security" merits a mention. While prolix on "choses in action", its advice under "chattels" is terse: "see Bailment; Trespass". Tucked away between "Real Evidence" and "Receiving Orders", we find of course "Real Property" with its long list of crossreferences to such topics as "free and common socage", "estates tail" and "*Shelley's Case*".

The traditional civil law is not strikingly different. Certainly in the realm of property the older versions have their own incantations that the student soon takes for creed, learning, for instance, that rabbits, fish, and pigeons are immovable (until they die), while the word movable used by itself does not include books, horses, or clothing (French Civil Code §§ 524, 533; Lower Canada Civil Code § 395).

---

* Professor of Comparative Law in the University of Oxford and Fellow of Brasenose College. A draft of this paper was presented to the W.G. Hart Workshop on property law held at the Institute for Advanced Legal Studies, London, August 6–8, 1993. The author was greatly assisted by the comments of several participants and in particular by those of James Harris, of Keble College, Oxford. A version appeared in (1994) 14 *Oxford Journal of Legal Studies* 82, and the author is grateful for permission to reproduce the (somewhat amended) text.

[1] The effect of the 1882 and 1925 Settled Land Acts was that the successive interests subsisted in a fund which was initially invested in land, but the investment could be changed at any time into stocks and shares (though the limited interests were still deemed to be land). Possibly the land itself can now be tied up without artifice: see Trusts of Land and Appointment of Trustees Act 1996, s.8(1) (England and Wales).

Both major legal systems, then, have their oddities. Yet it is unlikely that we are wiser than our forebears, for the rules and rituals they devised must have had reason in their day; perhaps it is our unthinking repetition that turns them into riddles. In common law countries, the formal presentation of the law of property, derived from long tradition and offered still by much modern doctrine, is based on four propositions. First, that the essential division is that between real and personal property. Secondly, that a string of special concepts applies always, but applies only to real property: the learning of estates (for life, in tail, in fee; in possession, remainder, or reversion; absolute, determinable or conditional), the use of powers of appointment (general and special), and, to control contingent vesting, the rule against perpetuities. Thirdly, that an essential division of property entitlements is between those recognised at law and those which subsist in equity. Fourthly, this last distinction turns on the concept of the trust, and a trustee is a "legal owner".

Depending on the authority and the purpose of the work, these four notions may be stated as axioms or may operate simply as background assumptions shared by expositor and reader. This paper puts forward some hesitant arguments against all of them. Its thesis is that when things are treated as thing, and whatever vocabulary the common-lawyers use, the modern law operates with a fairly uncomplicated set of basic concepts: ownership, trusteeholding, possession, servitude, charge, and publicity (through registration or possession). By contrast, when things are treated as wealth (whether they themselves be "real" or "personal") they attract the concepts and utilise the techniques of estates, powers, and perpetuities outlined above. It is further suggested that the traditional practice of describing a trustee as "legal owner" is both inaccurate and unnecessarily confusing.

This point needs preliminary clarification. It is true that, in relation to the trust property, a trustee has the powers to pursue and recover it which are one mark of ownership; but if the property vanishes, or perishes through some natural calamity, the loss does not fall on the trustee. Furthermore, there are two other essential features of the ownership relation, and one important consequence of each. First, someone who owns a thing may, with impunity, destroy it; and so may, of course, give it away for nothing. Secondly, by judicial execution an owner's things may be taken from her or him to serve as substitute performance of obligations incurred; and so, before that happens, things may be used by their owner as security for the performance of obligations. None of these propositions holds good in general for a trustee's relation to the trust property. It is not the trustee's to give away, and indeed in principle cannot even be lent without security. A trustee's *own* creditors – the epithet is both precise and revealing – may never levy execution on the things their debtor holds as trustee.

It must be admitted that this objection to calling a trustee an "owner" is made in vain. The practice is clearly useful to the legislator as well as the expositor. Nonetheless, the latest official example may perhaps demonstrate just how strange the usage is. The Trusts of Land and Appointment of Trustees Act 1996 (England and Wales) announces in section 6(1):

> "For the purpose of exercising their functions as trustees, the trustees of land have in relation to the land subject to the trust all the powers of an absolute owner."

Among the powers undoubtedly belonging to an absolute owner of land under English law are: power to make a perfect present of it, *inter vivos* or by will; to abandon it; or to mortgage it to raise money for a holiday. Trustees of land can do none of these things, a restriction inherent in the first phrase of the sub-section "for the purpose of exercising their functions as trustees". But this means that the sub-section has layers of meaning: its reference to "owner" refers to a wide range of powers, but all the pleasant ones are excluded by the word "trustees". In short the sentence imparts its intended meaning only to those who, being common-lawyers, already know what it means.

To turn now to things. The traditional concepts of the common law of property were created for and by the ruling classes at a time when the bulk of their capital was land. Nowadays the great wealth lies in stocks, shares, bonds and the like, and is not just movable but *mobile*, crossing oceans at the touch of a keypad in the search for a fiscal utopia. This is not to make light of the need for a home, or of the difficulties encountered by English judges in the absence of any customary or legislative system of matrimonial or quasimatrimonial property. Nor is it meant to denigrate the importance of land as one of the bases of the economic structure, and a factor whose cost enters into the price of everything. In terms of legal theory and technique, however, there has been a profound if little discussed evolution by which the concepts originally devised for real property have been detached from their original object, only to survive and flourish as a means of handling abstract value. The feudal calculus lives and breeds, but its habitat is wealth not land.

The argument can be more precisely stated by distinguishing, not between things as such ("corporeal/incorporeal", "movable/immovable"), but in terms of their function. A thing may be treated for itself and be possessed, used, and disposed of for its own qualities, however banal they be. In this case the legal regime applicable treats the object as unique: it is this house we own and live in, this book we sell and no other. On the other hand every thing may be treated merely as the clothing (*in-vestment*) worn by a certain amount of wealth. In this case the relevant law accords it the modest role of a member of a class, perfectly replaceable and subject to an implacable regime of real subrogation.

The distinction between the uniqueness of things considered for themselves and their total convertibility when treated as wealth does not follow the classic lines of fungibility: a pound of flour is unique if its owner wants to make bread with it; a Vermeer in the hands of a pension fund is just another investment. Nor is the distinction necessarily tied to the nature of the object in question: most things can be either possessed for their own sake or held as investments for their income stream or in the hope of capital appreciation. The law of property covers impartially the things we own because we need them, our home, food, and clothing, and those we own but could exist without, the flat we lease and do not live in, the first editions that we dare not read. In other words, in most legal systems things of the same type may be held by some as necessaries and by others as investments, while many persons hold part of their property as both. In defining and protecting entitlements, powers, and so on, the law does not need expressly and initially to distinguish between these purposes.

Nonetheless, such a distinction is attempted in what follows. It is beyond the author's powers to render the difference in simple English. In 1901 Josef Kohler used the terms *Substanzrecht und Wertrecht*, but the words do not translate readily.[2] In English, then, and for want of better, the expressions used are "things as thing" and "things as wealth".

2. Things as thing

The thesis advanced is that, when faced with things treated for themselves, the common law employs a set of concepts familiar to jurists from any country, such as ownership, possession, and publicity. But this approach is masked by certain habits which are bred into the common law systems and have laid down patterns of vocabulary which tend to control perception. First, when dealing with tangible things, a tenacious common law tradition commands us to distinguish, most scrupulously, real (*i.e.* immovable) property from personal property. The orthodoxy will be briefly summarised and followed by some notes of respectful disagreement.

Tangible immovables

The familiar doctrine attributes to the law of real property two sets of distinctive features concerning on the one hand the concepts said to be applicable, and on the other the remedies said to be available. As to the first, it is traditionally taught that real rights are to be classified by time: the learning of the "estate in land".[3] More precisely, all the holders of a *jus in re sua* have similar rights in space, rights of possession and use; it is the time from or for which these rights may be enjoyed that distinguishes one interest from another. Thus, some may hold them for ever, some for life, some for a time certain, from now, or from some future moment. All possess the power of alienation, but what they transfer is the entitlement to exercise the rights only for and from the relevant time. As to judicial protection of real rights, traditional doctrine insists that the courts are bound to restore them in kind only to the person ousted from real property.

---

[2] (1901) 91 *Archiv für die Civilistische Praxis* 155. Kohler's lengthy and lively account will be referred to below, but it covers only a few of the issues here addressed, and does so in the very different context of German legal dogmatics. Basically, he classes as substance rights the traditional figures of ownership, *usufruct*, and *usus*. The oldest value right is the pledge, but Kohler extends the general category to cover certain land burdens and the interests of some partners and of company shareholders. He emphasises the way in which the growth of value rights has greatly facilitated transfers of wealth, but does not develop any general concepts of real subrogation of the fund.

[3] See, for instance, Lawson and Rudden, *The Law of Property* (1982) pp. 88–98.

Those dispossessed of other things must, in principle, be content with substitute protection in the form of money.

A quite different view may be put forward. To treat immovable property as the object of entitlements corresponding to the classic estates in land (and all the possible combinations thereof) was found to be bad for the land, for families, and for the market, and was forbidden in England in 1882. The property legislation of that year (above all the Settled Land Act) is largely and fundamentally *jus cogens*, its application cannot be set aside by private parties, and it sets up a legal regime under which the object itself can always be sold. This statutory technique was strengthened and extended in 1925[4] so that it applies to virtually all situations where the legal relation between a person and an immovable object is less than that of absolute individual ownership. If the entitlement amounts to such an interest then, of course, it needs no legislator to say that the thing can be disposed of.

The details of the relevant legislation are too technical to be rehearsed in a brief paper. In general, however, the statutes ensure that where more than one person is entitled to the immovable, whether successively or concurrently, then their legal relation is shifted from the immovable treated as thing to the immovable treated as wealth. The thing itself can always be sold, though not for the exclusive benefit of the seller, and not automatically at the behest of the seller's creditors. To curtail the risk of this being attempted, the practice imposed by the legislation seeks to ensure that the price will be paid into safe hands.

Tangible movables

Where chattels are concerned, orthodox theory tells us that they may not be subjected to the conceptual structure appropriate to realty. In other words the relation between a person and a tangible movable is not that of the estate concept, but is one of ownership, possession, or security. This view is put forward by deservedly eminent jurists such as Roy Goode[5] and J. C. Gray,[6] yet it provokes two responses. First, the relation just described is virtually the same as that which today applies to realty when the immovable is treated for itself. Secondly, movables treated as investments are subject to the same legal regime as that of realty when treated as wealth, *i.e.* each movable is merely an entirely replaceable element in a portfolio. As such it may be held for life, in tail, and so on, in other words is subject to the familiar calculus of estate, and the risk of perpetuity.

---

[4] By the Law of Property Act 1925, the Settled Land Act 1925, and the Administration of Estates Act 1925.
[5] *Commercial Law* (1982) pp. 54–56.
[6] Gray, *The Rule against Perpetuities* (1942) pp. 821–826.

Industrial/intellectual intangibles

When we turn to intangibles, we see first that the fundamentals of the law of industrial and intellectual property are similar everywhere. Since the field developed outside the heartland of the two great traditions (it is in neither Justinian's Digest nor Coke's Institutes) both civil and common law have some initial difficulty in applying to it their basic concepts. Thus it is not treated at all in the great models supplied by the *Code Napoléon* and the *Bürgerliches Gesetzbuch*. It is covered in some civil codes of this century (Italy 1942, Russia 1964) but is dealt with, not in the section on property law, but in its own separate chapters. Furthermore, traditional civil law jurists are reluctant to speak of owning a patent or copyright.[7] In somewhat similar fashion, the common law hesitates to apply to this field the sacred learning of estates.

Yet all the doctrine accepts that the modern law allocates protection to those who hold patents, trademarks, copyrights and the like; that this protection is available *erga omnes* and thus constitutes, for a number of years, a zone of monopoly; that the person entitled can so to speak "abandon" the good by giving it away for nothing; can sell it outright or make another person pay for a licence to use it; and that the economic value which it has is available to its holder's creditors and so can be used as security for debts owed to them. What is noticeable is that, in general and as far as possible, the same basic notions of ownership, trusteeholding, possession, and security can be applied to all these intangible assets when they are treated for themselves. As their name, the noun "property" is now accepted, and German jurists describe a patent holder's entitlement as a "real right".[8] At the same time these things may play the role of investments for a pension fund or private fortune and so may become, at one remove, the objects of estates, contingent interests, and the whole traditional gamut of the classic land law.

Intangible claims

There is another great class of intangible objects for which English seems to have no intelligible word. For the simple *créance* or *Forderung*, our legislator uses the enigmatic phrase "things in action" (Law of Property Act 1925, section 136). Yet English has one short verb to denote the relation between the object and the person entitled to it; the obligation which is owed me, I *own*; I can "destroy" it by presenting it to the debtor; I can give it away; and it is, of course, available to my creditors and can be used as security for my debts. For well over a century these intangible entitlements, together with stocks and shares, have constituted by far the larger part of the wealth of any modern economy: the National Debt must have its correlative creditors.

---

[7] For instance, Kohler, *op. cit.* above, n.2, at p. 162.
[8] Mincke, *Die Akzessorietät des Pfandrechts* (1987) p. 94.

Furthermore, although these assets are intangible, long custom reifies them. From about 1,200 to 1,800 claims on the public purse were embodied in bits of wood, tallies, and were assignable at common law by simple delivery; an important fact overlooked by the generalisations which assert that choses in action were not assignable at common law. Since the days of the tally, the practice of treating such assets as corporeal is facilitated by the fact that their existence is normally attested by writing, treasury bonds, share certificates, commercial paper and so on. Today's short-dated gilt is quite recognisably the descendant of the tally. These intangible entitlements are thus brought into the physical world and recognised by their papers. All of this is merely a practical expression of the fact that, when treated for themselves, they are as far as possible subject to the same legal regime of ownership, possession, and security or pledge as that which governs tangible objects.

However, such assets have usually no significance beyond pecuniary value. Unlike other things, therefore, their primary function is to be treated as investment, as vessels into which wealth is poured and stored. As replaceable elements of a portfolio they may be the object, along with tangible things, of any legal relation, including that of estates.

3. Things as wealth

In examining things treated as wealth, or as investments of wealth, they must be considered first as members of a class and then as a class properly so-called. When treated as wealth, things do not, of course, change their physical form: they are still tangible or intangible, movable or immovable. But as each is perceived only as the external form of a value, no member of the class enjoys any privileged status. As an investment each individual object is treated in terms, not of its own inherent qualities, but of its opportunity cost. This last function betokens an important fact: as an item in a portfolio every thing can be changed or converted. Nothing is unique.

When one such object is replaced by another we must turn momentarily to the legal regime applicable to things treated as thing. If, for instance, it is decided, for reasons of investment strategy or tax planning, to sell a mansion house and a racehorse so as to buy some shares and an aeroplane, each of the four transactions will be governed by its particular legal rules, with its own form of transfer, its own register, and so on. But from the point of view of the portfolio, the sales and subsequent purchases effect merely a real subrogation whereby the things sold are transmuted into the sale price which then becomes the things bought. The fund has not changed: the accounts record on one side the disappearance of two assets expressed as sums of money, and on the other the acquisition of the price; the purchase money then leaves the accounts and the shares and patent enter them at asset value. The overall balance is still the same. Maitland said all this first, and put it best: "The idea of the trust-fund which is dressed up (invested) now as land and now as current coin, now as shares and now as debentures seems to me one of the most remarkable ideas developed by modern English jurisprudence".[9]

This is all very obvious when the portfolio has a single owner. But it is equally true if the fund has been settled (to put it succinctly) "on A for life without impeachment of waste, remainder to any widow who may survive him for life, remainder to his first and other sons successively in tail male, remainder to his sons in tail general, with cross remainders to his daughters in tail, remainder in fee simple to the right heir of A". The entitlement of each, in terms of rights, powers, and value, survives any replacement of one member of the class of investments by some other. The relation between the beneficiaries and the trust property is one which treats things as wealth and not as thing. What matters is not the object as member of the class but the class itself as the object of inherence of the estates intoned above. This class deserves attention both in its function and its management.

Function

As to function, what needs to be emphasised is the implications of the legal regime utilised by the common law to govern the birth, death, and transfer of the rights whose object is a class of investments. That branch of the law was born to deal with land, but it now affects real property not at all. When treated as thing, land can be owned, leased, and mortgaged but since 1882 it cannot be the object of any particular freehold estate: the phrase "fee simple absolute in possession" is merely traditional jargon for ownership or trustee-holding. The sacred Rule against Perpetuities has suffered the same fate. It never applies to things as thing, because as such they are not the subjectmatter of conditional limitations: the thing itself can always be sold. What the rule affects is the contingent entitlements to the subjacent value represented now by the thing, then by its price, and then by some new thing. Our very vocabulary reveals this. In Latin the word *fundus* meant a farm; but "fund" means the abstract value represented by a portfolio of investments. It is this fund whose function it is to form the object of the old concepts of estates, powers of appointment, conditions, and perpetuities.

This can easily be demonstrated from *Berry v Warnett*, which came before the House of Lords in 1982.[10] It was a case on capital gains tax, and that law is of no concern in this paper. What is interesting is the facts. The taxpayer owned shares and debentures in Rothschild Investment Trust Ltd, part in his own name and part through Lloyds Bank (Branches) Nominees Ltd. The two registered holders transferred the property to a company in the tax haven of Guernsey, Investors Trustees Ltd, which was to pay the dividends to the taxpayer for life.

---

[9] Maitland in *Selected Essays* (Hazeltine *et al.* eds. 1936) p. 134. See also Savigny, *System des heutigen Römischen Rechts* (1840 edn.) Vol. I § 56; Sombart, *Der Moderne Kapitalismus* (1919 edn.) Vol. II, pp. 119–20.

[10] 55 T.C. 92.

This leaves, by the application of legal logic, a fee simple absolute in remainder, which was sold to a Jersey company (another tax haven). The life estate was then transferred to a company (which held *pur autre vie*) in an even sunnier haven, the Bahamas. In contemplating the case, the reader is struck by five facts. First of all, this type of scheme is not at all uncommon. Secondly, three companies are created and manipulated as puppets, rather like the slaves to whom the Roman rich would entrust a *peculium*. Thirdly, although the objects involved are the intangible claims represented by shares and debentures, their owner used the ancient conceptual structure of life estate and remainder and then transferred separately each of these entitlements. One arrived in Jersey and one in the Bahamas but, fourthly, the investments as thing (and the share certificates) stayed in Guernsey. And finally, the only authority cited by their Lordships was William Shepherd's *Touchstone of Common Assurances*, first published in 1648.

Management: the trust

While fulfilling the function of being the object of inherence of these limited entitlements (identical with the old freehold estates), the fund needs to be managed. Here, of course, the common law uses the trust, a concept which is very hard to analyse.[11] For the reasons given in the introduction, it seems misleading to explain the trust by speaking of the trustee's legal *ownership*. Although trustees are far more than agents and hold more than a merely obligational claim in relation to the property, they cannot, with impunity, destroy or convert it (and if they do, time never runs in their favour). Nor is the property available to their creditors. One way of looking at the structure is to see the trustee as an office-holder and the property as going with the office. We are familiar enough with this technique in public law, and Honoré in fact points out that "trusteeship is a quasipublic office".[12] Furthermore, that shrewd outsider Max Weber describes the trust concept as *"ein Surrogat des Amtsbegriffs"*.[13]

Another approach is to see the relation between the trustee and the trust property as one between a person and things treated as thing but not as wealth. The utility of this view can be tested by applying it to the strangest thing of all: money. As regards the currency in our pockets, we own a number of tangible objects, coins and notes. We also own the thing in action, the (public law) claim, which the currency embodies (expressly, in the case of English banknotes, which still bear the words "I promise to pay the bearer on demand . . ."). We have unfettered access to all of money's functions. As it is a means of exchange, we can hand it over in return for other things. As it is legal tender, we can use it to extinguish our debts as they fall due. And it is a store of value which we

---

[11] A penetrating modern analysis will be found in Lupoi, *Trusts* (Giuffré, Milan, 1996).
[12] Honoré and Cameron, *Honoré's South African Law of Trusts* (4th ed., 1992) pp. 31, 44.
[13] Weber in *Rechtssoziologie* (Winckelmann ed. 1960) p. 162.

can enjoy to the full by acting irresponsibly, we can throw it into the sea, or simply give it away.[14] Trustees, by contrast, seem to have no access to the value stored in money. They "own" the chattels to the extent that they can recover them from thieves and the like, but if this proves impossible it is not the trustees' fortune which is diminished. They can utilise the currency as a means of exchange and a universal method of payment. But they cannot lawfully get at its value, for that must be stored in whatever replaces the currency, whether a tangible object, or stocks and shares, or the claim represented by a bank account in credit.

The orthodox explanation, given in terms of the traditional distinction between law and equity, provides only an historical and not a rational account of the trust. First, it does not explain the Scottish trust. Secondly, the separate English jurisdictions were fused long ago. And thirdly, the split between legal and equitable "ownership" seems to reflect that between things as thing and things as wealth for, as we have just seen, the trustee has no lawful access to the latter. There is a trace of this in the Law of Property Act 1925 which defines legal estates as "interests . . . in or over land", and calls equitable interests those "in or over land or in the proceeds of sale thereof" (section 205(1)(x)).

It will be objected that the crucial distinction between law and equity makes its appearance in the first clause of the first sentence of that statute, which is, after all, still the major English legislation in this field. Only a limited number of entitlements are, says the Law of Property Act, section 1(1), capable of subsisting "at law". All the rest "take effect as equitable interests". The counter to this objection is to point to section 2 which introduces a quite different, but more important, distinction: that between interests "capable of being over-reached" and the rest.[15] An interest capable of being over-reached is one that treats its object not as thing but as wealth. The same section's machinery for handling this over-reaching is expressed in terms of "capital money" which must, depending on the situation, be paid to the correct person, mortgagee, personal representative, or trustees. Thus what emerges as the crucial distinction of 1925 is cast in terms of the law of *things*, not that of *jurisdiction*. Things are divided, not according to any physical or innate characteristics, but according to their function in the legal relation: are they regarded for their own sake or as interchangeable investments of capital money. The juridical figures within the first class include a number of entitlements which can be "legal" (easements) or "equitable" (restrictive covenants). Those within the second class are interests which can amount to a fee simple absolute in possession (or any lesser estate) but whose function is to act as entitlements over wealth in a fund which may be invested from time to time in all manner of objects.

---

[14] It may be a crime to deface currency, but it seems, in England and Wales, to be lawful to destroy it.
[15] See Section 5 below, "co-ownership".

However it be analysed, the trust concept enables us to organise efficiently the relations between the trustee and a third party, and those between the trustee and the owners of beneficial entitlements. The contract of purchase of any object which forms part of the trust property treats it as thing, the buyer wants to acquire ownership and the usual guarantees of title, quiet possession, freedom from latent defects and so on. Similarly, a mortgage or charge of that object can confer a real right over the thing itself, but it is balanced by the sum advanced which swells the asset value of the fund. For their part the owners of beneficial interests (and their creditors) are concerned with the object as wealth and want their own fortune to be protected. The trust suits both sides because it is at once a screen and a pivot.

The trust-screen

In relation to a buyer, the trustee has the key legal power of sale, given by the trust instrument or by mandatory enactment. If the rights in the fund are held by co-owners, the trustees, who may be the co-owners themselves, hold under a statutory trust for sale of any immovables in the portfolio. If the rights arise among those entitled by succession on death, the personal representatives of the deceased are free to sell any given object in the inheritance; and if they arise by succession *inter vivos*, the life tenant has the statutory power of sale of land and (with judicial consent) of any tangible movables settled with the land. Similar techniques are incorporated by private (as distinct from statutory) provisions into *inter vivos* trusts of personalty, and all these powers of sale are accompanied by the capacity to incur the usual obligations in respect of warranties of title, quiet possession, and so forth.

The trust-pivot

Having disposed of the things and received their price, the trustee turns back to those who own the wealth. The sale has not impoverished them: *pretium succedit in loco rei*, and their rights are simply shifted to the money and to whatever is acquired with it. If they are life tenants they take the dividends, while the remainder (the "bare ownership" of civil law) is still the absolute entitlement to a capital value and to the income it will produce when the life interest ends. Its present "discounted" value can be readily determined.

If, despite all statutory and other precautions, a dishonest trustee sells an object and wrongfully appropriates the price, the buyer is safe. There is nothing particularly English, or "equitable", about the rule protecting a *bona fide* purchaser, for an even wider version is found in many legal systems for the situation where someone who holds a tangible movable with the consent of the owner transfers it (even for nothing) to an innocent acquirer. Furthermore, the civil law of unjustified enrichment ensures in this situation that if the thing is sold the seller owes its previous owner the price, and if given away the donee owes that owner the value. The debt, however, remains just that, *i.e.* part of the law of obligations, so that the defrauded owner is merely an unsecured creditor (*e.g. Burgerliches Gesetzbuch* §§ 816, 932). What may be peculiar to the common law is that it protects the injured beneficiaries also through the law of property, or at least by giving them priority. First of all, they may claim compensation for damage caused them by breach of the trustee's obligation and, to satisfy their claim, may go as unsecured creditors against the trustee's own property; and time never runs against them. But secondly, their relation to the asset sold is shifted to the money received, and they may follow this wealth into a bank account or into anything bought with it. Their right to this substitute thing takes precedence over claims by other creditors of the trustee.

Thus in the trust regime the technique of real subrogation has two functions. The first is peaceful: in an authorised sale by an honest trustee the price replaces the thing sold. The second is more hostile, enabling the beneficiaries to trace and seize anything acquired by breach of trust and, in priority to the trustee's creditors, to use it to satisfy their entitlement. Of course if the trustee destroys the trust property or sells it and squanders the proceeds, the beneficiaries are merely creditors of his or her private assets. But all real rights end with the destruction or disappearance of the object, here, the fund, in which they subsist.

The trusts convention

As a useful summary, it is worth recalling the 1984 Hague Convention on the Recognition of Trusts, which gives us, if not a definition, at least a description of the trust and its functions. The following key extracts help to show the two ways in which things can be treated: as thing or as wealth. Article 2 describes the trust and does so in terms of asset and fund, without mentioning "law" and "equity". The trust's main characteristics are (emphasis added):

> "(a) the assets constitute a fund and are not a part of the trustee's own estate;
> (b) title to the trust assets stands in the name of the trustee or in the name of another person on behalf of the trustee;
> (c) the trustee has the power and the duty, in respect of which he is accountable, to manage, employ or dispose of the assets in accordance with the terms of the trust and the special duties imposed on him by law."

Article 11 imposes on the High Contracting Parties a duty to recognise a trust which, by its own law, has been validly created and continues:

> "Such recognition shall imply, as a minimum, that the trust property constitutes a separate fund ... [and] shall imply in particular,
>
> (a) that personal creditors of the trustee have no recourse against the trust assets;
> (b) that the trust assets shall not form part of the trustee's estate upon his insolvency or bankruptcy;
> (c) that the trust assets shall not form part of the matrimonial property of the trustee or his spouse nor part of the trustee's estate upon his death;
> (d) that the trust assets may be recovered when the trustee, in breach of trust, has mingled trust assets with his own property ...".

These provisions thus protect the trust property from the trustee or the trustee's own creditors. Guarded by these rules, the fund as wealth (but no particular object as thing) may flourish as the object of inherence of the most elaborate, and old-fashioned, complex of "freehold estates". During the life of the trust each item in the fund may be disposed of for value, for it is the subjacent wealth which is the object of the beneficiaries "rights."[16] Those rights are still evaluated (as the freehold estates have long been classified) in terms of the time for which they entitle their holder to the income stream produced by the fund. They may be separated into bundles and allocated to different people, alive or unborn (subject to the perpetuity rule). The determinable, conditional, or absolute life estates, entails, and fees, whether in possession, remainder or expectancy, may all be given away by their owners, or sold, mortgaged or settled, and each owner's creditors may reach his or her share.

Private publicity

Transferees of these interests protect their entitlements in the fund by giving notice to its trustees, so that the trust instrument becomes a private register of dealings in aggregates of wealth, which happens to be invested in individual objects. This simple and inexpensive machinery furnishes a sort of "private publicity" whereby the transferees' rights come to the notice of, and so prevail against, all possible later acquirers of interests in the fund. Were it not so bad a joke, we might suggest that land as thing has its *Grundbuch*, but as wealth its Fundbook.

4. Some hesitations and refinements

It would be preposterous to propose that the suggestions advanced above reveal some new and profounder vision of the law of property; no crudely dyadic system can capture the many complexities of a living law. It is obvious, for instance, that the notion has little to offer as regards the interrelation of private and public law in such fields as planning, public housing, and compulsory purchase. In order to guard against misunderstandings, then, it may be useful to attempt some slight refinements of the distinction proposed and to make a few general observations on its relation to some contemporary complexities, particularly as they appear in the English land law of the late 20th century.

Corporeal/incorporeal

The distinction between things as thing and things as wealth is not the same as that between tangible and intangible (or corporeal/incorporeal). True, it may be rare that an intangible thing will be held for its own sake (although the moral

---

[16] Writing within a very different tradition, Kohler comes close to the view in the text: "value rights have their own nature, quite different from the rights in things, they can be movable while the thing is immovable, and vice versa . . . It is in fact a general feature of a value right that it goes its own way, different from that of the substance right" (*op. cit.* above, n.2, pp. 160–161).

right of an author provides an example). But tangible objects can certainly be held for their own sake or as wealth.

Use value/exchange value

A related comment might well be that the scheme put forward is no more than a ponderous restatement of the distinction between use value and exchange value found in some modern English property texts.[17] All that can be said is that neither of these two terms seems quite to express the points made above. Exchange value suggests a momentary monetary assessment at the time of purchase or sale, whereas the notion of a thing functioning as wealth is intended to detach the act of receipt from that of expenditure and to suggest the enduring subjacent value stored in a fund, where any given thing is merely a transient and entirely replaceable investment. Use is not hard to understand, but use value is very problematic, and its relation with exchange value is quite obscure. "The things which have the greatest value in use have frequently little or no value in exchange. Nothing is more useful than water; but it will purchase scarce anything; scarce anything can be had in exchange for it. A diamond, on the contrary, has scarce any value in use; but a very great quantity of other goods may frequently be had in exchange for it".[18] The problems raised so squarely by Adam Smith are beyond the present author's wit to solve.

A functional distinction

After a careful examination of the use of the word, Honoré concludes that "the investigation of things seems to peter out in a false trail".[19] This paper's distinction between things as thing and things as wealth is cast in terms, not of the meaning of the word thing, nor of the physical nature of any given object, but of the function attributed to the object in the relation being considered. It may well have no part to play in the situation where one person is undisputed, absolute, and unlimited owner, for, as there are no competing interests to manage or protect, there is little point in asking why its owner holds it; in fact, the joy of being absolute owner is that one does not have to answer that kind of question. It is clear, of course, that some things by their very nature are more fitted for one function than the other: we would be unwise to invest our life savings in milk, and unlikely to hold government stock for pure enjoyment. It is very difficult, however, to think of anything which could never, for some eccentric in a liberal legal system, serve one or other of the purposes.[20]

---

[17] See, for instance, Gray, *Elements of Land Law* (1987) pp. 375–376.
[18] *The Wealth of Nations* (1904 edn.) Vol. I, p. 31.
[19] "Ownership" in *Oxford Essays in Jurisprudence* (Guest ed. 1968) p. 107 at 130.
[20] It is within the author's personal knowledge that at least one shareholder in the New River Company Ltd declined to surrender his share certificates when the company was taken over in 1974. The holder preferred the things themselves, worthless as wealth but rich as symbol, to the expectation of dividends offered by the new shares in London Merchant Securities PLC.

As always, money is the mystery since it may be treated as an object or as a function.[21] It is tempting to say that, when considered as a measure, or a store, of value, money is never treated as thing, and that therefore currency held for its own sake would in that regard be chattel, not money. But this does not quite address one of the points made in this paper, namely that even chattels may be treated as things or as wealth. Thus I may hold the currency because I like to look at the coins and notes, treating them as thing, or because I expect their value to rise, treating them as wealth. Yet even here it seems we must distinguish: if their *price* rises, they are being treated as wealth but not as money; if, because of deflation, their *purchasing power* rises, they are money, pure and (anything but) simple.

5. Some modern English land law

This final section offers a few observations on the relation between the theory here proposed and some concepts and problems found in today's land law in England. For reasons of space, the basic background knowledge is taken as read.

Fee simple absolute in possession

The distinction between things as thing and as wealth is not the same as that between realty and personalty, nor as that between land and its purchase price. The contours may overlap, however, and the traditional common law concepts can be found on both sides of the division. Thus "fee simple absolute in possession" may denote a relation to land both as thing and simultaneously as wealth (the ordinary single absolute owner); or to the land as thing alone (where a trustee is tenant in fee simple absolute in possession, the trustee's creditors having no claim against the land's inherent value); or to the land as wealth alone (where it is held on a bare trust, with power to sell). In this last case we have two fees simple absolute in possession, that of the trustee (called "legal") and that of the beneficiary (called "equitable"); but only the latter and his or her creditors have access to the value of the land.

Fee simple in remainder

In modern English law, whether the traditional estates are classified as interests in land or in personalty may depend, not on their function, but on the management regime selected. For instance the tenant in fee simple absolute in remainder has, in that capacity, no relation to the thing as thing. But if at least some of the initial property be land, and if the system selected be that of the strict settlement, then the remainder is, for the purpose of dealing with it *inter vivos* or

---

[21] See Bernd von Maydell, *Geldschuld und Geldwert* (1974) pp. 8–10; Spiros Semitis, "Bemerkungen zur rechtlichen Sonderstellung des Geldes" (1960) 159 *Archiv für die Civilistische Praxis* 406; Georg Simmel, *The Philosophy of Money* (trans. Bottomore and Frisby, 1978); Goode, *Payment Obligations in Commercial and Financial Transactions* (1984) Chap. I.

on death, deemed to be land even though at the time of the relevant disposition all the land has long been sold and the price invested entirely in securities.[22] If the initial management regime be that of the trust for sale, the fee is deemed to have been always personalty. In terms of the distinction drawn in this paper, however, and whether technically called realty or personalty, it is and always was an interest in things as wealth.

Co-ownership

It is a serious question whether, under current English law, the same can be said of all modern co-ownership entitlements. Certain recent English decisions of the House of Lords have, under the doctrine of deemed "conversion" (of land into wealth and vice versa), taken the distinction more seriously, and applied it more rigorously than would the author of this paper. It would take too long to rehearse once more the details of this well-known litigation and legislation,[23] but in essence the problem arises where there are two creditors of a debtor who is registered proprietor (or paper owner) of a dwellinghouse.[24] The creditors are, first, the wife, lover, or some family member who has contributed to the acquisition of the house in such a way as to acquire a claim: as between this claimant and the registered proprietor, the claim is a real right, that of a co-owner, but, being unregistered, it is informal and is not, without more, effective *erga omnes*. The second creditor is a secured lender of the house, who has a claim backed by a (registered) real right. If the debtor's general assets were sufficient to meet both creditors, no problem would arise. But as the only asset is the house, the two creditors' real rights compete for priority.

The particular problem could be solved by a policy decision of the legislator. On the one hand, Parliament might agree that a lender's interest is merely in the thing as wealth, whereas a family member's interest is in the thing as a dwellinghouse, and so be led to lay down a clear if radical rule: that the real right of the creditor of a monetary obligation (the lender) is postponed to that of the creditor of an obligation in kind (the spouse, etc.). But a quite different policy might also be adopted, which held that the burden of a black sheep should fall on its kin rather than on a stranger dealing for value and in good faith; and this would lead to an equally clear if quite contrary rule. The first would not solve a conflict between a family creditor and a good faith buyer (as opposed to lender) and, in any case, no sweeping solution has ever been adopted.

Consequently, the courts were thrown back on the mechanics of the 1925 legislation which (until amended in 1996) imposed a trust for sale on co-owned

---

[22] Settled Land Act 1925, s.75(5), replacing SLA 1882, s.26(5). Such strict settlements as survive are doomed by the Trusts of Land and Appointment of Trustees Act 1996.

[23] For a concise statement see "Transfer of Land: Overreaching: Beneficiaries in Occupation" (1989) 188 Law Com. References to more recent material may conveniently be found in Maudsley and Burn, *Land Law: Cases and Materials* (1992) pp. 271 *et seq*.

[24] The problem has also occurred where the title was not (and was not required to be) registered but, for the limited purposes of this paper, such cases may be ignored.

property and imputed an overreaching effect only to sales effected by at least two trustees. The courts felt compelled by the fundamentals of that system to hold that the solution to the conflict between family creditor and monetary creditor might depend on the number of registered proprietors who effected the relevant transaction.[25] If the mortgage was effected by only one, the family creditor in occupation would win, her situation being described in terms of the thing itself: "to describe the interests of spouses in a house jointly bought to be lived in as a matrimonial home as merely an interest in the proceeds of sale, or rents and profits until sale, is just a little unreal".[26] But if the relevant disposition were made by two or more registered proprietors, the stranger wins, the interests of the family occupant being treated as wealth: "The beneficiary's possession or occupation is no more than a method of enjoying in specie the rents and profits pending sale in which he is entitled to share . . . ".[27] The reasons cited are not, of course, the only ones which led their Lordships to their conclusions. But they do illustrate the somewhat extreme distinctions which, in the absence of modern legislative solution, the judges are forced to draw.[28]

Leases

Like the fee, but in a rather different way, the lease is to be found on both sides of the division. If freehold owners treat their land as an investment they will often lease it. The tenant in turn may occupy the land and use it for its own sake, or may treat it as a source of wealth and sublease it. It is interesting to note in passing that, as a general principle, the numerous 20th-century statutes protecting farming, business, and residential tenants do so only for those who occupy.

Security interests

The final topic deserves a slightly more historical outline, for pledge seems to be the oldest of the institutions in which a person treats an object only and

---

[25] The Law of Property Act, speaking of course in terms of "legal" and "equitable" interests, provides that, in several common situations, a buyer of the former takes free of the latter whether he or she knows of them or not, provided the price is paid to the correct persons: s.2(1). Co-ownership was subjected to a trust for sale (ss.34, 36) and the requisite number of sellers to receive this prophylactic payment was at least two (s.27).

[26] *Williams & Glynn's Bank Ltd v. Boland* [1981] A.C. 487, *per* Lord Wilberforce at 507.

[27] *City of London BS v. Flegg* [1988] A.C. 54, *per* Lord Oliver at 83. His Lordship also (at 82–83) cited with approval the words of Cross L.J. that "Even to hold that [tenants in common] have an interest in the land for a limited period . . . would be inconsistent with the trust for sale . . ." (*Irani Finance Ltd v. Singh* [1971] Ch. 59 at 80).

[28] There are a number of much deeper analyses of this problem. Outstanding examples are: Anderson, "The Proper, Narrow Scope of Equitable Conversion in Land Law" (1984) 100 L.Q.R. 86; Harpum, "Overreaching, Trustees' Powers and the Reform of the 1925 Legislation" [1990] C.L.J. 277; Harris, "Legal Doctrine and Interests in Land" in Eekelaar and Bell (eds.), *Oxford Essays in Jurisprudence: Third Series* (1987) p. 167 especially at pp. 177–178. The Trusts of Land and Appointment of Trustees Act 1996 makes the formal structure much simpler and abolishes conversion.

always in terms of its value. The lender's interest is in repayment, and the thing pledged is entirely ancillary to that aim. Initially there is no right whatever to the thing as thing, for the Roman pledgee steals, who uses the thing itself.[29] Again, at Rome if a power of sale were given to and exercised by the lender, the borrower was entitled to any excess over the loan, interest or costs. Thus the lender was confined to a relation with the thing as wealth. Terms of the transaction (*lex commissoria*) whereby the pledgee might acquire ownership (and thereby treat the thing as thing) were forbidden by Constantine in AD 326. The only way the lender could acquire the thing to use at will was by a kind of foreclosure petition (*impetratio dominii*) addressed to the Emperor.[30]

In its own way, and of course with its own vocabulary, English law has traversed much the same path. The pledge is both simple and safe for both parties. But, as possession is transferred, it suffers from the fact that the lender's interest is purely in the thing as wealth, yet the borrower is obliged to give up any claim to the thing as thing for the period during which he or she is enjoying the wealth, *i.e.* the loan, which it has procured. This necessary severing of the possessory link between owner and object may be psychologically effective in stimulating repayment and redemption, but may be economically inefficient in denying the borrower the use of the object.

In the mortgage transaction (*hypotheca*), the lender's interest remains monetary, and the powers are much the same as those of the pledgee described above. The borrower, however, is enabled both to charge the thing as security for an advance and thus to realise some of the capital embedded in it, and simultaneously to enjoy the thing as thing by retaining possession for himself or herself; the entitlement to possession may also be exploited (by user, lease, hire and the like) in order to earn income. Further refinements are common. The object of the charge may be a thing as thing or a thing as wealth. One can lend on the security of a charge on a fee simple absolute in possession (whether held by a single owner or by a trustee with the appropriate power to mortgage) and protect the right by entry in the Land Register. One may, just as prudently, lend on the security of a mortgage of a fee simple absolute in remainder, and protect the right by notice to the trustees, *i.e.* by a kind of entry in the fund register.

The oldest and most stable means of treating a thing as wealth is to take it, or a mortgage of it, as security for the loan you make. This now forms the basis for one of the youngest and most mobile devices, by which first mortgages on English homes are transmuted into floating-rate bearer notes listed on the Luxembourg Stock Exchange: the magic of securitisation.[31]

---

[29] J 4.1.6.
[30] C 8.34 & 8.35.
[31] For the modern UK system see Bonsall, *Securitisation* (1990); Ferran, *Mortgage Securitisation* (1992). The development almost justifies the exuberance of Kohler's conclusion that "the creation of value rights alongside those in objects is one of the great achievements of humanity" (*op. cit.* above, n.2, p. 207).

13

Hohfeldian Use-Rights in Property

J.E. PENNER*

In this paper I shall examine one of the reasons why property is often considered to be a "bundle of rights".[1] It is not obviously wrong to think that an owner's right to his property can be meaningfully explained as a bundle of various rights to use it, which together comprise the total legal effect of owning it. Thus explained, property is a bundle of use-rights. On this version of the "property is a bundle of rights" view, we own a thing when we have a sufficiently large bundle of rights to use it in various ways, given a broad definition of "use". So, for example, if one has the right to consume a thing, to destroy it, to manage it for income, to transform it into a product, to sell it for profit, and so on, one is almost certainly the owner of that thing.[2] This view of the bundle of rights was the one that both the majority and the dissenting judges in the Supreme Court of California relied upon to decide whether John Moore had a property right to his spleen and other bodily cells of scientific interest.[3] The legal status of owner is therefore a matter of degree on this view: to determine that one has property in something is to determine the degree to which one has the rightful use of it, or the scope of one's use-rights in it. One reason for believing all of this, which I shall consider here, is that such a view may seem to follow from the well-known Hohfeldian analysis of rights.[4]

The Hohfeldian orientation to property

The Hohfeldian underpinning to the bundle of rights picture of property is well-known.[5] There are essentially two elements. First, there is Hohfeld's famous characterisation of rights *in personam* and rights *in rem* as "paucital" and "multital" rights, respectively:

---

* Department of Law, Brunel University.
[1] I have criticised this perspective on property in detail in Penner, "The 'Bundle of Rights' Picture of Property" (1996) 43 *U.C.L.A. Law Review* 711, but not in regard to the issues raised here.
[2] The classic specification of these different rights, and other incidents of property, is Honoré's "Ownership" in Guest (ed.), *Oxford Essays in Jurisprudence* (1961) pp. 104–147.
[3] See *Moore v. The Regents of the University of California*, 793 P.2d 479 (Cal.1990).
[4] Hohfeld, *Fundamental Legal Conceptions* (Conn., 1923).
[5] See Munzer, *A Theory of Property* (1990) pp. 15–27.

> "A paucital right, or claim (right *in personam*), is either a unique right residing in a person (or group of persons) and availing against a single person (or single group of persons); or else it is one of a *few* fundamentally similar, yet separate, rights availing respectively against a few definite persons. A multital right, or claim (right in *rem*), is always *one* of a large *class* of *fundamentally similar* yet separate rights, actual and potential, residing in a *single* person (or single group of persons) but availing *respectively* against persons constituting a very large and indefinite class of people."[6]

Secondly, we have Hohfeld's description of the fundamental legal conceptions as relations between individuals all of which constitute different kinds of right, *viz*. claim-rights, liberties,[7] powers and immunities; these rights are distinguished by their respective jural correlates, *viz*. duties, no-rights, liabilities, and disabilities. Combining these two elements to illuminate property in land, the analysis goes as follows:

> "Suppose, for example, that A is fee-simple owner of Blackacre. His "legal interest" or "property" relating to the tangible object that we call land consists of a complex aggregate of rights (or claims), privileges, powers, and immunities. First, A has multital legal rights, or claims, that others, respectively, shall *not* enter on the land, that they shall not cause physical harm to the land, etc. . . . Second, A, has an indefinite number of legal privileges of entering on the land, using the land, harming the land, etc. . . . Third, A has the power to alienate his legal interest to another, . . . to create a life estate in another . . . to create a privilege of entrance in any other person by giving "leave and licence". . . . Fourth, A has an indefinite number of legal immunities . . . Thus A has the immunity that no ordinary person can alienate A's legal interest or aggregate of jural relations to another person . . .".[8]

Thus the Hohfeldian scheme represents the owner as having an indefinite number of legal rights in respect of the property, and this bundle has two dimensions. First, because these rights are *in rem*, each particular right held against one legal subject is matched by an indefinitely large number of "fundamentally similar" rights held against the multitude of other legal subjects in the jurisdiction. Secondly, there are the different kinds of right – different claim-rights, liberties, powers and immunities.

There are a number of problems with Hohfeld's analysis of rights, not all of which are pertinent here.[9] What bears on our understanding of property is the

---

[6] Hohfeld, *op. cit.* above, n.4, at p. 72.
[7] The term Hohfeld uses is "privileges", but no one else does, and for all intents and purposes he means "liberties": see *ibid*. at pp. 44–50.
[8] *ibid*. at pp. 96–97.
[9] See Raz, *Concept of a Legal System* (2nd ed., 1980) pp. 179–181. With respect to property, one point is particularly important. Hohfeld appears utterly blind to liabilities which do not correlate with powers, that is, liabilities to the operation of law, many of which are of the last consequence as regards title to property. For example, we must not confuse the equitable share in a legal estate in land which arises on the basis of constructive trust because of the behaviour of the parties, that is by operation of law, and the similar share which is only created by the exercise of the powers of the court, as in the standard view of proprietary estoppel. See, *e.g.* Gray, *Elements of Land Law* (2nd ed., 1993) pp. 356–368.

general orientation of his scheme. The genius of Hohfeld's scheme, or fatal flaw, depending on your perspective, is his disintegrating urge to define each legal relation in its most spare possible form. Thus, every legal relation can only exist as between two individuals. Any legal relation which might more naturally refer to more than two is broken down to achieve this result. It is therefore impossible on his scheme to describe a general duty owed to everyone (*i.e.* all subjects of the law), or rights and duties in respect of a practice which involves the participation of all. Secondly, every legal relation can only refer to the act or forbearance of one of the parties to it. Thus, as we shall see, one cannot have a right to walk the streets which correlates with a duty on someone else (much less on everyone else) not to act in such a way as to interfere with one's doing so: such a relation comprises acts of both the right-holder and the duty-ower, and therefore is too complex under the Hohfeldian scheme, and must be broken down. The consequences of the Hohfeldian approach, as I hope to show, is that it leads us down a false turning in our exploration of the complex normative practice we call "property", and I shall therefore concentrate on those aspects of the scheme which make understanding property particularly difficult. It will make things clearer if I give a thumbnail sketch of my own view of property, which I have defended at length elsewhere,[10] but which I trust is plausible enough to convince the reader to proceed.

Property as the right of exclusive use

"Property" is a legal term of art which describes an institutionalised practice, the practice of the way we deal with things. It takes some doing to elaborate what counts as a "thing", why our labour is not a thing as far as the practice of property is concerned[11] but land or a sandwich is, but for the purposes of this paper we must live in faith that such an elaboration is possible.[12] The practice is framed principally in terms of what I have called "the right of exclusive use". If we describe that right properly, and elaborate what it entails in particular legal contexts, I have contended, one is able to make sense of the idea that property really is about the right to things, that is, a single, definable right to things, and thus is not to be understood as a bundle of rights to a thing. Here, two features of framing property in terms of the "right to exclusive use of a thing" are pertinent.

First, "use" has to be elaborated. The right protects not just "use", but also the owner's determination of the way that his property may be used. It is quite clear that we would generally baulk at the idea that property ownership gave us the right to the use of a thing, but not the right to decide which use that was. A simple point, perhaps, yet one I think which is often subconsciously glossed to ill effect. Concentration on "use" *per se*, rather than on the determination of

---

[10] Penner (1996) above, n.1; Penner *The Idea of Property in Law* (1997).
[11] For an excellent discussion of the considerations which indicate that labour is not a thing for the purposes of property, see Harris, "Who Owns My Body?" (1996) 16 O.J.L.S. 55 at pp. 65–75.
[12] I give one in Chap. 5 of Penner (1997) *op. cit.* above, n.10.

use, leads one to emphasise the tangible contact an owner has with his property at the expense of his intentions about disposing of the property in a way that may serve his interests, in particular his shared use of the property with others, or his licence or transfer of the property to others. The use of others is not a matter of the owner himself engaging the property and using it. Yet it is fully within the owner's determination of the use of the property and is equally protected by the right to property.[13] The right of exclusive use I describe comprises this broader notion of use and would be better framed in terms of a phrase like "the right exclusively to determine the disposition of the property" if that were not so long.

Secondly, our interest in the use of things (in this expanded sense) is the reason which grounds the institution of property, and thus the right of exclusive use. I hold the view that in order to make sense of norms, such as rights, duties, powers and so on, we must take into account the interest or interests which they serve or protect.[14] The interest we have in things is using them in various ways, which is why the right is framed in terms of use. Rights, however, correlate with duties, so when we look to understand the nature of any particular right we must always remember that it is a right-duty relation which is in question. Thus any right has in reality two sides: the right side and the duty side. Right-duty relationships protect interests of the right-holder, which is why naming a right often equally names the interest at stake, as the right to freedom of assembly does. But the protection of the interest is afforded through the imposition of duties on others. My right to my property correlates with the duty on others not to interfere with it. In this sense, the duties are the legal means by which the protection of the interest is legally institutionalised. But the law does not impose duties willy nilly. The imposition of duties is a measured response to the legal recognition of the (significant) interest at stake. The duties are crafted taking into account a number of factors, such as the importance of the interest, the relationship of the right-holders to the duty-owers, the knowledge a duty-ower may be expected to have, and principles like the harm principle, which, roughly speaking, rules out the imposition of duties to act morally unless such a duty is required to prevent harm to others. Thus the right-duty relationship manifests not only the interest of the right-holder, which justifies its institution, but to the particular means, the particular duties, the law sees fit to impose to protect it. Property protects our use of things in a very particular way, that is by prohibiting the interference of others. Thus the right of exclusive use does not serve or protect our interest in using things by *enabling* the owner to use his property in the way he wants – owning a piano does not entitle one to piano lessons – but

---

[13] Surely this is right; the point of property is not to enforce social isolation, but to allow the exclusion of those others whose interference would upset one's determination of use. That will require the exclusion of most others, but not all.

[14] See Penner (1997) above, n.10, Chap. 2. I rely extensively on the work of Professor Raz; see Raz, *Practical Reason and Norms*, (2nd ed., Princeton, N.J., 1990); "Legal Rights" (1984) 4 *Oxford Journal of Legal Studies* at p. 1, and "On the Nature of Rights" (1984) 93 *Mind* at p. 194.

only by providing him a realm of liberty, or freedom from constraint, in which he may determine its use without interference. Property is neither simply a right to exclude nor simply a right to use, but a right framed in terms of exclusion whose purpose is to serve and protect the interest in use. Therefore on my view anyone who takes one of either "use" or "exclusion" to be the essence of property misses the mark. In formal, practical terms, the right to property is a right of exclusion. But in justificatory terms, *i.e.* in terms of what interest property is there to serve and protect, *i.e.* what the right to property is a right to, property is a right to use.

Difficulties with applying Hohfeld's scheme to property

Liberties and claim-rights

For Hohfeld, A's claim right, or right "properly so called" correlates with a duty upon someone else, B, that B act or not act in some way. One cannot have a claim right to do (or not to do) something oneself. In contrast, a liberty-right is a right to do (or not to do) something oneself, but it does not correlate with a duty on any other person; it may only correlate with the no-right that someone else has. If I have a liberty to harvest clams *vis-à-vis* some other person, that person has "no right" that I don't harvest them. These requirements concerning the description of rights and liberties makes the scheme fiendishly hard to apply, since it is so at odds with our normal practice of thinking about and describing rights.[15] Thus, on the Hohfeldian scheme, since one cannot have the claim-right to do something oneself, one cannot have a right "properly so-called" to vote, or marry, or express oneself. Rights only refer to the duties others have to do or not to do things. "Rights" to do things oneself only fit into the category of "liberties", which correlate to "no-rights". I have a liberty to express myself if no one else has a right in regard to my expressing myself (if, in other words, I have no correlative duty in regard to my expressing myself). Thus rights to do things are framed in terms of the absence of legal norms. For this reason we are going to run into trouble describing use-rights in property as they are normally understood, since we normally think of these rights as rights to do something which correlate with duties on others. If I own a packet of cigarettes, my (use-)right to smoke them is normally regarded as correlating with a duty on others not to interfere with my smoking them. On the Hohfeldian scheme, there are no use-rights of this kind *per se*. Such a situation can only be described with two rights: my liberty to smoke my cigarettes (a right I have to do something) correlating with other's no-rights *and* my claim-right that you not interfere with my doing so.

Hart and Raz explain rights without similar counter-intuitive requirements. Their basic position is that the notion of right applies broadly to protect any kind of legally-recognised interest, including the right-holder's interest in doing or not doing something himself. Thus, one can have a right to a liberty, for

---

[15] Finnis, "Some Professorial Fallacies About Rights" (1971–1972) 4 *Adelaide Law Review* 377.

example, a right to freedom of expression, which correlates with a duty on others not to interfere with one's expression. As Raz has stated, whenever we claim a right we claim the existence of a duty on another (or others) of some kind.[16] On this view the liberty-"no"-right correlation is simply false as a description of legal relations. The liberty-no-right correlation is a description of the absence of any legal norm, not of the institution of one.

The Hohfeldian description of claim-rights and liberties has a pernicious consequence. If Hohfeldian liberties are regarded as legal relations, as rights freed from any necessary correlation to duties, then any freedom from constraint counts as a right, *i.e.* a liberty right. Some of these liberties, of course, will be paired with claim-rights, as is, for example, my liberty/claim-right to smoke the cigarettes I own: but not all. The ones that are not, however, are no less liberty rights for all that. We thus vastly expand the category of legal rights to include "rights" which the law could not care less about and in respect of which the law has never instituted any norms. Furthermore, the scheme does not distinguish between bare liberties of this kind and liberties which the law is not concerned to protect, but which, as Hart points out, benefit as a matter of fact from legal protection, like the liberty to scratch one's head.[17] That liberty is protected because everyone has a duty not to assault other people. Just because many such freedoms from constraint are the result of legal duties does not mean that these freedoms are the legally recognised interests which underlie and therefore shape or define the duty or duties. By contrast, true legal rights precisely reflect their correlative duty or duties, and the correct statement of the right is framed in terms of the interest or interests which justifies the imposition of those duties.[18] The law does not create any duties in order to allow a person to scratch his head, for the law, in this case at least, is not interested in securing trivial benefits. As I have said, to understand the nature of any right-duty relationship which the law institutes we must pay attention to the purposes for which it was instituted. Not every benefit falls within the purpose. This vital distinction is nothing more than the distinction between intended effects and side-effects.

Overlooking these points has a price. On the Hohfeldian scheme, an infinite number of liberties are elevated to rights simply because the test for liberty right-hood is the absence of any specific legal duty which applies to its exercise. This mistaken view is bolstered if, ignoring the distinction between the intended purposes behind the institution of norms and their side-effects, we regard the adventitious legal protection of some liberties as the legal imposition of duties on others to protect those liberties, with the result that we get the pair of claim-right and liberty by sleight of hand. Thus, for example, any liberty to use a thing which the duty not to interfere with property adventitiously protects is transformed into a liberty to use paired with a claim-right that others don't inter-

---

[16] Raz, "Legal Rights", above, n.14, at p. 20.
[17] Hart, *Essays on Bentham*, (1982) p. 171.
[18] See Penner, "The Analysis of Rights", forthcoming *Ratio Juris* (1997).

fere. At this stage we arrive at a perspective from which the idea that the right to property comprises a myriad of use-rights seems eminently plausible, since by this transformation we do seem to have such a myriad of use-rights. We shall return to this point below.

Multital and paucital rights

The multital/paucital analysis of rights *in rem* and rights *in personam* is deeply flawed.[19] Primarily, it simply ignores the fact that there can be rights or duties which are defined in respect of *practices* rather than personal relations between individuals. It is simply not true that each person owes a separate and particular duty to each and every owner in respect of each and every bit of his property. We all owe the single, general duty not to interfere with property that is not our own. It doesn't matter in the least to my understanding of my own duty in respect of the property of others, and thus the way in which I guide my behaviour in respect of that duty, whether I know who happens to own the individual houses I pass walking down the street. My duty does not change in the least if one of the houses is sold to a new owner. Something that is completely extraneous to the compliance with a duty, such as the knowledge of who owns the particular car I refrain from taking for a joy-ride, is not properly comprised in the description of that duty. This is simple common sense, and yet in Hohfeldian terms we cannot even express it, for any legal relation must exist between two specified[20] individuals.

The upshot of the multital rights analysis is that any right *in rem* is a bundle of rights, by definition. If we are willing to accept this kind of multiple rights analysis, it seems to follow that no further harm can come from splintering the right of exclusive use into a myriad of liberties to do this or that with one's property, each liberty constituting a legal relation with one other subject of the law. True, neither dimension of the bundle conceptually depends on the other. One might hold that the multital/paucital view is wrong, but subscribe to the fractionation of the right of exclusive use into a spectrum of individual use-rights of various kinds. Or one might accept that the right to property is the single

---

[19] See Penner (1997) *op. cit.* above, n.10, Chap. 2.
[20] *Specified*, not *specifiable*. Of course we might always in any particular instance specify the individual owners who currently benefit from my complying with my duty not to interfere with property; they are the owners who are within my scope of potential interference. And we can, at least theoretically, go through the burdensome task of listing all the subjects of a legal system and writing out the criss-crossing duties they owe to each other in respect of their individual property. But we don't, and we take no notice of the fact that we might do so in the way we govern our behaviour. Practical norms have to have practical content; there is no individual interpersonal relation-like content to an impersonal duty like the one not to interfere with the property of others. Hohfeld cannot dodge this point by making reference to the obvious fact that remedies for transgressions are always *in personam*, for Hohfeld clearly believed in a distinction between primary and secondary rights and duties; see Hohfeld, *op. cit.* above, n.4, at pp. 69–70, 111.

right of exclusive use I favour, yet hold that an owner holds an indefinite number of multital rights of exclusive use. But each of the two dimensions of the disintegration are natural outcomes of the general orientation of Hohfeld's scheme to analyse by parts in order to work a conceptual disintegration of complex legal relations. I hope it is now apparent how this would give credence to the "bundle of rights" picture of property. In particular, I think the scheme gives credence to the view that the right to property is composed of a series of use-rights, since it is plausible to claim that on an expansive definition of use like the one I have employed myself, above, a comprehensive series of use-rights might seem capable of exhaustively capturing all the content of the right to property. Nevertheless, I hope to show that the appearance is misleading.

Use-rights

There would seem to be no more secure proposition about the right to property than that it encompasses, or protects, or simply is, a right to use. As I have said, this is roughly, but only roughly, correct. The liberty to determine how things are to be used without the interference of others is the interest underlying the right to property, and the right to property is only explicable if we take that interest into account, since that interest justifies its legal institution and therefore shapes the contours of the right. Nevertheless, if we only consider our interests in treating some things as property we will fail to characterise it properly. There are many ways of serving that interest, in the same way that there are many ways of skinning a cat. The particular means of protecting this interest that concerns us here is the practice of property, and to describe this particular means we must have reference to the actual duties correlating to the right to property that the law imposes. Thus it is not difficult to point out problems which will arise when we try to define property in terms of use-rights.

Defining property in terms of use-rights clearly carries the imprint of Hohfeld's analysis. Failing to distinguish between mere liberties and liberties which are actually protected by rights, it does not allow us to distinguish an appropriate level of analysis which would generate a definitive use-right (a liberty to use), or a definitive bundle of them. The trivial and essential have equal standing when a correlation to "no-rights" is the test of membership. Secondly, the definition of use-right itself in this way, *i.e.* as a *liberty* to use, obscures the essential reference to the correlative duty that is part and parcel of any right. So, in the Hohfeldian mindset, treating use-rights as a defining feature of property disengages the interests protected by property from the means of their legal, institutionalised protection.

While the determination of the use of things is the interest underlying the right to property, no particular uses are favoured by law, and so none are individuable out of the right to property. Furthermore, and partly in consequence of this, the right to property does not *enable* use; rather, the right to property correlates with a duty on all but the owner of a thing not to interfere with it. Thus, the use of a thing by an owner is not enabled, rather the disabling of an owner's use is inhibited, because interferences are prohibited. Nor is the use of property positively required: in general we have no obligation to actively use our property in order for it to remain ours.[21]

In view of this, there is simply no basis in the legal institution of property rights to individuate or identify particular use-rights as legally recognised elements of the bundle. The picture that emerges is one we would expect from framing property in terms of the right of exclusive use, not a bundle of use-rights: the use of a thing guaranteed by property is co-extensive with the duty of non-interference imposed on others, not co-extensive with some (as yet unproduced) canonical itemisation of particular use-rights. Property does not endow an owner with a right to any particular set of uses of a thing (try thinking of any particular use or set of uses which would realistically reflect the ownership of all items of property, from a copyright to a piece of land), but rather protects his pre-existing non-legal powers to determine the use of a thing according to his own intelligence, talents, and magnanimity, whether extensive or paltry. What is essential to grasp here is that property endows an owner with no powers or capacities to use a thing whatsoever. It only protects what he otherwise already had, but was subject in the case of his control over things to the interference of others.

At first glance this will seem contentious, because it is clear that owners do have the legal power to licence the use of their property and transfer it to others, and so change the existing pattern of legal norms: licensees and transferees have rights they did not have before, and they arise through the exercise of an owner's legal powers. But these powers merely recognise pre-existing "social" powers a possessor of a thing already has regardless of whether there is a legal practice of property. No one is going to say that my ability to build a house on a patch of the earth arises because a legal practice affords protection to my doing so. Yet neither does my capability to share a bottle of wine, or give my guest a lamb chop for dinner; that social capability exists because I live in a society that understands what it is to share and give – the law did not create that understanding, though of course legal norms may shape it. The reason why the law must institute this recognition of pre-existing social capabilities in the form of legal powers, whereas the law need not do so in the case of my protected ability to build a house, *i.e.* by recognising a specific use-right, is explicable in terms of the general duty of non-interference. Because I am not necessarily connected to any of my property, it might as well be someone else's, anyone else's. Thus the duty on others, to be effective, must apply to everyone; this is the only appropriate "default" position. In order, however, to allow me the full use of my property, which includes my use of it with others, I must have the power to release those with whom I want to share the property or to whom I want to give it from their duty to exclude themselves from it in this instance.

---

[21] There are of course exceptions, such as the right of any person to a compulsory licence of a patent on the ground it is not being worked: Patents Act 1977 (c.37) s.48 (1), (3).

Hohfeldian Use-Rights in Property 173

A legal power, the power to alter the normative landscape in this way, is the only means of doing so. The interest underlying this power is the same interest underlying the general right of exclusive use, the determination of the use of one's property. The institution of this power is merely a legal recognition of the fact that anyone who would determine the use of a thing may wish to do so in a social context. That legal recognition does not, however, turn such social uses into the objects of particular reified use-rights which can take their place in a defined bundle, any more than the protection of a liberty to build a house on one's land does so; while I have the power to licence others to use my land just as much as I have the right to use it myself, I do not have a use-power or a use-right to throw a party that forms an elemental right in the bundle any more than I have a right to play solitaire. The power to share and give extends the ambit of my use, but it does not identify any one use or any series of uses which can be isolated and framed as individual rights.

Another tack which is sometimes taken to explain property in terms of use-rights is to treat these rights as rights to the value of using property. On this understanding, use-rights are transformed into rights to exchange-values, since these use-values are determined by the market. In the first place this view is susceptible to the same problem as use-rights simpliciter; if we cannot identify any list of use-rights, defining any list of value-rights which depend upon identifying valuable uses will be no more successful. There is a deeper problem though. It is true that property protects the value of a thing to the extent that the duty of non-interference protects whatever value an owner can extract from it in a condition of non-interference. In the same way, the right not to be assaulted protects the market value of an individual's bodily security. Nevertheless, the right to property is not the right to the value of the uses that an owner may make of it. The law is, in general, completely blind to the value that anyone else might put on the use of a thing,[22] in the same way that the right to bodily security is blind to the value of the use that an individual, or someone else, might make of his body. That is to say, the law does not ensure in any way that an owner achieves any value from his ownership while it is his. A guarantee of non-interference does not guarantee successful or valuable exploitation. This is a crucial point. While the result of property ownership might be that an owner can capture the market or exchange value of a thing, this result derives not merely from his having the right to property, but from his having exchange rights, *i.e.* those rights which arise because individuals may participate in the practice of contract. It is the individual's exploitation of his property rights *and* his contract rights together which will secure him an exchange value for the use of his property. The practice of contract, though it may work together with the practice of property, is conceptually independent of it, and it extends to different areas. Thus it permits the exchange of many other values besides those which are captured by the right of exclusive use of property; the practice also

---

[22] *cf.* Brudner, "The Unity of Property Law" (1991) 4 *Can. J. of Law and Juris.* 3 at pp. 34–35.

allows a person to capture the market value of his bodily security, allowing him to enter into agreements which secure him payment for acting (*i.e.* using his body) in various ways.

It is also probably worth pointing out that any right which is conceptually dependent for its existence on the existence of any actual value cannot but misdescribe the right to property, since a lot of property is literally useless, and thus valueless. If this were not true there would be no property in bad debts, worthless currency, nuclear waste, that is, in rubbish generally, and we know there is. It is no answer to this to say that any bit of property is *potentially* useful in some way, since that is just untrue, at least to the extent that "value" means anything like "actual value to humans in a particular social and historical context", which it surely must. Of course the duty of non-interference protects the value of using property, since it protects using property, but fastening on this value as a means of explaining property is bound to obscure any characterisation of the practice, since we need know nothing of the value of something, to the owner or anyone else, in order to correctly identify it as property.

Conclusion

It is the owner's liberty to use his property, now or later, which is evidently protected by property rights, not any particular active or passive engagement with his property, nor any bundle of all such uses. Property keeps the owner at liberty to do as much or as little with his property as he can. As I have tried to show here, the problem with treating use-rights as such as the central defining feature of property is that it emphasises one side of a coin, use, at the expense of the other, exclusion. I have also tried to show how Hohfeld's analysis of norms, in particular his description of liberties, suggests, if it does not require this flawed analysis. In contrast I have argued that we must explain property in terms of both use and exclusion, which may be thought of as the end and the means, respectively, underlying the legal institution of this practice.[23]

---

[23] This is a (very) revised version of a paper given at the W.G. Hart Workshop in July of 1993 at the Institute of Advanced Legal Studies. A section of the original paper concerning the conceptual analysis of legal concepts such as property is omitted; a vastly expanded version of that may be found in "The 'Bundle of Rights' Picture of Property" (1996) 43 *U.C.L.A. Law Review* 711 at pp. 767–799. I wish to thank the participants of the Workshop, in particular James Harris, Peter Jaffey, Stephen Munzer, and Bernard Rudden, for the benefit of their views and advice.

14

What is Non-Private Property?

J.W. HARRIS*

1. Introduction

Most speculative writing about property has been concerned, primarily, with individual private property – its nature and alleged justifications. However, political philosophers have often contrasted private property with "common property" and sometimes with "state property". Anthropologists and historians have added notions of "collective property", "group property", or "tribal property". Is there anything in the term "property" which makes all these expressions branches of a common conceptual tree?

Every-day political controversy includes disputes as to whether some particular resource ought or ought not to be held as private property. If it should not, seemingly interchangeable labels abound as to the sort of "property" regime which is the alternative to "private" property. In 1995 the British Labour Party abandoned its commitment to the "common ownership" of the means of production, distribution and exchange. In journalistic discussions of this issue, the term "public ownership" slips in and out as an apparent synonym for "common ownership". In what sense is any non-private conception of "ownership" still "ownership"?

Such questions cannot be answered unless we begin with a fixed marker, an explication of conventional assumptions about what it is for there to be "property" in, or for people to "own", resources – a starting-point made all the more necessary by the tendency for property-notions to balloon in all directions in the hands of contemporary social and economic theorists.

I have argued that the essentials of a property institution are trespassory rules and the ownership spectrum.[1]

By "trespassory rules" I mean any social rules, whether or not embodied in law, which purport to impose obligations on all members of a society, other than an individual or group who is taken to have some form of open-ended relationship to a thing, not to make use of that thing without the consent of that individual or group. The most hallowed such trespassory rule embodies the command "thou shalt not steal". Legal trespassory rules may be supported by

---

* Professor of Law at the University of Oxford and Fellow of Keble College.
[1] Harris, *Property and Justice* (1996).

criminal or civil sanctions, or both. In modern legal systems, they protect privileged relationships to land, chattels, money, and various sorts of ideational entities (intellectual property). As Bentham put it, the paradigm type of a property law is: "'Let no one, Rusticus excepted', (so we will call the proprietor) 'and those whom he allows meddle with such or such a field.'"[2]

By "the ownership spectrum" I mean the range of open-ended relationships presupposed and protected by trespassory rules. All attempts in the history of theorising about property to provide a univocal explication of *the* concept of ownership, applicable within all societies and to all resources, have failed.[3] Yet property talk, lay and legal, deploys ineliminable conceptions of ownership interests. They find their place within the ownership spectrum. At the lower end is what may be called "mere property". Mere property embraces some open-ended set of use-privileges over a resource and some open-ended set of powers of control over uses made by others. At the upper end of the ownership spectrum stands "full-blooded ownership". Full-blooded ownership entails a relationship between a person and a thing such that he or she has, prima facie, unlimited privileges of use and unlimited powers of control and transmission, so far as such use or exercise of power does not infringe some property-independent prohibition.

The content of ownership interests is a function of cultural assumptions. It varies with time and place. It may or may not comprise testamentary freedom. Indeed, an ownership interest may confer use-privileges and control-powers but no power to transmit, as when legislation grants security of tenure to particular classes of occupants.[4] Transmissibility is only a necessary feature of an ownership interest in the case of money.

The same property institution may recognise a variety of ownership interests over the same resource, as common law doctrines of estates in land illustrate. Since what is conveyed is always an estate in the land, it has been widely assumed that "ownership" is not a conception internal to English land law.[5] The truth is that ownership interests, of various kinds, are incidents of different estates and it is by reference to them that, both within and without the law, assumptions are made about what may be done to or with land.[6] Section 6(1) of the Trusts of Land and Appointment of Trustees Act 1996 enacts that trustees of land are to be vested with "all the powers of an absolute owner". Even a short leaseholder " . . . is able to exercise the rights of an owner of land which is in the real sense his land, albeit temporarily and subject to certain restrictions".[7]

---

[2] Bentham, *Of Laws in General* (1970) p. 177.
[3] See Honoré, *Making Law Bind* (1987) Chaps. 8 and 10.
[4] See Hand, "The Statutory Tenancy: an Unrecognised Proprietary Interest?" (1980) Conv. 351.
[5] See, *e.g.* Hargreaves, "Modern Real Property" (1956) 19 M.L.R. 14; Rudden, "Notes Towards a Grammar of Property" (1980) Conv. 325.
[6] *cf.* Harris, "Ownership of Land in English Law", in MacCormick and Birks (eds.), *The Legal Mind* (1986).
[7] *Street v. Mountford* [1985] A.C. 809 at 816, *per* Lord Templeman.

The items on the ownership spectrum are united in three respects only. First, they all involve a juridical relation between a person (or group) and a resource. Secondly, the privileges and powers which they comprise are open-ended – that is, they cannot be concretely listed. Thirdly, they authorise self-seekingness on the part of the individual or group to whom they belong.

Ownership interests are not reducible to the rules which protect or presuppose them. No enumeration of such rules, however exhaustive, could yield their content. They operate as unreflective organising ideas in countless social interactions, and have always done so. In the parable of the labourers in the vineyard in St Matthew's gospel, the land-owner takes it to be obvious that: "Is it not lawful for me to do what I will with mine own?"[8]

Ownership interests also interact with trespassory rules in legal reasoning. Their implicit normative force is taken to be a principled ground for giving some open-textured rule one interpretation rather than another – as when a court enjoined mere dissemination of information about etchings which plaintiffs had created and wished to keep private[9]; or where the Torts (Interference with Goods) Act 1977 was construed widely enough to make it wrongful for a railway authority (which wished to placate striking steel-workers) to retain, even temporarily, steel belonging to a company, that being conduct which denied to the plaintiffs "most of the rights of ownership"[10]; or where courts have ruled that neither the common law doctrine of necessity nor any principle of equity can be invoked as a defence to an owner's right to recover land by homeless people who squat in empty premises.[11]

Ownership interests are also presupposed by three categories of rules which, whilst not essential to the idea of a property institution, are universally to be found in all modern property institutions. These are "property-limitation rules", "expropriation rules" and "appropriation rules". They are addressed to holders of ownership interests as such. They are to be contrasted with "property-independent prohibitions". It is criminal to commit assault or homicide with a weapon, but it is completely irrelevant whether the accused owned the weapon or not. Property-limitation rules, like those contained in the law of nuisance, planning law, environmental protection law, industrial safety law and so forth, remove privileges and powers prima facie contained within prevailing conceptions of ownership interests. Expropriation rules, like those contained in the law of civil execution and bankruptcy, criminal forfeiture, compulsory purchase and taxation, empower the stripping of ownership interests. Appropriation rules, such as those contained in the law of succession, family law, social security law and public housing law, enable ownership interests in money or other resources to be conferred.

---

[8] Chapter 20, v.15.
[9] *Prince Albert v. Strange* (1849) 1 Mac. and G. 25.
[10] *Howard E. Perry and Co. Ltd v. British Railways Board* [1980] 1 W.L.R. 1375.
[11] *Southwark L. B. C. v. Williams* [1971] Ch. 1; *Department of the Environment v. James* [1972] 3 All E.R. 629; *McPhail v. Persons Unknown* [1973] Ch. 447.

There are other characteristic outworks from the core idea of the twinned conceptions of trespassory rules and the ownership spectrum. The most important are "non-ownership proprietary interests" and "cashable rights". The former (servitudes, mortgages and so forth) are protected by special trespassory rules which presuppose transferable ownership interests, but their content is not open-ended in the way that the content of ownership interests is. The latter (assignable interests in trust funds, bank accounts, shares and other choses in action) may or may not be the direct subject of trespassory protection, but the cash into which they are transmutable always is. For that reason, they are brought within the purview of property institutions. Expropriation rules and appropriation rules typically apply to cashable rights as they apply to ownership interests in money and other resources.

2. Communitarian property

Trespassory rules may accord ownership interests to two or more individuals jointly, to a group, or to a corporation.

It is of the essence of joint property that no trespassory rules regarding the asset in question subsist between the joint owners. The same may be true of group property. There can, however, be internal regulations allocating use-privileges and control-powers between members of a group, as will often be the case with associations like clubs or trade unions. Should such internal regulations encompass intra-group trespassory rules, then there will be individual property interests of one kind or another. Where regulation does not go that far, members are not vested with property which is independent of the group property. Each member differs from outsiders by virtue of enjoying, first, a share in the protection conferred on the group as a whole and, secondly, a right not to be excluded by other members of the group.

Corporate property is a sophisticated variant of group property. External trespassory rules vest use-privileges, control-powers and powers of transmission in the corporation and hence, via its constitution, in particular officers. Individual members retain the right to share in the wealth-potential of this protection but not, usually, the right not to be excluded from corporate assets. It is this facet of corporate property to which attention is drawn in the classic work on the modern corporation by Berle and Means, described by them as the "separation between control and ownership".[12]

Joint, group and (non-public) corporate property are all variations of private property. Joint, group and corporate owners are free to make such uses of their assets as they jointly or collectively decide, in accordance with the prevailing conception of the ownership interest in question, within whatever property-limitation rules apply to all owners. It is taken for granted that, to the extent that

---

[12] Berle and Means, *The Modern Corporation and Private Property*, Commerce Clearing House (1932); *cf.* Jones, "Forms of Ownership" (1947) 22 *Tulane L.R.* 82 at pp. 86–89, 93.

an individual owner may insist on the immediate return of his chattels which another is detaining, so may an owner-company.[13] If an individual owner of a factory is free to demolish it and thereby deprive thousands of employment, so too is a corporate owner.[14] The principle of no expropriation without compensation applies in the same way whether the property belongs to an individual or to a private corporation.[15]

A vast swathe of the private wealth in modern western societies is held in the form of joint, group or corporate property. In all variations, whatever latitude may be conferred on members to arrange their affairs at pleasure, internal regulation cannot exceed the tolerance accorded by the wider property institution. The general law lays down a framework within which partnership or corporate property must subsist. With all these must be contrasted a spontaneously evolved category of property-holding which has been of the greatest historical significance but which, for better or for worse, has been largely eclipsed in modern societies. So long as it survives and receives external trespassory protection without intrusion on its internal regulation, the relationship of the participants to the resource is essentially different from the varieties of joint private property just discussed. Any label for this relationship which borrows on the technical terminology of modern property systems would be misleading. I shall call it "communitarian property".

"Communitarian property" is a global term employed here to designate a wide range of land-holding arrangements which, in many parts of the world, used to subsist alongside conventional forms of private property.[16] The positive content would depend on social, economic and spiritual variables. Nothing unites the category except its negative contrast with individual or joint private property. It is a relationship which the wider society depicts by differentiation. It is not, of itself, an organising idea internal to the particular community, except by way of contrast with the otherness of individual or group private property.

Thus, "communitarian property" refers to a situation in which a community of persons has the following relationship to a resource, usually land. They have the benefit of trespassory rules excluding outsiders from the resource – in that sense it is their private property. However, whatever powers of internal division or transmission they possess are referable, not to the wider institution which contains the trespassory rules, but to internal regulations controlled by their mutual sense of community.

A surviving instance of communitarian property was recognised in the recent decision of the High Court of Australia in *Mabo v. Queensland*.[17] The court ruled that, according to the common law of Australia, the "radical title" to land acquired by the Crown on settlement was burdened with the "native title" of

---

[13] *Howard E. Perry and Co. Ltd v. British Railways Board* [1980] 1 W.L.R. 1375.
[14] *United Steel Workers v. United States Steel Corporation* 631 F.2d 1264 (1980).
[15] *Burma Oil Company (Burma Trading) Ltd v. Lord Advocate* [1965] A.C. 75.
[16] See Vinogradoff, *Outlines of Historical Jurisprudence* (1920) Vol. 1, pp. 321–343.
[17] (1992) 175 C.L.R. 1.

any aboriginal clan or group which was in occupation of any distinct portion of territory for so long as its descendants remained in occupation, unless and until native title was effectively extinguished by legislation or exercise of executive power, or surrendered to the Crown. The Meriam people were vested with such a title to the Murray Islands in the Torres Strait. So long as it persisted, the community's native title was subject to appropriate legal protection against all the world. All questions as to the rights of individual members of the community over their land were to be determined, as questions of fact, by reference to the particular evolving traditions of the group. It was not requisite to show that, internally, the members viewed their relationship to the land as an "ownership" interest, in any way comparable to the range of ownership interests known to modern legal systems. It was not an institution of the common law, but a special defeasible interest which the common law ought in justice to (and therefore did) recognise.

It is noteworthy that the High Court did not accept an alternative argument advanced on behalf of the Meriam people, that the group had acquired title to an ordinary fee simple estate by virtue of prior possession.[18] That would have meant that any group or tribe of native inhabitants would be as free to trade their land (if they all wished to do so) as are the members of any commercial partnership or other unincorporated association. They would have joint property within the institution, not communitarian property recognised by the institution. The court's ruling entailed, instead, that native title persisted only so long as a group retained some spontaneously evolving connection to the land, and could be disposed of to no one but the Crown.

3. State and public property

When a private owner of land, for his own commercial purposes, throws it open to members of the public he usually does not thereby forfeit the power to exclude particular individuals provided that such exclusion does not infringe anti-discrimination legislation. That has been ruled in relation to privately-owned shopping malls both by the English Court of Appeal[19] and by the Supreme Court of Canada.[20] A different view was taken by the Supreme Court of New Jersey.[21] It favoured the evolution of a new property-limitation rule whereby owners of commercial premises have, at common law, no right to

---

[18] See McNeil, *Common Law Aboriginal Title* (1989). All the members of the majority of the court were, however, influenced by McNeil's criticism of older views of the common law position, according to which the Crown, on settlement, acquired beneficial ownership of land along with sovereignty.

[19] *CIN Properties Ltd v. Rawlins, The Times*, February 9, 1995.

[20] *Harrison v. Carswell* (1976) 62 D.L.R. (3rd) 68. See also *Russo v. Ontario Jockey Club* (1988) 46 D.L.R. (4th) 359.

[21] *Uston v. Resorts International Hotels Inc.* 445 A.2d (1982).

exclude patrons unreasonably.[22] On this basis the Court ruled that the owners of a casino could not deny access to their blackjack tables to the plaintiff merely on the ground that he had devised a successful system for playing the game. In all these cases the point of departure was the assumption that, prima facie, private owners have powers of exclusion notwithstanding that their premises are normally open to the public.

The trespassory rules of modern property institutions typically include, amongst those to whom privileged uses and powers are afforded, agents of the state or of other public institutions. The assets to which they apply are commonly referred to as "state" or "public" property, as opposed to "private" property. Access to state factories, farms or offices may be prohibited to all except officials and those whom they authorise. Appropriation of state money or chattels will be criminal unless it was done in performance of an official function.

However, the privileged domain thus afforded to officials falls nowhere along the ownership spectrum since it lacks the crucial feature of legitimate, self-seeking exploitation. Exploitation is governed by conceptions of social function which vary according to the public enterprise in question, but which uniformly do not include the idea that the officials, or any personified complex of them, may, prima facie, do what they like with the assets.

The same is true of property dedicated to public use, but not vested in state organs. Charitable corporations and charitable trusts have emerged as mechanisms for discharging community-approved objectives with the co-operation of private initiatives. The powers of corporate managers and trustees are largely modelled on those inherent in ownership interests. However, they are not at liberty to exploit any such powers for their own benefit nor (unlike their counterparts in private corporations and trusts) to discharge them at the self-interested direction of any private class of citizens.

The content of the domain conferred on an official (or trustee) over state (or public) property in his charge is a variable composed of elements borrowed from ownership interests and elements deriving from the particular social function which that relationship is supposed to serve. For want of any better label, we may call such relationships "quasi-ownership interests". At one extreme, a state corporation may be vested with "ownership" of some industrial enterprise, have some of its powers and duties specified by statute in general terms, but for the rest be presumed to have virtually the same ownership privileges and powers as any private corporation would have – always bearing in mind the non-self-seeking limitation. At the other extreme, the majority of the rights, duties, privileges and powers of such a corporation are laid down in detail in legislative codes, ownership privileges and powers being resorted to only, if necessary, to fill in the gaps.

---

[22] The United States Supreme Court has fluctuated over the question whether private owners' powers of exclusion may be challenged on the ground that they infringe the freedoms of expression conferred by the 1st Amendment to the Constitution – see the decisions reviewed in *Pruneyard Shopping Center v. Robins* 447 U.S. 74 (1980).

Public parks fall towards the latter end of this spectrum. Some agency is vested with title to the park and is obliged to allow access for recreational purposes to members of the public. Even so, it has been ruled, the agency retains sufficient "ownership" to benefit from the common law rule by which chattels discovered in or attached to land belong, not to the finder, but to the owner of the soil.[23]

In English law, even public highways are the subject of quasi-ownership interests. Statutes vest in highway authorities the surface of the road and so much of the sub-soil and superjacent airspace as is needed for the discharge of statutory functions.[24] Such an interest has been held to constitute an estate in the land.[25]

When a court has to rule on the validity of the exercise of a power by a body vested with a quasi-ownership interest, it reaches a conclusion by some synthesis of legally defined, and residual ownership, privileges and powers. It has been held that a public authority, as "owner" of an airport, could lawfully exclude picketers.[26]

> "The B. A. A.'s ownership (unlike that of a private landowner) is subject to the right of the public to have access for the purpose of taking advantage of the services and facilities provided by the B. A. A. in pursuance of its statutory duty: . . . However, access for the purpose of picketing is not a right to which the B. A. A.'s ownership is subject." [27]

A private owner may prohibit hunting on his land for any reason that seems good to him, but not so a local authority "land-owner". The prohibition did not come within the statutory function for which the land was held, *viz*, the "benefit, improvement or development" of the area under the authority's control.[28]

In another case, the sensitive question of access by patients to their medical records has been dealt with in terms of a quasi-ownership interest. The Court of Appeal ruled that, although written medical records were "owned" by a health authority, the position at common law was as follows. The "owner" had no absolute right to deal with the records in any way it chose since its ownership was subject to its duty to act at all times in the best interests of the patient. Nevertheless, the health authority could, as "owner", refuse to disclose records to a patient if it considered that disclosure would be detrimental to the patient.[29]

Even money is the subject of merely quasi-ownership interests, comprised of an amalgam of ordinary ownership powers and powers derived from desig-

---

[23] *Waverley B.C. v. Fletcher* [1995] 4 All E.R. 756.
[24] *Coverdale v. Charlton* [1878] 4 Q.B.D. 104; *Rolls v. St. George the Martyr, Southwark (Vestry)* [1880] 14 Ch.D. 785; *Tunbridge Wells Corp. v. Baird* [1896] A.C. 434.
[25] *Tithe Redemption Commission v. Runcorn U.D.C.* [1954] Ch. 383.
[26] *British Airports Authority v. Ashton* [1983] 1 W.L.R. 1079.
[27] *ibid.* at 1089, *per* Mann J.
[28] *R. v. Somerset C.C., ex p. Fewings* [1995] 3 All E.R. 20.
[29] *R. v. Mid Glamorgan Family Health Services, ex p. Martin* [1995] 1 All E.R. 356. The matter is governed by the Access to Health Records Act 1990, in relation to records made after October 31, 1991.

nated functions, when it is vested in a public authority. In *Hazell v. Hammersmith and Fulham L.B.C.*;[30] the House of Lords held that interest swap transactions, entered into by a local authority as a speculation, were *ultra vires* its statutory powers and so unenforceable. "Individual trading corporations and others may speculate as much as they please or consider prudent. But a local authority . . . is a public authority dealing with public moneys . . . ".[31]

The ownership privileges and powers comprised within quasi-ownership interests may be removed by property-limitation rules applicable to ownership interests proper. Non-ownership proprietary interests avail against successors in title in much the same way whether those successors have ownership or quasi-ownership interests unless the legislative designation of functions is interpreted as an abrogation of inconsistent private proprietary rights.[32] However, the difference between them is typically reflected by the drastically foreshortened application to quasi-ownership interests of expropriation rules and principles. Most state and public property is not subjected to bankruptcy law or the law of criminal forfeiture, and it typically features differently in taxation law. That principle of statutory construction which presumes that Parliament does not intend to expropriate private property without payment of compensation has been held inapplicable to statutes which divest public bodies of their property.[33]

Quasi-ownership interests, lacking legitimised self-seekingness, are not private wealth. Their varying contours nonetheless reflect, in part, prevailing conceptions of ownership interests proper. All conceptions of state or public property build upon the twinned notions of trespassory rules and the ownership spectrum which constitute the core of all property institutions.

4. Common property

Political philosophers, from Plato and Aristotle to the present day, have contrasted both private and public property with "common property". Often enough, the term is used as a synonym for some form of group or communitarian property. It is also sometimes used to refer to an asset which is vested in a public authority with a quasi-ownership interest, where the discharge of the function for which it is so vested requires access to be afforded to members of the public on most occasions, like a park or a highway.[34] In English law the expression "common land" refers either to land which is subject to the rights of common (such as grazing rights) of a defined class of persons, or to land which is (or was) part of the waste land of a manor which is subject to public

---

[30] [1992] 2 A.C. 1.
[31] *ibid.* at 31, *per* Lord Templeman.
[32] *Kirkby v. Schoolboard for Harrogate* [1896] 1 Ch. 437; *Brown v. Heathlands Mental Health National Health Service Trust* [1996] 1 All E.R. 133.
[33] *R. v. Secretary of State for the Environment, ex p. Newham L.B.C* (1987) 85 L.G.R. 737; *Sheffield C.C. v. Yorkshire Water Services Ltd* [1991] 1 W.L.R. 58.
[34] See, *e.g.* Rose, "The Comedy of the Commons" (1986) 53 U. Chi. L.Rev. 711.

rights of access and recreation.[35] In either case there is an "owner" of the land, often a public authority vested with a quasi-ownership interest, whose title to the fee simple estate requires to be registered.[36] The owner retains residual rights in the soil, subject to the rights of commoners or of the public, and is protected by trespassory rules against unlawful interference with the land.

In so far as "common property" has a meaning distinct from these other forms of property, it designates a context in which no-one may, by virtue of an ownership or quasi-ownership interest, dispute the right of any other person to make use of a resource. In Hohfeldian terminology, all use-privileges correlate with ownership no-rights.[37]

In this sense the term "common property" may be employed as a way of pointing out that a particular resource has not been subjected to a property institution. It is so used judicially, on occasion, particularly in the context of ideas or information within the public domain.[38]

"Common property" means no property. It would be a redundant (indeed meaningless) concept in a society which knew nothing of property institutions.

5. Protected non-property holdings

Trespassory protection does not inevitably create even a quasi-ownership interest. Exceptionally, use of a resource may be banned to all persons save X, but X's use-privileges and control-powers over the resource are enumerated in terms of role-duties which borrow nothing from ownership conceptions. Such resources are removed altogether from the domain of property. They may be called "protected non-property holdings".

Consider the regime instituted in the United Kingdom by the Human Fertilisation and Embryology Act 1990 for embryos and live gametes. The Act prohibits storage and use of these materials to anyone except the holder of a licence granted by the Human Fertilisation and Embryology Authority. Licensees are permitted to store these products and their duties are elaborated in the Act and in regulations made under it. There is no reservation to the authority or to any licensee of a set of privileges or powers modelled on those inherent in an ownership interest anywhere along the ownership spectrum.

Such items are not common property, since access to them is not open to all on the same terms. Nor are they state or public property, since proprietary notions play no part whatever in determining how they must or may be used.

The conception which I have labelled "protected non-property holdings" has an important role to play in critical questions of property-institutional design.

---

[35] *Mid Glamorgan C.C. v. Ogwr* [1995] E.G.C.S. 12.
[36] Commons Registration Act 1975.
[37] Hohfeld, *Fundamental Legal Conceptions as Applied in Judicial Reasoning* (Yale University Press 1919) pp. 38–50.
[38] See, *e.g. International News Service v. Associated Press*, 284 U.S. 215 at 219, (1918) *per* Pitney J.

We may suppose, as to some resource, that it ought to be the subject of protected storage but that we should avoid borrowing ownership notions in relation to its use or disposal. That was the view taken by the Warnock Committee in relation to human embryos.[39] The same category of holding seems to apply to human organs which are subjected to the regulatory regime set up under the Human Organ Transplants Act 1989; and indeed has, in most societies, always applied to corpses. I have argued that, where there are good reasons for government information to be kept secret (that is, not to become "common property"), it ought to be the subject of protected non-property holdings.[40]

The government ought not to be free to act as its "owner".

6. The logical priority of private property

It is often claimed that property is a conception of which there are three parallel ideal types: private property, common property, and state or collective property.[41]

One can certainly imagine either a society in which there are no trespassory rules, or one in which such trespassory rules as there are protect only non-property holdings. But in either case, by assumption, whatever organising ideas controlled the internal regulation of resource-use they would not include any notion of property.

In all real societies, the internal utility of the concept of "common property" is limited to ruling out one kind of reason which might be advanced for denying that X is privileged to make some use of an asset. It excludes the possibility that X's use conflicts with Y's ownership (or quasi-ownership) interest. In that negative sense, common property presupposes private property. In contrast, the concept of state (or public) property presupposes private property in a positive sense. Every quasi-ownership interest borrows some of its content, great or small, from the open-ended privileges and powers which belong to the prevailing private ownership conception. State (or public) property is thus parasitic on private property. "Private property" is the logically prior concept.

7. The justificatory priority of "Common Property"

Influential political philosophers of the seventeenth century, like Grotius,[42] Pufendorf,[43] and Locke[44] begin their arguments for individualist private property regimes by positing a starting-point of common ownership. Granted that God had given all things to men in common it was possible, so they thought, to support a just evolution of private property-holdings. The crucial step, in the

---

[39] Report of the Committee of Inquiry into Human Fertilisation and Embryology 1984 Cmnd. 9314, 10.11.
[40] Harris, *op. cit.* above, n.1, Chap. 17 s. (iii) (B).
[41] See MacPherson, *Property: Mainstream and Critical Positions* (1978) Chap. 1; Waldron, *The Right to Private Property* (1988) Chap. 2.
[42] Grotius, *De Jure Belli ac Pacis* (trans. Kelsey, 1964) Book II, Chap. 2.
[43] Pufendorf, *De Jure Naturae et Gentium* (trans. Oldfather, 1934) Book IV, Chap. 4.
[44] Locke, *Second Treatise of Government* (Gough ed. 1976) Chap. 5.

view of Grotius and Pufendorf, was tacit agreement and, in Locke's view, creative labour. Sound or not, their arguments do not contradict my claim about the logical priority of private property. The conception of "common property" deployed by these theorists is not merely a situation in which there was no property. It entails a power in individuals, assuming the proper steps, to appropriate part of what was before such appropriation the property of no-one.[45]

Thus the whole notion is infused with the conceptual possibility of individual property. It would make no sense to speak of "common property", in the sense of that to which no-one presently has any special claim but parts of which may at any time be rendered the private property of individuals, unless we already had some notion of what it is for something to be the private property of individuals. Of course, speculators about original common property always do come to that subject armed with such a conception.

8. The historical priority of communitarian property

I have coined the term "communitarian property" to stand for any situation in which the members of a group have mutual rights over a resource, referable exclusively to their own traditions, but are protected against the rest of mankind by trespassory rules. If it were historically the case that individual appropriations arose, not from enclosures of what was previously owned by no-one, but by encroachments on what had already been possessed in the form of communitarian property, how could arguments which presupposed common property, even if abstractly sound, have any relevant application?

That problem came to the fore as a result of the researches of the historical school of jurists in the nineteenth century. They accumulated data suggesting that early Germanic and Slavic law had recognised communitarian property in land and pointed to comparable surviving institutions in medieval Europe and contemporary instances in other parts of the world. Maine collated all this information and made it the basis of a scorching critique of natural rights theories of property.[46] Many features of Maine's speculations have been disputed. Indeed, anthropological and ethnographic studies in the twentieth century reveal such a wealth of variety of property arrangments within primitive societies that any generalisations about historical priority must probably be rejected. Lawrence Becker so concludes:

> "Every attempt I have made is refuted by a counterexample actually observed in the field. The data indicate that, although property rights exist everywhere, what is necessary about them is just *that some exist*. It appears that many specific systems of ownership are compatible with any set of environmental conditions and social structures."[47]

---

[45] See Buckle, *Natural Law and the Theory of Property: Grotius to Hume* (1991) pp. 95–96.
[46] Maine, *Ancient Law* (Murray ed. 1906) Chap. 8.
[47] Becker, "The Moral Basis of Property Rights" in Pennock and Chapman (eds.), *Property Nomos* (New York University Press, 1980) Vol. xxii, p. 200.

Supposing, however, that, at least as to land, communitarian property did historically precede individual and group ownership interests. That would not affect my claim about the logical priority of private property. Communitarian property is a conception deployed by historians, comparativists and anthropologists, under various labels, in order to distinguish the relationship of a community to a particular resource from individual or group full-blooded ownership. Nothing but contrast with private property unites this category of resource-holding. This is confirmed by Paolo Grossi's survey of the debate sparked off among nineteenth century continental theorists by the publication of Maine's *Ancient Law*, between the proponents and opponents of "primitive communism".[48] What Grossi calls "collective property" played no role, as a distinct organising idea, within the societies in which it was found to have been present. It was an outsider's label.

> "Since it was historically just the historical and logical oppositum of ownership by a single proprietor, it is defined by a complex of alternative characteristics that emerge from that origin: the priority of the group and the subordination of individuals and their ends to the group; the priority of objective ends, of the economic nature, destination and use of things over subjective ends; the priority within the group of subjective situations of duty over those of power or right typical of the traditional jura in re."[49]

Grossi commends the social values served by surviving instances of what I have called "communitarian property". He recognises that the term "collective property" is ambiguous since it might be confused with socialist proposals for deliberately created property-holding entitlements, from which he distances his inquiry.[50]

Socialist theorists of the nineteenth century drew on similar historical information to that used by Maine as a basis for condemning and reconstructing capitalist private property. Communitarian property had once existed and, in a new socialist guise, it could be re-instituted. There were many variants – utopian, syndicalist and "scientific".

Marx contrasts all variations of private property with "social" or "collective" property.[51] According to Marx's theory of history, there was, at the dawn of history, universal communitarian property. Evolution in the forces of production resulted, inevitably but deplorably, in successive stages culminating with capitalist private property which will in turn, inevitably and triumphantly, be superseded by a new form of common ownership – "an association of free men, working with the means of production held in common, and expending their many different forms of labour-power in full self-awareness as one single social labour force".[52]

---

[48] Grossi, *An Alternative to Private Property: Collective Property in the Juridical Consciousness of the Nineteenth Century* (trans. Cochrane, University of Chicago Press, 1981).
[49] *ibid.* at p. 24.
[50] Grossi, *op. cit.* above, n.48, at pp. 22–23.
[51] Karl Marx, *Capital* (trans. B. Fowkes, Penguin Books, 1990) Vol. 1, pp. 927–930.
[52] *ibid.* at p. 171.

It is notoriously unclear whether this joint ownership entails literal common property – no-one who wishes to exert his labour-power on or with the means of production is to be excluded; or revived communitarian property – different associations jointly own assets from which members of other associations are excluded, and the owners arrange matters between themselves without reference to any external property institution; or, as those who have tried to implement the prophecy have generally assumed, the means of production are to be vested in state organs who will be endowed, by suitable trespassory rules, with quasi-ownership interests. All that need be noted here is that the supposed primitive communism of the past, and the joint ownership of the future, are alike analysed by reference to, and in contrast with, various species of private property.

Communitarian property, in a pure form, would entail that all internal decisions about resource-allocation are dictated by traditional notions internal to the group without any borrowing of proprietary conceptions from a wider society. Assuming that it ever existed, it is unlikely that it has anywhere survived the intrusion of the modern state. As a conception, it arises as a contrast to self-seeking private property notions, and with contrast comes contamination. Individual members of the Meriam people, whose communitarian property was recognised in the *Mabo* case, today own money and goods. In a sense, when communitarian property was pure it did not exist, for there was no-one around to point out the differences between it and property institutions.

9. Conclusion

So far as general justifications of property institutions are concerned, the inheritance of western political philosophy has bequeathed four kinds of arguments: alleged bases for natural rights; supposed inherent freedom virtues of property institutions; a raft of consequentialist claims; and appeals to the dominating considerations, either of equality of resources, or of convention. These are all property-specific justice reasons.[53] Many other considerations enter into arguments for the just society. But property-specific justice reasons are always addressed to private property. If their rejection yields the conclusion that, as to some resource, there ought to be no trespassory rules, then that resource is to be "common property". If they point to the desirability of some kind of trespassory protection, but also indicate, as to some resource, the injustice of individual self-seeking ownership, recommendations of various kinds may be put forward: group private property; group communitarian property either modelled (so far as possible) on the communitarian property of the past, or invented *de novo* for a newly constructed society peopled with reclaimed human beings; or a protected non-property holding; or some form of quasi-ownership interest vested in a public authority.

---

[53] See *Property and Justice,* above, n.1, Part 2.

In the politics of today, the latter is seen as by far the most popular alternative to private property. But then the variability within the notion of "quasi-ownership interest" should always be borne in mind. The mix of elements borrowed from ownership interests proper and those deriving from specific functions allows for anything from a public institution working the market for all it is worth (save that the institution is not supposed to promote private gain), to an authority with specified duties and powers where "ownership" serves only as a gap-filling analogy.

One of the leitmotifs of the last United Kingdom parliamentary election was a verbal dispute as to whether the government's programme for transferring hospitals from local public authorities to public trusts amounted to "privatisation". Clearly it did not, in the sense that the interest to be conferred on the trustees would entail the self-seekingness characteristic of ownership interests proper. Such trustees cannot give as a complete answer to any criticism, as private trustees and company directors may: "What we propose is in the best interests of the equitable owners (shareholders)". On the other hand, the programme had the effect of incorporating into the new quasi-ownership interests many more ownership powers, especially those connected with market transactions and the hiring and firing of staff.

The logical priority of conceptions of private property over those of non-private property demonstrates that, if we discuss the justice of property at all, private property is our focus. There can be no question of speculating about, approving or condemning public, common or communitarian property in isolation from private property.[54]

---

[54] Most of the research leading to this essay was undertaken while I was holding a British Academy research readership 1990–1992. I am grateful to the Academy for this assistance. It was first presented at the W. G. Hart Legal Workshop, at the Institute of Advanced Legal Studies, in July 1993, on "Concepts of Property in the Law". I have benefited from the discussion at the workshop. An earlier version was published in the *Law Quarterly Review* ((1995) 111 L.Q.R. 421).

PART III
RELOCATING PROPERTY'S ROLE

15

Theories of Property and Economic Development[1]

JOSHUA GETZLER*

Introduction

According to economic theory, the clear definition of property rights is essential for well-functioning markets. Comparatively little attention, however, is given to explaining the development of these rights. Economic reasoning suggests that markets themselves call property rights into existence: Persons contract to set up institutions enforcing stable, definite entitlements to scarce resources in order to facilitate investment, production and exchange. Thus, contracts constituting property rights and institutions precede those contracts dealing with existing property rights: both can be conceived as market transactions made in pursuit of gains. As McCloskey observes, in order to understand the emergence and function of property rights, economics "enlists the theory of self-interest to define the very object of self-interested desire".[2]

An historical approach to the development of property rights may suggest further explanations adding to the economist's parsimonious theory. Economic institutions and activities need not be subsumed within purely economistic interpretations; they are also susceptible to legal and historical analysis. Much can be learned from studying the ideas, institutions, and laws of property during England's pioneering industrialisation in the eighteenth and nineteenth centuries – the period known as the Industrial Revolution. This essay in the history of ideas describes the origins of the modern economic theory of property. The theory

---

* Fellow in Law, St. Hugh's College, Oxford, and Lecturer in Law, University of Oxford. The author wishes to thank Avner Offer, Jacob Metzer, Brian Bix, James Harris and Lucia Zedner for generous advice and helpful criticism; and Morton Horwitz for stimulating discussion.
[1] Reprinted from (1996) XXVI *Journal of Interdisciplinary History* at pp. 639–650, 669, with the permission of the editors of the *Journal of Interdisciplinary History* and the MIT Press. © 1996 by the Massachusetts Institute of Technology and the editors of the *Journal of Interdisciplinary History*.
[2] McCloskey, *The Applied Theory of Price* (New York, 1982) p. 359; Coase, "The Problem of Social Cost" (1960) III *Journal of Law and Economics* 1, reprinted in Coase, *The Firm, The Market and the Law* (Chicago, 1988) pp. 95–106; Demsetz, "Towards a Theory of Property Rights" (1967) LVII *American Economic Review* 347; Libecap, *Contracting for Property Rights* (1989) 1; Barzel, *Economic Analysis of Property Rights* (1st ed., 1989; 2nd ed., 1996); Eggertsson, *Economic Behaviour and Institutions* (1990) pp. 33–58.

traces back to nineteenth- and twentieth-century historical and social-scientific models of the Industrial Revolution. The sources of property theory in the world of the classical economists are now forgotten, and this lapse of memory has blunted the critical self-consciousness necessary for the theory to be effective and fruitful. The solution lies in a restoration of historical self-consciousness and an openness to alternative disciplinary historical approaches.[3]

Blanqui early suggested the concept of an "industrial revolution" commencing in mid to late eighteenth-century England and contrasting with the political revolution in France. Although some quantitative historians of the new economic history school have rejected the notion of a sudden sequence of rapid economic change in this period, the consensus of modern scholarship still accepts that a radical and unprecedented growth and restructuring of the British economy can be identified around 1800, making this period a watershed in human history.[4]

An older generation of institutionalist economic historians gave close attention to the impact of law and government on the course of the Industrial Revolution, examining poor laws, enclosure statutes, and labour and guild regulation; but these concerns were submerged with the rise of quantitative and neoclassical historical methodologies known as the new economic history. Crafts, in a survey of new Industrial Revolution historiography, concluded that "relatively little has been done . . . in seeking to investigate the impact of changes in the law and other institutional arrangements on economic efficiency." This statement perhaps underestimates the state of the art, for much has been achieved in disciplines contiguous to quantitative economic history. In particular, legal historians and legal economists have developed a variety of powerful interpretations explaining the role of property rights and legal institutions in fostering economic development; and this work is available to enrich and inform the history of industrialisation, as well as economic theory.[5]

---

[3] Field, "Do Legal Systems Matter?" (1991) XXVIII *Explorations in Economic History* 1 at pp. 2–7, 31–33; Alchian and Demsetz, "The Property Rights Paradigm" (1973) *Journal of Economic History* 16.

[4] Blanqui, *Histoire de l'Economie Politique* (1837) p. 389. See also Bezanson, "The Early Uses of the Term Industrial Revolution" (1921–1922) XXXVI *Quarterly Journal of Economics* 343; Mantoux, *The Industrial Revolution in the Eighteenth Century* (trans. Vernon, 1928); Floud and McCloskey, *The Economic History of Britain Since 1700, Vol. 1 1700–1860* (1st ed., 1981; 2nd ed., 1994); Mokyr, *The Economics of the Industrial Revolution* (1985); Mokyr, *The British Industrial Revolution: An Economic Perspective* (1993); Cannadine, "The Present and the Past in the English Industrial Revolution 1880–1980" (1984) CIII *Past and Present* 131; Wrigley, *People, Cities and Wealth. The Transformation of Traditional Society* (1987); Hoppit, "Counting the Industrial Revolution" (1990) XLIII *Economic History Review* 173; Berg and Hudson, "Rehabilitating the Industrial Revolution" (1992) XLV *Economic History Review* 24.

[5] McClelland, *Causal Explanation and Model Building in History, Economics, and the New Economic History* (1975); Mokyr (1985) *op. cit.* above, n.3; Mokyr (1993) *op. cit.* above, n.3; Crafts, "The New Economic History and the Industrial Revolution" in Mathias and Davis (eds.), *The First Industrial Revolutions* (1989) pp. 42–43.

Instrumental and expressive theories of property

Theories of property in the Western philosophical tradition divide roughly in two. There is a notion of property as pre-social, a natural right expressing the rights of persons which are prior to the state and law, this being the view of Hugo Grotius, Samuel von Pufendorf, John Locke, Immanuel Kant, and Georg W.F. Hegel; and there is a notion of property as social, a positive right created instrumentally by community, state or law to secure other goals – the theory of Thomas Hobbes, David Hume, Adam Smith, Jeremy Bentham, Emile Durkheim, and Max Weber. The expository line between these theories blurs, and their analysis has yielded a large and intricate philosophical literature. The concerns of this essay lie elsewhere, with the practical operation of concepts of property in law and economy, especially in England from 1770 to 1870.[6]

In the history of English political thought, it is the positive tradition of property theory that is most important in modern times, because it was integral to classical political economy and utilitarian philosophy. Yet, one of the few vigorous natural-right strands of the English political tradition, especially on the right of politics, has been the idea of the sanctity of private property rights – in particular, the immunity of individual property entitlements to the claims of public welfare. This idea is to be found in many distinct forms: one expression is the Lockean tradition, and another, the common-law tradition of Coke and Blackstone. The roots of English individualism and absolute respect for property have been traced back to England's distinct medieval system of landholding and property law; and a religious element may also be identified, for example, in the seventeenth-century Puritan insistence on the sanctity of property against monarchical authority.[7]

The naturalist ideology of the sanctity of property was especially appealing to the powerful class of landowners and to the legal functionaries that they supported. Other less powerful groups might stress different natural rights, such as customary communal rights or public rights to enjoyment of the land. The tension between contending property ideals held by different fractions of the propertied and unpropertied classes was evident throughout the span of industrialisation, from the late eighteenth century onward, reaching a final climax in

---

[6] See Becker, *Property Rights: Philosophical Foundations* (1977); Ryan, *Property and Political Theory* (1984); Waldron, *The Right to Private Property* (1988); Buckle, *Natural Law and the Theory of Property* (1991). For a critical review of the abstraction and ahistoricism of much recent philosophical analysis, see Becker, "Too Much Property" (1992) XXI *Philosophy and Public Affairs* 196.

[7] Locke, *Second Treatise of Government*, Chap. 9, ss.123–127, in Laslett (ed.), *Two Treatises of Government* (1963) pp. 395–397; Coke, *The First Part of the Institutes of the Laws of England, or, A Commentary on Littleton* (1628); Blackstone, *Commentaries on the Laws of England* (1765–1769) Vol. I, pp. 123–140; Macfarlane, *The Origins of English Individualism (1978)*; Little, *Religion, Order and Law (1970)*; Macpherson, *The Political Theory of Possessive Individualism: Hobbes to Locke* (1962).

the liberal assault on the landed interest during the late Victorian and Edwardian period.[8]

Property as certainty of expectations

The most powerful strain of property theory in economic thought has been instrumentalist rather than naturalist, as exemplified in Smith's *Wealth of Nations*, and later in the philosophy of Bentham – of all the philosophical radicals the most legalistic and attentive to the detail of social institutions. Bentham advocated a property regime promoting security of individual title, possession, and control to maximise the individual "calculation of chance" essential to capitalist production and trade. Property, according to Bentham, was "nothing but a basis of expectation," and the institution of property failed if expectations of obligation and interest were not made clear.[9]

The orthodox utilitarian claim that private property rights are desirable because they are conducive to certainty and efficiency was often challenged with another utilitarian argument that alternative forms of property can often do the job of resource allocation with more beneficial results than a regime of crystallised, sharply-defined individual rights of appropriation – for example, such non-private property holdings as the public trust, common rights, and other legal forms of public and communal goods. The later utilitarians and classical economists questioned the desirability of allowing any landed private property. Ricardo held that, in a mature capitalist economy, private landownership was an unproductive monopoly extracting rents from commerce and industry. Malthus gave this idea an optimistic gloss, holding that the idle and luxurious consumption of land rents helped to sustain effective demand and so promoted full employment of the economy's resources. Marx added that this monopoly was tolerated within the capitalist system only because landownership was the archetype of all private property rights, the model of capitalist power to appropriate surplus value. But these classical arguments are concerned exclusively with the optimal arrangement of resources for maximised production and welfare, rather than for countervailing values such as social equity or civic virtue. A more radical tradition argued that the rise of the possessive and atomistic individualism entailed by pure forms of private property holding produced an unjust and unattractive civilisation, whatever the aggregate utilities of production.[10]

---

[8] Thompson, "Custom, Law and Common Right" in Thompson, *Customs in Common* (1991) pp. 97–184; Offer, *Property and Politics, 1870–1914* (1981); Schlatter, *Private Property: The History of An Idea* (1951).

[9] Smith, *An Inquiry into the Nature and Causes of the Wealth of Nations* (Cannan ed. 1904), Vol. I, p. 267; Vol. II, p. 207. See also Smith, *Lectures on Jurisprudence* (1978) pp. 459–472; MacCormick, "Law and Economics: Adam Smith's Analysis," in MacCormick, *Legal Right and Social Democracy* (1982) pp. 103–125; Bentham, *Of Laws in General* (Hart ed. 1970) pp.111–112 and, generally, pp. 109–198; Bentham, *The Theory of Legislation: Principles of the Civil Code* (Hildreth ed. 1891); Hart, *Essays on Bentham* (1982).

[10] Malthus, *The Principles of Political Economy* (facs. repr. of 2nd ed. [1836], 1936); Ricardo, *On the Principles of Political Economy and Taxation* (Sraffa ed. 1951) pp. 67–84, 173–175,

Uncertainty of title and user

Historically the most infamous aspect of England's property law regime, which attracted the attention of generations of distinguished radicals from the seventeenth-century independents to Bentham and Lord Henry Brougham and others to follow, was the obstruction to free transfer of property, due to uncertainty of titles and the clumsiness of the legal process of conveyance. The heavy transaction costs of land exchange and succession had many causes: archaic, irregular, and obscure legal rules of tenure, copyhold and estates; monopolist charges extracted by the lawyers, who alone could define and convey those estates; the secrecy of titles desired by landholders who wished to protect their wealth from the threat of public taxation and private family claims; and overt legal barriers to transfer, which included family strict settlements and entails passing land exclusively to linear family descendants, and the residual precapitalist property forms of common rights. The radicals of the nineteenth century believed that removal of these institutional frictions would bring in a host of benefits: a shift of resources by auction to the most efficient users, a breakup of the great estates and power of the landlords, a reduction of the professional rents extracted by lawyers, and a readier assessment and taxation of landed wealth. A parallel movement can be seen in Germany with the Pandectist movement – a group of liberal lawyers and historians who believed that changing the law of tenures and estates could effect a quiet but profound social and economic revolution.[11]

This essay emphasises a different, less familiar story of conflict about the law of property, involving not the aspects of exchange and distribution but rather of production or user. Following Weber, we may ask, how did a country with such an irrational property system as England support the enclosure movement and industrialisation? How could developers calculate the risks of investment when labouring under such uncertain entitlements? Neither the rights of title and

---

181–190; John Stuart Mill, *Principles of Political Economy* (7th ed., 1871) Bk. II, Chap. 2, s.1, Bk. V, Chap. 2, s.7; John Stuart Mill, *Collected Works* (Robson ed. 1965) Vol. II, pp. 173–185, 199–217, Vol. III, pp. 819–824; Karl Marx, *Capital* (New York, 1967) Vol. III, p. 821; Harvey, *The Limits to Capital* (1982) pp. 330–372; Macpherson (1962) *op. cit.* above, n.6; Hill, *The World Turned Upside Down* (1975); Thompson, *The Making of the English Working Class* (1968); Thompson (1991) *op. cit.* above, n.7.

[11] Worden, *The Rump Parliament, 1648–53* (1974) pp. 105–118, 265, n.298; Rudden, "A Code Too Soon, The 1826 Property Code of James Humphreys: English Rejection, American Acceptance, English Acceptance" in Wallington and Merkin (eds.), *Essays in Memory of Professor F.H. Lawson* (1986) pp. 101–116. For a later phase see Offer, "The Origins of the Law of Property Acts 1910–1925" (1977) XL M.L.R. 505; Offer, *op. cit.* above, n.8; Anderson, "Land Law Texts and the Explanation of 1925" (1984) XXXVII *Current Legal Problems* 63; Anderson, *Lawyers and the Making of English Land Law 1832–1940* (1992); Getzler, Review Article, (1993) CIX L.Q.R. 684; Offer, "Lawyers and Land Law Revisited" (1994) XIV O.J.L.S. 269; Whitman, *The Legacy of Roman Law in the German Romantic Era* (1990); Whitman, "Why Did the Revolutionary Lawyers Confuse Custom and Reason?" (1991) LVIII *University of Chicago Law Review* 1321; Blum, *The End of the Old Order in Rural Europe* (Princeton, 1978).

transfer, nor the rights of amenity permitting the exploitation of vested resources were sharply delineated. The anomaly of industrialisation in an uncertain regime of property title and user constituted Weber's "England Problem", an exceptional case that seemed to contradict his general typology of legal and economic development in the West.

Weber and the institutional bias of English Law

To explain the anomaly of "backward" English law, Weber argued that during modernisation the procedural and institutional structure of the common law was functionally more significant than the substantive or normative content of its rules. Weber found a deep historical divergence between the rationalised German civil law, based on Roman law, and the customary and precedent-based English common law – a distinction that "originates from the autonomous development of the two different structures of domination":

> "In England there was centralised administration of justice combined with domination by notables; in Germany there was no political centralisation but a high degree of bureaucratisation. Thus the first country in modern times to have a highly developed capitalist economy, England, retained a less rational and less bureaucratic system of justice. The main reason why capitalism in England was able to come to terms so well with this situation, however, was that in that country the manner in which the courts were organised and the trial procedure, right up until modern times, were in fact tantamount to a virtual denial of justice to the economically weak. This fact, together with the time consuming and costly procedure for conveyancing land, which is also the result of the economic interests of the lawyers, has in turn also deeply affected the agrarian system of England in the direction of the accumulation and immobilisation of land."[12]

Weber did not make clear how the agrarian and industrial revolutions of the eighteenth and nineteenth centuries were promoted or influenced by large estates "immobilising" the land, or whether immobilisation meant restraints on the transfer of land in an imperfect property market or else concentration of property into monopolist holdings. Moreover, Weber's leitmotif of legal rationality as a general prerequisite of modernity and economic development is notoriously ambiguous. Weber often associated rationality simply with governance by rules. Hence, a rational legal system was "a logically clear, internally consistent, and, at least in theory, gapless system of rules, under which, it is implied, all conceivable fact situations must be capable of being logically subsumed lest their order lack an effective guaranty."[13]

---

[12] Max Weber, "The Development of Bureaucracy and its Relation to Law," from *Wirtschaft und Gesellschaft (Economy and Society)* (1922), reprinted in Runciman (ed.), *Max Weber: Selections in Translation* (1978) pp. 352–354.

[13] Weber's varied uses of the concept of formal legal rationality are examined in Giddens, *Capitalism and Modern Social Theory* (1971) pp. 178–184, 214–216; Holton and Turner, *Max Weber on Economy and Society* (1984) pp. 103–130; Kronman, *Max Weber* (1983) pp. 37–95; Rheinstein, "Introduction" in Rheinstein (ed.), *Max Weber On Law in Economy and Society*

The highest expression of this concept of rationality was held to be the developed Romanist law of the European countries, "the legal science of the Pandectists". However, legal rationality went beyond rule governance. Weber also stressed the role of law and lawyers in creating stability of property rights and predictability of contract enforcement through formal bureaucratic rule, whereby deliberately chosen norms were applied, rather than customary norms ("age-old rules and powers"), in order to resolve conflict and generate order.

In the exceptional case of England, Weber's main thesis seems to have been that the inequalities wrought by the adversarial and formalistic common-law system were a boon to the wealthy and energetic, who could carry out the transformation of the economy without challenge from the poor or the unproductive who could not afford to defend their rights. Weber also argued that the absence of formal legal rationality did not impede capitalist enterprise in England because the judges shared a developmental ideology with the entrepreneurial classes and were willing and able to mould the English system of precedent sufficiently to create legal conditions supporting certainty of business calculation. Weber characterised the English experience as a unique historical case, in which an irrational system of laws was controlled by pro-capitalist functionaries not generally present in other societies.[14]

Private law and public law adjustments to capitalism

Four criticisms of Weber

In his attempt to align the legal-economic facts with his theoretical models of legal rationality and the spirit of capitalism, Weber missed many of the influences that help to explain the adjustment of English property system to the Industrial Revolution. First, and crucial, was the ready adaptation of existing ancient law to modern economic functions – new private ordering using old legal forms. For example, trust law and the calculus of estates and perpetuities, designed for projecting family wealth across generations in a precapitalist soci-

---

(trans. Shils and Rheinstein, 1954); Schluchter, *The Rise of Western Rationalism: Max Weber's Developmental History* (1981); Stoljar, "Weber's Sociology of Law," in Sawer (ed.), *Studies in the Sociology of Law* (Canberra, 1961) pp. 31–56; Trubeck, "Max Weber on Law and the Rise of Capitalism" [1972] *Wisconsin Law Review* 720. For a sensitive appraisal of theories of rationality and modernisation, see Wrigley, "The Process of Modernisation and the Industrial Revolution in England" (1972) III *Journal of Interdisciplinary History* 225, reprinted in Wrigley (1987) *op. cit.* above n.3, pp. 46–74. Quotation from Rheinstein (ed.) (1954) *op. cit.* above, p. 62.

[14] See also Atiyah, *The Rise and Fall of Freedom of Contract* (1979) pp. 112–117; Horwitz, *The Transformation of American Law 1780–1860* (1977) pp. 1–30; Brooks, "Interpersonal Conflict and Social Tension: Civil Litigation in England, 1640–1830," in Beier, Cannadine and Rosenheim (eds.), *The First Modern Society* (1989) pp. 357–399. Alexis De Tocqueville maintained that in the case of France, in contrast to England, pre-revolutionary elites were restrained by a heavily centralising system of law, a system which the weak and poor could invoke to their advantage (*The Old Regime and the French Revolution* (4th ed., 1858; trans. Gilbert, New York, 1955) pp. 32–72, 289–300).

ety, provided the flexible instrument of equitable funds, allowing the accumulation and investment of circulating capital for business and municipal enterprise. Lease and mortgage law provided for the ready fragmentation of property interests that accompanied the capitalist division of economic functions. Legal tools for private planning of land use (easements, covenants) were extended, but ultimately there was little radical doctrinal innovation. Following Renner, private law can be seen here as an archaic form or institution that could sustain the new substance of capitalist property relations without requiring abrupt conceptual transformation.[15]

The disaggregation or fragmentation of ownership made possible by the common law in England contrasts with the abstract property norms of the modern European civil law, as promulgated in the great codes of the nineteenth century. The modernising drive, especially in Germany, towards "rational" forms of property, based on the Romanist concept of absolute ownership, owed more to the theorising of idealist philosophers and the preoccupations of classicist jurists and historians than to the needs of capitalist manufacturing and commerce. The German lawmakers resorted to Roman and civilian jurisprudence as they sought to frame the economic and social institutions of a new German nation-state; they believed that individual and absolute property was a universal progressive value that could overcome the subordinations and backwardness of unfree tenurial societies. But absolute property as often impeded the swift movement and deployment of resources and responsibilities necessary for development and modernisation. Examples of areas of difficulty in the German code included the legal aggregation of shifting capital resources in which management of capital is divorced from ownership, as well as the legal mechanisms for the transfer of title in complex sale of goods transactions passing property rights through a long chain of production and trade. English common law may have owned no developed theory of property as ownership, but the model of the fee simple provided a practical approximation of ownership that did all the necessary work. A feudal and therefore relativist system of property such as England's, which readily allows splitting of proprietary interests between many persons, creates intense complexities of

---

[15] See Holdsworth, *A History of English Law* (1925), VII; Lawson and Rudden, *The Law of Property* (2nd ed., 1982) pp. 76–113, 125n, 158, 176–204; Simpson, *A History of the Land Law* (2nd ed., 1986) pp. 208–291; Rudden, *The New River: A Legal History* (1985) pp. 208–248. For recent historical debates about the causal links between common law property forms and the modernising economy, see Cornish and Clark, *Law and Society in England 1750–1950* (1989) pp. 123–136, 166–172; Rubin and Sugarman, "Towards a New History of Law and Material Society in England, 1750–1914" in Rubin and Sugarman (eds.), *Law, Economy and Society in England, 1750–1914: Essays in the History of the English Law* (1984) pp. 1–123; Karl Renner, *The Institutions of Private Law and their Social Functions* (1949) pp. 81–250; Kahn-Freund, "Introduction," *ibid.* pp. 1–43. Similar ideas may be found in classical common law theory, *e.g.* Blackstone's metaphor for the law as an "old Gothic castle, erected in the days of chivalry, but fitted up for a modern inhabitant" (Blackstone, *Commentaries*, III, p. 268); Postema, *Bentham and the Common Law Tradition* (1986) pp. 3–38; Waldron, "What is Private Property?" (1985) V *Oxford Journal of Legal Studies* 313.

title, but an absolute property regime forced to disaggregate title by fictions faces still greater complexities. Therefore, Weber's legal "rationalism" was a conservative force, paradoxically bound more by time and place than was the pragmatic and evolutionary common law.[16]

Secondly, during the late eighteenth and early nineteenth centuries, the English common law was internally reforming and shedding some of its most archaic features. Milsom describes the long evolution of English law as a process of dethronement of the jury by the judge; that is, the wide discretionary power of juries to determine fact and discover customary norms was replaced by judicial power to define the law and to restrict narrowly the issues of fact going to the jury. Moreover, the style of judicial reasoning shifted from the arcane craft of classifying disputes within the medieval forms of action to a process describing substantive principles by which to resolve present litigation and set precedents for the future. In other words, the English common law was developing into a "mandarin" system of professionalised, bureaucratic, predictable norms more akin to the European civilian systems. Weber recognised that rational legal procedures could count for more than rational legal rules and concepts, and acknowledged that "it was not, indeed, the greater appropriateness of the *content* of Roman law to the needs of emerging capitalism which was responsible for their victory on the Continent: all the specific legal institutions of modern capitalism are in fact alien to Roman law and are of medieval origin." Roman law generally enjoyed the more rational procedures; but English law also moved slowly toward "rational procedures of evidence" in order to benefit the merchant class.[17]

The third argument acknowledges the evolutionary internal development of the common law, yet holds that the flexibility, predictability and rationality of this legal order remained deeply flawed. The solution ultimately lay not in the courts, but in Parliament. When common-law adaptability and reform finally reached its limit, public and especially private and local legislation were readily made available to create the legal structures for development. Examples include eighteenth- and early nineteenth-century parliamentary enclosure; incorporation of business enterprises and limitation of their liability for property

---

[16] See Whitman (1990) *op. cit.* above, n.10; John, *Politics and the Law in Late Nineteenth-Century Germany: The Origins of the Civil Code* (1989); Jolowicz, "Political Implications of Roman Law" (1947) XXII *Tulane Law Review* 62; Birks, "The Roman Law Concept of *Dominium* and the Idea of Absolute Ownership" [1985] *Acta Juridica*, pp. 1–37, 19–25; Nicholas, *An Introduction to Roman Law* (3rd ed., 1962) pp. 145–153; Harris, "Ownership of Land in English Law" in MacCormick and Birks (eds.), *The Legal Mind. Essays for Tony Honoré* (1986) pp. 143–161; Kronman, *Weber* (1983) *op. cit.* above, n.12, pp. 134–146.

[17] See Milsom, *Historical Foundations of the Common Law* (2nd ed., 1981) pp. 33–50, 70–81, 243–246; Milsom, *Studies in the History of the Common Law* (1985) pp. 149–189; Baker, *An Introduction to English Legal History* (3rd ed, 1990) pp. 63–111. See also Pollock and Maitland, *The History of English Law Before the Time of Edward I* (2nd ed., 1898, reissued 1968) Vol. II, pp. 598–674. Quotation from Weber, "The Development of Bureaucracy and its Relation to Law", p. 353.

damage as well as debt; compulsory acquisition and other statutory powers for transport and urban development; monopolist protections of vested property and its profits against the competitive market; and reform of entrenched common law rules curbing powers of ownership, sale and succession.[18]

Fourthly, the unwieldy and uncertain features of English private law were further offset by another dimension of public law – the success of the post-1688 Constitution. The settlement of 1688–1689 was built around the regularity of rule-bound taxation by Parliament dominated by a self-governing propertied class, making possible a system of stable public credit that protected the English State from financial crises, especially in wartime. This condition, in turn protected property from arbitrary exactions by a centralising state, and fostered a relative certainty of expectations vastly overshadowing the uncertainties of title and possession cultivated by the ramshackle common law. In other words, the costs of irrational private law were balanced by the benefits of a legitimate and effective system of public taxation. A stronger governmental participation in the definition and control of private property rights at the microeconomic level might have undermined the legitimacy and success of the larger fiscal system. North has argued that stable taxation and the resulting security of property rights was the key exogenous, or non-economic, factor making Britain's pioneering industrialisation possible.[19]

Legal uncertainty and analysis of the institution of property in capitalism

How do these large theories help explain the practical links between property law and economic change? What was the effect of particular legal forms and institutions on the activities of entrepreneurs and capitalists as they sought to innovate in early industrial societies? The classical economic and the Weberian perspectives, whilst suggestive, have proved to be inadequate in matching the data. The highly unstable regime of land titles provided by common law and statute in English history requires a more discriminating explanation of the relationship between property, law and economic development at the level of entrepreneurial decision-making. Guidance is available in the ideas of the institutional economists and the legal realists of early twentieth-century

---

[18] See Cornish and Clark, *op. cit.* above, n.14, pp. 1–196; Dicey, *Law and Public Opinion in England in the Nineteenth Century* (2nd ed., 1914); Simpson, "Legal Liability for Bursting Reservoirs: The Historical Context of *Rylands v. Fletcher*" (1984) XIII *Journal of Legal Studies* 209 at pp. 251–254; Simpson (1986) *op. cit.* above, n.14, pp. 270–291.

[19] Dickson, *The Financial Revolution in England: A Study in the Development of Public Credit, 1688–1756* (1967, reissued 1992); Mathias and O'Brien, "Taxation in Britain and France, 1715–1810: Comparison of the Social and Economic Incidence of Taxes Collected for the Central Government" (1976) V *Journal of European Economic History* 601; Beckett, "Land Tax or Excise: The Levying of Taxation in Seventeenth- and Eighteenth-Century England" (1985) C *English Historical Review* 285; Brewer, *The Sinews of Power: War, Money and the English State, 1688–1783* (1989); North, *Structure and Change in Economic History* (New York: 1981) pp. 147–170.

America – economists and lawyers such as Commons, Hale, Hohfeld and Cohen. These writers, like those of the German historical school, theorised about the origins of property rights as part of their criticism of analytical economics.[20]

Property is a bundle of nested rights

According to the early institutionalists, property is more than merely a right of exclusive possession against all the world. It is a bundle of nested rights, that is, rights building upon each other, which include (1) possession of the physical thing owned; (2) rights to exploit, change, re-order, and manage; (3) rights to the flow of income from rights 1 and 2; (4) rights to transfer, exchange, and destroy rights 1, 2 and 3; and (5) rights to transfer right 4.

Modern legal and economic uses of the concept of property tend to emphasise the abstract rights 3, 4 and 5, shifting from the "physicalist" notion of property represented by rights 1 and 2. The right to flow of income and the right to transfer (and thus capitalise) this right become a paramount means of evaluating, dealing and allocating resources; the value of an asset is determined by the present net value of income flow and the transferability of that flow. The company share or investment equity and the bond investment exemplify this transformation of property to a dephysicalised expectation of income divorced from association with the *res* or real object. A telling example is the longstanding English practice of referring to land values in terms of yearly rent, and of real capital values as so many year's purchase.[21]

Property is a coercive monopoly subject to competitive injury

In the institutional perspective, property rights, whether held to be natural or social in their philosophical foundation, are in their actual operation coercive

---

[20] McCloskey, *Applied Theory of Price* (1st ed.) p. 358 (2nd ed.) p. 339; Commons, *Institutional Economics* (New York, 1934); Commons, *Legal Foundations of Capitalism* (New York, 1924); Hale, "Coercion and Distribution in a Supposedly Non-Coercive State" (1923) XXXVIII *Political Science Quarterly* 470; Hale, *Freedom Through Law: Public Control of Private Governing Power* (New York, 1952); Hohfeld, *Fundamental Legal Conceptions as Applied in Judicial Reasoning* (New Haven, 1919); Cohen, "Property and Sovereignty" (1927) XIII *Cornell Law Quarterly* 8; Cohen, "The Basis of Contract" (1933) XLVI *Harvard Law Review*, 553. For modern surveys see Horwitz, *The Transformation of American Law: The Crisis of Legal Orthodoxy, 1870–1960* (New York, 1992) pp. 145–246; Duxbury, "Robert Hale and the Economy of Legal Force" (1990) LIII *Modern Law Review* 421; Samuels, Institutional Economics (1988); Samuels, *The Economy as a System of Power* (1979) Vol. I, pp. 334–393.

[21] *cf.* Lawson and Rudden, *Law of Property* (1982) *op. cit.* above, n.14, p. 1, n.39; Honoré, "Ownership" in Honoré, *Making Law Bind: Essays Legal and Philosophical* (1987) pp. 161–192; Finnis, *Natural Law and Natural Rights* (1980) pp. 169–173; Offer, "Farm Tenures and Land Values in England, c.1750–1950" (1991) XLIV *Economic History Review* 1; Dickson, *op. cit.* above, n.18; Pocock, *Virtue, Commerce and History* (1985) pp. 51–71, 103–123; Vandevelde, "The New Property of the Nineteenth Century: The Development of the Modern Concept of Property" (1980) XXIX *Buffalo Law Review* 325.

rights over the actions of others. Property generally is a form of control of necessary resources vested in certain groups or individuals, their rights being established by public power of law; private property, in practice, functions as a delegation of public power to a monopoly right holder.[22]

This coercive monopolist right is not absolute but can take the form, in Hohfeld's analytic language, of a right proper, a privilege, an immunity, or a power. Thus, a property right need not impose correlative duties of noninterference upon all third parties, but can legitimately be subjected to redistribution or destruction by the operation of other common law rights, by markets, or by regulatory legislation.[23]

The monopolist right of property is diminished primarily by the prospect of competitive injury to physical control and income flow caused by the actions of rival property holders in exploiting their holdings, in the absence of any contractual relations between the rivals specifying the allocation of risks, externalities and other costs. It can be difficult for the law to discriminate between legitimate price competition and coercive interference with assets, and even more difficult to balance competing physical calls on resources; there is a complex "relationship between the 'right' to private property and the legitimacy of injurious competition". In the words of Holmes "[t]he absolute protection of property, however natural to a primitive community more occupied in production than in exchange, is hardly consistent with the requirements of modern business." The economy translates the conflicts and uncertainties of the market into a spectrum of risks that entrepreneurs assume according to their preferences. Moreover, the uncertainty of title and user rights gives rise to competition for the physical control and integrity of resources.[24]

Property takings and delictual compensation policies

The traditional utilitarian insistence on the certainty of individual vested rights neglects the contending needs for the continuous reformation and destruction

---

[22] Hale, "Coercion and Distribution" above, n.20; Cohen, "Property and Sovereignty" above, n.20; Duxbury, "Robert Hale" above, n.20; Horwitz, *Crisis of Legal Orthodoxy*, above, n.20, pp. 160–167. Locke's concept of property as a natural right made effective by social contract is compatible with this analysis (Locke, *Second Treatise of Government*, Chap. ix, ss. 123–127, 395–397).

[23] Hohfeld, *Fundamental Legal Conceptions*. On some of the juristic and economic implications of Hohfeld's analytical scheme: Finnis, *Natural Law and Natural Rights*, pp. 198–230; Duncan Kennedy and Frank Michelman, "Are Property and Contract Efficient?" (1980) VIII *Hofstra Law Review* 711; Singer, "The Legal Rights Debate in Analytical Jurisprudence from Bentham to Hohfeld" [1982] *Wisconsin Law Review* 975; Horwitz, *Crisis of Legal Orthodoxy*, pp. 151–156.

[24] The early modern common law could regard the income generated by a fixed capital investment as protected from interference no less than the physical asset itself. *cf. Sury v. Pigot* (1625) 79 E.R. 1263; 81 E.R. 280 (K.B.). For analysis of common law attitudes to price competition see *Charles River Bridge v. Warren Bridge* (1829) 7 Pick. 344, 352 (Mass.); Horwitz, *Transformation of American Law, 1780–1860*, pp. 130–139; *idem, Crisis of Legal Orthodoxy*, (see nn.20 and 22) p. 154; Holmes, *The Common Law*, p. 80; and see *idem*, "Privilege, Malice, and Intent" (1894) VIII *Harvard Law Review* 1.

of entitlements as an aspect of asymmetric information and risk under capitalism. One task of an effective legal system is to resolve this tension between certainty and contingency in order to prevent property hardening into a rent-extracting monopoly. The pre-eminent solution of the law is to allow the more efficient actor or user to capture, expropriate, or diminish another's right to a resource, on condition of consensual purchase or the payment of delictual or tortious compensation (outside legitimate price competition in which no compensation is required). But compensated takings or interferences can still present a major threat to the stability of entitlements. Compensation is not always forthcoming, nor need it preserve the status of the dispossessed owner. The law can simply refuse to recognise a person's property right as attracting remedial protection, as in the case of the extinguishment of "uncertain" and "unreasonable" common rights during enclosure. Alternatively, the invasion of a recognised legal right can be held to be reasonable, and hence without negative legal sanction – *damnum sine injuria*, in legal phrase, or damage without right, infringement or breach of duty. Another solution is to do away with rigid individual entitlements altogether and create new forms of communal or public goods governed by flexible, discretionary standards of "reasonable usage" that are simpler and cheaper to police than sharply defined standards of private ownership.[25]

The early institutionalists tended to assert blandly that compensation policy and the choice of property forms were questions involving pragmatic shaping of entitlements in the communal interest by the state. More recently, however, economists and legal theorists with less faith in the expertise and neutrality of state regulation have sharpened the characterisation of such policies, suggesting that the legal system often embodies political choices made in an arena of conflict. They have cultivated a number of theories explaining the evolution of property rights in the period of modernisation in Britain and America,[26] ranging from Marxist class and interest group analyses, to transaction cost and game-theoretic theories, to thick legal-historical descriptions of the origins of property. Space does not permit a full examination of these new methodologies; but in their attention to the detail of legal and historical data they are a

---

[25] Coase, "The Problem of Social Cost"; Calabresi and Melamed, "Property Rules, Liability Rules and Inalienability: One View of the Cathedral," (1972) LXXXV *Harvard Law Review* 1089; *Ashby v. White (The Aylesbury voters case)* (1703) 92 E.R. 126, 137; 90 E.R. 1188, 1189 (K.B.), *per* Holt C.J. Examples of communal goods can be found in natural resource law from the mid-nineteenth century in England and America. See Rose, "The Comedy of the Commons: Custom, Commerce and Inherently Private Property", (1986) LIII *University of Chicago Law Review* at pp. 711–781; idem, "Crystals and Mud in Property Law", (1988) XL *Stanford Law Review* at pp. 577–610; *idem*, "Energy and Efficiency in the Realignment of Common-Law Water Rights", *Journal of Legal Studies*, (1990) XIX at pp. 261–296; Merrill, "Trespass, Nuisance, and the Costs of Determining Property Rights" (1985) XIV *Journal of Legal Studies* at pp. 13–48.

[26] All contemporary "law and economics" scholarship, whether written from a neo-classical or radical viewpoint, has been strongly influenced by public-choice theory: see, *e.g.* Posner, *Economic Analysis of Law* (4th ed., Boston, 1992) pp. 519–537; Kelman, *A Guide to Critical Legal Studies* (Cambridge, Mass., 1987) pp. 114–185.

signal advance over prior abstract theorising about the institutions of property.[27] "The rational study of law is still to a large extent the study of history" wrote Holmes in 1897,[28] and one hundred years of reform, legislation, and social transformation have not outdated his dictum.

Summation and envoi

According to classical social and economic theory, markets are constituted by the development and trade of clearly defined property rights. Conversely, markets constitute property rights themselves through transactions between private individuals who wish to define and stabilise their entitlements and thereby maximise investment, production and exchange. The legal and institutional history of the development of property rights in industrialising England shows that there was a large public and political dimension to private property rights that transcended market behaviour and that there was an inherent instability in property as a monopolist power to enjoy resources continually threatened by competitive injury from rival developers. Weberian and economic theories describe property simply as a basis of certainty and prediction. Parsimonious explanations such as these are valuable as a basis for useful generalisation; but new property theory and new historical arguments suggest that legal institutions of property have a more complex role in shaping the course of economic development. It is ironic that property-rights theory, which was first cultivated to correct the exaggerated abstraction of classical social and economic theory, should now itself stand in need of fresh infusions of legal, institutional, and historical thought.

---

[27] See further the full article from which this essay is drawn, above, n.1, at pp. 350–369.
[28] Holmes, "The Path of the Law", (1897) *Harvard Law Review* X 457 at p. 469.

16

Telling Stories: Rights and Wrongs of the Equity of Redemption*

DAVID SUGARMAN** and RONNIE WARRINGTON***

Introduction

One of the protections the legal system developed to safeguard land was the equity of redemption. Largely the creature of the seventeenth and eighteenth centuries, this intricate body of legal doctrine minimised the possibility that landowners would lose their land when they mortgaged it. The courts applied the equity of redemption irrespective of the terms of the agreement between the parties and their manifest intentions. The rights of the landed were thus entrenched as against lenders, even though this might involve the courts re-writing the transactions between the parties. Only in 1914 did the courts substantially recast the doctrine.[1]

In this essay we explore the complex interplay between the legal, economic, political and cultural dimensions of the equity of redemption. The creation and development of the equity of redemption was part of a wider trend within land law concerned with the preservation and consolidation of landed wealth. This topic has already received extensive treatment within the context of the debates surrounding the strict family settlement and primogeniture.[2] Nonetheless, the

---

* David Sugarman was primarily responsible for the Introduction, Part II and the Conclusion of this essay; and Ronnie Warrington was primarily responsible for Part I. This essay is an abbreviated and updated version of a chapter in John Brewer and Susan Staves (eds.), *Early Modern Conceptions of Property*, 1995 pp. 111–143.
** Professor of Law, Department of Law, Lancaster University.
*** Formerly, Senior Lecturer, Department of Law, Lancaster University.
[1] In *Kreglinger v. New Patagonia Meat & Cold Storage* [1914] A.C. 25.
[2] See, generally, English and Saville, *Strict Settlement: A Guide for Historians* (1983); Bonfield, *Marriage Settlements, 1601–1740* (1983); the essays by Chesterman, English and Spring in Rubin and Sugarman (eds.), *Law, Economy and Society, 1750–1914: Essays in the History of English Law* (1984); Spring, *The English Landed Estate in the Nineteenth Century: Its Administration* (1963); Thompson, *English Landed Society in the Nineteenth Century* (1963) and "English Landed Society in the Nineteenth Century" in Thane *et al.* (eds.), *The Power of the Past* (1984); Stone and Stone, *An Open Elite? England, 1540–1880* (1983); Erickson, *Women and Property in Early Modern England* (1993); Cannadine, *The Decline and Fall of the British Aristocracy* (1990); Beckett, *The Aristocracy in England 1660–1914* (1986); Offer, *Property and Politics, 1870–1914* (1981); Spring, *Law, Land and Family: Aristocratic Inheritance in England, 1300 to 1800* (1993); Anderson, *Lawyers and the Making of English Land Law 1832–1940* (1992); Habakkuk, *Marriage, Debt and the Estates System: English Landownership 1650–1950* (1994); Thompson (ed.), *Landowners, Capitalists and Entrepreneurs, Essays for Sir John Habakkuk* (1994).

nature and significance of the equity of redemption has been neglected by almost all but legal historians.[3] More generally, the larger cultural and political significance of property law, in the sense of inventing and policing certain ideas of "Englishness", justice, citizenship and, therefore, the legitimate distribution of power, merit greater attention. It is these facets of property law, as exemplified by the development of the equity of redemption, that we hope to illuminate.[4]

In the first part of this chapter, we analyse the battles waged by judges and jurists to create, extend, and, occasionally, hold in check, this new jurisprudence. We then examine the circumstances that sustained its development. Finally, we briefly consider why a seemingly indestructible doctrine of land law was suddenly and significantly reforged in 1914.

I. THE RISE OF THE EQUITY OF REDEMPTION

1. Mortgages and the equity of redemption

Historically, a mortgage arose where an owner of property (usually land) required money and arranged to transfer the property to a lender as security in return for a loan. The loan agreement would generally provide for a re-conveyance of the property to the borrower at a specific date on repayment of the money borrowed and the interest due. If the loan was not repaid, the property became forfeited to the lender.[5] At common law, the date for repayment had to be strictly adhered to. Even one day's delay in tendering repayment could result in the borrower losing the entire property to the lender, though the amount of the loan was far less than the value of the land.[6]

---

[3] One notable exception being, Melton, *Sir Robert Clayton and the Origins of English Deposit Banking, 1658–1685* (1986). On mortgages and legal history, see Yale, "Introduction: An Essay on Mortgages and Trusts and Allied Topics in Equity" in *Lord Nottingham's Chancery Cases* Vol. II (Seldon Society, Vol. 79, 1961); and Barton, "The Common Law Mortgage" (1967) L.Q.R. 83.

[4] This essay is part of a larger study of the economic, political and cultural significance of law and lawyers in early modern and modern England. See, also, Sugarman and Rubin, "Introduction: Towards A New History of Law and Material Society in England 1750–1914" in Rubin and Sugarman (eds.), *op. cit.* above, n.2, pp. 1–123; Sugarman, *In the Spirit of Weber: Law, Modernity and "the Peculiarities of the English"* (1985); Sugarman, "Legal Theory, the Common Law Mind and the Making of the Textbook Tradition" in Twining (ed.), *Legal Theory and Common Law* (1986) pp. 26–61; Sugarman "Simple Images and Complex Realities: English Lawyers and their Relationship to Business and Politics, 1750–1950" (1993) 11 *Law and History Review* 257; Sugarman, "Bourgeois Collectivism, Professional Power and the Boundaries of the State: The Private and Public Life of the Law Society, 1825–1914" (1995) 3 *International Journal of the Legal Profession* 81.

[5] While the form has changed (see the Law of Property Act 1925, ss.85 *et seq.*), this centuries-old concept is still the basis of the law today.

[6] In the landmark decision in *Kreglinger v. New Patagonia Meat & Cold Storage*, above, n.1, the leading judgment of Lord Parker (at 47) surprisingly appears to get this wrong.

This interpretative stance was challenged by the courts of equity. Dating from at least the turn of the seventeenth century, the courts of equity determined that the strict date for repayment was somewhat irrelevant. Accordingly, the lender's claim to the property became subject: "to a right called the equity of redemption, which arose from the court's consideration that the real object of the transaction was the creation of a security for the debt. This entitled the [borrower] to redeem (or recover the property), even though he had failed to repay by the appointed time".[7]

Time was not to be the essence of the agreement. Although the mortgagor's legal right to redeem the property was lost after the expiration of the time specified in the contract, in equity the mortgagor had an equitable right to redeem on payment within a reasonable period of the principal, interest and costs. A reasonable period could in some cases span many years. The rights of the mortgagor were further enhanced by the rules governing foreclosure.[8]

The discretion to allow the borrower to get back property notwithstanding the contractual terms soon hardened into a right.[9] In addition to this right (the fully-fledged equity of redemption), the courts developed various analogous protections for borrowers. Partly under the umbrella of that seemingly tautological maxim of equity, "once a mortgage always a mortgage", the courts also laid down that the borrower's right to get property back could not be rendered ineffective either by postponing the right for some unacceptable period or by making the right subject to some penalty, such as the borrower being deprived of some or all of the property mortgaged on exercising the right to redeem. What became known as a "collateral advantage", that is, the lender asserting a claim to some or all of the borrower's property irrespective of repayment of the loan, was outlawed.

2. The establishment of the equity of redemption

It is generally agreed that the exact origin of the equity of redemption in its modern form is probably lost. A. W. B. Simpson suggested that the chancery courts were prepared to relieve mortgagors from strict forfeiture conditions from the fifteenth century.[10] But although there are examples to support this, these probably relate to what Simpson calls "peculiarly scandalous cases". The most common example of this would be where the mortgagee was repaid entirely from the rents and profits of the property and still refused to re-convey the

---

[7] Fisher and Lightwood, *The Law of Mortgages* (Tyler ed., 1977) p. 7.
[8] Equity developed the decree of foreclosure, an order of court, made on application by the mortgagee, declaring the equity of redemption at an end and thus leaving the mortgagee with the fee simple absolute. But if the property was worth more than the amount owed by the mortgagor, the court would order a sale of property, the mortgagee taking the money owed to him, the remainder going to the mortgagor.
[9] See, generally, Turner, *The Equity of Redemption: Its Nature, History and Connection with Equitable Estates Generally* (1931).
[10] Simpson, *An Introduction to the History of Land Law* (1961) p. 227.

property to the mortgagor. Richard Turner, the leading historian of the equity of redemption, concluded that the equity of redemption arose during the reign of Elizabeth I.[11] While the court of chancery did grant relief to mortgagors during this period, there are only two reported decisions where relief was given after a forfeiture. It was probably not until the start of the seventeenth century that courts began to grant relief to borrowers as a matter of course, without looking for the special circumstances that would have previously been necessary to activate equity's conscience. The courts gradually extended the list of circumstances that they regarded as causing the special hardship necessary for the court's protection. Thus, the jurisdiction to intervene which had originally operated only in exceptional circumstances became the rule; and the cases where no relief was granted became the exception.[12] Despite the attempts of the Commonwealth Parliament to limit the effectiveness of the right to redemption, and the effort of common lawyers to defeat the equity of redemption on the grounds that it was only a mere chose in action, that is, not a real property interest but merely a personal right recoverable by a suit at law,[13] the mortgagor's claim to preferential treatment as against the mortgagee, irrespective of the terms of the contract, was established.

3. The jurisdiction consolidated

The courts quickly established that the mortgagor (the borrower) could not be prevented from redeeming, either before or after the contractual redemption date.[14] Put simply, the date was fully effective against the lender, but rather less than effective against the borrower. Although later courts stressed that in certain circumstances the mortgagee may be prevented from redeeming early,[15] the vital principle that a mortgagor cannot be prevented from seeking the return of the mortgaged property has been taken to be established in the seventeenth century by Lord Nottingham.

Lord Nottingham was instrumental in starting the shift of the equity of redemption from a "thing" to an "estate" in equity, that is, in conceptualising the equity of redemption as a kind of real property rather than as a kind of chattel property. Increasingly, mortgagor's claims were given precedence over other interests to which they had earlier been postponed: for example, mortgagor's claims came to take precedence even over a real property claim like the wife's right to dower. In *Attorney General v. Pawlett* (1667),[16] Lord Hale first char-

---

[11] Turner, *op. cit.* above, n.9, p. 26.
[12] Turner, *op. cit.* above, n.9, pp. 26–27. Our account of the development of the equity of redemption in Part One of this essay is largely derived from Warrington, "Law and Property: the Equity of Redemption Re-examined, An Essay in Socio-Legal History" (Ph.D. thesis., University College, London University, 1982) Chaps. 7–9.
[13] *Roscarrick v. Barton* (1672) 1 Ch. Cas. 216.
[14] See, *e.g. Talbot v. Braddil* (1681) 1 Vern 394.
[15] *Brown v. Cole* (1845) 14 Sim 427.
[16] Hardres 465.

acterised the equity of redemption as a title in equity. According to Lord Hale, a trust was contractual in nature, while the equity of redemption was proprietorial. Lord Nottingham took this further by distinguishing the trust (binding in particular) from the equity of redemption (binding in general).[17] Lord Nottingham wrote that equity suffers no land to be lost, "if in a convenient time it may be redeemed . . . " and that equity would always allow a mortgage to be redeemed.[18] "No words of Scrivener nor any invention of Counsel can make that which was intended as a mortgage to work as an absolute assurance . . . ".[19] In *Jason v. Eyres* (1680), as judge rather than historian, Lord Nottingham declared: "That no Mortgage by any artificial words can be altered, unless by subsequent agreement".[20]

Although the principle in *Jason v.Eyres* was clear enough, an early nineteenth-century commentator, R. H. Coote, argued that the decision should have gone against the mortgagor on the same principle on which Lord Nottingham was reversed in the case of *Newcombe v. Bonham* (1681).[21] The history of this important decision is of some interest. In his version of the case, Lord Nottingham is reported as not only using the maxim "once a mortgage always a mortgage", but as stating that the agreement "being but a security, the same could not be extinguished by any covenant or agreement at the time of making the mortgage".[22] Yet the decision was, after some hesitation, reversed by Lord North. The agreement in the case was part of a family settlement where the mortgagor was permitted to redeem during his own lifetime only. Lord North thought that, therefore, on the original borrower's death, the right to redeem was at an end since otherwise inter-family arrangements might be upset because of the "indefinite" possibility of redemption.

Lord North's decision on the grounds of family security illustrates the problems that might be caused by a mechanistic interpretation of the equity of redemption. It foreshadowed difficulties equity would face with its own creation at a much later period. The point at issue was how far should courts take on themselves the duty to interfere in private arrangements. Two years later in *Howard v. Harris* (1683),[23] on similar facts, Lord Nottingham made the same decision. This time Lord North upheld the judgment, but again dropped hints that in cases of family settlements the courts might not interfere.

Other decisions which seem to prevent redemption such as *Isham v. Cole* (1639),[24] where confronted with a 33-year mortgage, it was stressed that "this Court doth hold it a dangerous Precedent to relieve Mortgages after so long an

---

[17] See, further, Turner, *op. cit.* above, n.9, pp. 54–55.
[18] *Lord Nottingham's Manual of Chancery Practice and Prolegomena of Chancery and Equity* (Yale ed., 1975) p. 280.
[19] *ibid.* p. 282.
[20] 2 Chan. Cas. 33 at 35.
[21] 1 Vern 7; 1 Vern 214; 1 Vern 232; 2 Vern 264.
[22] *op. cit.* above, n.18, at 266.
[23] 1 Vern 33; affirmed 1 Vern 190.
[24] 1 Chan. Rep. 127.

Elapse of Time",[25] or *Floyer v. Lavington* (1714)[26] where redemption was not permitted after 60 years, or *Mellor v. Lees* (1742)[27] where the court appeared to accept the perpetual mortgage of a rent charge, were equally by-passed as either erroneous or decided on "special circumstances".[28]

There were other instances where the exceptions appear to have almost challenged the basic equitable jurisdiction itself, although, significantly, until the end of the nineteenth century none of them actually did so. But despite these exceptional areas,[29] the move to establish a strong equity of redemption became too powerful to resist. To put it as Turner would, in terms of personalities, the tide turned in favour of Lord Nottingham.

Lord Nottingham was also responsible for settling that mortgagees' (that is, the lenders) rights were mere personality. In *Thornborough v. Baker* (1675) he explained this by saying: "For in natural justice and equity the principle right of the mortgagee is to the money, and his rights to the land is only as a security for the money . . . ".[30] The property, that is the land, really belonged to the borrower; the lender was only entitled to the money. Even Lord Mansfield seems to have had no doubts that in this area of the law the position of the landed gentry should be privileged irrespective of the intentions of the parties.[31]

Despite these legal developments, numerous lenders tried to circumvent the equitable protections. But time and again the courts stressed they would strike down the actual terms of a contract.[32] Claims that the mortgage had subsisted for too long to permit a redemption were also rejected.[33] Nor were the courts impressed when the mortgagee claimed to have suffered particular hardship or taken unusual risks.[34] This justice was not an abstract principle. It turned upon the assumptions of those who were deciding what was or what was not "just". And for most judges most of the time, justice in this context meant the restoration of landed property to the original owner.

As already suggested, Turner reduces much of his history of the equity of redemption to the "personality" of the Chancellors. This allows him to move straight from Lord Nottingham, the father of the equity of redemption, to Lord Hardwicke, who became the most important figure in the story by "consolidating" the work of Lord Nottingham. Lord Hardwicke's influential tenure as Lord Chancellor from 1736 to 1756 helped to settle equity as a system of general rules. If nothing else, Lord Hardwicke's claim to the central position in the story

---

[25] *ibid.* at 528.
[26] 1 P Wms 268.
[27] 2 Atk 494.
[28] See, *e.g.* Coote, *A Treatise on the Law of Mortgages* (1821) pp. 41–42.
[29] A major exception was created in the nineteenth century in relation to mortgages on West Indian Estates.
[30] 3 Swans 628; 36 E.R. 1000 at 1001.
[31] 1 Eden 177; 96 E.R. 67 at 84.
[32] See, *e.g. Spurgeon v. Collier* (1758) 1 Eden 56; 28 E.R. 605 at 606.
[33] See, *e.g. Cornel v. Sykes* (1660) 1 Chan. Rep. 193.
[34] *Newton v. Langham* (1675) 2 Chan. Rep. 108; 21 E.R. 630.

is assured by his famous decision in *Casborne v. Scarfe* (1735).[35] While this case is by no means the first to define the equity of redemption as an estate,[36] the importance of the equity of redemption as the equivalent of ownership limited through time is fundamental. It provided the legal foundation to underpin the "fairness" of the courts' interference in contract. Not only was this just, it was technically correct. Although doubts lingered in the minds of some judges for a century or more as to the accuracy of characterising the equity of redemption as an estate, for practical purposes they were of no further significance.[37] By 1822, Thomas Coventry could write as incontrovertible: "An equity of redemption will follow the custom as to the legal estate".[38]

A similar transformation took place to the rules governing what were termed "collateral advantages". These rules policed any additional benefit that the mortgagee had extracted from the mortgagor, additional that is to the interest and the principal owed to the mortgagee. As with the rules relating to attempts to limit rights to redeem, anything that allowed the mortgagee the slightest opportunity of obtaining the mortgaged property itself was, by definition, oppressive or unjust.

When doubts were cast on these decisions by Lords Lindley, Romer, Jessell and others at the end of the nineteenth century, many reasons were given as to why the collateral advantage rules should not be followed. But as we shall see, the crucial thing was that the late nineteenth century courts no longer found these decisions "just" or "reasonable". According to Lindley L.J., delivering judgment in 1898, to call a normal collateral agreement unconscionable, "would shock any business man . . . ".[39] Perhaps it would, and in this area at least, so far as his Lordship was concerned, what did not shock a business man did not shock him.[40]

In summary, the general effect of the rules governing the equity of redemption was to protect the owners of landed wealth as far as possible. The rules never purported to allow borrowers to escape from the actual debts they contracted, but the courts took it upon themselves to decide the limits beyond which lenders of money secured on landed estates could not go. In the mid-nineteenth century, the jurisdiction was seemingly incontrovertible. Even as late as 1912, Lord Halsbury spoke of "this equitable doctrine which, I agree, is now part of the jurisprudence of this country".[41]

---

[35] 1 Atk 598; for the notes, see 2 J & W 194; 37 E.R. 600. On Lord Harwicke's contribution to the law, the best modern account is Croft, "Philip Yorke, First Earl of Hardwicke – An Assessment of his Legal Career", PhD. Cambridge University, 1982 and the same author's contribution on Lord Harwicke's use of precedent in Equity in Watkin (ed.), *Legal Records and Historical Reality*, (1989) Chap. 8.
[36] Lord Hardwick's own notes refer to several earlier decisions.
[37] See Turner, *op. cit.* above, n.9, pp. 71–87.
[38] Powell, *A Treatise on the Law of Mortgages* (5th ed., Coventry ed.) (1822) Vol. 1, 265.
[39] *Biggs v. Hoddinott* [1898] 2 Ch. D. 307 at 321; see, also at 320.
[40] Lord Hardwicke's relation to the landowners of his time is vividly described in Thompson, *Whigs and Hunters: the Origin of the Black Act* (1977) especially at 208 *et seq.*
[41] *De Beers Consolidated Mines v. British South Africa* [1912] A.C. 52.

4. Little short of ideal

Why was this highly interventionist jurisdiction fair; and how was it justified? Judges and jurists tended to adopt two intersecting rationales for this special jurisdiction. First, one distinctive strand of Equity's broad and highly discretionary jurisdiction in Fraud concerned the protection of young heirs. In these cases it would be argued that landed heirs should be relieved from their bargains to borrow money, convey land, buy horses, jewellery, etc., because these bargains were unconscionable and fraudulent. They were fraudulent and unconscionable because the young heir concerned was in "necessitous circumstances". Because they felt impelled to undertake the sort of bargains that others would scorn, they were the obvious targets of what were characterised as "unscrupulous money-lenders" or "rogues" selling goods at a high price. It was co-extensive with these developments that equity developed and consolidated the equity of redemption. The doctrine was intended to protect the landowner from the money hungry activity of commercial interests. The anomalous character of this protection for the "necessitous" is evident when one considers the many other instances in which starker necessitousness did not postpone debts due.

Secondly, it was emphasised that the court's function was to ensure that ultimately land was returned to its "rightful" (often meaning historical or traditional) owner. Even when the terms of the contract unequivocally pointed to an agreement to transfer the ownership of the land in exchange for money, goods or services, the courts were seemingly loath to accept it at face value.

As the story was told by Turner, the development of the equity of redemption was a minor miracle. Speaking of Lord Hardwicke's role in the development, he could hardly contain his enthusiasm. His Lordship had created a body of law that was "fair", "rational", and "noble", ". . . a structure which soon became one of the most important features of English land law, having a far reaching effect upon the internal economic position of the country".[42] Although Turner conceded that the end result was not quite up to the high standard of Roman law: "The conceptions upon which the rules in application are based are sound in character and little short of the ideal".[43] He even allowed his enthusiasm to go so far as to suggest a comparison between the creation and development of the equity of redemption and the development of new symbols in mathematics making possible further advances into "unknown realms of mathematical speculation".[44] Here was a doctrine that could indeed perform miracles.

Ironically, Turner completely failed to comprehend that this near perfect doctrine had been substantially re-cast by the House of Lords in *Kreglinger v. New Patagonia*,[45] a case which he describes but whose significance escaped him. In this case, their Lordship's sought to cut back the long-standing doctrine that all

---

[42] Turner, *op. cit.* above, n.9, p. 136.
[43] Turner, *op. cit.* above, n.9, p. 137.
[44] Turner, *op. cit.* above, n.9, pp. 137–138.
[45] [1914] A.C. 25.

collateral advantages in favour of the mortgagee, that is, something granted to the mortgagee in addition to the return of the loan and interest, were invalid. These contracts were no longer viewed as automatically unfair and unconscionable. The result was that the equity of redemption had been significantly weakened. One conception of fairness (the fairness needed to protect and entrench the superior position of the landed oligarchy) had been largely supplanted by another conception of fairness (the fairness demanded by the financier) which appeared to demand the rigorous enforcement of the letter of contracts. Since Turner treated the development of the equity of redemption as intrinsically natural, desirable and superior, thereby abstracting the history of the doctrine from the context within which it was inscribed, he was unable to recognise that when circumstances changed the doctrine might no longer appear so natural and superior.

II. Another Way of Seeing: the Economic, Cultural and Political Dimensions of the Equity of Redemption

1. England's patrician polity, the law of real property and myth-making

What were the particular circumstances that sustained the construction and expansion of the equity of redemption, and enabled the landed elite to exploit it? First and foremost, was the fact that until the 1870s England was a "patrician polity".[46] Until the 1870s, the landed establishment owned about four-fifths of the land in the British Isles. Their political, economic and cultural hegemony was exemplified by their pre-eminence in government, parliament, the law, the church, the civil service and the armed forces.

In Britain, land was sacred: it denoted status and citizenship. Most landowners were faced at some time or other with pressure to sell their land. Writing in 1827, Sir James Graham recognised the problems that heavy indebtedness caused many country gentlemen, and conceded that sale was a possibility:

> "But what agony of mind does that word convey? The snapping of a chain, linked perhaps by centuries; the destruction of the dearest attachments, the dissolution of the earliest friendships, the violation of the purest feelings of the heart."[47]

This reluctance to sell was part of a larger ethos: namely, the landowners' desire to create and maintain a dynasty. As Edmund Burke put it, landownership was: "a partnership not only between those of the living, but between those who were living, those who were dead, and those who are to be born".[48] Most large landowning families schemed with varying degrees of success to ensure that the interests of future generations were secure. The legal system played a

---

[46] Cannadine, *op. cit.* above, n.2, p. 37.
[47] Graham, *Corn and Currency* (1827) p. 25.
[48] Quoted in Beckett, *op. cit.* above, n.2, p. 49.

decisive role in these developments. As Maitland observed, "our whole constitutional law seems at times to be but an appendix to the law of real property".[49]

The landed elite and the law were intensely bound together. From 1621 until 1844, the kingdom's supreme judges were not the professional lawyers of Kings Bench or Chancery but England's nobility assembled in parliament. The largest owners of property became the highest judges of the law of property. Even after 1844, England's most senior judges and law officers continued to be peers in part because the House of Lords remained the kingdom's supreme court of judicature.[50] The close relationship between the landed establishment and the law was reinforced by the fact that a significant proportion of the aristocracy took up the law in some form up to as late as the 1880s.[51]

In myriad ways the law constituted and symbolised the elevated position of the landed establishment.[52] Of major importance to the landed oligarchy was the fabrication of a system of equity alongside the common law from the fifteenth century onwards. The Court of Chancery was the great conduit of this equitable jurisdiction, a jurisdiction which tended to moderate the rigidities and formalism of the common law, particularly as it affected the landed. The close relationship between land and the law was further entwined with the privatisation of the process by which land ownership was transferred (conveyancing). In an elaborate process of judicial construction, the Statute of Uses of 1536 was interpreted so that conveyancing came to be undertaken by private contract, designed and overseen by lawyers, rather than involving the supervision of the courts. Nowhere was this dependence upon the legal profession more evident than in the extensive use that large land owning families made of the strict settlement, a legal device developed during the seventeenth century to forestall estate fragmentation.[53]

The attitude that it was the landowners' natural privilege to take loans on security and then be relieved from the terms of the bargain, persisted until well into the nineteenth century. Lord Guildford borrowed money at 60 per cent when an expectant heir and then successfully claimed that the strict terms of the bond that he gave against the expectancy should not be upheld. The exchange between counsel for the lender and Lord Guildford shows his Lordship denying that he even understood the meaning of "sixty per cent". "I did not know whether it high or low interest; I thought money-lenders always charged that amount" he said. Asked whether he thought the rate too high, he replied: "I think they ought to let me have money at a lower interest; because

---

[49] Maitland, *The Constitutional History of England*, (Fisher ed. 1908) p. 538.
[50] Hart, *Justice Upon Petition* (1992); Stevens, *Law and Politics: the House of Lords as a Judicial Body 1800–1976* (1979).
[51] Abel-Smith and Stevens, *Lawyers and the Courts* (1967) pp. 53–77, 187–209; Cannadine, *op. cit.* above, n.2, pp. 250–255.
[52] In peacetime, at least until the end of the eighteenth century, the taxes levied on land were less than those borne by trade: Colley, *Britons* (1992) pp. 64–65.
[53] See, generally, the references above, n.2.

Telling Stories: Rights and Wrongs of the Equity of Redemption 217

they know perfectly well that I was certain to come into the property, and that I could pay them and I was quite right to borrow the money if I wanted it."[54]

To emphasise the significance of England's landed polity does not require that we marginalise the significance of commerce, and from the late eighteenth century to the Thatcher era, Britain's industrial and manufacturing economy. The significance of credit, and the relations of mutual dependence that it gave rise to helped to bind together landowners, bankers and shopkeepers. Indeed, the equity of redemption helped to foster increased consumption and the expansion of credit by convincing more landowners that the risk of losing their property by way of mortgage was minimal. Most lenders, on the other hand, succeeded in protecting themselves by using bonds for security of rent rather than the actual land itself. Thus, use and avoidance of the law might go hand-in-hand.

2. The narratives of the equity of redemption

In addition to being an important instrument for preserving and consolidating landed wealth, the equity of redemption was also a set of political and cultural codes. It was a repository of stories signifying the central importance of the landed aristocracy and gentry to English society. It assumed a certain ordering of preferences and rights: of what was proper and illicit; and who and what should be recognised, protected and excluded. What we see here is the construction of memory, consciousness and identity, a process binding together and privileging particular conceptions of "justice" and "Englishness". [55]

In order to appreciate these links, we must consider how the equity of redemption exemplified a wider language and imagery, melding religious, historical and legal symbols and tropes into a reservoir of political language which embodied a particular national mythology. The close association of Protestantism, the sanctity of property and a unique legal order with the English (and British) nation was the product of the seventeenth and eighteenth centuries. The translation of the Old Testament into the vernacular and its dissemination, along with other leading Protestant texts (Bunyan's, *Pilgrim's Progress*, Foxe's, *Book of the Martyrs*, etc.), helped to forge a national discourse among rich and poor alike in which the English became God's chosen people, the defenders of Protestantism, forever locked in battle with the forces of Satan, Catholicism and despotism.[56] The great meta-narratives were often superimposed onto Biblical narratives, telling stories of steady progress, or of a once simple, golden age now debased, or of loss, struggle and redemption.[57] Particularly relevant here is the language of

---

[54] See *Aylesford v.Morris* (1872) 42 LJ Ch. 146 at 151–152.
[55] *cf.* Merry, *Getting Justice and Getting Even* (Chicago, 1990).
[56] Smith, *The Politics of Language 1791–1819* (1984); Cressy, *Bonfires and Bells* (California, 1989); Joyce, *Visions of the People* (1991) *op. cit.* above, n.52, pp. 173–174; Colley, Chap. 1.
[57] Other significant idioms which influenced political discourse include the languages of commercial society, republicanism and humanism.

precedent and the ancient constitution: the idea of English law as immemorial custom, rooted in the distant past, the feudal law, the only law that England had known, the great palladium of individual freedom and liberty.[58] In this brogue, rights were largely determined by appeals to the past. The sanctity of the law of real property, for instance, derived from the insistence of the common lawyers that this branch of law was specially privileged because its authority could be sought in time immemorial. Central, here, was the idea that the English were exceptionally fortunate – bathed in the King's Peace, sustained by Magna Carta, and thereby secure in the protection of their property and person.[59] In these ways the longevity and sanctity of England's religion, law and history were interwoven to create a common identity.

This imbrication of the languages of religion, history and law is significant with respect to narratives of the equity of redemption. To redeem has long meant to buy back a thing formerly possessed. But it also has other meanings touching upon the honour, status, and liberty of the redeemer which may be relevant in understanding why equity sought to intervene in the private world of agreement and accord. Thus, it was honourable people who sought to redeem their pledges, that is, buy back a thing formerly possessed; and the act of redemption was itself a symbol of their honour and gentility. To disable persons of standing from redeeming their pledges would therefore touch the position and honour of that individual. If the law placed obstacles in the way of the redemption of land, previously honourable people would be dishonoured and bondage might ensue. In this sense to redeem one's land was an act of liberation, akin to the paying of a ransom, and yet another meaning of "to redeem".

Even more potent was the image of the aristocracy and landed gentry, clothed in the title associated with Christ himself, as the redeemers of English society. Viewed from this optic, the landed gentry embodied the same elevated role in secular society as that performed by Christ in the spiritual world. The redeemer was someone especially worthy of or entitled to deliverance from sin and damnation. In the context of the equity of redemption, the law incorporated the imperative that the landed should be saved from excommunication; that is, losing their land and therefore their souls. Moreover, their curse might also be ours too. Thus, to grant redemption to the landed gentry was to preserve and redeem English society as a whole. Ultimately, their ownership interests were imagined as having a sacred quality: the preservation of the rights of the landed oligarchy guaranteed the continuance of divine favour, stability, and national identity.

3. Property, citizenship and the constitutional idiom

The legal community, personified above all by Lord Mansfield, had exhibited great ingenuity in developing a commercial common law sensitive to the needs

---

[58] See, Pocock, *The Ancient Constitution and the Feudal Law* (1987).
[59] Thompson, *Magna Carta* (Minnesota, 1948); Pallister, *Magna Carta* (1977); Goodrich and Hachamovitch, in Fitzpatrick (ed.), *Dangerous Supplements* (1992) pp. 172–173.

of commercial society.[60] But co-existing uneasily alongside these innovations was England's law of real property; and it was here that Mansfield locked horns with Blackstone. It was Blackstone who led the attack on what he and other judges regarded as Lord Mansfield's innovatory approach to real property, an approach that others stigmatised as Scottish, Romanist and alien.[61] In Blackstone's view:

> "... the law of real property in this country is now formed into a fine artificial system, full of unseen connections and nice dependencies, and he that breaks one link of the chain endangers the dissolution of the whole".[62]

The landed elite were entitled to their privileged status because they were part of an elaborate structure that held the nation together. Significant tinkering with the law of real property and the rights of the landed threatened to destroy English society.

Blackstone's passionate defence of the sanctity of land, with its attendant celebration of the common law, was reiterated by Edmund Burke.[63] For both Blackstone and Burke, any erosion of property opened the floodgates to radical reform, levelling and anarchy. In his celebrated *Reflections on the Revolution in France*, Burke argued that the concentration of large tracts of landed wealth in the hands of the few was both necessary and desirable; and that land must remain unfettered for such consolidation created: " ... a natural rampart about the lesser properties in all their gradations".[64] Again, the rhetorical thrust of these narratives was to demonstrate that the privileged position of the landed was just, and that its special prerogatives also served the best interests of the nation.

From this perspective, the narratives, symbols and rhetoric of the equity of redemption was part of a larger, conservative discourse which confined citizenship to the owners of real property, idealising an "independent" aristocracy mindful of all "the people". In so doing it designated some categories of persons as different from others, implicitly negating certain individuals and social relations, while claiming to be neutral. For example, it was defined against more inclusive notions of citizenship such as plebeian and radical notions of common law rights to land as public or communal property[65] and those customary

---

[60] See, generally, Oldham, *The Mansfield Manuscripts and the Growth of English Law in the Eighteenth Century* (North Carolina Press, 1992).
[61] See, *e.g.* Lord Camden's Argument in Doe on the Demise of Hindson. . . .Wherein Lord Mansfield's Argument in Wyndham v. Chetwind is Considered and Answered (1766).
[62] Fifoot, *Lord Mansfield* (1936) at p. 159, n.2, citing Justice Blackstone in *Perrin v. Blake* (1772). See, further, Lieberman, "Property, Commerce and the Common Law: Attitudes to Change in the Eighteenth Century" in Brewer and Staves, (eds.), *Early Modern Conceptions of Property* (1995) pp. 144–160.
[63] *cf.* Pocock, *Politics, Language and Time* (New York, 1971) in the chapter entitled "Burke and the Ancient Constitution".
[64] Burke, *Reflections on the Revolution in France* (O'Brien ed. 1968) p. 140.
[65] On communitarian, radical and other alternative conceptions of property and citizenship see, Hill, "The Norman Yoke" in his *Puritanism and Revolution* (1955); Smith, *The Gothic Bequest*

use rights in commons pertaining to gleaning, grazing, hunting, wood-gathering, etc., rights which were increasingly attacked in the eighteenth and nineteenth centuries by more exclusive uses of land.[66]

The common law also starkly distinguished between the British subject, who could own real property, and the alien, who could not. Throughout the eighteenth century, Catholics and Jews were treated as non-British. Immigration controls were properly installed by 1793, and the liberalisation of naturalisation was frustrated until 1836.[67] Of course the most obvious exclusion from the languages of property and citizenship were women. Much of the law (like much elite and popular culture) was intensely patriarchal, and the equity of redemption was no exception. As The Bible and the classic European texts, like Homer's *Odyssey* and Plato's *Symposium*, told and retold the heroic tale of how males took charge of heaven and earth, so the narratives of the equity of redemption was part of an exclusionary canon which celebrated "manliness" and represented women as different human subjects within a particular hierarchy.[68]

4. Room for manoeuvre

The equity of redemption exemplified but one of the several languages that together characterised the law of real property and contemporary debates concerning personhood. The languages of religion, history and the law had worked together to create a fixed and coherent conception of national identity through the narratives of their discourses. But as the Bible's stories had lent themselves to radically different interpretations, so also the narratives of history and the law. The languages of precedent, the common law, the ancient constitution and constitutionalism were together the major shared political idiom within which politics was spoken. But they were sufficiently ambiguous that they could be appropriated in different ways by unequally situated social groups. These groups sought to have their representations of the world recognised.[69] Thus, liberals and radicals claimed more comprehensive rights of political participation through expanded conceptions of property and citizenship.

(1987); Chase, *The People's Farm* (1988); Claeys, *Machinery, Money and the Millennium* (1987), *Thomas Paine* (1989), and *Citizens and Saints* (1989); Yeo, "Socialism, the State, and Some Oppositional Englishness" in Collis and Dodd (eds.), *Englishness: Politics and Culture, 1880–1920* (1986) p. 308; Horne, *Property Rights and Poverty* (North Carolina, 1990); Sapiro, *A Vindication of Political Virtue: The Political Theory of Mary Wollstonecraft* (Chicago, 1992).

[66] Hay *et al.* (eds.), *Albion's Fatal Tree*; Thompson, *Customs in Common*, Chap. iii; Linebaugh, *The London Hanged* (1991).

[67] With respect to Catholics, see Colley, *op. cit.* above, n.52, at pp. 19, 325–333 and Bossy, *The English Catholic Community, 1570–1850* (1975). On the treatment of Jews and aliens, see Henriques, *Law of Aliens and Naturalisation* (1906) and *The Jews and English Law* (1908); and Bevan, *The Development of British Immigration Law* (1986) pp. 50–64.

[68] See Staves, *Married Women's Separate Property in England*; Spring, *Law, Land and Family*; Erickson, *Women and Property in Early Modern England*; Menafee, *Wives for Sale* (1981).

[69] See, Bourdieu, "The Force of Law" (1987) 38 *Hastings Law Journal* 805; and Epstein, "Understanding the Cap of Liberty" (1989) 122 *Past & Present* 76.

Moreover, the moral justification for aristocratic rule could be turned on its head as liberals and radicals alike questioned its moral and economic basis in a world increasingly dominated by the language of economic freedom. From Adam Smith's criticism of strict settlements, to Ricardo's critique of unearned rents, from John Stuart Mill's advocacy of the reform of the law governing land tenure to Maitland's admonishment of primogeniture, the wisdom of limiting power in a landed elite was increasingly scrutinised in late Georgian and Victorian England. And from the 1870's to the First World War, "the land question" was revived, and the reform of primogeniture, entails, strict settlements, etc., became a major political issue.[70] By this time, the reasons for the equity of redemption – the strong desire of the owners of property to retain their hold over it – looked increasingly anachronistic. The rate of return on land significantly declined and the economic development of land fostered by coal, railways, urbanisation and the employment of professional land agents, all encouraged the landed to dispose of their land:

> "Land started to come on the market during the 1880s and 1890s ... The real tidal change arrived in the years 1910–14 ... In one week during June 1910 over 72,000 acres in thirty-six counties were offered for sale in England, and during the corresponding week a year later the total rose to 98,000 acres. [By] the outbreak of the First World War it was calculated that perhaps 800,000 acres had changed hands over the previous five years."[71]

5. The metamorphosis of the equity of redemption

As we have seen, there have always been some members of the judiciary who took issue with the doctrine of the equity of redemption even in its seventeenth- and eighteenth-century heydays. These misgivings grow louder from about the middle of the nineteenth century. Those elements of resistance within the discourse itself were galvanised anew as a more middle class judiciary found themselves privileging a social group, the landed, who no longer seemed to need nor merit this privileging. The period from the late eighteenth to the late nineteenth century witnessed a "shift in emphasis from property law to contract...."[72] [The] equation of general principles of contract law with the free market economy led to an emphasis on the framework within which individuals bargained with each other ...".[73]

Law was one of several discursive processes which helped to forge these new representations of the social world and personhood, determining who could

---

[70] Offer, *op. cit.* above, n.2.
[71] Beckett, *op. cit.* above, n.2, p. 85. As the rationale for the equity of redemption was re-worked from above so it was also re-worked from below with the democratisation of the mortgage and the rise of building societies.
[72] Atiyah, *The Rise and Fall of Freedom of Contract* (1979) p. 388.
[73] *ibid.* p. 402.

speak and how. These narratives celebrated commerce, the crucial economic role played by the middle classes, the freedom of the market, self-help and a less aristocratic notion of property and personhood. Freedom of contract served to fuse the tradition of the ancient constitution to a new emphasis on business and the town as the expressions of a liberal sense of evolutionary progress and national advance.[74] These narratives presented the middle classes as the real guardians of society.[75]

The members of the judiciary closely involved with the equity of redemption at the end of the nineteenth century and the beginning of the twentieth century had lost their aristocratic bias and were strong advocates of the new contract orthodoxy.[76] The mortgagor it argued was "usually a grown-up man, with a very clear vision of his own interests, and quite able to take care of himself even without the Solicitor who is generally found at his elbow".[77] Hence, presumably, there was no need for the classic equity of redemption. For these judges, their role was not to protect one species of property, land, but to protect contractual rights generally, that is, to protect forms of property including rights in land, but not privilege rights in land. If the courts were still to interfere with bargains freely made as the equity of redemption demanded, what would happen to sacred *laissez-faire* doctrines? Faced with these two apparently conflicting positions, the courts decided, after some hesitation, that freedom of contract as they understood it meant more to them than anything else, including the classic form of the equity of redemption. From this perspective, the metamorphosis of the equity of redemption was part of a late exorcism of sixteenth, seventeenth and eighteenth century notions of the place of land and the landed in English property holding and a manifestation of alternative conceptions of justice and Englishness.

The victory of freedom of contract over property had less to do with the intrinsic superiority of the arguments concerned than the circumstances in which they were expressed, which enabled certain groups to exploit them. From the Third Reform Act to the First World War, debates concerning citizenship intensified and progressive liberals sought to transcend the atomistic individualism of classic liberalism. In the eyes of old liberals like the constitutional lawyer, Albert Venn Dicey, the much-feared age of collectivism had arrived.[78] From this perspective, the upholding of freedom of contract with respect to the equity of redemption, and by implication minimal state interference, was itself an attempt to entrench the individualism of classic liberalism in a period when it

---

[74] *cf.* Joyce, *op. cit.* above, n.56, p. 177.
[75] Joyce, *op. cit.* above n.56, p. 185.
[76] Lord Jessel, for example, thought it unarguable that freedom of contract was necessary for property-owners: *Wallis v. Smith* (1882) 21 Ch. D. 243 at 266. See, too, his notorious celebration of freedom of contract in *Printing and Numerical v. Sampson* (1875) LR 19 EQ 462.
[77] (1899) 15 L.Q.R. 3.
[78] Dicey, *Law and Public Opinion* (1914).

seemed increasingly under attack. Such, then, was the context within which the equity of redemption was reformulated by the House of Lords in 1914.[79]

Conclusion

The belated metamorphosis of the equity of redemption, and therefore of the transformation of property, from older monopolistic forms of ownership grounded in the privileges of status to newer contractual, individualistic, and free-market forms of ownership, testifies to the tenacity of what some commentators have called the backward or feudal dimensions of modern English society.[80] Yet as with so much of English property law, its pre-modern form was deceptive and paradoxical.[81] The tenacity of the equity of redemption demonstrates that in some areas of property relations commercial prosperity was parasitic upon the stability, strength, and survival of the landed gentry. The mortgage, and the doctrine of the equity of redemption which accompanied it, facilitated both, on the one hand, the qualification, alienation, and fragmentation of property, and, on the other hand, the concentration of landed wealth and more absolute and exclusive property rights. The rise and tenacity of the equity of redemption highlights some of the ways in which certain areas of property law privileged the rights of the landed for a longer time-span than is often assumed; yet at the same time, fostered the extension of commercial contracts sustained by credit. From an economic perspective, the equity of redemption created a legal bulwark safeguarding land (and the landed) from the encroachments of capital, while helping to fashion the mortgage as a major vehicle for economic development. From a legal perspective, although the creation and development of the equity of redemption has been taken as exemplifying the law's increasing commitment to the notion of property as individual absolute dominion, it also illustrates the extent to which the law routinely fostered the qualification of property and restraints on alienation. Although the ideology of absolute private property denied those social and collaborative dimensions intrinsic to human endeavour, in practice the law continually threatened to undo the viability of one of the central tropes of eighteenth and nineteenth century political discourse. In these ways it could be both feudal and modern.

---

[79] In *Kreglinger v. New Patagonia Meat & Cold Storage* above, n.1. For a detailed analysis of how this case re-made the doctrine of the equity of redemption, see Warrington, *op. cit.* above, n.12.

[80] See, for example, Anderson, *English Questions* (1992); Mayor, *The Persistence of the Old Regime* (1981); Wiener, *English Culture and the Decline of the Industrial Spirit 1850–1980*; Habakkuk, *Marriage, Debt and the Estates System* (1994); *cf.* Thompson, "The Peculiarities of the English" in his *The Poverty of Theory and Other Essays* (1978) and Wood, *The Pristine Culture of Capitalism* (1991).

[81] Sugarman and Rubin, "Introduction: Towards A New History of Law and Material Society in England 1750–1914" in Rubin and Sugarman (eds.), *op. cit.* above, n.4; Sugarman, *In the Spirit of Weber, op. cit.* above, n.4; Wood, *The Pristine Culture of Capitalism* (1991) at pp. 45–54; Gordon, "Paradoxical Property" in Brewer and Staves (eds.), *Early Modern Conceptions of Property* (1995) at pp. 95–110.

In a society where there were few legal restrictions with regard to who might buy and sell land and where it was seldom in short supply, the law facilitated the preservation and consolidation of what the landed already possessed. The equity of redemption should be seen as part of a wider movement throughout most of western Europe during the sixteenth and seventeenth centuries when legal devices of various sorts were introduced to prevent estate fragmentation. What distinguishes England from much of Continental Europe is that these rules were enforced until the end of the nineteenth century, and, in the case of the equity of redemption, to the First World War.

These efforts at preservation and extension did not invariably work. Thus, they were also important as symbols of power, knowledge, justice, and Englishness, of what was legitimate and illegitimate, conceivable and inconceivable, public and private. Under this wider optic, the law of property was, amongst other things, an important form of story-telling. It provided *post-hoc* explanations for particular relationships between people.[82] Certain forms of property relations, and, therefore, the ability to exercise power over other people, were rendered more natural than other types of relations.

Much has also been made of the deference to the aristocracy and its values by the rising business and professional classes, and the cohesive self-confidence of the aristocracy until at least 1914.[83] In so far as this is correct, it requires that further consideration be given to the law of property as an instrumentality and as a symbol which isolated and privileged certain groups so as to make their actions intelligible and legitimate. Within the dynamic field of political struggle, significant tracts of the law of property and, therefore, the core of the common law helped to generate "knowledges" that tended to render aristocratic rule natural and essential. Other branches of property law, however, were more openly supportive of "commerce". It is, perhaps, this contradictory juxtaposition that helps to explain England's distinctive route towards modernity.[84]

---

[82] See, Rose, *Property and Persuasion* (1994).
[83] See the references above in n.80.
[84] See, further, Sugarman and Rubin, "Introduction: Towards A New History of Law and Material Society in England 1750–1914" *op. cit.* above, n.2, at pp. 1–123; Sugarman, *In the Spirit of Weber op. cit.* above, n.4.

17

Pragmatism and Property

ALAN RYAN*

1. Wider and narrower versions of the subject

The topic I have chosen is at its most interesting and engaging an ill-defined one. Pragmatism supplied the intellectual underpinnings of a substantial part of American jurisprudence in the first half of the century; this was the period in which the Supreme Court of the United States eventually reversed its earlier commitment to the sanctity of property rights, unfettered freedom of contract, and a view of the tort of interference with trade that made trade union organising as precarious in the United States as it had been in late nineteenth century Britain. To take all that seriously, I should have to write a book rather than a paper, and expand my topic to embrace the entire history of American law outside the criminal law, divorce law, and civil rights, and (given the extent to which the jurisprudence of the 1950s and 1960s might plausibly be described as a jurisprudence in which freedom of the person came to be decisively dissociated from freedom of the proprietor) perhaps even including those topics.

To narrow my focus, I have chosen to concentrate on one philosophical figure – John Dewey – and have chosen to emphasise the extent to which his views on the rights of property and their relationship to the rights of the community were those we associate with *British* social theory, in the shape of the political theory of the English idealists and turn of the century "New Liberalism". This emphasis casts, I hope, a new light on his more familiar role in the American movement in social science and legal theory aptly baptised "the revolt against formalism."[1] In other work on Dewey, I emphasise the extent to which his social and political thought, dominated as it was by references to "democracy," was none the less a form of liberalism and specifically of the "new liberalism" familiar from the writings of late nineteenth century British thinkers such as Green, Hobhouse, Ritchie, and, more surprisingly, Bertrand Russell.[2] Here I rely on such plausibility as that other work possesses, in order to focus on Dewey's legal theory.

---

* Warden of New College, Oxford.
[1] White, *Social Thought in America: The Revolt Against Formalism* (New York, 1973).
[2] For a difficult, and overcompressed, but tremendously helpful account of the transatlantic affinities between American, French, German and British writers in the period 1880–1920, see Kloppenberg, *Uncertain Victory* (New York, 1986).

2. The pragmatic stance

In general, pragmatism, or, as it was equally usually called, "instrumentalism", or (the label preferred by Dewey) "experimentalism", thought of the law as it thought of all social arrangements, in practical, means-end terms. The British observer is sometimes hard put to it to distinguish a pragmatist view of law in general, and so of property rights in particular, from a broadly positivist and utilitarian view.[3] Pragmatism's debts to a more idealist, Hegelian or "Fichto-Kantian" moral tradition makes the comparison not quite apt. That is, pragmatist ethics and jurisprudence were committed to a consequentialist view of social and political arrangements, but the consequences were not utilitarian ones. As we shall shortly see, the kind of categories that Dewey employed were deeply imbued with idealist overtones: democratic society was essentially a system of communication, and the object of such a society was to become ever more organic, making it possible for individuals more truly and more fully to share in the intellectual, moral, political and material resources of their society and allowing the society to use the individual's talents and resources more fully in the process. Moreover, the insistence on a consequentialist view of ethics was far from entailing that means were neutral and only to be judged by their efficacy in promoting the ends we were intent on promoting. One interesting feature of any comparison with more positivist and utilitarian accounts of law, then, is that pragmatism is *not* deeply committed to the doctrine of the separation of law and morals that is embedded in Bentham's distinction between positive and censorial jurisprudence, and defended more recently by Hart in his long running debate with Fuller.[4] This makes pragmatism something other than an absolutely natural bedfellow, not only of English positivism, but of American legal realism as well, and makes the familiar Dewey-Holmes alliance harder to characterise than one might think.[5] Holmes was quicker to observe that the law should be understood from the point of view of the bad man trying to find out what he could get away with than one can imagine Dewey being. Dewey's discussion of Austin on sovereignty, for instance, argues the obvious case that Austin's account of the law as the word of the sovereign and his account of the sovereign as a determinate person or body of persons receiving the habitual obedience of the bulk of the population and not himself or themselves giving habitual obedience to another rests on an implicitly social account of law – that is, that what

---

[3] Not only British observers; James W. Ely, Jr., *The Guardian of Every Other Right* (New York, 1992) writes of the effect of progressivism and the New Deal in popularising a positivist and utilitarian conception of ownership. See, too, Schultz, *Property, Power and American Democracy* (New Brunswick, 1991).

[4] Summers, *The Instrumental Theory of Law* (Ithaca, 1972).

[5] There are two overlaps here, in fact. Oliver Wendell Holmes Jr. was a good friend of William James, and is famous for declaring, after he had read Dewey's *Experience and Nature* that he now felt he had encountered the cosmos from the inside, and had come closer to the mind of God: "Thus methinks might God himself have spoken", though he did go on to say that he felt himself in the presence of a somewhat inarticulate deity.

backs the sovereign is the social habits that induce us to obey. Like Durkheim, and in that sense like later American writers such as Dworkin, Dewey takes this to mean that law binds only by being taken as morally authoritative.[6]

Because pragmatism was in aspiration a *Lebensphilosophie* in the grand historical manner, it had much more to say besides the near banality that law is a means to both individual and social ends. Not only did Dewey resist a sharp dichotomy between means and ends, the usual dichotomy between individual and social ends was itself something that he resisted. His vision of society as an organic union of individuals and of individuals as essentially social meant that what others might see as devices to promote a reasonably harmonious co-ordination of the separate aims of separate individuals, he was much more likely to see as expressions of a common purpose. He was, for instance, much more concerned that trade unions should improve the social standing and self-respect of their members than that they should just put more money in their pay-packets. In the American battle between socialists like Debs who saw trade union activity as a step towards a more or less insurrectionary socialism and reformers like Gompers, who just wanted the workers to screw as much as they could get from the employers without the latter going broke, Dewey stood in no-man's land. The teachers' unions he belonged to were affiliated to the American Federation of Labor, but he opposed both the class war and narrowly monetary goals.

Early in his career, he complained that economics was somehow relegated to the realm of the merely "natural," as though it was the nature of work and industry to be governed by the law of the jungle. "We admit, nay, at times we claim, that ethical rules are to be *applied* to this industrial sphere, but we think of it as an external application. That the economic life is *in itself* ethical, that it is to be made contributory to the realisation of personality through the formation of a higher and more complete unity among men, this is what we do not recognise; but such is the meaning of the statement that democracy must become industrial."[7] Pragmatism's conception of the social and individual ends that property rights are to serve is not exhausted by the concept of utility or even of welfare in a fairly broad sense. Pragmatism's "experimentalism" extended to ends as well as means; for pragmatists in general, and for Dewey especially, there was no sharp means/ends distinction, and the absence of this distinction was important to all of them, and a point on which he insisted at length. This emerges in some famous set piece confrontations such as Dewey's debate with Trotsky in the late 1930s; in Dewey's eyes, it was not simply bad luck that the Russian Revolution was corrupted by the violence and dictatorship resorted to by the Communist Party of the Soviet Union, and it followed therefore that any sort of socialism worth espousing in the west must be one that was implemented by procedures that themselves were plausibly part of the end result aimed at by socialists.[8]

---

[6] Dewey, "Austin's Theory of Sovereignty" in *Early Works*, Vol. 4, pp. 70*ff*.

[7] Dewey, "The Ethics of Democracy" in *Early Works* (Southern Illinois) Vol. 1, p. 248.

[8] This battle was fought out in *Their Morals and Ours*, Novak (ed.), with contributions from Dewey, Trotsky, and Novak.

Dewey's nice little contrast between the "planned society" and the "planning society" is a pregnant one. The *positive* abolition of private property was Marx's youthful term for the socialism he looked for, and it is not unduly fanciful to see such an aspiration in Dewey's own liberal socialist agenda. The political programme implied by such views, taken narrowly, would have fit neatly within the programme of the British Labour Party at any time between 1935 and 1950, but what made Dewey unusual in the United States was not just that he was a social democrat in a country where there were almost none, but that he was not *balancing* liberal values against socialist measures; rather, it was supposed to follow from the philosophical methodology that "our" institutions, modern forms of private property among them, would when analysed reveal potentialities for a more humane and intelligent management of the world and our social lives alike, which they also frustrated. Dewey's somewhat amorphous concept of an "end in view" presupposed that ends were "ends-as-secured-in-such-and-such-a-way" and that means were never pure instruments of the goals they served. The standard English view that the Labour Party might pursue socialist measures to achieve liberal ends was not a pragmatist trope.

3. American and British spectacles

American readers find it easy enough to distinguish pragmatism in the law from utilitarianism and Austinian positivism, if only because the latter made surprisingly little impact on American jurisprudence.[9] What American readers are more likely to have trouble with is distinguishing between pragmatism and legal realism. The pragmatic concern with "law in action" and the pragmatic hostility to purely conceptual schemes looks like realism. That is, pragmatists were unpersuaded that the search for "bright line" conceptual distinctions was the proper foundation of intelligent jurisprudence; so were the legal realists. All the same, there is a distinct difference of temperament between pragmatism and the tougher sort of legal realism. Although I shall show in due course that Dewey's naturalism and the deflationary line he took about such issues as the "personality" of corporations pulls him away from Hegelianism, as it pulls him away from Gierke's nostalgia for the corporation's premodern ancestor, and even from Maitland's attempts to show that what is worth having in Gierke can be had consistently with moral and methodological individualism, I suggest that it makes better sense to locate Deweyan pragmatism with tender-minded late nineteenth-century neo-Hegelianism than with tough-minded 1950s realism. Neo-Hegelianism is only Dewey's starting point, to be sure, but its influence throughout his life ensured that the other was exceedingly unlikely to be his destination. This is perhaps put too enigmatically to carry conviction; let me gloss it briefly. Dewey's philosophy was naturalistic and in that sense "anti-metaphysical"; he described himself as having when young been much taken

---

[9] Horwitz, *The Transformation of American Law*, Vol. II, 1870–1960 (OUP, New York, 1992) at p. 242 which mentions this with some surprise; it makes it the odder that Dewey should have written about Austin at all.

with Hegel's analysis of social institutions as the work of "objective mind", but having then come gradually to see that the Hegelian apparatus could be ditched but the insights it had offered be preserved. This all happened rather gradually, but there is a very clear contrast between the extreme ends of the process: early Dewey is theologically minded, treats idealism as the philosophical arm of the theological interpretation of the world, and follows T.H. Green in claiming that "the world" is more than merely natural, while late Dewey is sociologically and social psychologically minded, and entirely opposed to any idea that there are principles of a non-natural kind at work in the world. What persists, however, is the thought that the world is replete with *meaning*. Although Dewey is an anti-formalist, he is not a cynic or a sceptic or a hardboiled case; judges can, must, and do *interpret* the law, and this is not a process of making it up, nor is it a process of merely rationalising views that they hold for who knows what reason. All interpretation is to a degree indeterminate, so Dewey does not suppose that judges will always come to identical views, any more than a bunch of physicists confronted with the same data will always come to the same view of what it means. That, however, is far from saying that the data may not make one interpretation more or less compelling than another.

4. Biographical interlude

Although there has been a startling revival of interest in Dewey during the past ten years, he is not a household name among British legal scholars, so a short biographical sketch may not be out of place. (The already over-informed or biographically allergic should turn to section 5.) Dewey was born in Burlington, Vermont, in 1859; he died in New York City in 1952. He is often, but misleadingly, described as a Yankee, and even as a "Yankee saint". It is misleading because he was hostile to many of the most distinctive features of New England life; most importantly, he thought that even the rather liberal Congregationalist Christianity in which he had been reared was calculated to produce "an inward laceration," and that its unhealthy concentration on the gap between fallen man and a punitive heavenly judge greatly diminished the value of Christian teaching, especially by devaluing the intelligent management of everyday social life. Less saliently, but perhaps as importantly, he disliked the New England emphasis on "respectability", seems to have had an unforced liking for the immigrant working people who laboured in Burlington mills and lumber yards, and seems at an early age to have decided that in almost all conflicts between capital and labour, the right lay with labour.[10]

Dewey found himself, so to speak, as a professor of philosophy in the midwest; he *was* archetypically American, but it was a mid-western archetype that he fitted. He did his graduate work at Johns Hopkins, taught at the University

---

[10] Jane Dewey's biography of her father that serves as a preface to Schilpp (ed.) *The Philosophy of John Dewey* (New York, 1939) pp. 3–45 quotes his remark about "an inward laceration"; similar phrases occur throughout his work.

of Michigan from 1884–1894, at Chicago for the next decade, and at Columbia from 1904 to his retirement. He wrote constantly, from the moment he left his undergraduate college in 1879 to his ninetieth year. His *Collected Works* run to 37 volumes. He stood in an interesting and awkward relationship to the great philosophical and theological tradition. He lost his faith early, but preserved all his life the belief that philosophy's task was to preserve in a "non-supernatural" form the insights worth carrying on from Christianity, and in 1935, his little book, *A Common Faith*, defended the idea that a "religious" view of the world could and should survive the death of "noun religion". He argued in *Reconstruction in Philosophy* that it was time for philosophers to turn away from "the problems of philosophy" to "the problems of men", but added that when they turned their gaze in a practical direction, they were to bring their philosophical skills with them. Philosophy so conceived was to be a form of "cultural criticism" or rather "the criticism of criticisms". Whether he ever knew how like Young Hegelianism this sounded, and how nasty Marx had been in mocking the idea of a "*kritische Kritik*" we may never know. But the affinity is not accidental.

Dewey's own philosophy was developed piecemeal; he greatly admired T.H. Green, but thought that even Green's view of the eternal self in which we saw our better natures reflected was too "dualist" for moral comfort. He turned to a purer Hegelianism than Green's "FichtoKantianism", but rather soon decided that Hegel's prioritising of mind over matter was another needless dualism, and that the absolute was too like the Calvinist God worshipped by his mother. He then adopted what he called "experimentalism"; the individual human being is a problem-solving organism, who must adapt himself to his environment and adapt his environment to himself. Society, too, is a problem solving organism. It is faced with the same tasks as the individual, needing both to adapt and adapt to its internal environment – that is the needs and beliefs of its members – and its external, physical, social, and political environment. Progress consists in bringing these processes under more intelligent and more conscious control; the technique of so doing is essentially an experimental one, and the great obstacles to progress are whatever habits of inertia and fear get in the way of experimentation.[11]

He was revered by teachers, perhaps because in "My Pedagogical Creed" he praised teachers as "truly doing God's work" and said that a proper education was in effect the worship of the true God. He wrote voluminously and interestingly on education, but may well have had much less influence on American education than either his critics or his supporters suggest; his ideas were not utopian, but they demanded extremely well trained teachers and teacher-pupil ratios that neither the United States nor the United Kingdom has ever been willing to pay for. Politically, he was mostly on the wrong side; he supported American entry into the First World War, but decided immediately after Versailles that this was a frightful mistake, and remained an isolationist until Pearl Harbour; he opposed the New Deal on the grounds that it was insufficiently radical. He

---

[11] Dewey, "From Absolutism to Experimentalism" in *Later Works*, Vol. 5, pp. 147–160.

was vastly admired as a sort of sage or prophet of democracy, and on the whole deservedly; he was an astonishingly steady and sensible thinker, and what he wrote was intrinsically extremely interesting. The fact that it was couched in the drabbest prose any American philosopher has ever produced may have made readers in the 1920s and 1930s feel that it was doing them good, but the revival of interest in his work over the past ten years plainly owes everything to the way his work satisfies our need for a moral and political philosophy that explores the middle ground he explored – neither laissez-faire nor revolutionary, neither individualist nor collectivist, communitarian but liberal, progressive but able to make sense of our attachments to the past.

5. The political implications of Deweyan pragmatism

Dewey's politics were those of a mild liberal socialist. The most characteristic of his essays in this vein was *Liberalism and Social Action*, published in the mid-1930s. He was in innumerable essays elsewhere fiercely critical of Roosevelt and the New Deal – what others called social experiments, he thought was mere thrashing about in the ruins of a decayed system – but he did not criticise the New Deal from the standpoint of gung-ho revolutionary social engineering. It is very noticeable, and necessary for us to notice here that the primary target he picked for intellectual assault from 1900 to 1940 was old-fashioned laissez-faire liberalism. I have not found any references to Albert Jay Nock, who revived the concept of libertarianism, and who attacked Roosevelt from the standpoint of the absolute sanctity of private property rights at much this time – Dewey is rarely very specific about just whom he is attacking – but Dewey's argument essentially is the familiar one that property rights exist in order to promote social well being, and that if social well being requires economic planning, individual property rights take second place.

At the end of the First World War, a *New Republic* essay on "What are We Fighting For?" struck the characteristic note: under the impact of war, American industry had become more organised and more efficient, and the government had had to play a more active role in the economy. Property had given way to organisation, and the war would be justified as a war to make the world safe for democracy if Americans remembered the lesson that individual property rights were instruments of social organisation, not something on which their owners could stand firm at the public's expense.[12]

This, of course, is what we should expect. The interest lies in the moves by which he defended such a view. One familiar argument that Dewey evaded rather than decided was the old argument that what individuals did with their property was voluntary and non-coercive, that it was an expression of uncoerced individual will, and that it was therefore not morally problematic in the way the essentially coercive interventions of the State were. Dewey took it for

---

[12] Dewey, "What Are We Fighting For ?" in *Middle Works* Vol. II, pp. 93–97.

granted that there was a continuum between the wholly voluntary and the wholly forced, and thought it was just obvious that society worked by *making* individuals toe the line where necessary. Most such making was not violent, but it was the exercise of power or "force" in general. Law was thus coercive, but Dewey did not make a great deal of the fact. He did not rely on it as a way of overthrowing the laissez-faire liberals' attachment to the old ideology that relied on sharpening the distinction between the non-coerciveness of proprietary and contractual relations and the coerciveness of State action.

He was thus not concerned to do what Robert Hale did in the mid-1920s. Hale disturbed everyone who believed in the absoluteness of the distinction between freely made contractual agreements for the use of one another's property and the coercive acts of the state by arguing that property was coercive all the way through. Ownership gave the owner a coercive power licensed by the state. You are, on Hale's view, coerced into paying me rent for the occupation of the house I own, and coerced into hiring my bicycle rather than riding off on it at your pleasure. I coerce you with the state's assistance. It follows that *all* contracts had a coercive element in them (a coercive element additional to that imported by the familiar thought that behind all my agreements there stands the power of the state to make me perform or make me compensate you for non-performance).[13] Dewey operated at a higher level of abstraction, and wanted to fry other fish. Taking it for granted that law coerces us, he wanted to separate out regular, predictable planned forms of coercion – you *have* to pay rent for my flat, but you expect to do so, you know how much, it isn't collected at gun point, and so obviously on, from arbitrary and unpredictable violence. In the contexts where he tackles such matters it is not property but international law that he has in the forefront of his mind. In the philosophy of law generally, his aim was always the same as in his philosophy of ethics, science, religion and nature – to persuade his readers to step out of an inherited framework in which concepts such as property and personality did battle, and to look instead at the social context in which arguments took place, and at the social forces that law tried to control.

6. "My philosophy of law"

Dewey's late essay on "My Philosophy of Law" (1941) can easily strike a reader as excessively methodological and abstract. In this, too, it is like altogether too much of his work. The point of it is easier to see against the background of three aspects of legal theory that even now are not wholly absent from the scene. The first is an excessive individualism. Attachment to this is not limited to any particular jurisprudential school; one might even accuse Holmes of going down the individualist track when he declared that the point of law was to enable the bad man to know at what point the law would impose sanctions upon

---

[13] Horwitz, *The Transformation of American Law* (New York, 1992) pp. 163–165.

him. Dewey's claim that "law is social through and through" is not the boring platitude that he cheerfully confesses it might be taken for. It is an insistence that law is to be understood as part of a network of ways we have of regulating all manner of human interactions. Dewey always held that individuals were one with their biographies, and their biographies were one with their absorption of and action upon their environments.

This was not a matter of outside social forces shaping a plastic human nature, either, but a matter of the interior development of individual character. Merely biological identity was neither here nor there; at most biological identity provided a platform for the individuality that came out of the creative transformation of the social conditions in which we operated. This is all part and parcel of Dewey's alienation from volitional and will-based theories of legal personality and hence of property, and reflects the pragmatist readiness to see the law essentially as an instrument of social policy, not as the defender of individuals *against* the claims of policy in the manner of Dworkin's "rights as trumps" thesis, nor as the device that crystallised our unique status as beings whose wills brought value and meaning into the world in the manner of Hegel's discussion of "abstract right." Of course, in saying this, one needs to be careful not to throw out the baby with the bathwater. Dewey certainly held that thought was the offshoot of action; he borrowed from G.H. Mead the interesting idea that "the psychical" or mental life generally came into existence because of an arrest or bafflement in human activity. So thought is entirely implicated in intelligent doing, and thus to those things that one thinks of as belonging to the domain of the will. The point, rather, is that Dewey does not give any particular place to the thought that individuals want to stamp their will on the world – which is Hegel's starting point in *The Philosophy of Right*. Property rights are part of the bundle of rights and duties that help us to join in the life of the wider society.

The second is the search for timeless and abstract principles to constrain current legal arrangements. Dewey agreed that law must in some sense be relatively fixed. He likened the nature of law to the banks of a river; the banks clearly did much to channel the river and dictate where and how fast it flowed. Compared with the water flowing between them the banks appeared relatively fixed, stationary, and solid. This, however, is only a question of degree. As the river takes its passage between the banks, it erodes them, silts up regions of the river and scours out others, and over a sufficiently long period carves out an entirely new course for itself. The law, on this account, is a structure both *of* the social process and *in* the social process. It hardly needs to be emphasised that this, too, is a view that closes the gap between law as the expression of social policy and law as a barrier to it. Dewey has some interesting passing observations about the way in which the Austinian theory of law as the expression of the will of a sovereign can and cannot be squared with such a vision. The view of law as the dictate of the sovereign was, he claims, not accidentally connected to the period of legislative innovation and administrative reform during which it emerged. It expressed, though it did not overtly side with, the view, new to the nineteenth century, that we could legislate for ourselves and get an intelligent grasp on the social and economic order through legal regulation without waiting centuries for judicial decision-making to amend the law for us. The brevity of its heyday in turn reflected the fact that the social sciences had shown how much more powerful than any determinate human superior or human superiors were social forces and social customs.

The third background, then, was the hankering after some external standard by which to decide whether to make new law, how to decide whether existing law was adequate, and by which judges might be guided in their decision-making. Dewey was writing at a time when conservative Americans were, as they periodically have done, urging that law must be tested by its conformity to natural law, and that the American constitution tested the validity of legislation and tested the validity of the decisions of lower courts by their consilience with the law of nature. He also had in his sights, as he always did, empiricists who proposed to draw a sharp line between mere facts and the values by which we were to assess the facts' desirability. He argued, as always, that if we considered facts as something "over and done with," the fact/value distinction made some sense; but social facts were never over and done with. They were, he said in one of his eloquent but utterly obscure colloquialisms, always "goings-on". The underlying thought is not obscure or difficult, though it remains mysterious why Dewey supposed that its mere recognition would do so much good. To talk of social facts is to talk of forms of social organisation and interaction – conflict as well as co-operation – that have continuing consequences. Any account of them requires at least a rough and ready prediction of their consequences; it can only be rough and ready, since those consequences will partly be determined by how cleverly or ineptly human beings react to the situation these facts create in the near future in bringing about their consequences for the further future. Law, however, *is* what it functions *as*. To see law in a functional light, says Dewey, will be the beginning of wisdom when it comes to using the law for social reform.[14]

This functional theory of law is, obviously enough, consistent with a social democratic conception of the place of law in reforming the economic and political system of the United States. It hints already that in Dewey's perspective, there will be less room than in many others for anyone to complain that in its concern for the rights of labour a reforming administration is likely to trample on the rights of property. For, on this view, the rights that property now possesses cannot be understood without reference to the kind of social function we now expect property to perform. If property rights are an obstacle to social

---

[14] It occurs to me that it is possible that Dewey's view was something like Charles Taylor's view in "Neutrality in Political Science" that the social sciences provide knowledge of the consequences of social change for the well being of the members of our society, and that this knowledge is just the knowledge we employ when deciding what policies to adopt. See Taylor, "Neutrality in Political Science" in Ryan (ed.) *Social Explanation* (1973) pp. 139–170.

change and co-operation between management and labour, then they are not rights. Readers of T.H. Green, Hobhouse, and even Bradley will recognise in such thoughts affiliation with English idealism. Green's analysis of a right as a capacity to contribute to the common good was taken over by Hobhouse; while Bradley proposed as the route to discovering whether we had a *right* that we ask the question, "am I in this the expression of law?", which is rather different from the question, "will the law back me up?"

The obvious complaint against all such analyses is that they miss out what "rights as trumps" may make too central, but what we hardly want to throw out entirely, the role of rights in protecting individual aims and actions *no matter what*. I have elsewhere argued that *property* rights in particular are best analysed in utilitarian and functional terms, and that they do not deserve as much respect as rights of conscience, rights of bodily integrity, rights of political agency and the like. Nonetheless, there are features of these more basic rights that property rights do implicate, and to the extent that they do, I would not wish to embrace a wholly functionalist (in Dewey's sense) view of them. Much less would I wish to be thought to endorse Dewey's analysis of all rights in such terms. My own inclination would always be to draw a line – not, sadly, a "bright" line – between the personal rights I would want to give "trumping" status to, and most property rights; I would not wish to make property rights manipulable for properly approved public purposes by making all rights so. The upshot of Dewey's views, following the idealist tradition, is that he does just that.

7. "Early" Dewey

"Early" Deweyan reflections on these matters are scattered and incidental. It is worth observing perhaps that his first essay on democracy insists that a democracy of voting rights needs to be rounded out by a democracy of wealth; he did not have a particular, socialist vision in mind of what all this might entail – indeed, all his life it was hard to pin him down on institutional formulae – but he certainly meant at least that measures ought to be taken to reduce the increasing gap between rich and poor. Since this was written some seven years before *Pollock v. Farmers' Loan & Trust* (1895), the high water mark of judicial obstruction of a federal income tax, it was a contribution to an argument that had been going on for the previous 20 years or so about the authority of the government to interfere with the marketplace in order to realise any social policy whatever. The courts were engaged in confining government to the tasks of policing property rights and helping owners to implement their intentions in the disposal of their property; redistribution was what was supposed in contemporary jurisprudence to be off limits. (It is hard to repress some amusement at the repetitive quality of American discussions of ownership; Professor Richard Epstein's recent work on takings has resurrected a tendency in dealing with property rights that was alive and well in 1895, and seemed to have died some 45 years afterwards.)

Dewey's intellectual affinities at that point lay with British writers rather than American ones. He had been bored with the syllabus at the University of Vermont, and had refreshed his mind with the English reviews of the day: the *Fortnightly*, the *Pall Mall Gazette*, the *Westminster,* and the *Nineteenth Century* among them; his interest was stirred by Darwin and Huxley, Maine and Morley, rather than his intuitionist philosophy instructors. It is somewhat mysterious to me that he so early took up the concept of "democracy" as the guiding thread of his social thought; but when he did so, it was in the spirit of T.H. Green, which is to say that it had less to do with the formal institutions of voting rights, judicial review, checks and balances, the separation of powers and the other resources of American democracy than with the idea of democracy as reflecting in everyday life the Kantian principle of respecting each person as an end in himself, and – a notion that was developed over his lifetime – of enhancing democracy as a system of "communication".

Dewey was not, so to speak, Jürgen Habermas *avant la lettre*; but he did – especially in *Democracy and Education* (1916) – emphasise open, free, equal and deep communication as the essence of democracy. As a notoriously opaque writer, he was doubtless speaking out of a full heart when he stressed the "joy" that unfettered communication could yield. Property thus appeared to him in his earliest years as an obstacle to democracy. The essence of property rights was that their holder could stand on them without regard to considerations of public policy. Oddly, Dewey did *not* so far as I have been able to discover, ever take two routes in discussion that one would have expected him to take, and that he might certainly have taken if he had wanted to borrow more than he apparently did from the English idealists. In the first place, he seems not have thought that if property expresses the will of the individual, it is essential to everyone to have *some* property, and therefore did not go on to argue that some measure of redistribution was required or some other pressure had to be exerted to make the United States more a "property-owning democracy." He seems to have decided early on that the derivation of property rights from a volitional base was a waste of intellectual effort; and in the second place, he seems not to have been tempted by the thought – mentioned more than once in that late flowering of idealist social theory, *Property: Its Duties and Rights*, a work that he could not of course have known of at this point, since it was published 25 years later – that if society was in some fashion endowed with "personality" public ownership could be understood as an expression of public personality and so be seen as a natural extension of the moral principles that underlay our respect for private ownership.

Dewey's passion for T.H. Green and Hegel makes one curious about his hostility to volitional theories of ownership. I wish it were possible to discover whether Dewey ever read O.W. Holmes's *The Common Law*, with its complaints against the use of ingenious Kantian constructions to explain the law of property; we do know that he read Holmes's later shocker, "The Path of the Law" and that Holmes read Dewey with interest and pleasure. It is not unlikely that

Pragmatism and Property 237

Dewey had read Holmes's earlier book, and it may well have been one reason why he did not embrace the idealists' line on property. Another is intrinsic to Dewey's own way of thinking, but was not fully in place until late in the 1890s when Dewey ceased to be a disciple of Hegel and adopted the naturalist, experimental view of philosophy he held to for the next 50 odd years. For Dewey, the will was not a very significant concept. More to the point, however – it makes all the difference when Dewey discusses the hotly disputed question of the nature of corporations and what flows from it – Dewey thought that the very notion of a *person* was essentially conventional.

8. Corporate personality

According to Dewey's notion of a person, the logical order was not one that begins with a "natural" or pre-legal conception of human personality, then moves to an understanding of proprietorship that expresses the interesting fact of that personality's being endowed with will; Dewey's account of this ran the other way. We used the concept of a person to help us order our social arrangements. The "individual" was a social construct. It did not follow that there were "no" individuals, and the element of artificiality in our conception of personality did not mean that personality was not "real." Bridges, as Dewey tartly observed, were artificial, but they were anything but unreal. When Dewey applied this to the question of whether corporations were natural entities, possessed personality, and were thus proper candidates for protection under the Fourteenth Amendment guarantees of due process, the result was simultaneously satisfactory and oddly empty.

It was satisfactory inasmuch as Dewey probably put the last nail in the coffin of a form of conceptualist thinking that hoped to derive the legal status of corporations from a contemplation of that dreadful question whether a corporate *personne légale* or *personne morale* is "really" a person at all; American thinking about corporations and corporate ownership (both its ownership of assets and its shareholders' ownership of it) is a much explored subject, and Berle and Means's *The Modern Corporation and Private Property* is rightly one of the best loved discussions of it. Dewey's contribution was apparently decisive in shutting down the conceptual wrangling, but 65 years later it seems empty because once Dewey had declared that it was up to courts, legislatures and the informed citizenry to mould their understanding of the personality of corporations to the purposes of the legal system generally, the most interesting argument was going to take place somewhere else, namely among lawyers wrestling with the question whether shareholders had too few rights against the officers of a corporation; whether governments had to treat corporations as sensitively as they treated individuals because whatever a corporation lost would in the end be a loss suffered by assignable individuals; or whether individuals had chosen to forfeit such consideration by seeking profitable investments in the arm's length way that the corporate form allowed them, and so on. It is something of a puzzle that Dewey should have been allowed to have the last word. As Morton Horwitz observes, it is extremely implausible to suggest that just about *any* conception of corporate personality would be consistent with just about *any* way of treating corporations. Whichever way round the argument goes – from conception of personality to appropriate legal policy or from legal policy to conception of personality as rationalisation of it – it is hard to think that it is an accident that the Supreme Court's passion for providing corporations with Fourteenth Amendment due process safeguards co-incided with attempts to ascribe "personality" to corporations.

9. Dewey's impact

It would be unfair and untrue to suggest that Dewey had nothing to contribute to such arguments. The contribution comes indirectly, however. If we return to early Dewey, we find him thinking that the great barrier to democracy as communication is conflict of interest; it distorts what might otherwise be a more or less communicative relationship centred on how we are to co-operate for mutually acceptable ends and turns it into a conflictual one. That is, the great enemy of communicative democracy is whatever tends to narrow the interests and render us defensive and self-protective. *Some* security is essential if life is to proceed at all, but too much emphasis on the security of property is just deadening and isolating. Dewey was a fiercer critic than his walrus moustache and heavy glasses suggested he knew how to be, and he wrote some quite unkind things about Maine's *Popular Government*; generally in the 1880s and 1890s, Dewey fought off any suggestion that the modern world was intrinsically unsatisfactory.

Romantically backward-looking writers such as Renan were particularly a target for criticism, and Dewey spent a good deal of ink – carbon probably, since he seems to have written by "hunt 'n' peck" typing almost as soon as the first semi-portable typewriters became available – defending a secular faith in the modern world, faith, that is, in the possibilities of modernity. Maine was not a romantic, backward-looking critic, but someone who feared the loss of the gains for progress that liberal society and liberal economics had achieved. Dewey hardly bothered to distinguish him from other anti-democratic conservatives, however. Though he was not just nostalgic, he was needlessly fearful, and his defence of the *laissez-faire* economy, together with its exclusion of the working class from political influence struck Dewey as absurdly pessimistic and simply a matter of turning his back on the new ways of "associated living" that the modern world offered. To the degree that private property bred the kind of terror that Maine displayed, it needed reformation.

Dewey also in those years held straightforward doubts about the impact of large concentrations of property on social peace and also on the welfare of the poor. There is next to nothing in his work that addresses all this directly, but letters to his family when he arrived in Chicago at the height of the Pullman Strike in 1894 leave no doubt about his sympathies. He sided unequivocally with the workers and against the employers, and thought it absurd to talk of the rights of property in face of the realities of Pinkerton agents and the Illinois National

Guard. Publicly, however, he wrote next to nothing on the subject, and became interested in real politics only after moving to New York. One might unkindly wonder whether Dewey practised a certain amount of self-censorship during his years at Chicago. John D. Rockefeller, the founder of the University of Chicago, used one of his many secretaries as a spy and watchdog and on the strength of his reports had Thorsten Veblen pushed off the faculty, and incidentally ensured that institutional economics, the solitary native contribution to the dismal science that the US has produced, should flourish elsewhere – mostly at Madison, Wisconsin. Dewey maintained that there was no heavy handed repression in evidence; my own suspicion is that he would not have noticed it unless it affected the Department of Philosophy and the Law School.

In any case, Dewey's radicalism was of a nature to give the *status quo* something of a headstart. Though he later wrote to a friend, declaring himself an optimist about things in general and a pessimist about things in particular, the American social and legal order counted for these purposes among things in general. His radicalism consisted in complaining that his society failed to live up to its better nature. (One has to be careful saying any such thing, not only because it assimilates Dewey to the Hegelians he repudiated but because he was decidedly unhappy about any social theory that drove a wedge between the ideal and the actual. Nonetheless, it is the only account that makes much sense.) This was radical enough for him to be able to believe that capitalism was a failed economic experiment and failed because it was at odds with the aspirations after intelligent social control that the modern world had come to embrace and which were indeed one of the defining features of modernity.

Nor is this a strain sounded only in his youth. There is in Dewey – it comes out very clearly in *Individualism Old and New* (1931) many years later – a romantic streak that objects to the property relations of modern capitalism not only because they foster the growth of anonymous corporations (so much, one might sometimes be tempted to say, for the insight that the legal personality of corporations is simply a reflection of whatever we choose to *make* of corporations) within which work is boring and routinised, but they lead owners as opposed to workers into a moral dead end. Property exists for the sake of creative and imaginative work, but the owners only exist to exploit the work of others. It is a safe bet that Dewey never read Marx's *Economic Philosophical Manuscripts* – he could have done, and it is even possible that Sidney Hook urged it upon him in the late twenties and early thirties when Hook was trying to persuade Dewey that part of Dewey's own genius was to have brought to a humane completion what Marx had struggled with – but there is an odd echo of the theory of alienation here.

More commonly, Dewey lines up with the standard modern view. That is, property is a "bundle of rights and duties," and from this it follows that the determination of just what ought to be included in that bundle is a matter of convenience. As an anti-conceptualist, Dewey would have argued against any attempt to discern the "essence" of proprietorship, and would have been sceptical of the utility of trying to draw sharp lines between real property and chattel property, or between property-based claims and non-property-based contractual ones. In that sense, Dewey's way of thinking contributes to the broad current that can accommodate "the new property" without strain. But, Dewey did not entirely wish to go down that track, and the reason is obvious enough. He wished to argue two things simultaneously; he wanted to fight off *laissez-faire* liberalism, a form of social thinking that may or may not have been on the retreat in 1935 when he published *Liberalism and Social Action*, but which is certainly the target of that little book. *Laissez-faire* liberalism is, or was, a liberalism of property rights, and therefore any attack on it was an attack on any simple appeal to the rights of property.

In the second place, he wanted to emphasise the claims of "intelligence" against what he perhaps unfairly always represented as intelligence's only rivals – tradition and violence. The liberalism of *Liberalism and Social Action* is astonishingly underdescribed; it turns out to be whatever the method of intelligent social action dictates. Non-violent social change with the object of making society more democratically hospitable to the plurality of individual projects available to us, as illuminated by modern science and as provided for the technology built on that science is about what it amounts to. Organising the economic relationships on which that society is to be built is something that we cannot describe in any brief or simple fashion; we do know that it will require more conscious and collective control than nineteenth century *laissez-faire* envisaged, and we also know that it will not involve forced collectivisation and nationalisation.

What this entails for property rights is mostly negative. It can't be said that Dewey really got very much further than these statements of "neither too far towards collectivism nor back towards individualism." By the end of the thirties he was in his eighties, and had certainly retreated a little towards a more Jeffersonian and less Herbert Crolyesque conception of the promise of American life.[15] It seems plausible to view him at the end of the day as a welfare state liberal or moderate social democrat, who would have been happy in the postwar Labour Party if only it had allowed a good deal more room for workers' self-management in its nationalisation plans. Oddly, he and Bertrand Russell got on very badly in philosophy, but held similar political opinions on everything except the two world wars – Dewey supported the First World War and was an isolationist until Pearl Harbour. There is a great deal of Dewey in Russell's *Principles of Social Reconstruction* and a great deal of Russell in

---

[15] Croly, *The Promise of American Life* (1908); Croly argued that America must pursue Jeffersonian goals by Hamiltonian means, that is, that the freedom of the individual was no longer promoted by a state that left individuals to enrich themselves as they saw fit. This meant that he, for instance, did not deplore the rise of the corporation, but saw it as a step towards the modest degree of collectivism he thought the federal government had to learn to practise. Dewey never gave a clear answer to the problem of reconciling his distaste for the modern corporation as an institution and his wish for a more organised and integrated economic order.

Liberalism and Social Action. Which is, roughly, to point to a coincidence of understanding between "New Liberalism", and pragmatism, and thus between one strand of British and American social thought in the first half of this century that is surprising in view of the apparently distant relationship between the practitioners of jurisprudence on opposite shores of the Atlantic. Its bearing on property in particular is as indirect as I, at least, would have guessed it would be. I have for 25 years thought that in liberal democratic societies the rise of the "bundle of rights and duties" of property diverted the interest of political theorists – not that of lawyers on their daily rounds – away from property as the subject it had been in Kant, Marx, Locke or Hegel and on to the broader subject of what rights and duties we generally wished to secure. There is, I think, a sort of dialectic at work in which more expansive and more deflationary views of property compete for our allegiance. Dewey's views belong firmly with the deflationary side, and my own view is that for political good sense rather than intellectual excitement that is the side to be on. That leaves, of course, plenty of room for an account I have not tried to give here, comparing the expansive view of the rights of property owners popular at the end of the nineteenth century with the recent resurrection of such views under the umbrella of the "takings" provision of the US Constitution.[16] It is that that accounts for my offering this rather broad brush view of a Deweyan vision of the place of property in social theory rather than anything more meticulous and detailed.

---

[16] See, of course, Epstein, *Takings: Private Property and the Power of Eminent Domain* (Cambridge, Mass., 1985).

18

Socio-Legal Concept of Property Rights in Town Development

A Critical Approach to Comparative Studies on Urban Planning Laws in Eastern and Western Countries

MICHIATSU KAINO*

1. Introduction

Modern thinkers, from John Locke onwards, suggest that property is the essence of political freedom. Although Locke was not concerned with the analysis of the concept of property itself, we can recognise this view in his famous remark that every man has a property in his own person.

However, there is surely a distinction between property which is very personal and much more productive but anonymous forms of property such as capital. Can we justify anonymous productive capital on the same grounds as intimate private property?

Can great landed estates be justified in terms of his theory?[1] Here I would like to mention that the Lockean concept of property was linked to Western ideas of civilisation, that is, cultivation of the physical surroundings of human society. Therefore even interaction with nature meant the transformation of a given society into a much more civilised one. Thus, changing types of property themselves could be understood as a reflection of progress in a certain society.

On the other hand, property rights are regarded as assets inherited from traditional society. In certain countries rights in land reflect historical elements of society, which sometimes means that they express a continuous human relationship through the land. For example, there is some Englishness in English landed property, that is, her land tenures symbolise the continuity of the forms of landholding from her feudal periods. It goes without saying that continuity

---

* School of Law, Nagoya University, Japan.
[1] See Locke, *Two Treatises of Government* (Laslett ed., 1963), especially Chap. V Second Treatise. For interesting discussion of Locke's property theory in terms of intellectual property see Hughes, "The Philosophy of Intellectual Property" in 77 *Georgetown Law Journal* 287 at pp. 297–305. An interesting discussion of body rights can be found in Munzer, *A Theory of Property* (1990) pp. 41 *et seq.*

in the form of land tenures does not necessarily mean that England is still a feudal society. However, because of the development of the trust, which was said to play an important role in transforming English feudal tenures into a much more modern land-ownership from around the fifteenth century, English land law seems to retain a unique character. Therefore the English notion of a fee simple estate in land, for instance, often includes or has to be accompanied by various estates such as the fee tail or life estate. Thus property can be seen as a variable bundle of rights, a mechanism for allocating the enjoyment of property to each successive generation.

These bundles of rights imply that the power and privileges of people or groups of people derive from the estate relationship, not from an anterior or superior idea of property.[2]

In various Asian countries, discussion of property in land is much more focused on the revenue from the land. British administrators, Raffles, for example, who wished to collect taxes from a village, villages or a certain plot, had recognised that the "owners" of the land are the persons or group being responsible for paying tax on it. Peasants, on the other hand, had the option of leaving a village and settling elsewhere, so long as there were vacant lands.[3]

This suggests a unique conception of property rights differing both from modern Western ideas and those of contemporary Asian countries. Nevertheless, if we assume that (at the relevant period) powers to appropriate meant property rights, then such powers probably belonged to a village or rank and not to individuals. It appears that we should use property as a descriptive term only where a superior authority is able to enforce rights and redress wrongs according to some law recognised as binding by and upon the people concerned. Otherwise, the position of a group and its members is expressed in relation to its surroundings.

In the absence of a superior authority, it might be correct to recognise that there would be a strong claim to land; however, even in such circumstances, assertion would be in favour of the person who first cultivated the land.

In societies where this relation and a group element supersedes appropriative property, such ideas about property are not compatible with the ideas of property originating in Western countries. It might be very useful to consider the process of urbanisation in the West and East, since in the types of formation of urban societies themselves, we could perhaps find different reflections

---

[2] See Kaino, *A Study of History of Landownership in Modern England* (Igirisu TochishoyukenHo Kenkyu) (Tokyo, Iwanamishoten,1980).

[3] Kaino, "Toshikeisei ni okeru Tochishoyumondai no Jakkan no Kosatsu", *Hosei Ronsyu, Nogoya University Journal of Law and Politics* 132; see also Hooker (ed.), *The Laws of South-East Asia*, Vol. 2 (Singapore, 1988); Harding (ed.), *The Common Law in Singapore and Malaysia* (Malaya Law Review, Butterworths, 1985); in Japanese, the late Professor S. Shinobu, *Raffles* (Tokyo, Heibonsya, 1963) is the most valuable work and very informative book which referred to original historical documents and materials even during the period of the Straits Settlements.

of land tenures as well as ideas of landownership in these different cultural and historical environments. Cities are spatial expressions of society which are not a mere occasion for the development of social structure, but a concrete expression of the historical nexus at which the society is located.

This paper examines the striking contrasts in modern urban planning law between Western and Eastern countries (especially the Association of South-East Asian Nations – ASEAN). Although the allocation of material resources, as we may say, is a primal and universal concern of human societies, Japan was and still is, at this point, in a backward state. In examining the case of Japan, we will analyse the processes that created the opportunities for the Japanese to industrialise. This will reveal how land monopoly undermined the public interest in the land and left the people living in a miserable physical environment. The type of urbanisation and institutional framework for the organisation of space in Japan seems to be a hybrid, so that Japan can be used as a paradigm for exploring the laws whereby Western or Eastern countries structure and transform urbanisation. In my conclusion, I would like to emphasise that market-orientated or product-orientated systems of property have often operated as a means to destroy traditional communal elements which are indigenous to developing countries.

2. Method and criteria

It is important to note sociological factors relating to legal systems which have been introduced from the West through industrialisation and urbanisation. Product-orientated systems often conflict with the indigenous system so that the various institutional and legal frameworks that have been introduced face serious harmonisation problems with the indigenous systems in traditional societies. Three factors may affect urbanisation trends. The first is the market system in which land is assumed to be a commodity which has a value in the market like other commodities. The second is the political power system which includes not only national or official political power, but also autonomous systems or traditional communal ties which can be recognised as the "unofficial" or "private sector" of the political economy. The third is the spatial element of the environmental system, the outcomes of the activities of individuals and communities in building cities, including the decision-making processes.

Many cities in ASEAN countries have a rich cultural heritage, as well as traditional communal elements which are indigenous to each country. In Japan, as a result of rapid urbanisation, and the so-called "scrap and build" way of city building, there has been a negative impact on the citizens' quality of life, as well as on the communal elements of local life in each city. There used to be close ties among people, which can now only be found in rural areas; and even there they are rapidly disappearing.

Communal ties in developing countries, however, sometimes become a means for reducing the negative environmental impact of urbanisation. Such historically-conditioned elements should be reflected in legal systems in the West, as well as in developing countries. Urban space is not a mere occasion for the development of social structure, but a concrete expression of the historical nexus at which a society is located. Therefore, a deep structural analysis of the law in terms of its role as an urbanisation regulator in developing countries may reveal similar problems at a very different legal phase in Western countries.

The word "law" tends to mean "justice according to the law", and in short, "adjudication". Within it we see an issue-oriented approach, where one of the important elements is certainty in which the outcomes are predictable. However from the Eastern viewpoint, if I may make such a rough generalisation, the notion "according to law" is not always accompanied by adjudication.[4] There is no comparable idea of the rule of law in the United Kingdom, and hence the law covers much more limited fields of society in substitution for traditional communal elements which have been rapidly disappearing in Japan as well as in Western societies. Therefore law for urbanisation in West and East cannot be easily summarised, for in the East the law is not always the process of reasoning to logical conclusions, but is the dynamic process of inquiring into the traditional elements of the society itself, and its legalisation or judicialisation is always done to forward development ends which are assumed to be shared by the local people.[5]

3. The rise and fall of the myth of land-ownership in contemporary Japan

In developing countries, the results of urbanisation are often over-urbanisation and consequently social instability. By contrast, Japan, despite being a late starter in industrialisation, has been able to create a relatively stable urban society because its cities were largely formed at the same time as Japan was undertaking industrialisation.[6]

Urban problems in Japan began to be seen as major social problems after the Second World War. The area of land covered by new urban development in the 30 years since the Second World War is equivalent to the total urban area built up in Japan since the beginning of history.

However, the retention of village-type mutual-assistance patterns had made it easier for incoming populations to adapt and therefore had prevented urban

---

[4] McAuslan, comment in UNCRD Regional Development Dialogue (Grant ed.) Vol. 13 (Spring, 1992).

[5] Kaino, "A Changing Structure of Urban Land Tenures and Town Planning Laws in the ASEAN Countries", *Hosei Ronsyu (Nagoya University Journal of Law and Politics)* No. 126 (March, 1989); Sofa (ed.) *Towards a Political Economy of Urbanisation in the Third World Countries* (1985) especially the Introduction.

[6] Land problems in post-War Japan were clearly analysed in Harrison, *The Power in the Land* (1983) pp.162 *et seq*. I owe so much to his analysis of contemporary land problems in Japan.

problems from becoming too serious. Although Japan has been quickly transformed into an urbanised country, a large number of people flowing from rural villages into Tokyo, Osaka, Nagoya and other big cities commonly maintained their social ties within their home communities. Even during the period of rapid economic growth in the 1960s, these so-called "dekasegi" type workers (that is, a kind of internal *Gastarbeiter*) streamed back to the rural communities in time of recession functioning as a kind of shock absorber to control the total labouring population in urban areas. On the other hand, however, because of these unsettled urban residents, the concept of "citizen" has not become established in Japan's metropolises, and thus there is no real orientation on the part of citizens toward making their cities into communities that are pleasant to live in. This is often cited as the reason for the low level of amenities in Japan's big cities, where "workaholics" are said to live in "rabbit hutches".[7]

The main feature of residential patterns in Japanese cities is the neglected distinction between areas or streets in which members of different socio-economic classes reside. While individual residences may be the object of social evaluation, little attention is paid to the street and residential area. One of the disadvantages of this is that no interest is taken in the residential environment, particularly in the area between public and private spaces. This in turn has a very close bearing on the lack of progress registered in improving the housing environment.[8]

"Living together", on the other hand, appears to have had a remarkable impact upon the formation of metropolitan areas in Japan. Japan lacks such a custom of living together so that people of similar background, culture and lifestyle live in one place to the exclusion of others; hence, the so called "sprawl" phenomenon. In Japan, therefore, one can scarcely find the kind of beautiful and well-organised suburban areas that one can easily see, for instance, in the United Kingdom and the United States.[9]

The recent land price explosion began in 1986–1987 and continued until 1989. The average price in the 23 wards of Tokyo increased by 78 per cent between January 1, 1986 and January 1, 1987. Although the process of speculation usually comes to a stop when price levels no longer correspond to any economic rationality, the consequences of such surges for displacement of housing and the spread of urban functions is difficult to reverse or repair. Without entering into a global analysis of the Japanese economy it is extremely difficult to advance an explanation of this phenomenon which puzzles everyone, even Japanese experts themselves. Some suggestions can be offered. First, it was

---

[7] Japanese "dekasegi" type workers are discussed by Kurasawa, in "Social and Cultural Issues in Japan" in Sazanami (ed.) *Metropolitan Planning and Management* (Japan Society for the Promotion of Science, 1982).

[8] *ibid.* at p. 118.

[9] It is very interesting to read comparison of different evaluations of urban development between Japan and Western countries. A full discussion can be found in Iida, *Metropolitan Issues in Japan* in Sazanami, above, n.7, at pp. 58–59.

quite clearly related to the increase of speculative land transactions. Secondly, the increase in land prices is due to a disequilibrium between supply and demand in the market for office space. In the early 1980s demand was high due to the development of Tokyo as an international financial centre. This situation arises from the rapidly increasing demand for office space. New Japanese words such as "Jiage" – depicting the tearing up from the roots of the ground when tenants were forcibly evicted to make space for office developments in metropolitan centres – had been born and became popular around this period.[10]

The uniqueness of Japanese land law must be borne in mind. According to English law as well as Continental (French or German) law, land not only means every species of ground, soil or earth, but also includes houses and other buildings on it; and with the conveyance of the land, the structures upon it pass also. However, under Japanese law, land and buildings are treated as independent objects of realty, subject to independent rights. Each is handled in accordance with its individual legal identity, subject to separate conveyancing or mortgaging. It was customary that land-ownership rights and rights of ownership of the buildings on that land were the property of separate individuals. Therefore, it became necessary to protect buildings on another person's land, and also the rights of tenants who live in a building which is owned by a lessee of the land. These are so-called "building tenants" as opposed to "land tenants". Thus an enormous amount of case law relating to special protection for these tenancies has grown up around the Land Lease Law and Housing Lease Law which were introduced in 1921, and amended quite recently.

This unique character of Japanese land law is said to bring about the strange phenomena of "white land": land which has no specific lessee's right is much more expensive than one with such right, *i.e.* land with buildings is less expensive than land with no buildings at all. However, building tenancy or land tenancy has been protected as the means to secure tenants' rights to settle and to live in cities, since public sector housing was very weak even after the Second World War.

Access to home-ownership and a better quality of life in cities should have become central policy issues; but they have rarely figured in Japanese general elections. It is clear that recent trends in prices have resulted in an increase in tax receipts for the State (succession duties, taxation of increases in values). Although there is now an emerging problem of social inequality between the haves and have-nots (the price of an average condominium apartment in the Tokyo region was approximately nine times an ordinary worker's annual income in 1989), the mythology of land price, that is to say the myth that the price of land will rise without limit, has been believed and even supported by a lot of people (including "rabbit hutch owners") and especially by a number of major companies. It should be noted here that the high market value of land and property markets are of considerable importance in the economy as a whole.

---

[10] See especially OECD Report of the Groups on Urban Affairs, 1990.

The financial equilibrium of a number of major companies depends to a great extent upon the value of their property portfolio, in as much as banks take account of this in their lending policy towards companies. The rapid price increases in 1986 and 1987 created a gap between the market value of property portfolios of companies and their accounting value registered in the company's books. This led to a number of speculative stock operations.

These developments could be linked with the system of land-ownership itself and consequently could become "barriers" to a solid national consensus on basic principles regarding land, such as the preference for public welfare. Therefore a variety of public relations and educational activities like the campaign to emphasise the importance of land politics should be undertaken. But we have not succeeded in it.[11]

4. Basic issues in ASEAN countries

The inner city problems of the ASEAN countries differ from those in Western countries but resemble closely the case of Japan which I have just outlined. While the industrialised countries search for better living standards, many ASEAN cities still function as a refuge for displaced persons, such as the urban poor. While the field of comparative urban research has grown significantly, it has generally lacked a firm theoretical framework within which to examine cross-culturally the socio-economic processes which have accompanied the rapid growth of most of the cities in the ASEAN countries. It is now generally recognised that the historical process of urbanisation in these areas might be radically different from that in the highly industrialised societies, and that the ecological or class structure of human societies in these areas should, therefore, be examined from their own view-points.

It is true to say that the expansion of the cities is unplanned and uncontrolled, but illegal settlements of the poor often work far better than official housing schemes purporting to help them. One of the most neglected aspects of the urbanisation process in the ASEAN countries relates to the phenomenon of circulatory migration between rural and urban areas. The so-called Kampong (or Kanpung) redevelopment is especially noteworthy since it indicates differences in approach to both nature and to the logic of processes of urbanisation between Western and Third World countries. Kampong should not be seen as the result of disorderly urbanisation and unplanned expansion, but should be studied as one of the expressions of "harmony" among rural/urban elements as well as the proper means to stop the expansion of town areas simply by force of the market.

We should particularly note the relationship between socio-political, and especially legal, elements indigenous to those countries and those systems

---

[11] I owe so much to Professor Yamada's very stimulating thesis in "Home Ownership under Modern Capitalism", an unpublished paper presented to the Department of Land Economy, University of Cambridge, 1994.

which have been introduced from the West through industrialisation and urbanisation. The latter product-orientated systems often conflicted with the former, giving rise to serious problems of harmonisation. I shall consider the structural position and function of the indigenous laws of the ASEAN countries in terms of the State laws, which are by and large based on received Western law, through examining the actual interaction between received law and indigenous ones in the field of town development. For case studies on urban development, I will sometimes refer to four ASEAN cities. These are Bangkok, Kuala Lumpur (abbreviated to K.L.), Jakarta and Singapore. The Indonesian islanders encountered the British law during the nineteenth century and later on were introduced to the legal system of the Netherlands. Similarly, in that period, the then Straits Settlements – today Malaysia and Singapore – and Brunei, the former British-protected Sultanate, were placed under the common law of England.

How then is it possible to observe and analyse the whole structure of the law of these countries in the context of their own cultural background or as a result of the conflicts of the indigenous elements and the received ones? These legal elements are, as it were, revived in the current situation in that modernisation and industrialisation have been affected greatly by these elements.[12]

5. Historical background and ideas of property

Japan used to be an agrarian society in the Far East, but its traditional values were no match for the thrusting wave of merchants following after General Perry's U.S.A. warship just before the Meiji period about 150 years ago. To resist this threat, Japan had to modernise her political and economic institutions. She had to change her method of extracting agricultural surplus.

The land tenure system was reconstructed by the Land Tax Revision Act 1873. The title deeds introduced by that Act were issued for each plot of land to those customarily considered to be in possession. The land tax was converted into an annual tax of three per cent of the assessed value of the land. Some peasant cultivators formerly bound to the land by feudal ties became independent proprietors. However, more than 50 per cent of the total number of peasants were wholly or partly tenants of other people's land at the beginning of the Meiji period. Rents for those tenant farmers had to be paid in kind and continued to amount to half of an average crop.

As for the compensation for the privileged classes of the old regime, the Meiji Government provided government bonds and salaries, and these new officials played an important role after the Meiji Restoration. As Professor Dore suggested those who controlled policy during the Meiji period were not landed gentlemen, unlike the situation in England at the comparable stage of

---

[12] The notion of reception is important even after the ages of colonisation; see Bartholomew, "English Law in Partibus Orientalium" in Harding (ed.), above, n.3, at p. 13 *et seq*. A general description of the conflicts between Western law and indigenous law is very difficult but see Hooker (ed.), above, n.3, where the introduction is particularly useful.

industrialisation, but were bureaucrats who depended on the State for their income and salaries.[13]

The above-mentioned title deeds recognised only one form of property, namely, unconditional ownership. Hence all other rights were swept away and various customarily recognised rights of permanent tenancy failed to gain legal recognition. Naturally many disputes occurred concerning conflicting claims to the land and finally the Civil Code Act of 1898 recognised customary rights as a kind of property right with a maximum limit on their duration. However, because of the difficulty of bringing cases to court, customary rights faded away or became mere tenancies at will of the people who owned the title deeds to the land.

These reforms were largely influenced by Western notions of absolute ownership. Many communal village lands to which no right of ownership attached were also taken over by the state or became the property of powerful individuals who could influence the procedure for issuing title deeds.

It should be noted, too, that traditional self-sufficient type villages (where everyone knew everyone else and everyone co-operated for the management of common pasture and forest land) were gradually absorbed by newly created village administrative units and, through them, a new dimension of loyalty was added with the development of a national State.[14]

Soon after Japan's defeat in the Second World War, the allied occupation brought measures of economic democratisation. Among these, land reform was the one of most outstanding importance. These drastic reforms swept away the old tenancy system at a single stroke. The question of the actual size of holdings apart, as far as the system of land-ownership is concerned, Japan can now be aptly described as a country of owner-farmers.

Although the post-war reform sought to increase the number of owner-occupiers, the reform succeeded in consolidating the system of land monopoly, with the privileges enjoyed by an enlarged class. There is no society of private ownership of land where the benefits of publicly created land values are so effectively subject to private appropriation as in Japan of post-war years. The former tenants were not slow to cash in on the need for development land. Dispossessed land-owners claimed that land which was taken from them for the price of a sparrow's tears was now being sold as building land at 5,000 times the purchase price in growing urban areas.[15]

We can see very different notions of ownership in land in South East Asia. As for the common law, it began to spread at the beginning of the seventeenth century and eventually encompassed all of North America, parts of the Mediterranean and the Middle East, etc. The introduction of the common law

---

[13] My discussion of the history of modern land law reform in Japan especially for readers of English owes so much to Professor Dore's important and interesting work, *Land Reform in Japan* (1959) pp. 14–15.
[14] *ibid.* at pp. 14–22.
[15] Harrison, above, n.6 at pp. 168–169.

to South-East Asian countries is therefore only one example of a much larger movement over the so-called "common law world". These countries, therefore, share a common heritage of common law where the introduced English common law was the law of general application and there was no suggestion of special law area or law population as in the Netherlands East Indies.

Penang, Malacca, and Singapore, which together comprised the Strait Settlements, were acquired at different dates. However, as far as Singapore was concerned, in the short time between its establishment in 1819 and its incorporation into the Strait Settlements in 1826, judicial matters were organised through a set of Regulations ("Raffles Regulations" of 1823). With the granting of the Second Charter in 1826, the three territories had a unified legal system as the Straits Settlements. The Straits continued under the British East India Company government until 1857, when with the demise of the company, the India Office assumed control. This only lasted until 1867 when the transfer to the Colonial Office took place for the remaining years.[16]

Dutch rule over the Netherlands East Indies was quite different from British. Its main characteristic was, in short, the long-standing and complex formulation of laws which remained a feature of the Netherlands Indies. It included a scheme of cultural division of native (adat) law and European law. A kind of "internal private international law" resulted from these divisions.

Large tracts of privately owned lands in the Netherlands East Indies had been transferred, and the problems which arose were settled by colonial government. However, the final resolution of the problems was done only in 1958 by the post-independence national government of Indonesia.

The colonial State claimed sovereign domain over the territory of the Netherlands East Indies and had alienated much of it (the realm of Jakarta and Batavia). Raffles followed this precedent and granted territory during the short period of British rule. The property rights were, roughly speaking, the most comprehensive forms of ownership under European feudalism. The landlords, some of whom were originally native heads but many of whom were Chinese or European, possessed power not only over land and water, but also over the native population.[17]

6. Communal ideas of property and town development – the case of Indonesia

The dualism of the land tenure system in the Republic of Indonesia was abolished by "Act No. 5 of the Year of 1960 concerning Basic Regulations on Agrarian Principles". According to the enacting clauses of the Act, it was enacted "considering (a) that in the State of Indonesia, of which the structure of its society including its economic system is especially of agrarian nature, its earth,

---

[16] Hooker (ed.), *A Concise Legal History of South East Asia* (1978) at pp. 123–124; Professor Hooker is the most important scholar of South-East Asian laws and my analysis generally owes much to this and his other work.
[17] Burns, *The Netherlands East Indies: Colonial Legal Policy and the Definitions of Law* in Hooker (ed.), above, n.3, at pp. 285–286.

water and air space being the gift of God, have a very important function in the Construction of a just and prosperous society", and also "considering (b) that the Agrarian Law" which is valid today, is partly based on aims and principles of the colonial government and its influence, and is thus "in conflict with the interest of the people and the State in the completion of the present National Revolution and the over-all development", (c) that the above-mentioned Agrarian Law is dualistic in regard to the validity of the Adat (Customary) law, existing besides the mentioned Agrarian Law, which is based on Western law, and (d) that for the indigenous population, the aforementioned colonial law does not guarantee legal security.

This Act also expressed a very interesting notion of communal property as follows:

> "(a) that in connection with the considerations as above, it is deemed necessary that a National Agrarian Law is established, based upon the Agrarian Law concerning land, which law should be simple and should guarantee legal security for the whole of the people of Indonesia, without neglecting elements based on religious law;
> (b) that the National Agrarian Law shall enable the functioning of the earth, water and air space as mentioned above, and shall be in line with the interests of the people of Indonesia and at the same time meet the needs which are required at present in all matters pertaining to agriculture;
> (c) that this National Agrarian law must be the realisation of the spiritual fundamentals of the State and ideals of our Nation, as is laid down in the Preamble of the Constitution, *i.e.* Belief in the One and Supreme God, Humanity, Nationalism, Democracy and Social Justice;
> (d) that the National Agrarian Law shall be an implementation of the Presidential Decree of 1959, Article 33 of the Constitution, which obliges the State to regulate land property and to guide its utilisation, so that all land throughout the Nation's sovereign territory be used for the maximum prosperity of the people, individually as well as mutually;
> (e) that in connection with all that, it is deemed necessary to lay down the principles and to compose new basic provisions in the form of an Act, which will become the basis in composing the abovementioned National Agrarian Law."[18]

It was often said that Western or European ideas of development or progress were based on obvious political, economic and military superiority.

Together with this was the belief in the validity of European experience or science as a method of classifying, describing and analysing South-East Asian cultures. By the early years of the twentieth century, this position was widely criticised. The main negative result of the Euro-centric position was to obscure many of the complexities of Asian culture. So far as law is concerned, it resulted in misunderstanding or distortion and narrow ideas of laws by enshrining

---

[18] As to the above, Agrarian Law of 1960, see Hooker, *Concise Legal History* above, n.16, at p. 207.

them formally into statutes and judicial decisions. The actual or real laws in these areas might be hybrid ones, some of which still operate today.

This might be true of ideas of property, especially notions of land-ownership, as with the communal ideas of land in the Agrarian Law cited above. Apart from the provision of the Constitution of the Republic of Indonesia which refers to the communal systems of economy based on the family system, Gotong-Royong in villages in Indonesia and perhaps Pansa-Sila of Sukarno's administration, there survive and still operate various kinds of social systems of mutuality or communal ideas in South-East Asian countries. Those should be compared with self-reliant communities such as Barangay in the Republic of the Philippines, Semaul in South Korea and also with Mura (village community) especially in pre-war Japan.

However I should refrain from estimating these communal elements, for these ties sometimes imply a very feudal relationship within the group, and the making of individualistic arrangements was, on the other hand, the process of modernisation in Western countries. Apart from current debates on Lockean natural rights (as alienable or inalienable), I should like to note here that there has been a very strong tradition of common ownership in these ASEAN countries, and it was very rare to need a solution to the historical conflict between the liberal principle of individual property right and the democratic principle of majority rule.

At any rate, these communal ideas or systems have almost disappeared in Japan with the rapid growth of its economy especially during the 1960s. The bare rule of "market theory" becomes much more dominant in the process of urban development especially since the period of the second oil crisis in the late 1970s, when the price of land in Tokyo metropolitan region rose so crazily that it became a matter of great concern that people had to leave the town centres of many big cities, sometimes driven by the above-mentioned "Jiage".

7. Management of Malaysian, Thai and Singaporean cities

Since the attainment of internal self-government, and ultimately, of independence from the United Kingdom and separation from the neighbouring State of Malaysia, Singapore's development with gleaming blocks of high-rise flats, most of them concentrated into "new towns", is enormous. What is the source of this achievement with its attendant management skill?

The condition of Singapore when occupied by Raffles in 1819 seems almost precisely similar to that of Penang. Raffles entered into a series of agreements and treaties with the local rulers. Thus Singapore and the islands immediately adjacent are stated to be at the entire disposal of the British Government, and the laws of Malays shall be respected in so far as not contrary to reason, justice or humanity, but in other cases English law will be applied. This was not a necessary consequence in the Dutch or even French possessions.

By the earlier nineteenth century, the principles of common law and equity were received as part of the law of Singapore and Malacca which together with

Penang were administered as part of British India. The operation of the Charter meant that the English doctrine of tenure and estates operated in Singapore and in the other two Straits Settlements. Therefore all land was in theory vested in, first the East India Company, subsequently in the British Crown and currently, by virtue of Article 160 of the Constitution, in the State. The allocation system of landholding, by which in theory no individual can actually "own" land, applies in Singapore.[19]

In general, however, the Malay legal systems, largely customary but with some parts written, had a distinct existence; but with the advent of Islam there arose conflict between Malay custom and Islamic law. In some respects Malay *adat* was more generous than Islamic law. In spite of Islam the equitable and practical principles of Malay traditional custom were too ingrained in the Malay mind to be abandoned. In particular in *adat*, there seems to be some sort of communal and patriarchal elements. Through the consultation with chiefs by the Ruler, and the administration of justice through territorial magnates, as it were, the *adat* was aimed at harmony.[20]

Thailand is unique in South-East Asia in that it was never colonised. However, the borders which Thailand now holds were defined by imperial pressure in the late nineteenth and early twentieth centuries under which Siam lost territory. From the point of view of legal history, therefore, the first experience of European law by Siam was through treaties which granted extra-territorial rights and consequences which flowed from them.[21] Thus between 1855 and 1900, Siam was locked into a set of engagements, treaties and orders with the European powers. Reforms were undertaken to accomplish State construction in Siam. King Chulalongkorn had grasped the essential point that the legal changes demanded by the Europeans required also the adoption of European principles on the fundamental question of the distribution, organisation and delegation of political power. Professor Petchsiri said "In the late nineteenth century, King Chulalongkorn led the country to adopt the Western course of development and legal system while neighbouring countries fell prey to colonialism." He also said

> "Thailand is a country with a long history of established indigenous legal system since the thirteenth century. It was revived in the following century, and subsequently altered and codified. The final indigenous law reform was the codification of all the laws in the early nineteenth century which resulted in the Law Code of 1805. The indigenous system was not entirely replaced until the early twentieth century."

The earlier Thai law is *dharmasastra* or *thammasat* which is sometimes called the Code of Manu and is of Hindu origin, but is not identified with the

---

[19] Ricquier, *Land Law and Common Law in Singapore* in Harding (ed.), above, n.3, at pp. 233–235.
[20] As to the Islamic influence on Malay, see Hooker, above, n.16, *Concise History* at pp. 51–68.
[21] See Hooker, "Introduction: European Laws in South East Asia" in Hooker, above, n.3, at p. 22.

Hindu original – that is to say, *thammasat* developed in response to the needs of the Thai people.[22]

We should refer again to the problems of communal consciousness in land ownership. In Thailand, the legal forms of interests in land seem to be similar to English common law, represented by the notions of estates such as freehold and leasehold; but there might be different parallel ideas of land-ownership which are perhaps based on some indigenous laws or "living laws".

In the future, I would like to inquire into the process of the Agricultural Land Reforms during the 1970s. Here, I should like to point out some interesting topics in land-sharing which may point to solutions to the land price problems that we experience in contemporary Japan.

In Bangkok, the capital of Thailand, there are "official projects" involving so called landsharing which arise from negotiated agreements between slum dwellers and landlords to share the land. There is ample evidence that governments cannot produce housing units which the poor can afford. It has been suggested that governments act to make land tenure secure, and to enable people to build and improve their houses by themselves.

In the attempt to establish land rights in slums and squatter areas, government usually finds itself in the position of an arbiter between the conflicting claims of landlords on the one hand and slum dwellers on the other. The general claim of landlords, whether private or public, is that the government must protect their legal rights to the land and assist them in clearing the slums so that they can exercise their right to use the land as they see fit.[23]

Land-sharing – the partition of the land into two patterns, one for use by the landlord, and one for use by the present occupants of the site – looks like a typical example of an alternative idea to the land-ownership in Western countries including Japan. Town planning laws should be reconsidered from these viewpoints of ASEAN people.

8. Conclusion

Community can not be created under a physically isolated situation. Only by group sympathy or by symbiosis, do we proceed beyond the boundaries of a very limited and conflicting sphere of private property concepts. Locke raised a problem of the distribution of property that is categorically unsolvable. If we could not avoid a view of the community as a single product-orientated unit, Locke's *Two Treatises of Government* would be meaningless in a certain sense. What Locke posits as "independence" is based on the notion that a man of property is less likely to be dependent upon another man's goodwill than someone with nothing to sell except his labour. However property is, as history demon-

---

[22] Petchsiri, *Eastern Imposition of Western Criminal Law* (1987) pp. 10–11.
[23] Angel and Boonyabancha, "Land Sharing as an Alternative to Eviction in Third World" *Planning Review* (May, 1988) Vol. 10, No. 2.

strates, the condition of a state in which liberty is possible. The man of property was pre-eminently someone charged with the maintenance of conditions of liberty for everyone.

Independence has been linked with the idea of citizenship[24] which is again a very Western tradition. However, as the communal elements in Eastern societies indicate, a proprietor has a duty to look to the benefit of the community to which he belongs. What is fundamental for the relationship between property and democracy is that a right to own private property has an important effect on the citizen's relationship with the State. Unconcern with distribution or complete indifference to the poor is another aspect of Western enthusiasm for property which should be overcome by the development of the system of communality or symbiosis which we often come across even in urban areas in Eastern countries. Emerging democracies in developing countries as well as in the former socialist countries will appreciate that ownership could overcome people's political dependence on the State.

But the mere development of ownership and monopolisation of the land without communality and a relationship of "living together" would bring about what has been called the "tragedy of the commons" (Harding). Citizenship should include a certain system of creating normative and communal relationships with private property in order to change its mere monopolistic nature into communal or symbiotic ones. Then the notion of private property itself should play an important part within a constitutional democracy.[25]

---

[24] As to citizenship, preliminary discussion can be found in Marshall and Bottomore, *Citizenship and Social Class* (1992).
[25] Waldron, *The Right to Private Property* (1988) pp. 300–301; see also Munzer, above, n.1 at pp. 42–43.

19

Hegel and the Social Dynamics of Property Law

M.G. SALTER*

Introduction

The purpose of this paper is to reconstruct those aspects of Hegel's account of property law that have retained a measure of contemporary relevance. One strength of Hegel's analysis is that it re-opens the question of which areas of social life should fall within the domain of private property rights. He addresses this question independently of any "cold war" predisposition in favour of either wholesale state nationalisation or unregulated free markets. By contrast, his analysis brings out the one-sided quality of contemporary neo-liberal ideologies that treat private property as an inherently good and liberating thing, whilst decrying public property as inherently disempowering.

In his *Philosophy of Right*[1] Hegel presents an account of property law involving a logical sequence of development that unfolds over three distinct stages: the formalism of abstract right, the moralistic contribution of Equity and a law-in-context approach (PR: 30, 32). Property rights perform a different role in each phase. However, Hegel's developmental view of modern society reconstructs property as a complex totality evolving towards maturity in each of its three stages (PR: 45).[2] Although the third contextual phase represents both a culmination and fulfilment of its predecessors, the two earlier stages still make an indispensable contribution to the overall progression (PR: 30, 32). Hegel's teleological and evolutionary model of both property law and modern society more generally, allows us to make value judgements about what does and does not constitute "progress" within social and historical developments. This is despite the fact that the sequences are of a logical and conceptual, rather than wholly empirical, nature.

For Hegel historical progress involves both comprehending and fulfilling modernity's core principle of subjective freedom. This principle is articulated

---

* Department of Law, Lancaster University.
[1] (trans. Knox): hereafter cited as "PR" followed by the paragraph number.
[2] Benson, "The Priority of Abstract Right, Constructivism, and the Possibility of Collective Rights in Hegel's Legal Philosophy" (1991) 4 Can. Jnl. Juris. 257; see Stillman: "Hegel's Analysis of Property in the Philosophy of Right" (1989) 10 Cardozo L. Rev. 1031 at p. 1048.

by an individualistic and "negative rights" standpoint. That is, one that insists that freedom consists in *freedom from* all external restrictions upon voluntary action, with individual choice taken to be an absolute value. Progress also requires the liberation of humanity from unwarranted historical restrictions upon its inherent power for self-determination, *i.e.* the capacity to determine both the detailed contents and form of our own will (PR: 10, 27, 57). Hegel claims that there is an *internal connection* between the project of establishing the *social and historical preconditions* for human liberation, and his three-stage developmental sequence of property law (PR: 46, 221).

1. The contradictions of abstract right

The first developmental phase of modern property law is the emergence of the distinctly individualistic orientation of early modern capitalism. The "possessive individualism" of capitalist ideology is articulated by a legalistic perspective which Hegel terms *abstract right*;[3] but which is now more commonly referred to as the black letter tradition.[4] Hegel begins his account of property law *from inside* the individualistic orientation of abstract right. He then follows through the logical and social consequences of how it both defines and applies its central categories (PR: 2, 31). He shows how this perspective interprets the social world so that central categories of property law, such as possession and ownership, are divorced from their social context; and then relocated within a quite distinct realm of interpretation where they function as lawyers' specialist *terms of art* (PR: 37). In this way, abstract right sets up a legal realm of abstract legal forms and categories. Adopting a lofty attitude of superior indifference, this realm stands over and above the world of everyday life over whom it demands absolute jurisdiction nonetheless. Abstract right strives to become a closed, autonomous and self-justifying sub-culture that is oriented only towards the legalistic interpretation of the technicalities of lawyers' law. The assumption here is that semantic and definitional considerations concerning "what constitutes the essential meaning of, say 'possession'?" can, in themselves, supply an adequate basis for resolving property disputes.

Abstract right insists that all relevant legal arguments must refer back to the strictly legal meaning of doctrinal precedents expressed in primary materials such as statutes and case-law. It bases the *authority* of the various principles and rules of positive law upon the principle of "positivity". In other words, that a given law (even one allowing slavery and the sale of children) is valid simply because *it is* traditional law. Hence, the longevity of a legal principle, or its consistency with other traditional aspects of institutional life, are seen as sufficient grounds to accept its legal validity (PR: 3, 57).

---

[3] See Brudner, "Hegel and the Crisis of Private Law" (1989) 10 Cardozo L. Rev. 949.
[4] See Schauer "Formalism" (1989) 97 Yale L.J. 509; McBarnet and Whelan, "The Elusive Spirit of the Law: Formalism and the Struggle for Legal Control" (1991) 11 M.L.R. 848.

Abstract right's treatment of law as a wholly separate and technical realm means that whatever is identified within ordinary life as an urgent social problem, such as mortgage debt, need not fall within the definition of what counts as a "legal problem" for property law. Instead, this approach routinely filters out all moral and ideological aspects of the immediate case. It does so in order to maintain the autonomy of "strict law" understood as a coherent, consistent and self-sufficient system of lawyer's law (PR: 3). Hence, what is absolutely prohibited by the formalism of abstract right is for a judge to go beyond or disregard the authority of existing precedents. This is particular true where the judge's aim is to meet the requirements of rational social policy or morality.

The individualistic standpoint of abstract right focuses upon single persons considered in isolation from their network of specific social, political and economic attributes and roles.[5] Hegel argues that, in one sense, abstract right does respect the claims of modern individualism. Property rights are reduced to a situation in which one legal subject is able to claim that this "thing" is mine alone, and that the property "right" which is granted by the law is "my right". Hence, this approach portrays legal subjects as self-centred individualists who exist only for themselves, and who lack all sense of communal ties and social responsibilities. Because abstract right views individuals as a disconnected mass of atomistic "subjects", anxious only to preserve and enforce their strict legal rights, it is necessary to use the institutional force of law to coerce them to respect the rights of others.

Within the individualistic perspective of abstract right, the unequivocal right of individuals to exercise a far-reaching and rich variety of private property rights is fundamental. This right represents an *absolute basis* for their recognition as fully-enfranchised and rights-bearing "persons". Private property provides the basis for other basic civic rights, including freedom of contract, the right to a private life and liberty from state regulation and control. One consequence of abstract right defining private property as absolute is that the negative rights of property owners take precedence over any competing social policy requirements relating to, say, the imposition of public planning or rent controls (PR: 37).

At least as a primary and undifferentiated starting point, Hegel accepts the validity of a fundamental distinction made by abstract right between the subject and object of property ownership (PR: 2, 41). However, he also shows how the individualistic perspective of abstract right does not, as it claims, *simply describe* the inherent and natural character of property relations. Instead, this approach *reinterprets, and thereby transforms*, these relations according to its own legalistic requirements. Hence, what abstract right assumes to be a self-evident "starting point", *i.e.* the "natural rights" of a private legal subject, is really secondary and derivative. For Hegel, this so-called "starting point" is, in

---

[5] Stillman, *op. cit.* above, n.2, at pp. 1032–1023, 1038, 1065.

fact, produced socially through an underlying interpretative process that transposes everyday problems into specifically legal categories.

On the basis of this legalistic abstraction, abstract right produces a highly simplified account of property ownership. The subject of legal rights is portrayed as equipped with both free will and a fully matured form of personality. This subject is then seen by abstract right as confronting various undifferentiated, external objects of ownership, which themselves lack personality, rights or free will (PR: 41, 42, 44). Unlike objects, which can only exist in a wholly external fashion, human subjectivity can relate consciously to, and act purposely upon, both itself and its needs (PR: 42). The basic subject/object distinction made by abstract right excludes any mediation of supposedly extraneous social, historical or ideological factors *on both sides of their relationship*. This is because property relations are portrayed in terms of a solitary individual, confronting an unshaped, natural object which is similarly abstracted from its particular social and historical contexts.[6] This view requires that the objects of property law must be single, external things that are wholly distinct from the internal, subjective constituents of the personality of individuals (PR: 65–66, 75).

Within this simplified perspective of abstract right, an object becomes "property" only when a legal subject puts his or her will into it by appropriating this object as a means for a subjective end. This is something that all individuals have an absolute right to do with respect to unowned property (PR: 44). Such appropriation combines material and symbolic aspects. It requires various kinds of deliberate physical action to be performed, such as entering into occupation, the exercise of effective control of its use and acts which symbolically "mark out" the property, *e.g.* by fencing it off (PR: 44, 51, 54). However, in order to transform mere physical possession into a fully fledged property right, would-be owners must also make a public claim to ownership whose validity others can freely recognise (PR: 45, 51). A free-market contractual process including the exchange of ownership between (formally) equal parties aids such social recognition. Here, contracting parties relate to one another through the medium of owned objects, and thereby come to recognise each other as the rightful owners of what they exchange (PR: 40, 72–73).[7]

Hegel's "immanent critique" of abstract right argues that its standpoint contains a partial truth insofar as it subverts feudalism's oppressive hierarchical framework of collective social control by asserting the individual's formal right to self-determination. This demand for universal rights is made quite independent of any individual's formal status within a social hierarchy established on the basis of inherited property relations. By abstracting the self-consciousness of individuals from their immediate historical circumstances and social contexts, the bonds that confine them within their customary ways of life are gradually corroded. Traditional bonds are then replaced by the distinctly modernist

---

[6] *ibid.* at p. 1033.
[7] *ibid.* at p. 1034.

standpoint of individualism. This standpoint insists that all communal claims must prove themselves to be valid to the personal satisfaction of those individuals whom these claims affect (PR: preface). When we understand social life in terms of this individualism, we also define ourselves relative to our capacity to exercise negative rights involving unrestricted freedom of choice.

This type of self-understanding is clearly subversive of a fixed social hierarchy which rigidly divides the population on the basis of property ownership, *e.g.* into landed aristocracy, freeholders, tenant farmers, serfs and landless labourers. On the basis of entailed property and primogeniture, the feudal hierarchy once ensured (and – in some respects – still does ensure) that individual rights are passed down to the eldest son from one generation to the next (PR: 46, 178–180).[8] The inevitable result is that the relative political and civic rights of individuals depend upon the individuals pre-ordained position within an essentially static system of property relations (PR: 35, 40). By contrast, the negative rights orientation of abstract right claims to treat all individuals on the principle of the rule of law, *i.e.*, the formal equality of all citizens under the same law irrespective of their particular relationship to property (PR: 221). Abstract right can operate as a progressive force by introducing into social life a modern conception of subjective freedom. For Hegel, this conception represents a vital, if ultimately insufficient, constitutional principle on which to build a democratic, self-governing state (PR: 5–7, 25).

Hegel bases his appreciation of this progressive aspect of abstract right upon a belief in the internal connection between private property and the task of securing the preconditions for genuine human freedom. He argues against various feudal, religious or customary encumbrances and restrictions upon the comprehensive exercise of property rights, including the prevention of the right to sell "settled" landed estates, or to otherwise freely dispose of them through a will. Such encumbrances amount to an irrational type of restriction upon the scope of free personality which effectively entrap owners reducing them, in practice, to the status of mere trustees of what is "their" property in only an impoverished sense of the term.[9] Thus, feudal restrictions represent the very opposite of the distinctly modern principle that private property should serve the self-development of human subjects, and not vice-versa.

These restrictions on the alienation of property also impede the emergence of a fully rational modern state. In such a state, individuals' "negative rights" would be given full weight irrespective of what is being chosen, *i.e.* the particular *content* of such willing (PR: 5–6, 13). It follows that all "paternalistic" restrictions on freedom of contract imposed, say, by trust conditions or other bequests, should be abolished, even where these are specifically designed to protect the welfare of the individuals concerned. Negative freedom is incompatible with

---

[8] In "modern" Britain, primogeniture has yet to be fully abolished in respect to qualification for membership of the House of Lords and accession to the monarchy.

[9] See *Hegel's Political Writings* (trans. Knox, 1964) p. 308.

entailed property since it must include the right of owners to choose to remove their will from the property by contracting to sell it. Hence, within abstract right property should, *at the absolute will of the owner* be treated as *fully alienable via the market-place* (PR: 53, 65). By undermining those feudal restrictions on the alienability of property that treat all individuals as, at best, mere tenants of the crown, abstract right also promotes the fundamental principles of the capitalist economy. In turn, this type of economic and social system assures that private property represents a commodity that can be freely and wholly bought, sold and mortgaged through an unregulated market (PR: 53).

Hegel claims that abstract right has been a progressive force insofar as it limits ownership to single external things. This limitation insists that the type of possession, ownership and control which subjects have in themselves, *i.e.* in their own minds, wills, bodies and other personal capacities, *is different in kind* from that which they exercise over external objects. One important constitutional implication of this principle is that our potential for self-determination should be recognised as *an inalienable end in itself.* As such, it should be legally protected against being treated as the property of another (PR: 185, 206).

Individuals should not be allowed by law to alienate their own innate capacities for freedom. For example, Hegel opposes the idea that it should be permissible for individuals to agree to sell their personality, bodies and talents to the permanent service of another as, say, a servant, serf or slave (PR: 57, 66). To enter into such an agreement would be to treat various essential and subjective components of the free personality, which themselves form an indivisible whole within the internal realm, as though they were merely external and impersonal entities (PR: 67). Such contracts are self-contradictory and ethically wrong, irrespective of any social welfare policies of the government since they both recognise and deny the free will of the individual.[10] What is more, no legal code that formalises the social injustice of slavery can ever offer an inclusive, coherent definition of either citizenship or property rights (PR: 2).

However, in marked contrast to abstract right for which individual freedom is the fixed and natural starting point, Hegel offers a *developmental* account of the evolution of the human subject. Here, the subject is seen as dependent upon an on-going project of socialisation, education and cultural integration. This process is oriented towards the eventual creation of a rational form of social and economic organisation (PR: 47, 57). In Hegelian terms, individuals must evolve from an immature condition of being free "in themselves", *i.e.* in principle only, to exercising that form of effective self-determination which makes them free "in and for themselves", *i.e.* in concrete social practice (PR: 10, 24, 41). He stresses that individuals need to acquire for themselves the pre-conditions for a being able to exercise a concrete form of freedom. This form of freedom requires the establishment of the supportive institutional context of a self-determining social

---

[10] Stillman, *op. cit.* above, n.2, at pp. 1044–1046.

order (PR: 185, 187, 206, 258). This project requires individuals not only to act co-operatively with others upon the substantive material of both natural and social worlds, but also to learn from both the planned and unintended consequences of such action. By reflecting upon the intended or unintended results of their actions, the rational powers of human will can further develop and mature through its constant use.

Control over material objects, such as agricultural land, and the investment of valuable resources of time, labour and money into such objects opens up owners to the particular vulnerabilities which affect that specific kind of property. It also limits their range of possible actions to those which this specific type of property allows. Without drawing upon this accumulated knowledge, the possession of property rights can always turn into a liability by undermining the plans and actions of owners. In sum, and contrary to abstract right, Hegel argues that freedom from external dependencies is not a fixed starting point of property rights but instead represents a project involving a continuous struggle against countervailing forces.

To develop into a fully fledged person also requires individuals to appropriate, in an active purposeful fashion, their own potential for freedom and self-determination. Individuals must not only shake off all unjustifiable restrictions upon their self-determination, but also *take full possession and control over their lives as willing, thinking and acting persons* (PR: 48). The potential for individuals to mature into free self-determining personalities must itself be actively appropriated by individuals themselves as an indispensable part of their citizenship of the modern world (PR: 56). The evolutionary and educational aspect of freedom forms part of a larger scale social and political project of self-development. The progressive realisation of this project involves a long-term historical and constitutional struggle for self-determination against a wide range of formidable social, natural and ideological limitations (PR: 63).

Within a struggle for self-determination whose overall character defines the modern epoch, the practical exercise of a full range of property rights plays a vital role as a means to realise the higher end of genuine freedom. According to Hegel, private property serves this purpose by allowing individuals to both express and extend their own personality into a material realm which they themselves have extensively shaped and dominated through physical action (PR: 41). Property rights lay out an external realm in which human subjectivity can – through work, speech and social interaction – externalise both its will and practical capacities (PR: 41). Prior to the embodiment of their intentions and plans within the surrounding social and natural world, the freedom of property owners exists only as a merely subjective and formal – and hence notional – capacity. Once appropriated, the otherwise alien and external material of nature can be progressively transformed, through personal and employed labour, so that it comes to take an objectively realised form: one which increasingly embodies the owner's subjective intentions, ideas and desires independent from the dictates of traditional customs (PR: 56). Hence, possession of private property rights facilitates the externalisation of subjectivity. As a result, having such rights represents an important means through which practical freedom and personality can go out from its self-enclosure within the interiority of a subjective realm. In addition, possessing property rights enables individuals to further realise, within an objective realm, their potential for substantive freedom and self-development (PR: 8, 41). Since all those who are members of a modern constitutional state governed by the rule of law have a democratic right to fully realise their subjective freedom and actualise their particular talents, interests and needs, it follows that every citizen should enjoy a right to own private property (PR: 49).

Despite his acknowledgement of the progressive role of abstract right, Hegel criticises abstract right for not honouring its ideologically important promise to fully protect the individuality of individuals. Each party to a property dispute is seen by this formalistic orientation as an *abstract universal*. This view disregards all those particular social contents (including gross inequalities of wealth, influence and bargaining power) which differentiate, say, landlords from tenants (PR: 49). Hegel argues that abstract right defines the subject as free in a wholly indeterminate and formal sense; yet ignores the existence of those specific contextual factors that, in practice, clearly impede the effective exercise of such freedom (PR: 35). In this way, abstract right corrodes important *substantive* aspects of free individuality leaving its individualistic ideals disappointed as "an unaccomplished end": one that, in principle, cannot be realised without transforming the totality of its underlying perspective (PR: 25).

What is more, the process of abstracting real life individuals from their network of family and other contextual relations means that the legal subject *becomes fictionalised*. It becomes transformed by abstract right into a *specifically legalistic invention* because individuals are treated as distinguishable from each other *only* upon distinctions drawn from the internal resources and specialist categories of property law itself. Here, individuals are re-interpreted only in terms of a formalistic and legalistic mentality that is projected upon them without any awareness of either the violation this produces or its own limits.

Hegel's *Phenomenology of Spirit*[11] argues that the only common element that the formalistic schema of abstract right recognises is the empty identity of "sameness" which one legal subject shares indifferently with every other atomised "individual". This schema defines the life-situations of actual persons impersonally, and hence de-personalises them. Real life individuals are represented as *no more* than the empty space of hollowed out "legal persons" whose distinguishing features within everyday life are thereby made to count for nothing. Thus, each party to a property dispute can receive "equal treatment" from a formalistic system of law only in the *sense of an equal measure of alienation*. Each party is alienated from both their own definitions of their situation, and any shared moral and social values and other cultural mediations drawn from

---

[11] (1967) translated by J. Baillie.

their participation within a complex web of social, family and economic relations. Hegel claims that, in practice, the much-vaunted individualism of abstract right is self-contradictory. It represents an attack on the complexity and self-definitions of real individuals since: "to describe an individual as a "person" is to use an expression of contempt".[12]

Hegel also criticises the formalism of abstract right as a type of interpretation that allows oppressive forms of social power to both underlie, and find expression via, an apparently neutral and abstract schema. Such formalistic interpretative practices allow irrational social content to escape from rational scrutiny. He further claims that it is the *particular characteristics* of the concrete relations that connect groups of persons and their interests to others that underscore many of the conflicts over property. Since abstract right individualises such conflicts, it necessarily glosses over the social character of conflicts of group interests. This legalistic perspective also fails to address property law's own role in both supporting and reproducing those asymmetrical social relations that tend to encourage all manner of conflicts over the ownership of resources.

According to Hegel, the formalistic orientation of abstract right is also defective on the grounds that legal form always depends for its substantive content upon historically specific social and economic phenomena. Yet the latter are primarily located beyond the confines of lawyers' law (PR: 3). Since legal form and social content presuppose one another as two sides of a unity, each should be analysed in terms of the other (PR: preface, 57). However, to bring out the mutual dependence of form and content undermines a basic tenet of abstract right by *introducing a social dimension* into property law from the very beginning (PR: 50).

This argument represents a fundamental criticism of abstract right's claim that judicial decisions can be made exclusively on the basis of judges giving the correct interpretation of the strict legal meaning of autonomous legal forms. Hegel's demonstration of the need to relate legal form to substantive content also destroys the cherished distinction between "strictly legal" issues (which are supposed to be wholly internal to a discrete realm of private law), and those which refer to "external" social policy questions. He shows that no matter how apparently technical the legal issue, the basic rationale and definitions of property still have to be established collectively with reference to specific social purposes. It now becomes clear that although abstract right attempts to exclude policy and ideological factors, it does this upon the hidden basis of these very same factors, especially *its own* neo-liberal ideological commitments. In practice, these latent commitments clearly operate to privilege negative rights and free-market individualism, and therefore rule out policies of socialist collectivism oriented towards the realisation of various social and economic welfare entitlements.[13]

---

[12] *ibid.* at pp. 503–504.
[13] See Benhabib, "Obligation, Contract and Exchange" in Pelczynski (ed.), *The State and Civil Society: Studies in Hegel's Political Philosophy* (1984) pp. 160–166.

Abstract right cannot, however, publicly acknowledge its dependence upon these underlying ideological value commitments. To do so would be to admit that it violates the central formalistic distinctions upon which its own entire perspective is based (PR: 37).[14] For example, Hegel suggests that it is wrong to classify property law as an essentially private law subject. The very either/or distinction between what is supposed to be inside and outside property law, between what is strictly legal and what is part of social policy, is untenable. This distinction collapses once we recognise that *the whole* of this discipline is determined by policy considerations based upon specific ideological commitments.

For Hegel, the credibility of the neo-liberal perspective of abstract right breaks down whenever it is over-extended to cover *all realms* of social interaction. Many such realms are structured around communal principles that are completely incompatible with the self-regarding individualism of this perspective. When over-extended, neo-liberalism shows itself to promote only an abstract, immature and partial conception of freedom: one which can supply neither the underlying ethos nor sufficiently rich forms of social experience, within a variety of institutional settings, to support the emergence of well rounded individuality. That is, a socially responsible form of individuality that is capable of exercising positive ethical duties of care towards the welfare of others (PR: 5, 34, 38). Instead, the concealed, but still effective, implementation by abstract right of a neo-liberal ideology ends up, in practice, violating the very values of human freedom which this ideology claims to promote. It promotes an abstract ideal of freedom based on the model of "freedom of contract". This model encourages individuals to enter into decisions that then render them vulnerable to the unpredictable operation and changes of unregulated market forces. In practice, such forces often make ideological promises of greater individual freedom seem formal, hollow and notional. This is because the content of what is willed by freedom of choice is typically supplied by an independent, external force operating independently of, and unaccountable to, any rational considerations (PR: 6–7, 12). Abstract right's definition of freedom in terms of negative rights ignores the fact that these are: "neither self-generating nor self-maintaining but rather rely on norms and values that are external to and prior to rights".[15] Negative rights must, according to Hegel, be fused with equal legal recognition of the importance with welfare entitlements – thereby creating a synthesis that includes both aspects (PR: 6–7).

He further argues that the free-market necessarily creates chronic social inequalities of wealth, status and power which market forces cannot correct. In

---

[14] Reyburn notes: "Abstract right thus is formal or immediate, in that it does not make explicit the further principles of the rational community within which alone it can exist." *Hegel's Ethical Theory* (1921) p. 123.

[15] Stillman, *op. cit.* above, n. 2, at p. 1039.

turn, such inequalities violate the integrity of personality by treating the most economically vulnerable members of society, such as children, spouses or employees, as little more than commodities. Once such groups are defined in this way, their social value is then determined largely by the price for which their services can be exchanged on the market-place (PR: 43, 75, 174). Although this instrumental "reification" of the body and personality of human subjects, who are thereby treated as mere resources to exploit, is one of the hallmarks of free-market systems,[16] such reification is also self-defeating. It leads to a contradiction in that such reification violates the core subject/object distinction on which the neo-liberal ideology of abstract right is itself founded. Hence, such reification is based upon a basic category mistake: one that, under modern conditions, Hegel identifies as both ethically wrong and self-contradictory (PR: 48).

According to Hegel, the various inadequacies and contradictions which result from the practical application of neo-liberal assumptions should confine abstract right to the strictly commercial sphere of the private sector. This is because the egotistical and remorseless assertion by individuals of their private property rights, regardless of their impact upon the welfare of others, produces a morally defective – and ultimately self-defeating – orientation, especially within family life and public service (PR: 35, 38, 40, 75). Instead, property relations must themselves be adjusted to accommodate the specific ethos and imperatives of these particular areas of social life, e.g. by treating family assets as communal (PR: 170–72). According to Hegel, even within the commercial sphere of economic exchange, the one-dimensional, free-market orientation of abstract right needs to be supplemented, modified and limited by a rich variety of complex moral, familial and social policy considerations. These include interventionist government policies involving the regulation of trade, consumer protection, taxation and general economic management. Such interventions are needed to counteract disequilibriums (such as monopolies) within market conditions. They are also required to off-set those social control problems created by the emergence of an alienated "underclass" which necessarily emerges as a by-product of free-market policies (PR: 185, 238, 241–8).

Under modern conditions, a legitimate state must follow policies that combine respect for individual rights with effective recognition of a diverse range of social welfare needs. He argues that taxation for the sake of funding public services, such as education, communication and social welfare work, represents the state's own rightful share of the individual's resources (PR: 35).[17] This argument is especially pertinent in the present context where the negative rights orientation of abstract right is frequently over-generalised. In Britain since 1979 "possessive individualism" has become all-pervasive official ideology: one that tries to treat *all* important social relations as based ultimately upon private

---

[16] Hegel, *Aesthetics* (trans. Knox, 1975) p. 149.
[17] Stillman, *op. cit.* above, n.2, at p. 1071.

property and freedom of contract (PR: 38).[18] For Hegel, such an over-extension, which is also found within the law and economics scholarship,[19] fails to recognise that the place of negative property rights is little more than *one partial moment* in, and phase of, a far larger process of human liberation. In turn, this process both encompasses and limits private property rights. This larger process not only unfolds the self-cancelling implications of a neo-liberal ideology, but also develops the political will expressed via the social policy of a potentially rational social order (PR: 64).

Hegel offers an alternative account of property law which – contrary to both black-letter and law and economics scholarship[20] – highlights the *mediation* of property relations by social, ideological and moral values. What is owned is a legally recognised interest in *the value*[21] of an object that itself can be intangible (PR: 43, 63). This "right to a right" itself depends upon continued acceptance of the norms of a large scale system of social recognition. This re-introduces moral considerations into the heart of property relations.[22]

2. The social need for the remedial morality of equity

Hegel argues that the realisation of justice is an immanent moral ideal which is located at the heart of the concept of law in general (PR: 33). Yet – contrary to the legalistic claims of abstract right – this internal ideal cannot be reduced to – or grounded upon – established positive law (PR: 3). Equity entails the *ad hoc* exercise of equitable principles and maxims that, for moral reasons, deliberately departs from, or suspends, the application of strict legal rules. The resulting disruptive effects of Equity upon a rigid system of self-sufficient and consistent precedent are often necessary in order to both dissociate law from unjust rules, and to further rationalise legal doctrine (PR: 223). Contrary to abstract right, law should not act as though logical consistency and doctrinal certainty were absolute values. Instead, society must reform the doctrinal content of positive law so that it accords with those universal principles that can withstand critical examination (PR: 3). For Hegel, the contradictions of abstract right point towards the need for an alternative agenda: one that, acting as a corrective, reconnects strictly legal "rights" with Equity's traditional role of accommodating various universal claims of "justice and good conscience".

In order to meet Hegel's criteria of a legitimate modern state, social policies on property ownership must necessarily build in a moral dimension to legal

---

[18] See Brudner, *The Unity of the Common Law: Studies in Hegelian Jurisprudence* (1995) especially, Chap. 2; Radin, "Property and Personhood" (1982) Vol. 34 *Stanford Law Review* 957.
[19] See Posner, *Economic Analysis of the Law* (1977); Epstein "Why Restrain Alienation" (1985) 85 Colum. L. Rev. 970.
[20] See Epstein, *Takings: Private Property and the Power of the Eminent Domain* (1985) pp.138 et seq.; Posner, *Economic Analysis of Law* (3rd ed., 1986) p. 30.
[21] Cullen, *Hegel's Social and Political Thought* (1979) pp. 16, 43–46.
[22] Hegel, *System of Ethical Life* (trans. Harris, 1979) p. 118.

judgements: one which cannot itself be based solely upon private property or contractual relationships. Despite reversing each assumption of abstract right, *e.g.* by giving priority to substantive over wholly procedural, technical and/or formal considerations, Equity is often able to generate a more adequate view of property law. Often only Equity is able to do justice to the moral dimensions raised by particular property disputes (PR: 223).

Recognising this dimension allows Equity to redefine the character and purpose of property law by limiting the obstinate assertion by property owners of their strict legal rights irrespective of any underlying bad faith.[23] The discretionary operation of equitable remedies is also vital. It allows a more flexible interpretation of law to take place in particular contexts where a rigidly mechanical application of technical rules as part of a "universal legal disposition" would otherwise create gross injustice (PR: 223). Hegel gives the example of someone who is forced by extreme circumstances to appropriate another's property in order to protect life (PR: 127). Without the ethical supplementation provided by Equity, positive law could allow the indiscriminate granting of formal legal remedies to be used cynically by property owners. Such remedies can be abused as a vehicle for fraudulent and unconscionable action (PR: 102, 127). Thus, property law only becomes legitimate *as law* through the contribution of Equity. This is because Equity synthesises the purely technical – and hence amoral – formalism of strict individual rights, with a more ethically-sensitive response to the particular circumstances. In turn, this enables Equity to "reach its decision in the interests of the individual case in its *own* right" (PR: 223).

At this second, moralistic stage, the individualism of property rights is cancelled as a self-sufficient standpoint. Yet, at the same time, it is also preserved as a minimal but necessary component of a more adequate orientation towards property law (PR: 253). Equity's ethical supplementation of positive law plays an important function in rescuing individuals from the contradictions that arise if they orientate themselves towards the ethical obligations of these communal spheres in exclusively rights-based terms. The latter's one-sidedness tends to misrecognise, distort and undermine the underlying rationale of these realms by, for example, undermining the mutual trust and solidarity that is necessary for family life (PR: 158).[24]

Yet Hegel does not *reduce all* property law issues to equitable considerations. This is because both the source and trajectory of property rights transcends the abstract realm of "morality" whose obligations are expressed as wholly formal "ought" statements. These set out universally valid demands that are then supposed to be immediately binding upon the interior realm of an individual's conscience (PR: 33, 34). It is impossible to base specific legal doctrines upon inherently vague, moralistic and subjectively variable notions of con-

---

[23] Hegel, *Philosophy of Mind* (trans. Wallace, 1971) p. 513.
[24] Stillman, *op. cit.* above, n.2, pp. 1058–1061.

scionability and good faith (PR: 15–18, 33, 133–40). In this respect, the moralistic realm of Equity addresses the relation between the distinct internal contents of an individual's subjective will, *i.e.* questions of her good faith and intent, and a wholly formal conception of what is deemed to be morally good "in itself". In this respect, it constitutes a form of natural law. These formal and indeterminate conceptions are then wrongly considered to have a timeless meaning and integrity quite independent of any historical, ideological and social considerations (PR: 3, 141). Equity's moralistic view ignores the objective force of those social, cultural and economic factors that encompass, support and *mediate between* the interior realm of individual conscience at one extreme, and abstract moral imperatives at the other (PR: 33, 34).

3. Contextualising the abstractions of property law

Hegel terms the third and final stage within Hegel's logic of property law "ethical life". This stage aims to remedy the abstract quality of its predecessors. It does so by focusing upon the importance of those historically specific contextual features and relationships which shape both subjective and objective aspects of property relations. This stage unifies the equally one-sided contributions of abstract right and Equity by fulfilling – in the concrete existence of particular social institutions – the potential that was promised, but not delivered, by these earlier phases (PR: 33). Hegel now addresses the impact upon property law of various social, political, institutional and economic circumstances. Together with their associated roles, relations and goals, these circumstances combine to provide both the overall settings in which, and the medium through which, the concrete lives of property relations are actually played out.

This third contextual stage invites us to study the social reality of property *as it is actually lived* under prevailing ideological and economic conditions. This means analysing the specific details of our involvement within a complex network of substantive, yet historically specific, social roles and welfare needs. Such contextual analysis allows the subject of property rights to be identified not as an empty, formal abstraction, but rather as a socially and materially embodied human being. As a result, we must analyse how individuals interact with (and against) various others from within their particular socially defined and structured position, such as landlord, mortgagor or farmer. Only at this law-in-context stage is it finally possible to recognise the sheer embeddedness of the subject. That is, its state of being firmly situated within the historically specific goals and structures of particular social institutions. The latter's operations are themselves largely conditioned by the general ethos and policies of a specific cultural tradition.[25] The result is that contextual analysis needs to totalise these various relations into a comprehensive overall picture.

---

[25] *ibid.* at p. 1035.

Hegel portrays individual owners as real life individuals belonging to different kinds of communities. It is the collective ideals, division of labour and assorted rules for interaction of these various communities that largely shape the habits, self-identity, beliefs and overall life-chances of their members (PR: 257). Hegel analyses the subject of property rights in more concrete, empirical terms in order to give full weight to the impact of the individual's involvement within a complex and differentiated network of relations. These include:

1. Family relations (often involving meeting the various needs of child care);
2. Economic relations within the production of goods and services (as, say, an employee or employer) and
3. Citizenship obligations directed towards, and social-welfare entitlements derived from, the public life of the wider community (including both the local and national state).

When understood within their broader institutional context, we can analyse how property constitutes a form of natural law which plays an important *cultural role* in both the socialisation, and hence integration, of children; and in materially supporting the ethical unity and independence of the family unit across successive generations (PR: 173–174). In terms of their social function, property rights are important in providing citizens with a sense of possessing an immediate personal stake in the public realm, a sense of belonging to a community with whom they identify. This integrative role is particularly important to off-set the threat of alienation from community life that the individualistic orientation of modernity permanently threatens.

The *objects* of property law are also re-defined in contextual terms so as to take into account the force of those social, economic and cultural factors which have already shaped, worked over and mediated their nature. For example, by transforming owned things (such as agricultural land or company shares) into a valuable source of wealth, income and power. Hence, we can now recognise how the relationship between the subject and object of property relations, i.e. between owners and their property, is *mediated on both sides* by the conditioning impact of cultural, economic, social policy and constitutional factors.[26] Taken together, these specific factors determine the overall meaning and purpose of property relations by, for example, imposing various planning restrictions on the use of agricultural land and industrial sites.

This third perspective allows us to redefine what counts as an "issue" within property law to include various historical changes in the socially organised response to some of our most urgent material needs, such as housing, security,

---

[26] Hegel's analysis of constitutional change in Britain culminating in the 1832 Reform Act repeatedly stresses the connection between private property and the domination of vested interests within the political and legal systems; see *Hegel's Political Writings op cit.* above, n.9, at pp. 295–330.

the maintenance of the integrity of homelife. For example, Hegel's early writings at Jena between 1802–1804 give decisively historical orientation and social analysis of the origins of legal concepts of property; whilst in his "*System der Sittlichkeit*" (1802) Hegel links these conceptions to various core historical developments within both the economic life and political economy of society, including the relationship of law to the material "system of needs" of civil society. The latter include the need to both categorise and socially process *the economic value* of the abundance of goods produced through machinery and factories.[27] Here Hegel's analysis raises important questions about the law's own role in determining the rightful ownership of the profits from the expenditure of capital, skill and labour.[28] Hegel also views property rights as historical artefacts that emerge from cultural relations of social identity and status that variously connect the material needs of owners, workers, traders and consumers.[29] Hence, one essential aspect of property is that the ownership interest in, and right to, the quantitative economic value is expressed as market price, as well as the control of its use (PR: 63). Here property becomes understood in terms of rights over definite "assets" with the money functioning as a *symbol for the quantitative extent* of the interest (PR: 204).

Hegel contextualises property law as itself one of many mediating relations at work in the social construction of the significance and (material and cultural) *value* of property. We can now understand property as an on-going historical construct whose significance is both assembled and reiterated through the complex mediation of a series of distinct realm forms of social life. These forms include the family, commerce and the judicial determination of constitutional rights and individual freedom. This process of mediation by contextual factors (including legal regulation) is so pervasive that what, in Hegel's view, is truly owned is a form of legal interest in something. As a social construct, the object of ownership need not itself be tangible.

According to Hegel, a rational modern state should play an active role in maintaining the overall institutional, legal and economic framework of social policy. It is only a framework of this kind which allows individuals, families and groups to flourish and develop a purposeful life which is fulfilling for themselves (PR: 260). However, the State's own authority cannot be based upon property or contractual relationships. Under emergency conditions, the state is positively obliged to appropriate private property in order to protect the territorial integrity and well-being of society as a whole. Hegel also recognises that the particularistic orientation of property rights should not play a central role in the public sector. In this sector, an orientation towards the universal communal good – independent of private vested interests – is absolutely vital (PR: 75). Since the modern state is not itself a single divisible object, we cannot

---

[27] *System of Ethical Life*, at pp. 37–38.
[28] ibid.
[29] *System of Ethical Life*, at p. 121.

understand either its offices or interaction between public officials wholly in terms of private ownership or contractual agreements. Hence, official posts, including judicial appointments, should not be privately owned, bought, inherited and sold as family or commercial assets – as was once the case with army commissions and parliamentary seats in England during the 19th century (PR: 75, 277).

Thus, during this final stage, Hegel analyses property rights as a totality as collective expressions of the political will of an entire community (PR: 3–4). We should, therefore, analyse each dimension of property rights (including notions of property claims in and over human bodies) as a further development of the trajectory and embodiment of political will expressed concretely within social policy (including the latter's articulation within legislation). As a result, we need to understand that the *source* of property rights lies firmly within the sociological realm. That is, within the historically concrete norms of a specific cultural tradition and intersubjectivity at a particular moment of its evolutionary development.

In this way, the contextual account that arises only during the final phase of Hegel's evolution sequence comes to recognise the central importance of those political dimensions of ownership that form the preconditions for the rational ordering of social life more generally. The legal recognition of private property rights is now seen as valid only insofar as it makes a positive contribution to the wider project of cultural self-determination. This is a project that itself requires the overcoming of those unjust features of social life that cannot withstand critical scrutiny, such as homelessness, systematic poverty and pervasive social alienation.

20

Hegel on Private Property and Public Access

WILLIAM N. R. LUCY*

Starting points

It is often assumed that there is an important conflict, perhaps even a contradiction, between claims to private property in land, on one hand, and claims of public access to it, on the other. The conflict is manifest in the dispute, common to many industrialised countries, between those who have private property in land and those who claim access rights to that land for recreational purposes.[1] This essay assumes that this conflict operates at least at the level of normative justification. By "normative justification" I mean to refer to arguments that provide reasons why either private property or public access should be taken seriously or regarded as compelling considerations in practical deliberation. One such argument in favour of private property is considered here – the argument offered by G. W. F. Hegel. I seek to show that this apparently successful justification can also be used to justify public access claims, the putative opposite of private property. Hegel's normative argument is therefore indeterminate in the sense that a justification for access can be generated within the interstices of its justification for private property. Before examining that argument, a brief analysis of the notions of private property and public access is offered.

Private property and public access

A complex view of property shows it to be not a thing but a set of relationships between persons and things.[2] Superficially, any relationship appears to be

---

* Law School, University of Hull. Thanks to Francois Barker, Alan Brudner and the participants at the 1993 W. G. Hart Workshop for helpful comments. This paper was originally published as a section of a much longer essay co-written with Francois Barker which appeared in (1993) VII *Canadian Journal of Law and Jurisprudence* 287. The arguments of that essay provide support for those stated somewhat briefly here. Many thanks to Francois Barker, the Journal and its editors for permission to reprint.

[1] I am concerned only with justifications for and access rights to land. For evidence of the dispute between landowners and access-seekers in England, see the publications by, *inter alia*, the Countryside Commission, Country Landowners' Association and Ramblers' Association. The latter organises an annual day of civil disobedience and mass trespass under the title of "Forbidden Britain".

[2] Honoré, "Ownership" in *Making Law Bind* (1987) pp. 181–184. Ultimately all property (even

between the "owner" and the "thing" in question but, since the "thing" is obviously not in a position to exercise rights or be bound by duties, the relationship must be seen as one between persons in relation to things. Notions of property and ownership are far from being absolute and simplistic in nature. Rather, they are *relative* ideas based upon a complex web of legal relationships between persons that can include a wide range of combinations of Hohfeldian claim-rights, liberties, powers and immunities.[3] The web of relationships that envelops land can be extremely complex since, as a perpetual commodity, land is prone to a historical accretion of a variety of rights and duties – mortgages, leases, easements, restrictive covenants, rights of entry and access, planning or zoning restrictions and so on, many of which can be "owned" and enforced by different people. These relationships between "owners" and others must be governed by rules which dictate who, in what circumstances, has rights to control, use and access those objects and who, in what circumstances, is under correlative duties to respect those rights. The concept of property can thus be defined as a set of rules governing the allocation and control of, as well as access to, resources (Waldron, pp. 31, 32, 35).

What, then, is distinctive about a *private* property system? For Waldron, the organising idea behind private property is that "in principle, each resource belongs to some individual" (Waldron, p. 38). Metaphorically speaking, each object or resource in a society has a label attached to it sporting the name of a member of the society who is regarded as the owner of the resource. This is the person whom society and the legal framework regard as the final arbiter of the way in which the resource in question is used (Waldron, pp. 38–39). Given that property is a system of rules governing relations with regard to the control of, and access to, resources, private property occurs where these rules "are organised around the idea that resources are on the whole separate objects each assigned and therefore belonging to some particular individual" (Waldron, p. 38). Since that individual is the final arbiter of the way in which the resource is used, she must have fairly extensive rights of control (including the ability to exclude others from the resource), use and alienation.[4]

What, then, of the idea of access? According to our analysis of private property that concept entails, at the abstract level, something like a name-object rela-

---

intangible) may involve material objects, *e.g.* models or drawings for patents and copyrights: see Munzer, *A Theory of Property* (1990) p. 73.

[3] See generally Honoré *op. cit.* n.2; Hohfeld, *Fundamental Legal Concepts* (New Haven, 1919) pp. 35–64; Becker, *Property Rights* (Boston, 1977) pp. 11–15; Simmonds, *Central Issues in Jurisprudence* (1986) pp. 129–132; and Waldron, *The Right to Private Property* (1988) pp. 27–28. For an argument that complexity imperils the concept of private property see Grey, "The Disintegration of Property" in Pennock and Chapman (eds.) *NOMOS XXII Property* (New York, 1980) pp. 69–85.

[4] On the importance of the relationship between private property (or ownership) and excludability see: Honoré, *op. cit.* above, n.2, at pp. 166–168, 181 and 184; see also Munzer, *op. cit.* above n.2 at pp. 89–90.

tion. Clearly when some thing is held in this way by someone an access problem is possible: the access claim can be directed at that particular thing held by that particular person. The essence of this situation is that T has something S needs to use, but not necessarily consume, for one or more of her important purposes. Any old purpose of S's will not be sufficient to raise an interesting access problem – her trivial interest in determining how quickly T's car accelerates could not come close to conflicting legitimately with T's private property claim over it. The conceptually interesting questions that arise in relation to the notion of access cannot be tackled here. One question that flows immediately from the previous example raises the issue of which purposes can generate an access claim. Another question that the notion of access raises within the confines of a private property system is the significance of the apparent incompatibility between private property and a regime of public access, on the one hand, and the seemingly compatible relationship between private property and private (contractual) regimes of access, on the other. In what follows, I concentrate upon the conflict between regimes of private property and public access.

Hegel on private property

The argument of this section is that the justification for private property offered in Hegel's *Philosophy of Right*[5]: (i) at least establishes a prima facie case for private property; but (ii) that the steps in the argument, and the values it tracks, might be successfully used by a proponent of public access.

For Hegel private "property is something everyone needs in order to develop his freedom and individuality" (Waldron, p. 351) or, alternatively, to become a person. It would be a mistake to think that personhood begins and ends with property since, like everything else in Hegel's philosophy, achieving personhood is a developmental process. Initial steps toward this goal occur when the will takes control of its wants and desires, on the one hand, and its body, on the other. This, however, does not take the will beyond its own subjectivity, the transcendence of which is another requirement of personhood. That step can be taken in a number of ways, the most important of which for our purposes is through the embodiment or externalisation of the will in property. This takes the will beyond the realm of pure subjectivity and into contact with, and control over, elements of the world beyond itself. The process of ethical development into personhood involves a move from subjectivity to universality and is both temporal, because it takes time, and spatial, in the thin sense that it involves the will taking control over things in the world. It seems clear that the key ideas in the Hegelian justification of private property are: (i) control by the will of its body, wants, desires and some things in the world; (ii) the disciplining of the will, found in its being stabilised and constrained by its prior willing

---

[5] (1952) translated and with notes by Knox. In notes and text I refer to, as is customary, section numbers rather than page numbers.

1. Between wantonness and personhood[7]

The first steps towards achieving personhood for Hegel involve obtaining some degree of control over one's desires and wants. This could be initially expressed as the realisation that one is something different from one's wants and desires. Rather than being solely the locus of these things one must, to be a person, be something more than the ebb and flow of a stream of different wants and desires which can flash into and out of existence like a strobe-light, and that "more" must be something other than the physical parameters – one's body – within which those wants and desires occur.[8] In what does personhood consist, then, if it is something other than either one's wants and desires, or one's body? The Hegelian answer is: one's will, if it is free. The free will, which is not free in the sense of being arbitrary, enables a selection of wants and desires and thereby entails some degree of control over those wants and desires. As Waldron puts it, persons "take themselves to be capable of abstracting their will from given impulses and inclinations, and so the needs and wants on which their will settles take on the character of resolutions or chosen ends rather than mere natural afflictions" (Waldron, p. 353). Moreover, resolving upon ends is eventually more than merely randomly hitting upon some such ends rather than others: those ends "become the rational system of the will's volitions"(H:PR, S19). Reflection about the ends one resolves upon and the best way to pursue them leads the will beyond its own subjectivity: "when reflection is brought to bear on impulses, they are imaged, estimated, compared with one another, with their means of satisfaction and their consequences . . . In this way reflection invests this material with abstract universality and in this external manner purifies it from its crudity and barbarity"(Hegel, section 20).

One's will must also take control of one's body in order for personhood to be possible:

> "I am alive in this bodily organism which is my external existence, universal in content and undivided, the real precondition of every further determined mode of existence. But, all the same, as person, I possess my life and my body, like other things, only in so far as my will is in them".

---

[6] Anyone familiar with Waldron (Chap. 10) will recognise our indebtedness to his treatment of Hegel. About control, Ryan, *Property and Political Theory* (1984) p. 122, says that "Hegel identified *taking in order to control* as staking the initial claim to ownership" (emphasis in original).

[7] On being a wanton see Frankfurt, *The Importance of What We Care About* (1988) pp. 16–22. As Waldron rightly notes (p. 352) there are echoes of Hegel here.

[8] Of course, this claim need not be read as a denial of anything Hegel says about the importance of embodiment: see Hegel, section 47 and section 48.

(Hegel, section 47, footnote omitted). Yet bare, passive possession by the will of one's body or, for that matter, of any kind of "external" property, is not enough for Hegel. In relation to the body the will controls it through processes of "development" and of "training" which increase its "dexterity" (Hegel, section 52 and section 57 (Hegel's additional notes to his original lectures) and Waldron, p. 362). This way of possessing or controlling the body is different from the way in which animals can be said to possess their bodies and serves as one distinction between them and persons.

2. The will and embodiment

Control over one's wants and desires, on the one hand, and over one's body, on the other, is not the only kind of control necessary for personhood: it also requires that the will be externalised or embodied in nature. This is a matter of extending the will's control into aspects of the external world. Achieving this kind of control serves further to break down the limits of the will's subjectivity and is a step towards an appreciation of what Hegel calls the "universal". Waldron is thus quite correct when he says that for Hegel "ethical development in general involves some sort of "transition" from the inner subjective world to the external objective world"(Waldron, p. 355). Property is a crucial way of facilitating this transition. Hence: "by appropriating, owning, and controlling objects, a person can establish his will as an objective feature of the world and transcend the stage in which it is simply an aspect of his inner and subjective life" (Waldron, p. 356); " . . . my will, as the will of a person, and so as a single will, becomes objective to me in property" (Hegel, section 46).

In what, exactly, does embodiment or externalisation consist? Put brutally, would we know an instance of the will being externalised or embodied were we to see it? Waldron's answer very usefully draws together a number of strands in Hegel, particularly his discussion of the way in which the will comes to possess and control its wants, desires and body, which we have already outlined, and his account of the way in which the will possesses, controls and alienates external things in the world beyond its wants, desires and body. On that basis he concludes that "[a] person's will is embodied in an object to the extent that (1) his will has made a difference to the object and (2) the object, affected in this way by his will, itself makes a difference in turn to his willing" (Waldron, p. 370). The way in which the will makes a difference to an object is by taking it into its possession and changing or marking it: the will is embodied in the object in so far as some feature or property of the object can only be understood by reference to some human purpose.[9] So, for example, the sawing down and dismantling of a tree and the reassembly of some of its constituents as a desk

---

[9] Ryan puts it concisely when he says that "[t]he world literally takes on human purposes": "Hegel on work, ownership and citizenship", Pelczynski (ed.), *The State and Civil Society* (1984) p. 185. See also Ryan, above, n.6, at pp. 122–157.

is a purposive process – the language of the description makes any other conclusion impossible. The change in the tree is only explicable to us as a conversion to human purposes, an instance, for Hegel, of objectifying, externalising or embodying the will in nature. Note also that on Waldron's account embodiment is a two-way process, the will controlling aspects of the external world and the changes it has effected therein alter, limit or constrain one's future willing. So, for example, one can no longer resolve that the tree-desk bear fruit.[10] This view could also be applied to the will's control, development and changing of its body and its wants and desires: present changes therein, brought about by the will, can constrain future willing in exactly the same way.

Setting aside the usual difficulties of expression in Hegel, we can say relatively clearly that the will needs property to overcome its subjectivity and that that "overcoming" is a crucial step in the process of development into personhood and full freedom: "[a] person must translate his freedom into an external sphere in order to exist as Idea" (Hegel, section 41). However, exactly why this requires a regime of private property, as opposed to a regime of common property in which some possessory and use rights are recognised, is more than a little opaque.

3. The normative basis of private property

Hegel never seriously addresses this issue. The only argument he explicitly offers in *Philosophy of Right* to establish the connection between the will's need to transcend its subjectivity and private property clearly fails. The argument is that since one's will becomes objective to one in property, "property acquires the character of private property" (Hegel, section 46). This falls far short of being a compelling argument specifically for private property. At most it shows that persons must possess some property and that requirement could conceivably be satisfied by a regime of common property. Waldron fills this argumentative gap in the following Hegelian way: private property is required for the will's transcendence of its subjectivity, through externalisation or embodiment, because transcendence and embodiment must be relatively long-term processes (see Waldron, pp. 373–374). Remember, the journey to personhood is both temporal and spatial, the underlying themes of this journey being those of achieving control and self-discipline (over one's wants and desires, one's body and one's external world) as well as the transcendence of subjectivity. Now, if embodiment in the external world is to serve a role in this long-term process, then the things that one's will becomes embodied in must be controlled by one and exercise their limiting, controlling or disciplining effect upon one's will, for a substantial amount of time. Hence if "an object can embody a will – by registering the effects of willing at one point of time and forcing an individual's will-

---

[10] Unless, that is, the Emperor Caligula is one's role model. He, remember, asked for the moon: see the eponymous play by Camus.

ing to become consistent and stable over a period" then that "effect can be lost if others are also working on the object for purposes of their own in the meantime" (Waldron, pp. 373–374).[11] This is why a property regime which incorporates the idea of a name-object relation is normatively necessary.

What are we to make of the three steps of the Hegelian justification? Do they add up to a compelling, or just a prima facie plausible, argument? One objection needs to be dismissed immediately. In relation to Hegel it is often said, echoing his own words, that his particular arguments cannot be accepted without also accepting the whole philosophical panoply. Yet why ought we to accept such an intellectually disempowering claim? While it is undoubtedly true that all the particular arguments are formulated on the basis of certain framework assumptions, there is no *a priori* logical block to testing the steps in such arguments for consistency, coherence and plausibility regardless of their framework assumptions. Again, there seems no logical block to supporting particular arguments with different framework assumptions. If the contrary is maintained then specific arguments and examples need be provided. Only that will do, not a general invocation of this claim.

A second objection appears more problematic. It holds, *inter alia*, that the argument for private property as we have sketched it invokes substantive ethical considerations. That is a mistake because the arguments of abstract right lack any ethical substance.[12] Hence the justification for private property we have, however plausible, is not truly Hegelian. This objection reduces to two issues: (i) do the arguments of the abstract right have any prescriptive power?; and if so, (ii) what is the source of that power? Few would disagree that the answer to the first question must be yes. The key issue is whether or not at least

---

[11] This view is also held by Knowles, "Hegel on Property and Personality" (1983) 33 *Philosophical Quarterly* 45 at p. 57 and expressed by Munzer thus: "stable possession and use are necessary to achieve some abiding ends": Munzer, *op. cit.* above, n.2, at p. 79.

[12] This is the view of Benson, "The Priority of Abstract Right and Collectivism in Hegel's Legal Philosophy" in Cornell, Rosenfeld and Carlson (eds.) *Hegel and Legal Theory* (1991) p. 201, n.24. He also suggests that Hegel's argument for private property does not justify some private property for all but just the capacity or freedom to appropriate property. The power of this argument turns, initially, upon the interpretation of (Hegel, section 49 (additional note to Hegel's original lectures)). Benson's interpretation is, however, informed by the claim that the abstract right lacks ethical substance: it therefore stands or fails with that claim. Some (perhaps too tenuous) support for the latter claim may be found in Ryan's view that Hegel's argument "is not exactly a moral defence of property": above, n.6, at p. 139. Alan Brudner has put to us a slightly different version of this objection. An Hegelian defence of private property which holds that property is something everyone needs in order to develop their freedom and individuality, and which purports to be rooted in the abstract right, is mistaken because it incorporates something into abstract right that should not be there, namely, considerations of the good: see Hegel, sections 37 and 129. This assumes that freedom and individuality qualify as the good in the relevant sense, that is, in the sense which should be excluded from abstract right. But this is by no means clear in light of Hegel, section 37 (additional notes) and section 129 (additional notes)) and translator's note 4 at p. 320. Moreover, we are not uncomfortable with the claim that abstract right tracks some abstract conception of the good where that means "good for all persons qua persons" (translator's note, *ibid*) rather than "good for specific individuals". We think it is the latter sense that is excluded from abstract right, not the former.

some of the prescriptive power of those arguments derives from substantive ethical concerns. If particular arguments in the abstract right are considered then it is undeniable that some of them appear to invoke substantive ethical judgments – most obvious is Hegel's claim that the Roman law provision making children the property of their parents was "unjustifiable and unethical": Hegel, section 43. This example, and there are others (see (Hegel's original remarks on the text) Waldron, pp. 345–347), presents a large difficulty for proponents of this objection. For they need an argument which, contrary to appearances, can show that statements such as these either have no ethical prescriptive power or are unrelated to the main body of the argument in the abstract right. Until that task is discharged this objection cannot be taken seriously.

The argument so far shows, I hope, that the Hegelian justification passes a threshold requirement of prima facie plausibility. Therefore the way is open to consider whether or not that justification for private property can also support an argument for access.

4. The access argument

Control, self-discipline and the transcendence of subjectivity are the values tracked by private property. Is there a plausible way to show that these values are also tracked by access? Can the justification for access have exactly the same substance and structure as the justification for property? Despite unpromising appearances I think it can. What follows is an argument to show that to a large degree the proponent of access can use the Hegelian argument for private property to justify access. After sketching the argument I outline some snags that its proponents must address.

The argument has three steps, all of which echo aspects of the justification for private property. First, I outline the way in which access rights facilitate the will's control of some, albeit very special, things just as property rights facilitate the will's control of some things in the world. There is, however, an important qualitative difference between the things the will controls through property rights and access rights. Far from weakening the argument for access, that qualitative difference strengthens it. There is also a quantitative difference between the control property rights and access rights yield, though I do not think this seriously impairs the argument for access. The second step consists of a demonstration of the way in which access rights, like property rights, involve the transcendence of subjectivity. The third step shows how the will develops in being constrained and limited by access rights in the same way as it is developed through the limits and constraints encountered in its externalisation or embodiment in property.

The kind of control had by one who has access rights to the private property of another is not control over a thing in the way in which Hegel usually envisages the subject of property rights (see, *inter alia*, Hegel, sections 44, 45, 47, 52 and 56–63). Hegel's account of contract also concentrates, almost to the point of being misleading, upon control over and exchange of things (see, *inter alia*, Hegel, sections 68, 71 and 80). Yet when one has a right of access the most one can do is control the actions of others, most significantly, the actions of owners of private property. For example, one could compel them to facilitate access to their property, to refrain from obstructing those who have access. This might involve prohibitions upon the activities in which owners of private property in land can engage: for example, a regime of public access rights would surely prohibit land owners making their land either impossible or highly risky to traverse. But the object controlled is disanalogous to the thing controlled by the bearer of a property right since that which is controlled is itself a bearer of rights, developing towards full personhood and freedom. If one has access rights to the property of another, then one has some degree of control over another will. Are there any Hegelian objections to this?

It would be a mistake to make too much of Hegel's arguments against slavery here. He reconciles himself to slavery as a historical contingency but rejects it as inappropriate to epochs in which the will is further advanced toward freedom (Hegel, section 57 (Hegel's remarks on the text and additional note to Hegel's original lectures).[13] In such epochs slavery is undoubtedly illegitimate. It is also a matter of controlling, albeit almost completely, another will. Yet it surely cannot be argued that access rights are even remotely analogous to slavery. For one thing, the degree of control is much lower here; for another, the degree of control access rights give one will over another is more like the control the institution of contract allows, and that institution is one which Hegel embraces with the same enthusiasm he has for private property. Nor can it be assumed that Hegel's objections to slavery, which also function as both his objections to treating another will as a thing, and as an argument showing the legitimacy of the will controlling external, will-less bits of the world (Hegel, sections 44 and 52), rule out all and any control of one will over another. This cannot be so if contract is ethically required. For in an important sense contract is just a matter of two or more wills controlling one another. What else can be involved in a contract for wages, the legitimacy of which is not questioned by Hegel (Hegel, section 80)? It might be objected that this point equivocates on the exact contours of the will. And so it does. Yet the equivocation cannot be resolved in a way that squares Hegel's treatment of contract and the denial mistakenly attributed to him – of the legitimacy of one will exercising limited control over another. It can plausibly be said that the invocation of the labour contract to illustrate the fact that Hegel allows wills to control one another mistakenly assumes that a constituent element of the will is the capacity to labour. But it is not. Neither labour nor the capacity to labour are among those things which Hegel regards as inalienable because constitutive of the will. Inalienable constituents of the will or the person are for Hegel "substantive characteristics, which constitute my own private personality and the universal essence of my self-consciousness . . . my personality as such, my universal freedom of the

---

[13] For useful discussion see Ryan, above, n.9, at pp. 186–187 and above, n.6, at pp. 122–123.

will, my ethical life, my religion" (Hegel, section 66). Only if we regard capacities such as the ability to labour as not constitutive of the will or the person can we make sense of Hegel's point that "[o]bjectively considered, a right arising from a contract is never a right over a person, but only a right over something external to a person or something which he can alienate" (Hegel, section 40 (his remarks on the text)). This reformulation of the contours of the will cannot support the claim that for Hegel any control by one will over another is illegitimate because some external, alienable "things" are inextricably linked to the will. Because the will is embodied, having contractual control over another's labour power must of necessity entail some control over that other's will. Obviously this control does not, and for Hegel cannot, extend to the constituents of the person or the will. But it is nevertheless control. Henceforth, when we speak of one will controlling another will we mean "controlling the nonconstitutive elements of another person, which, because of embodiment, must entail some very limited, indirect control of the will". That is necessary for contract to be ethically permissible. It is that kind of control over another that access rights also entail.[14]

The tenor of Hegel's treatment of contract is such as to suggest that contract is not only ethically permissible but ethically necessary. One reason for this is found in the apparent importance of the right to alienate property – contract is surely an indispensable means to that end. There are, however, the seeds of another argument to show the ethical necessity of contract in Hegel and these seeds also serve to show the ethical significance of access rights. The argument begins by noting that the object controlled by a regime of access rights, while exactly the same as the object controlled by labour contracts, is qualitatively different from the object controlled by property rights. Different because ethically more significant. Ethically more significant because that which is controlled, albeit in a very limited way, is another will, another person capable of freedom and a bearer of rights. Since the object of control is a bearer of rights, the controlling will cannot do just anything to it: the range and exercise of control must be severely curtailed. In fact, the reason Hegel offers to show the permissibility of the will controlling things in the world – thereby embodying itself in property – shows the ethically greater significance of what is controlled by the holder of access rights or of rights under a contract for wages. The thing controlled by the will when it is embodied in property "has no end in itself . . . is not a thing in itself" (Hegel, section 44 (and additional notes to the original lectures)) This is proven when the will takes control of the thing, "endowing . . . [it] with a purpose which is not its own" (Waldron, p. 356). However, what the will as a bearer of access rights or rights under a labour contract controls is something

---

[14] Rosenfeld divides the Hegelian person into an alienating ego contractans and an inalienable will: "Hegel and the Dialectics of Contract", in *Hegel and Legal Theory* above, n.12, at p. 245. See also, in the same volume, Stillman, "Property, Contract and Ethical Life in Hegel's *Philosophy of Right*" at pp. 210–212 and Benhabib, "Obligation, Contract and Exchange: On the Significance of Hegel's Abstract Right" in Pelczynski (ed.), above, n.9, at p. 163.

which is an end in itself, something capable of formulating its own purposes, something which has ethical significance in itself – another will. Thus there is indeed a qualitative difference between those things controlled under a regime of property rights as compared with those "things" controlled under contractual or access rights. Yet the difference is not such as to weaken the argument for access; if anything, it is strengthened since the constraint and discipline required of a will which controls, in even a limited way, another will is greater than the constraint required of a will controlling some external bit of the world. (While there are some ways in which the will just cannot treat another will, it seems that a will can treat property in a far greater variety of ways.) This issue arises again in the third step of the access argument which concerns the benefits for the will of embodiment.

In what way do access rights lead to the transcendence of the will's subjectivity? Remember that property rights take the will beyond itself since they entail the will endowing things in the world with purposes. The will thereby appreciates that there is some general thing beyond itself, one of the constituents of which are those particular things the will takes under its control. The will transcends its subjectivity in exactly the same way in exercising the control contractual and access rights give: the will thereby appreciates that there are also other purpose-bearing and rights-bearing "things" in the world.

Moreover, for Hegel the recognition of other wills is as ethically important as, if not more ethically important than, the recognition of a world beyond the particular will. This is so because such recognition is a prerequisite for property and contract. The *Philosophy of Right* "begins from the standpoint of a social totality in which the right of individuals to be recognised as persons has become established as an intersubjective practice".[15] The importance of this starting point is evident from Hegel's treatment of the struggle for recognition between lord and bondsman in *Phenomenology of Mind*.[16] In essence, that struggle consists of the working out of the process by which wills come to concede one another's independence and inalienability, despite their initial tendency to domination (for the best way to ensure that one's will is recognised is to force others, as the lord forces the bondsman, to recognise it without reciprocal recognition). This process of mutual recognition presupposes some framework of constraints upon the way in which one will can relate to another, constraints which in *Philosophy of Right* are manifest in, *inter alia*, the argument against slavery. These constraints also serve to map out the terrain of property and contract, telling us what can be the subject matter of contract (not the inalienable constituents of the will) and why private property is important (a free will must express its purposivity in the world in a relatively long-term way). Hence it is

---

[15] Benhabib, *ibid.* at p. 168.
[16] Translated with an introduction and notes by J.B. Baillie (revised second edition, 1949) pp. 228–240. For a helpful treatment of this issue see Bernstein, "From self-consciousness to community act and recognition in the master-slave relationship", in Pelczynski, above, n.9.

not an exaggeration to say that the control contract and property give one will over another and some things in the world is a "culmination"[17] of the struggle for recognition. Certainly, contract and property presuppose that the struggle has been resolved and they therefore serve to reinforce the recognition of one will by another as a will, a locus of ethical significance.[18] So too with the control that access rights give one will over another: they presuppose and restate, or are a "culmination" of, the process of recognition, since they are very limited controls over another will already recognised as a (property) right-bearer.

The third step concerns embodiment. We noted above that the best understanding of the will's embodiment in property holds that it is a two-way process: the will must have made a difference to an object by imposing purpose upon it and the imposition of purpose constrains the will's future willing. (Our example was the tree-desk: having been made into a desk it can no longer be willed that it bear fruit.) Is there anything similar to embodiment when the will has access rights? Bearing in mind that no "thing" is controlled when a will has such rights, it seems unlikely. However, there is some limited control over another will and that control, despite the emphasis of our discussion so far, is a two-way process. The control over another will cannot be and clearly is not absolute: the most that can be done by the bearer of access rights is that some aspects of the land owner's behaviour will be constrained – she cannot plant a minefield on property to which others have a right of access. Further, there are also likely to be a range of constraints upon the access bearer's exercise of her rights. The bearer of access rights cannot do just anything to the property of another, nor impact in any old way upon the property owner's behaviour: the access bearer will be constrained in relation to the degree of access she has to the property and in the way in which she exercises her right. She may, for example, be duty-bound to do no unnecessary damage to the landowner's property. Surely we have here a situation in which the will is disciplined, and constrained by, its willing, although the constraint comes not from the effects of irredeemably endowing some thing with purpose but from the fact that the object controlled – from the perspective of the access right-bearer, the property owner, from the perspective of the property owner, the access bearer – is another will, a rights bearing "thing" capable of freedom.

This situation of mutual recognition and constraint is analogous to the contractual relationship. Contracts are essentially lists of rights and duties which the parties have agreed to. The control each has over the other is limited by the express terms of the agreement and the background assumptions of the practice. Those assumptions include principles about, *inter alia*, capacity to con-

---

[17] The phrase is Rosenfeld's: above, n.14, at p. 239. He says of contract that its "primary purpose ... in Hegel's system is to give determinate content to the [sic] reciprocal recognition rather than merely to facilitate the acquisition of coveted goods", *ibid*.

[18] For what looks like a Hegelian statement to this effect see Hegel, section 40: "it is only as owners that two persons really exist for each other".

tract, responsibility and fairness. It is not implausible to regard some of these as doctrinal manifestations of the recognition of another as a right-bearer and person. Hence, the rationale for doctrines such as duress and fraud is found in the injunction to respect another will or person (see Hegel, sections 88 and 90–93). The will is constrained and disciplined by the terms of the contract itself since, once the will has entered into a contract, the scope of its future willing is restricted – in Elster's useful phrase, contract is a strategy of pre-commitment.[19] If the constraint upon the will caused by its embodiment in property serves to stabilise and discipline the will, then so too does the constraint upon the will found in contractual rights. Access rights also serve to constrain the will. In the exercise of those rights the will must move carefully, structuring its action in the world around the premise that it has very limited control over something of crucial ethical significance which must be respected. If that is not a constraining, disciplining and educative influence upon the will, then it is difficult to imagine anything which would qualify as such.

In so far as my characterisation of Hegel's justification for property was an accurate one – I claimed that the values it tracked were the will's control, self-discipline and transcendence of subjectivity – it seems that those values can also be tracked by an argument for access rights. At least, I hope to have established a prima facie case to show the indeterminacy of this particular justification – its structure and values do seem also to justify what is often assumed to conflict with private property. However, setting aside the exegetical problems which are bound to arise, the proponent of access faces two initial snags with this argument which may serve to deny it even prima facie plausibility. The first holds that the argument makes much of the analogy with contract. Too much, in fact, since there is a strong disanalogy between it and a regime of access rights. The second snag is that the argument relies upon too close an analogy between access rights and rights to private property.

While it is true that both contract and a regime of access rights or, for that matter, any regime of rights whatever its content, presupposes that the struggle for recognition has been overcome and amounts to the culmination of that struggle, the two are significantly dissimilar. The disanalogy lies in the fact that the disciplinary and constraining effects of contractual obligations are consensually created by the parties to the contract: "[t]heir implicit identity is realised through the transference of property from one to the other in conformity with *a common will* and without detriment to the rights of either. This is contract" (Hegel, section 40, emphasis added). Clearly, some public access rights in some societies lack this consensual element since they are statutory impositions upon land-owners.[20] In itself this is not yet a devastating criticism of the argument

---

[19] Elster, *Ulysees and the Sirens* (1979).
[20] Some examples from English law are: Highways Act 1980, ss.26 and 31; The National Parks and Access to the Countryside Act 1949, s.65. However, the majority of access rights in England and Wales are the product of custom and common law.

for access because a structurally similar argument can be made against the Hegelian defender of property and contract. For, although in the abstract right sections of *Philosophy of Right* Hegel insists upon the crucial significance of contract and property for ethical development, by the time we reach his discussion of ethical life, civil society and the State, we find that the sphere of free contract, for example, is severely curtailed. Hegel has no objections to large scale interventions into what libertarians would regard as the purely private realm of contract, for example, to fix prices (Hegel, section 236). This surely is a denial of one aspect of the common will expressed by the parties to a contract since the common will would not extend to matters such as price. Hence if the absence of consent is embarrassing to the proponent of access rights, then it is equally embarrassing to the Hegelian defender of contract.

This point illustrates the difficulty of using the arguments in the abstract right as standards against which to judge existing social practices and institutions. For, as the remainder of *Philosophy of Right* shows, this is not at all a Hegelian strategy. While property and contract are instantiated in civil society they are also mitigated and constrained by it, perhaps, more accurately, made possible by it.[21] Moreover, this process of mitigation is so marked that it has been said that "[a]lmost nowhere in the [Hegelian] state exist the principles of private property and free contract".[22] The reason behind this process of derogation from the principles of property and contract could well be Hegel's alleged belief that property and contract, though "primary in logical order, [are] therefore primitive and less developed than later attitudes and institutions in contributing to mature human freedom".[23] This debate cannot be entered here. Suffice it to say that the difficulty raised serves to suspend judgment on the power of this first snag. Moreover, it is plainly not impossible for some public rights of access to have their basis in consent.[24]

The second snag has two parts. First, it might be urged that there is no real analogy between access rights and property rights because, although both allow a will some degree of control, the latter allow far more control. Further, it could be maintained that this quantitative difference is so great as to amount to a qualitative distinction between the two, showing the illegitimacy of access rights and the legitimacy of property rights. It is hard to deny that, in most circumstances, there is indeed a quantitative difference in the degree of control both sets of rights confer. Yet the most obvious rejoinder is a point we have often made thus far: the "thing" which is controlled under access rights, another will, is something of greater ethical significance than the "thing" controlled by the

---

[21] As Rosenfeld, above, n.14 at p. 247, observes: "[b]ecause the same process that sustains contract eventually leads to its dissolution, contractual relations must be bounded by noncontractual ones".

[22] Stillman, above, n.14, at p. 219.

[23] Stillman, *ibid.* at p. 221.

[24] See, for English law examples, Highways Act 1980, s.25; National Parks and Access to the Countryside Act 1949, Part V.

holder of property rights (some will-less bit of the world). Moreover, even if we concede as valid, though it looks fishy, the move from quantitative to qualitative difference, the argument to the illegitimacy of access rights brings with it unwelcome consequences. The most obvious is that if access rights must go, then so too must rights under a labour contract. The control arising from labour contract rights is circumscribed by the terms of the agreement and, more importantly, by the fact that the control is over some thing with ethical significance; thus there are some ways in which it just cannot be treated. But this is exactly the basis of the constraints upon the control that a regime of access rights can confer. In this respect access rights and contract rights appear to stand or fall together.

The second part of the snag consists of the claim that property rights are different from access rights because one can alienate one's control over property but not, in regimes familiar in many societies, one's public access rights. Therefore the argument to justify property cannot rightly be used to justify access. Two points need clarification. First, although Hegel undoubtedly thinks it important that one be able to alienate many of the things one owns, it does not seem possible, at least at the stage of ethical development of abstract right, for a will to do without any property. It does not have to follow from this that the will cannot alienate all its property. However, it *might* follow if we note that property is required in order to discipline and develop the will and, until such time as that is achieved, all wills must have property and cannot therefore alienate all of it. Until this stage of ethical development is completed there are some very limited constraints upon alienation. Moreover, it could be suggested that the constraints upon alienation might be even more severe because Hegel "does not show that *alienable* property is needed in order for humans to be free persons" (Waldron, p. 369; emphasis in original). Hence Hegel is mistaken in thinking that alienability is important for the same reasons that having some property is important. If this is true the argument about alienability becomes even more problematic.

The second point requiring clarification is this: there are some things the will takes control of and holds as property which, as we have often noted, cannot be alienated. These are the things constitutive of the will. The fact that Hegel speaks of the will having property in these things suggests that alienability is not as crucial as we may first think. The question is simple: must the idea of alienability always be a criterion of the concept "private property"? Alan Ryan thinks so. He doubts that the word property is rightly applied to those inalienable aspects of the will.[25] Yet the difficulty here lies in establishing that alienability is always and ever a criterion of property. This difficulty is especially acute if it is accepted that conceptual definition and elucidation is not a matter

---

[25] He says that, on reading the conjunction of property and inalienability in Hegel, one might well "conclude that lives and liberties simply are not property in any useful sense of the term": above, n.9, at p. 187.

of giving the necessary and sufficient conditions for a concept's instantiation. Rather, if this task is a matter of tracing family resemblances between what appear to be similar but different instantiations or conceptions of a concept, any such claim as Ryan's is difficult indeed to defend (see Waldron, pp. 30–31).

These points considerably weaken the argument from alienability. If the access proponent's reply to the first snag is also compelling, then the access argument at least achieves the threshold requirement of prima facie plausibility. That, of course, is a confession and avoidance: confession that the argument cannot be taken further here and a temporary avoidance of the problems involved in making it stronger.

Important published works of contributors

J.W. Harris

Variation of Trusts (1975)
Law and Legal Science (1979)
Legal Philosophies (2nd ed., 1997)
Cross and Harris, *Precedent in English Law*, (4th ed., 1991)
Property and Justice (1996)

Deryck Beyleveld

A Bibliography on General Deterrence Research
The Dialectical Necessity of Morality
Beyleveld and Brownsword, *Law as a Moral Judgment*
Beyleveld and Brownsword, *Mice, Morality and Patents*

Roger Brownsword

Brownsword and Adams, *Understanding Law*
Brownsword and Adams, *Understanding Contract Law*
Brownsword and Adams, *Key Issues in Contract*
Brownsword and Beyleveld, *Law as a Moral Judgment*
Brownsword and Beyleveld, *Mice, Morality and Patents*
Brownsword, Howells and Wilhelmsson (eds), *Welfarism in Contract Law*

Stephen Munzer

A Theory of Property
"Validity and Legal Conflicts" (1973) 82 *Yale Law Journal* 1140
"Retroactive Law" (1977) 6 *Journal of Legal Studies* 373
"The Acquisition of Property Rights" (1991) 66 *Notre Dame Law Review* 661
"Aristotle's Biology and the Transplantation of Organs" (1993) *Journal of the History of Biology* 109
"Transplantation, Chemical Inheritance, and the Identity of Organs" (1994) 45 *British Journal for the Philosophy of Science* 555
"Elickson on 'Chronic Misconduct' in Urban Spaces: Of Panhandlers, Bench Squatters, and Day Laborers" (1997) 32 *Harvard Civil Rights & Civil Liberties Law Review* 1

Antonello Miranda

Il testamento nel diritto inglese. Fondamento e sistema
Introducing the Italian Legal System
"Telematica e diritto di informazione" (1981) Vol XXXIX, II *Atti dell' Accademia di Scienze, Lettere ed Arti di Palermo* 1
"Scelte esistenziali ed educative die minori in diritto inglese ed italiano" (1981) *Rass. Civ.* 1022
"Codificazione e Common Law" (1987) Vol VII *Atti dell'Accademia di Scienze, Lettere ed Arti di Palermo* 137
"La disciplina giuridica inglese delle case mobili" 1987 *Rass. Civ.* 738
"Il Mobile Homes Act 1983" (1987) *Rass. Civ.* 838
"Diritti dei genitori ed interesse del minore new caso In Re Baby M" (1987) *Dir. Fam e delle Persone* 1515
"Banks Liability in Contract for the Use of Safe Deposit Box" (1988) *Company Lawyer*
"La giurisprudenza per massime ed il valore del precedente" (1988) *Riv. Crit. Dir. Priv.* 513
"Live and Let Die: tre questioni di vita e di morte" (1991) *Vita not.* 716
"The negligence saga: Irragionveolezza ed ingiustizia del danno nel risarcimento delle 'pure economic losses'" (1992) I *Riv. Dir Civ.* 387
"Autonomia privata e contratti gratuiti atipici" (1993) *Vita not.* 967
"Nobilis in mobile: verso la (nuova) frontiera del danno ingiusto" (1993) *Vita not.* 1561
"A neverending story: la fideiussione omnibus" in Draetta and Vaccà (eds) *Diritto e prassi degli scambi internazionali, Le Garanzie Contrattuali* (1994)
"In vitro veritas?: infertilità e diritto tra dubbi ed incertezze" (1994) *Vita not.* 411
"Questioni di famiglia" (1994) *Vita not.* 1460
"Un problema di coerenza sistematica: la violenza nel matrimonio" (1995) *Vita not.* 469
"L'Insurance Ombudsman" (1995) *Vita not* 60
"Lo strano caso del 'Dr Jones and Mrs White' (ovvero della lesione delle aspettative del presunto beneficiario di un lascito testamentario)" (1995) *Vita not.* 1558
"Giudici senza pace" (1995) *Vita Not* 1558
"Successione e famiglia di fatto" (1996) *Vita not* 1
"I signori della terra: nuovi confini di un vecchio rapporto" (1996) *Vita not.* 2
"'Surfing Contracts': luce nuova sulla conclusione del contratto mediante mezzi elettronici (1996) *Vita not*

Deborah Fisch Nigri

"Investigating Computer Crime in the UK" (1992) 8 *Computer Law and Security Report*

"Crime e Informática: Um Novo Fenomeno Juridico" (1992) 100 *Revista Trimestral de Jurisprudencia dos Estados* 41
"UK Data Protection: The UK Data Protection Registrar's Annual Report; Data Protection Court and Tribunal Cases in the UK and their Implications" (1992) 21 *Privacy Laws and Business Newsletter*
"Computer Crime: Why should we still care" (1993) 10 *Computer Law and Security Report*

Gerard McCormack

The New Companies Legislation
Reservation of Title (2nd ed. 1995)
Registration of Company Charges
Proprietary Claims and Insolvency

Wolfgang Mincke

"Eine vergleichende Rechtswissenschaft", *Zeitschrift für Vergleichende Rechtswissenschaft* 83 (1984) p. 315 (auch ins Japanische übersetzt erschienen)
"Die Kohärenz juristischer Aussagen", *Archivum Juridicum Cracoviense* (1990) p. 5
"Die Problematik von Recht und Sprache in der Übersetzung von Rechtstexten" *Archiv für Rechts und Sozialphilosophie* (1993) p. 446
"Sale and lease back, art. 3:84 lid 3 BW, eigendomsvoorbehoud en de numerus clausus. Opmerkingen na aaneiding van het arrest Sogelease", *Nederlands Tijdschrift voor Burgerlijk Recht* (1995) p. 175
"Objects of Property Rights" in van Maanen and van der Walt (eds) *Property Law on the Threshold of the 21st Century* (1996) p. 651

Richard Nobles

Pensions Employment and the Law
Controlling Occupational Pension Schemes
"The Pensions Act 1995" (1996) 59 MLR 241

Joshua Weisman

The Condominium Law: A Study of Its Operation
The Land Law: A Critical Analysis
The Security Interests Law
"Copyright Law of Israel" in Nimmer and Geller (eds) *International Copyright Law and Practice Law and Property: General Part (*in Hebrew)
Law of Property: Ownership and Concurrent Ownership (in Hebrew)
"Restrictions on the Acquisition of Land by Aliens" (1980) 28 *American Journal of Comparative Law* 39

Alison Clarke

Emmet on Title (assistant ed)
"Ship Mortgages" in *Palmer and McKendrick's Interests in Goods*
"Insolvent Families" in *Rajak's Insolvency Law: Theory and Practice*

William Swadling

Editor of the *SPTL Reporter*, the Society of Public Teachers of Law newsletter, and co-editor of *Trust Law International*

Bernard Rudden

Soviet Insurance Law
The New River
The Law of Mortgages (co-author)
Source-Book on French Law (3rd. ed., 1990)
Basic Community Laws (6th ed., 1995)
Comparing Constitutions
Basic Community Cases (2nd ed., 1997)

J. E. Penner

The Idea of Property in Law
"Nuisance and the character of the neighbourhood" (1993) 5(1) *J. of Environmental Law* 1
"The 'Bundle of Rights' Picture of Property" (1996) 43(3) *UCLA Law Review* 711
"Voluntary Obligations and the Scope of the Law Of Contract" (1996) 2(4) *Legal Theory* 325
"The Analysis of Rights" (1997) 10 Ratio Juris
"Basic Obligations in Birks" (ed.) *The Classification of Obligations*

Joshua Getzler

The History of Water Rights at Common Law (forthcoming)

David Sugarman

Sugarman (ed.) *Legality, Ideology and the State*
Sugarman and Rubin (eds) *Law, Economy and Society, 1750–1914: Essays in the History of English Law*
Sugarman and Teubner (eds) *Regulating Corporate Groups in Europe*
Law and Social Change in England, 1780–1900
Sugarman and Dezalay (eds) *Professional Competition and Professional Power: Lawyers, Accountants and the Social Construction of Markets*
A Brief History of the Law Society
Sugarman (ed.) *Law in History: Histories of Law and Society*

Ronnie Warrington

"Pashakanis and the Commodity Form Theory" (1981) *International Journal of Law and Society* 33
"Land Law and Legal Education: Is there Justice or Morality in Blackacre?" (1984) 18 *The Law Teacher* 35
Douzinas, McVeigh and Warrington, "Thrashing in the Dwellinghouse" (1989) *Modern Law Review* 50
Douzinas, Warrington with McVeigh *Postmodern Jurisprudence*
Douzinas and Warrington *Justice Miscarried*

Alan Ryan

The Philosophy of John Stuart Mill
The Philosophy of the Social Sciences
Property and Political Theory
Property
Bertrand Russell: A Political Life
John Dewey and the High Tide of American Liberalism

Michiatsu Kaino

A History of Law of Land Ownership in Modern England (in Japanese)
A History of Ideas of Property in Modern Europe
European Land Law
Modern Urban Land Law in England, France, Germany and America
"Some Introductory Comments on the Historical Background of Japanese Civil Law" (1988) Vol. 16 No 3 *International Journal of the Sociology of Law*

Michael Salter

"On the Idea of a Legal World" (1994) *Int'l Jnl of the Legal Profession* 283
"Hegel and Constitutional Law" (1994) *Journal of Law and Society* 464
"A Dialectic Inspite of Itself: Overcoming the Phenomenology of Legal Culture" (1995) Vol. 4 *Social and Legal Studies* 453
Salter and Bogusa-Tych, "Comparing Legal Cultures of Eastern Europe: the Need for a Dialectical Analysis" (1996) Vol. 16, no. 2 *Legal Studies* 157
"Habermas's New Contribution to Legal Theory" (1997) *Jnl of Law and Society*

William Lucy

Explaining and Understanding Adjudication (forthcoming)
"Adjudication for Pluralists" (1996) 16 *Oxford Journal of Legal Studies* 369
Lucy and Mitchell, "Replacing Private Property: The Case for Stewardship" (1996) 55 *Cambridge Law Journal*
"The Common Law According to Hegel" (1997) 17 *Oxford Journal of Legal Studies*

Index

abstract right
    abstract legal forms and categories, legal realm of, 258
    commercial sphere, confined to, 267
    contradictions of, 258–268
    existing social practices and institutions, judging, 287
    freedom, definition on terms of negative rights, 266–268
    ideological value commitments underlying, not acknowledging, 266
    immanent critique, 260
    individualistic standpoint, 259
    judicial decisions, basis of, 265
    law, treatment of, 259
    meaning, 258
    negative rights orientation, 261
    neo-liberal perspective, credibility of, 266
    oppressive forms of social power, allowing, 265
    positive law, basis of, 258
    progressive force, as, 262, 264
    property ownership,
        simplified account of, 260
        subject and object, recognition of, 259, 260
    sameness, empty identity of, 264
    sub-culture, 258
    subject, defining, 264
administration
    procedure, 122
administrative receivership
    procedure, 122
affiliation
    complication of, 39
    surrogate, 39

articles of association
    alteration of,
        benefit of company, for, 73, 74
        case law, 71–73
        discrimination by, 75
        expropriation, conferring power of, 74
        judging, principle for, 74, 75
        power of, 71–76
        prejudicial, protection against, 71
        special resolution, by, 69
    compulsory expropriation, provision for, 67–70, 76, 77
    contractual status, 68
    expulsion clauses, 70
    judicial intervention in context of, 69
    unfair prejudice petitions, 75, 76
artificial insemination
    development of techniques, 39
    homologous, 40
    pre-embryos. *See* **pre-embryos**
ASEAN
    cultural heritage of cities in, 244
    indigenous laws, 249
    inner city problems in, 248
    Kampong redevelopment, 248
    land ownership, 250
    urbanisation process, 248

bankruptcy
    amount received from estate, limiting, 126
    bankrupt's home, special significance of, 122, 123
    development of law, 122
    individual rights, preventing enforcement of, 122, 123

bankruptcy *(cont.)*
    isolation of secured creditor from, 126, 129
    pre-bankruptcy entitlements, respecting, 126
    private rights, interference with, 124
    property rights, respecting, 122
    secured creditors opting out of procedure, 124

capitalism
    institution of property in, 202–206
    modern, property values of, 239
    private and public law adjustments, 199–202

charges. *See* **security interests**

chattels
    property regime, 150
    things or wealth, treatment as, 160

choses in action
    property, as, 2

citizenship
    independence, link with, 256

common law
    archaic features, shedding of, 201
    commercial, development of, 218
    inequalities of, 199
    Roman law contrasted, 198
    Singapore and Malacca, in, 253, 254
    South East Asia, in, 250, 251

community
    creation of, 255

company law
    compulsory expropriation. *See* **compulsory expropriation**
    contracting out, limits on, 68

compensation
    delictual, 204–206

compulsory expropriation
    articles of association, alteration of, 71–76
    provisions of, 67–70, 76, 77
    disclosure of information, alleging lack of, 64, 65

compulsory expropriation *(cont.)*
    erroneous advice, takeover based on, 65
    fairness, 64
    options for, 76
    reduction of capital, in course of, 67
    situations of, 61
    statute, by,
        application to court, 63, 64
        Companies Act provisions, 61
        European Convention on Human Rights, provisions of, 62, 63
        introduction of, 62
        private property rights, protection of, 62, 63
        reduction of capital, 67
        schemes of arrangement, 66
    valuation of shares, 75, 76

computers
    information age, in, 48–50
    protection of assets held in, 60
    telecommunications, alliance with, 48

Constitution, English
    post–1688, 202

contract
    control by, 285
    ethical development, significance for, 287
    Hegel's treatment of, 283
    obligation as product of, 87
    property rights, protection of, 99, 100
    services, for, 87

corpse
    property in, 1

crime
    definition, 54
    property, concept of, 54

democracy
    concept of, 236
    wealth, of, 235

developing countries
  communal ties in, 244
Dewey, John
  biographical sketch, 229–231
  democracy as guiding thread of work, 236
  early reflections, 235–237
  impact of, 238–241
  philosophy of, 230, 232–235
  pragmatism, view on, 225. *See also* **pragmatism**
  radicalism, 239
Directive on the Legal Protection of Biotechnology
  revision, 23
duress
  doctrine, rationale for, 286
  unjust enrichment, effect on, 134

economics
  ethical rules, application of, 227
embryos
  protected non-property holdings, 184, 185
English law
  evolution of, 201
  institutional bias, 198, 199
equity
  fabrication of system, 216
  law distinguished, 155
  property law, redefinition of character and purpose of, 269
  remedial morality, social need for, 268–270
equity of redemption
  anachronistic reasons for, 221
  circumvention, attempts at, 212
  collateral advantages, 213, 215
  consolidation of jurisdiction, 210–213
  construction and expansion, circumstances of, 215
  contract orthodoxy, 222
  duration of mortgage, 211, 212

equity of redemption *(cont.)*
  establishment of, 209, 210
  estate in equity, as, 210, 213
  fairness, 214, 215
  generally, 5
  increased consumption, fostering, 217
  justification, 214
  land, safeguarding, 207, 223
  legal, economic, political and cultural dimensions, 207
  mechanistic interpretation, 211
  metamorphosis of, 221–223
  narratives, 217, 218
  nature and significance of, 208
  origin of, 209, 210
  redeem, meaning, 218
  right of, 209
  tenacity of, 223
  title in equity, as, 211
  trust distinguished, 211
  value, 119
  wide movement, part of, 224
European Convention on Human Rights
  conflicts between rights, 16
  human rights instrument, as, 15
  Principles of Generic Consistency, conflict with, 16
  private property rights, protection of, 62, 63
European Patent Convention
  Contracting States, agreement to terms, 18
  critical cultural morality, 12, 13, 18, 20, 21
  human rights, acceptance of, 15
  Principles of Generic Consistency, acceptance of, 19
  genetic engineering, applications concerning, 10
  human rights, commitment of Contracting States to, 13
  light regulatory regime, intention for, 17

European Patent Convention *(cont.)*
morality,
authority, delegation of, 12
candidates for, 11
consensus against granting
patent, 12
Contracting States, of, 12, 13
critical cultural, 11, 12, 21
cultural, 11, 12, 20, 21
EPO Guidelines, 11
exceptional exclusion on
grounds of, 12
interpretation of, 10, 11
patents contrary to, 10
personal, of examiners, 11, 12
Principles of Generic
Consistency, incorporation of, 11
quality threshold, 21, 22
quantity threshold, 21
specific established moral
theory, 11
patentability under, 10
recognised human rights, subject
to, 16
European Patent Office
moral jurisdiction, extent of, 12
morality, Guidelines on, 11
inconceivability test, 20, 21
patents for human gene sequences,
grant of, 9
expropriation
compulsory. *See* **compulsory
expropriation**
rules, 177

foetus
fertilised ovules, and, 42–44
protection of, 43
fraud
doctrine, rationale for, 286
freedom
innate capacity, alienation of, 262
nature of, 258

freedom *(cont.)*
negative rights, definition in terms
of, 266–268
preconditions, securing, 261, 262

genes. *See* **human genes**

highways
ownership, 182
human body parts
derived-status strategy, 35, 36
dignity, sale offending against,
affronting, insulting or
demeaning, 32
degradation, concept of, 33
Kantian argument, 26, 27
means of, 31–34
morality, relevance to, 33
particular person, of, 34
price, equation with, 28, 34
worth, awareness of, 32
donation,
law requiring, 25
sale distinguished, 29
integration strategy, 35
market, participation in, 26, 36
meaning, 25
personal identity, bound up with, 30
politicising, 36, 37
property discourse, 37, 38
property rights in,
case against, 25, 26
commodities, treatment as, 26
context of, 25
division, fallacy of, 34–36
human dignity, argument from,
26–28
Kantian arguments against,
26–31
moral and legal rights, idea of, 27
sale, recognition on, 25
uneasy case against, 38
sale of,
allowing, effect of, 25

Index

human body parts *(cont.)*
- dignity, means of offending, 31–34
- donation distinguished, 29
- inappropriate, where, 25
- isolated and frequent, 29
- money, obtaining, 36
- money, receipt of, 31
- moral objection, vulnerability to, 29, 30
- objection to, 30
- strength of reason for, 30, 31
- self, as part of, 28

human genes
- patents,
  - applications, processing, 23
  - Directive on the Legal Protection of Biotechnology, 23
  - donation of tissue, 20
  - European Patent Office, grant by. *See* **European Patent Convention; European Patent Office**
  - human dignity, criterion of, 23, 24
  - morality of, 9, 19–22
  - number of, 9
  - recognition of human rights, significance of, 13–17
  - *Relaxin* opposition, 19–22
  - technical criteria, doubts about, 23

human nature
- individual character, development of, 233

human organs
- protected non-property holdings, 185

human rights
- claim-right, as, 14
- commitment of EPC Contracting States to, 13
- conflicts between, 16
- dialectically contingent argument, 13–15
- humans, possession by, 15
- recognition, significance of, 13–17

independence
- citizenship, link with, 256
- meaning, 255, 256

individuals
- evolution, developmental account, 262
- potential for freedom and self-determination, appropriation of, 263

Indonesia
- land tenure, 251
- property, communal ideas of, 251–253
- town development, 251–253

Industrial Revolution
- English property system, adjustment of, 199, 200
- law and government, impact of, 194
- period of, 193, 194

information
- appropriation, question of ownership in, 55
- Canada, notion of protection in, 49
- commercially valuable, 57
- computer system, unauthorised removal from, 55
- computers, use of, 48–50
- confidential,
  - conceptual objection to categorisation as property, 53
  - property in, 53, 54
  - rights in, 52
  - taking of, 53
  - trade secret protection, 53
- copyrighted work, infringement of, 50
- criminals, exploitation by, 48
- economic, cultural and political asset, as, 49
- intangible assets, as, 48
- intrinsic characteristics of, 48
- legal property, concept of, 50–59
- medium, association with, 57

Information *(cont.)*
  owner, importance for, 54
  ownership of, 56, 57
  property rights in,
    adjustment of law, 59
    balancing interests, 58, 59
    civil law, 52–54
    criminal law, 54–57
    full scale, 59
    private and business level, at, 52
    recognition of, 52
  property, as, 2
  proprietary protection, deserving, 60
  proprietary rights, attribution of, 48
  theft of, 49, 55
  unfair obtaining of, 59
insolvency
  procedures, 122
intellectual property
  property, as, 2
  protection of, 151

Japan
  agrarian society, change from, 249
  economic democratisation, 250
  industrialisation of, 244
  land and buildings, independent treatment of, 247
  land law, 247
  land price explosion, 246, 247
  land tax, 249
  land tenure, 249
  land-ownership, rise and fall of myth of, 245–248
  property portfolios, value of, 248
  residential patterns in, 246
  social inequality in, 247
  unconditional ownership of property, 250
  urban society, stability of, 245
  urbanisation, 246
  white land, 247

land
  immobilisation of, 198
  multitude of rights in, 88
  nationalisation of, 3
  patrician policy, 215
  sanctity, defence of, 219
land tenure
  co-ownership, 161, 162
  continuity, 242, 243
  fee simple absolute in possession, 160
  fee simple in remainder, 160
  Indonesia, in, 251
  Japan, in, 249
  lease, 162
  long-term leases. *See* **long-term leases**
  Singapore, in, 254
  state ownership, based on, 105
law
  abstract right, treatment by, 259
  coercive, 232
  dictate of sovereign, as, 232
  equity distinguished, 155
  fixed nature of, 233
  functional theory of, 234
  justice according to, 245
  new, external standard for, 234
  positive, basis of, 258
  things, of, 155
leases
  long-term. *See* **long-term leases**
  thing or wealth, as, 162
liberties
  claim right, 168–170
  conditions of, 255, 256
  legal relations, as, 169
local authority
  swap transactions by, 183
long-term leases
  fictitious, 114
  holding of land by, 3
  inherent difficulties of, 116
  Israel, term in, 112

Index   303

long term leases *(cont.)*
land tenure, as form of, 106
limits on maximum duration, 115
planning objectives, attainment of,
  Australia, in, 108, 109
  experience of, 109
  historical background, 108
  Hong Kong, in, 108, 110
  Israel, in, 109
  positive planning, 110
  review of, 110
  sanctions, 108
  Singapore, in, 108
premium, payment of, 111, 112
reasons for adopting,
  aliens, restricting acquisition by, 113
  ideological grounds, 106, 107
  Israeli law, under, 106
  land use control, 108–110
  number of co-owners, limiting, 114
  public and private interests, 107
  religious motives, 106, 107
  revenue, source of, 110–112
  socialist ideology, 107
  socio-economic conditions, response to, 105
  speculation, prevention of, 112
  utilitarian grounds, 107–114
revenue, source of,
  criticism of, 111
  increase in value of land, 110, 111
  premium, payment of, 111, 112
  rent, increase in, 111
scope of right, changing nature of, 116
substitution for ownership, as, 116
system of ownership based on, 105
term, 114–117

Malaysia
cities, management of, 254

medical records
patients' access to, 182
money
means of exchange, as, 154
object or function, treatment as, 160
quasi-ownership interests, 182
mortgage. *See also* **security interests**
bundle of rights, 120
date for repayment, adherence to, 208, 209
duration of, 211, 212
equity of redemption. *See* **equity of redemption**
lender, interest of, 163
loan agreement, 208
protections, development of, 209
rights under, 121
thing or wealth, as, 163
underlying debt, value in, 118, 119
where arising, 208

Netherlands East Indies
Dutch rule over, 251
norms
interests served or protected by, 167

occupational pension schemes
defined benefit, 89
ownership
appropriation rules, 177
bundle of rights analysis, 4
co-ownership, 161, 162
disaggregation, 200
expropriation rules, 177
fragmentation, 200
highways, of, 182
interests,
  categories of rules presupposed by, 177
  rules on, 177
  same resource, over, 176
  trespassory rules, interests interacting with, 177

ownership *(cont.)*
  Japan, in, 249
  marks of, 147
  parks, of, 182
  property-limitation rules, 177
  quasi-ownership interests, 182, 183, 189
  responsibility for tax, and, 243
  social policies, 268
  South East Asia, in, 250
  spectrum, 176, 177
  subject and object, recognition by abstract right, 259, 260
  volitional theories of, 236

patents
  human genes, for. *See* **human genes**
  inventiveness, system centred on, 17
  life, on, 9
  modern biotechnology, applications involving, 18

pension fund
  contributions, owners of, 95
  disputes, perspectives in, 91–93
  members' benefits as property, 97
  members, claim of ownership by, 94, 102
  ownership of, 90, 94–97
  property, as,
    identification of rights, 98
    ideology of, 93, 94
    lawyers' view of, 90, 91
    lay perceptions of, 89, 90
    members' benefits, 97
  property rights in, 94
  property rules, application of, 3
  settlor, 96
  surpluses,
    intention as to, 92, 93
    parties benefiting from, 91
    use of, 91
  trust doctrine, development of, 94–98

pension fund *(cont.)*
  winding up, disposal of assets on, 96, 99

pension schemes
  amalgamation, 97
  contract of employment, perspective of, 100, 101
  contractual entitlements, 98–101
  employer, powers of, 100

personality
  corporate, 237
  individual character, development of, 233

personhood
  journey to, 279
  steps to achieving, 277
  will and embodiment, 278, 279

planning law
  Asian perspective, 5
  Western and Eastern countries, in, 244

pragmatism
  American jurisprudence, underpinning, 225
  Dewey, views of, 225
  Deweyan, political implications of, 231, 232
  experimentalism, as, 226
  instrumentalism, as, 226
  legal realism distinguished, 228, 229
  means and ends, dichotomy between, 227, 228
  neo-Hegelianism, 228
  practical terms, view of law in, 226
  utilitarianism and positivism distinguished, 228

pre-embryos
  biological material, as, 45
  custody of, 40
  entitlement to property, 46
  fate, deciding, 42
  fertilised ovules and implanted embryos, difference between, 42–44

Index

pre-embryos *(cont.)*
  human subjectivity of, 40
  legal status of,
    choice of solution, 41, 42
    propositions, 41
    question of, 40
    rights, gradation and balancing, 42–44
  ownership, acquisition of, 45, 46
  pregnancy, beginning of, 44
  property in, 44–47
principles of generic consistency
  acceptance of, 11
  conformity, need for, 13
  criterion of legal validity, as, 15
  human rights instruments, consistency of, 16
  strained interpretation of, 16
private property
  argument for, ethical considerations, 280
  distinctiveness of system, 275
  Hegel, view of, 276–289
  justification for, 276, 286
  logical priority of, 185
  normative basis of, 279–281
  public access to,
    conflict of claims, 274
    control, as, 281, 282
    Hegelian argument for, 281–289
    idea of, 275, 276
    justification for, 281
    plausibility of argument, 289
    property rights, analogy with, 287–288
    rights, thing controlled under, 287
    statutory imposition of, 286
    struggle for recognition, overcoming, 286
    transcendence of will's subjectivity, rights leading to, 284
progress
  social and historical developments, within, 257

property
  absolute, 200
  alienation, restrictions on, 261
  aliens, inability of, to own, 220
  analysis, problems of, 1
  Asian countries, discussion in, 243
  autonomy over, 6
  bundle of rights, 164, 203, 233, 239
  cashable rights, 178
  categorisation problems, 118
  certainty of expectations, as, 196
  civil law protection, 51
  claim right, 168–170
  coercive monopoly, as, 203, 204
  collective, 175, 187
  common, 175
    internal utility, 185
    justificatory priority, 185, 186
    meaning, 183, 184
  common law conception of, 50, 148
  communitarian,
    Australia, in, 179, 180
    historical priority, 186–188
    internal decisions, 188
    meaning, 179
    mutual rights, 186
    surviving instances of, 187
    trespassory rules, 178
  concentrations, effect of, 238
  concepts of,
    developing nature of, 51–57
    English and French, 78
    German and Dutch, 78, 79, 81
    Swedish and Finnish, 79
  contractual agreements for use of, 232
  control by, 285
  corporate, 178–180
  corpse, in, 1
  criminal law protection, 51
  definition, 50
  division of entitlements, 147
  duties as to, 167

property *(cont.)*
  economic theory of, development
     of, 193, 194
  elusive idea of, 1
  entailed, conflict with negative
     freedom, 261, 262
  erosion of, 219
  essence of political freedom, as, 242
  estates in, 147
  ethical development, significance
     for, 287
  exclusion of patrons from, 180, 181
  exclusive use, as right of, 166–168
  feudal system, 200
  free transfer, obstruction of, 197
  frontiers of, 1
  group, 175, 243
  Hohfeldian orientation, 164–166
  ideology of, 93, 94
  industrial/intellectual intangibles,
     151
  information as. *See* **information**
  information industry, role in age
     of, 2
  institutions, 4
     essentials of, 175
     justification of, 188, 189
  instrumental and expressive
     theories of, 195
  intangible, boundaries of, 2
  intangible claims, 151, 152
  joint ownership, 187, 188
  judges as owners of, 216
  legal definitions, 146
  legal relations, definition of, 166
  legal term of art, as, 166
  liberties, 168–170
  Lockean concept of, 242
  mere, 176
  non-ownership proprietary rules,
     178
  non-physical forms of, 50
  obligations,
     characteristics of value, 86
     contract, product of, 87
     object of, 85–87

property *(cont.)*
  need for, 82–84
  relationships, as, 82
  rights in value, as, 88
  transfer of, 83
  value of, 85–88
  orthodox assumptions,
     challenging, 3
  ownership. *See* **ownership**
  patrician policy, 215, 216
  political issues, introduction of, 221
  private. *See* **private property**
  protected non-property holdings,
     184, 185
  public, open to, 180
  public use, dedicated to, 181
  real and personal, 50, 54, 147
  rearrangement of categories, 84
  relativity of notion of, 52
  rights. *See* **property rights**
  set of relationships, as, 274, 275
  social, 187
  social reality, 270, 271
  state, 175
  substance and value rights,
     separation of, 88
  taking of, 204–206
  tangible and intangible, 50, 54
  tangible contact of owner with, 167
  tangible immovables, 149, 150
  tangible movables, 150
  things covered by, 148
  things or wealth, as, 4
  transfer,
     contract for, 87
     novatio, 82
     obligations, of, 83
     performance of, 86
     relationships, of, 82
     Roman law standpoint, 83
  transmissibility, 176
  tribal, 175
  useless, 174
  value of use, 173
  vulnerabilities affecting, 263

Index 307

property *(cont.)*
  will's embodiment in, 278, 279, 285
property law
  abstractions, contextualising, 270–273
  approaches to, 219
  cultural and political significance, 208
  development, stages of, 257
  early modern capitalism, emergence of, 258
  economic change, practical links with, 202
  equity, redefinition of character and purpose by, 269
  ethical life, 270
  Hegel's account of, 257
  languages of, 218, 220
  objects, redefinition of, 271
  relations, mediation of, 268, 272
property rights
  absolute or relative, 80, 84
  body parts, in. *See* **human body parts**
  bundle of, 164, 203, 233, 239
  categorisations of, 80–82
  classification, approaches to, 80
  clear definition, need for, 193
  collective expression of political will, as, 273
  contract, use of to protect, 99, 100
  creation of, 51
  development, historical approach to, 193
  Deweyan perspective, in, 5
  disappearance of, 53
  German Civil Code, in, 81
  in personam, 164, 165, 170, 171
  in rem, 164, 165, 170, 171
  industrialising England, in, 206
  inherited assets, as, 242
  liberties, and, 168–170
  markets as, 206
  markets, called into existence by, 193

property *(cont.)*
  meaning, 51
  multital, 164, 165, 170, 171
  need for clear definition of, 5
  paucital, 164, 165, 170, 171
  primary and secondary, 84
  relationships between persons, classification in terms of, 81
  Scandinavian concepts of, 81
  social change, as obstacle to, 234, 235
  subjective, 80, 84
  tangibles, to, 51
  transfer of, 82
  use-rights,
    bundle of, 164, 172
    definition in terms of, 171
    exclusive, 166–168
    interference, prohibiting, 171, 172
    proposition of, 171
    value of use, as rights to, 173, 174
    way of use, determining, 166
  utilitarian and functional terms, analysis in, 235
prospective purposive agent
  Principles of Generic Consistency, acceptance of, 11
public parks
  property rules, 180

rationality
  concept of, 198, 199
restitution. *See* **unjust enrichment**

schemes of arrangement
  compulsory expropriation under, 66
security interests
  bankruptcy law,
    pragmatic argument in, 126–129
    pre-bankruptcy entitlements, respecting, 126
    property argument, 124, 125

security interests *(cont.)*
    property rights, respecting, 122
    secured creditors opting out of, 124
    secured creditors' rights, respect for, 125, 126
    charged assets, ownership of property in, 125
    credit-worthiness, checking, 128
    debenture, transaction at undervalue, 119, 120
    debt recovery, 128
    defaulting borrowers, 128
    options to purchase, 120
    over-valuation of,
        rights aspect, 120, 121
        value aspect, 118–120
    pre-emption rights, 120, 121
    property categorisation problems, 118
    property category misconception, 121–124
    protection of, 3, 4
    real nature of, 125
    rights in, 125
    risk, 127
    sui generis right, 126
    thing or wealth, as, 162, 163

shares
    compulsory expropriation. *See* **compulsory expropriation**
    trading, 2

Singapore
    cities, management of, 253, 254
    land tenure, 254

slavery
    Hegel's arguments against, 282

social policy
    state, role of, 271

statutes
    names of, 146

Straits settlements
    acquisition of countries, 251

telecommunications
    computers, alliance with, 48

Thailand
    cities, management of, 254, 255
    landsharing, 255

theft
    computer system, information in, 55, 56
    information, of, 49, 55
    intangible property, of, 54
    statutory provisions, 56
    things in action, of, 56

things
    corporeal and incorporeal, 158
    function, distinguished in terms of, 148
    in action, 151, 152
        theft of, 56
    investigation of, 159
    law of, 155
    thing, as, 149–152
    use value and exchange value, 159
    wealth, treatment as, 148, 152–158

title
    complexities of, 200, 201
    equity in redemption as, 211
    uncertainty of, 197
    unstable system of, 202

trade
    interference with, 225

trespass
    protected non-property holdings, 184, 185
    trespassory rules,
        communitarian property, 178
        legal, 175, 176
        meaning, 175
        ownership interests, interaction with, 177
        privileged uses and powers, 181

trust
    beneficiaries, 153
    concept of, 147
    equity of redemption distinguished, 211
    function, 153, 154

trust *(cont.)*
  Hague Convention, 157, 158
  historical account of, 155
  management, 154–156
  ownership of subject of, 93
  pivot, 156, 157
  private publicity, 158
  resulting, 135, 136, 140
  screen, as, 156
  subrogation, technique of, 157
trust for sale
  number of co-owners, limiting, 114
trustee
  dishonest, sale by, 156
  legal owner, as, 147
  powers of, 147, 148, 176
  trust property, relationship to, 154

unjust enrichment
  duress, effect of, 134
  failure of consideration, on, 135, 136
  free acceptance, on, 137
  law of obligations, as part of, 130
  legal response to, 4
  mistaken transactions, 133, 134
  new property right generated by, 132
  property law, not comprised in, 130
  proprietary restitution,
    arguments against, 144, 145
    arguments in favour of, 139–143
    claims involving, 133
    equity, relief in, 141, 142
    failure of consideration, on, 135, 136
    free acceptance, on, 137
    grant of rights, effected through, 130
    knowledge, trusts raised through, 141
    meaning, 131–133
    payments in anticipation of contract, 137
    policy, arguments from, 142, 143

unjust enrichment *(cont.)*
    policy-motivated, 137, 138
    principle, arguments from, 139–142
    qualified consent, on, 135–137
    resulting trusts, 135, 136, 140
    rights *in rem*, reversal of unjust enrichment by, 131
    risk of insolvency, plaintiff not accepting, 142, 143
    vitiated consent, on, 133–135
    when granted, 133–139
    wrongs, for, 138, 139
  qualified consent, on, 135–137
  substitution of assets, 131
  survival of ownership, 131
  underlying invalidity of contract, on, 139, 140
  undue influence, in case of, 135
  vitiated consent, on, 133–135
  windfall, as, 143
urbanisation
  ASEAN countries, in, 248
  Japan, of, 246
  law for, 245
  negative environmental impact, 244
  trends, factors affecting, 244
user
  uncertainty of, 197

voluntary arrangements
  procedure, 122

will
  constituent elements of, 282–283
  control by, 283
  embodiment, and, 278, 279
  other, recognition of, 284
  property, things taken hold of and controlled as, 288
  subjectivity, transcendence of, 284
  wants and desires, selection of, 277

W.G. Hart Legal Workshop Series

Volume 1
Property Problems From Genes to Pension Funds
(Editor J.W. Harris)
ISBN 90-411-9643-9